Charles Bosson

History of the Forty-second regiment infantry

Charles Bosson

History of the Forty-second regiment infantry

ISBN/EAN: 9783337268756

Printed in Europe, USA, Canada, Australia, Japan

Cover: Foto ©ninafisch / pixelio.de

More available books at **www.hansebooks.com**

HISTORY

OF THE

FORTY-SECOND REGIMENT

INFANTRY,

MASSACHUSETTS VOLUNTEERS,

1862, 1863, 1864.

BY

SERGEANT-MAJOR CHARLES P. BOSSON.

BOSTON:
MILLS, KNIGHT & CO., PRINTERS, 115 CONGRESS STREET.
1886.

PREFACE.

THIS history of the regiment was undertaken by me at the special request of several officers who knew I had written, soon after the term of service expired, considerable matter relating thereto, for my own amusement and instruction. Without this foundation to work on, written when memory was fresh, it is doubtful if a history of the regiment could be written, for references to many soldiers' diaries disclosed the fact that nearly all did not contain detailed accounts of events occurring at the time entries were made. Few soldiers thought any memorandum of theirs would ever become useful for a purpose of this kind. Access to the regimental books and files of papers has greatly facilitated this history.

I have not been able to write a satisfactory account of Companies C and H on detached service, or of Company K on detached service, in charge of pontoons. I found it impossible to obtain information in a way to be of service.

I proposed to publish *Descriptive Lists* of each company of the regiment. Upon investigation, and a comparison of lists in possession of the War Department, the regimental descriptive books, and orders of detail, I found such a marked difference in Christian names and surnames the idea was abandoned; besides, such lists would prove misleading, as many men enlisted under a false age; those who were too young gave in their age several years older than they were, others, too old, made their age to meet the requirements of law. The original *Descriptive Lists* were made up in a hurried, loose manner, few officers realizing their importance in after years.

It is probable certain facts in these pages will appear to some readers at this day far different than they would had the history been published within a few years after the war closed. We have grown older and wiser than we were in 1862 and 1863.

If any of my old comrades in arms shall have passed a pleasant hour in reading this history, I shall feel amply repaid for time and trouble in its preparation.

CHARLES P. BOSSON.

CONTENTS.

CHAPTER I.
ORGANIZATION OF REGIMENT—CAMP AT READVILLE—DEPARTURE FOR NEW YORK 1

CHAPTER II.
EN ROUTE—CAMP AT EAST NEW YORK—ON TRANSPORTS, 19

CHAPTER III.
ON BOARD TRANSPORTS—THE SAXON—QUINCY—CHARLES OSGOOD—SHETUCKET—QUINNEBAUG 38

CHAPTER IV.
GALVESTON 61

CHAPTER V.
AT CARROLLTON—BOUND FOR GALVESTON—ARRIVAL OF COMPANIES—CAMP MANSFIELD—DETAILS . . . 140

CHAPTER VI.
FEBRUARY—AT BAYOU GENTILLY—MORE DETAILS . . 154

CHAPTER VII.
ENLISTED MEN PRISONERS AT HOUSTON—MARCH FOR THE FEDERAL LINES—ARRIVAL AT NEW ORLEANS . . 173

CHAPTER VIII.
AT BAYOU GENTILLY—MARCH—APRIL 197

CHAPTER IX.
AT BAYOU GENTILLY—MAY 226

CHAPTER X.

BAYOU GENTILLY — JUNE — FAREWELL TO GENTILLY CAMP — IN NEW ORLEANS 239

CHAPTER XI.

BRASHEAR CITY 252

CHAPTER XII.

ACTION AT LA-FOURCHE CROSSING 286

CHAPTER XIII.

JULY — IN NEW ORLEANS — AT ALGIERS 310

CHAPTER XIV.

COMPANIES C AND H ON DETACHED SERVICE AT CAMP PARAPET 331

CHAPTER XV.

COMPANY K IN CHARGE OF PONTOONS — BATON ROUGE — TECHE CAMPAIGN — SIEGE OF PORT HUDSON — DONALDSONVILLE — RETURN TO REGIMENT 352

CHAPTER XVI.

AUGUST — AT ALGIERS — BOUND NORTH — ON BOARD "CONTINENTAL" — ARRIVAL HOME 378

CHAPTER XVII.

ADVENTURES OF CORPORAL WENTWORTH AND PRIVATE HERSEY 389

CHAPTER XVIII.

OFFICERS IN CONFEDERATE PRISONS — HOUSTON — STATE PRISON — CAMP GROCE — CAMP FORD — EN ROUTE HOME — AT HOME 415

CHAPTER XIX.

IN SERVICE FOR ONE HUNDRED DAYS — ORGANIZATION — READVILLE — OFF FOR WASHINGTON — AT ALEXANDRIA — AT GREAT FALLS — RETURN HOME 442

ILLUSTRATIONS.

	PAGE.
FIELD AND STAFF OFFICERS	1
KUHN'S WHARF, GALVESTON	81
HEADQUARTERS AT BAYOU GENTILLY	161

CHAPTER I.

ORGANIZATION OF REGIMENT — CAMP AT READVILLE — DEPARTURE FOR NEW YORK.

AT the time (August 4th, 1862) a draft was ordered by President Lincoln for three hundred thousand militia to serve for a period of nine months, Colonel Isaac S. Burrell was in command of the Second Regiment, Massachusetts Volunteer Militia — an old militia organization of the State. General Orders No. 25, issued July 1st, 1862, by the Commander-in-Chief of the State troops, Governor John A. Andrew, notified the militia to prepare for a call to service. General Orders No. 34, issued August 13th, 1862, by the same authority, notified the volunteer militia they would be accepted for nine months service.

In common with other organized and uniformed militia organizations in the State, the colonel was instructed by officers and men of his command to tender the regiment as volunteers for nine months service, and to obtain permission to recruit up to the requisite strength. Public opinion was opposed to a draft at that time, and Governor Andrew, by accepting the services of such militia bodies as volunteered, affording every facility in his power to enable them to recruit up to the full maximum of strength, avoided the necessity for a draft, made available the services of those officers who eventually recruited their companies to a war strength, and the rank and file already enlisted in the militia — a very fine nucleus to commence with. The intermixing of raw recruits with men of some experience of the duties of a soldier tended to greatly facilitate the mobilization of the States' quota, and hastened the departure of regiments to the field in a tolerable good condition for immediate duty.

The Second Regiment, M. V. M., was one of the regiments accepted. As there was already a Second Regiment (three years troops) in the field, orders were issued designating the regiment as the Forty-Second Regiment, M. V. M., and was ordered into a camp of instruction at Readville, August 26th, 1862.

The old Second Regiment, M. V. M., a part of the First Brigade, First Division, State Militia, had just completed the five days camp duty with the brigade at Medford, required by law, from August 13th to 18th, and the regimental guard, Company C, Captain Leonard, left at Medford in charge of the camp equipage, since that encampment ended, in anticipation that the regiment would be immediately ordered back, was ordered August 22d to strike camp, proceed to Readville early next day, and pitch tents upon high ground very near to the Boston & Providence Railroad track. The camp was laid out by Quartermaster Burrell and Adjutant Davis, assisted by men of Company C. Colonel Burrell assumed command of all troops rendezvousing there until Brigadier-General Peirce was placed in command.

In addition to this guard, the first detachment of about one hundred men, occupied this camp on the afternoon of August 26th, and from that time until the regiment was complete (November 11th), recruiting, equipping, and instruction occupied the time. The Ninth Battery, Captain De Vecchi (enlisting for three years), Eleventh Battery, Captain Jones, Forty-Third Regiment, Colonel Holbrook, Forty-Fourth Regiment, Colonel Lee, and the Forty-Fifth Regiment, Colonel Codman (all enlisting for nine months), were encamped in tents and barracks at the same place and at the same time. The whole force formed a post, commanded by Brigadier-General R. A. Peirce, of the State Militia.

The officers of the old Second Regiment, M. V. M., that went into camp with the intention of entering the service, if successful in recruiting men to complete their companies and the Forty-Second Regiment, were: —

Colonel — I. S. Burrell.
Lieutenant-Colonel — T. L. D. Perkins.
Major — George W. Beach.
Adjutant — Charles A. Davis.
Quartermaster — C. B. Burrell, *vice* James W. Coverly, resigned.
Surgeon — John A. Lamson, resigned August 28th, 1862.
Company A — Captain, Wm. A. Brabine; Lieutenants, Wm. Kilner and John H. Stevens.
Company B — Captain, Albert H. Townsend; Lieutenants, Artemas Webster and Wm. B. Rand.
Company C — Captain, O. W. Leonard; Lieutenants, I. B. White and Geo. H. Drew.
Company D — Captain, George Sherivé; Lieutenants, Wm. H. Cowdin and D. F. Eddy.
Company E — Captain, Samuel C. Davis; Lieutenants, David Hale and Henry Pierce.
Company F — Captain, Wm. H. Russ; Lieutenants, Wm. A. Clark and James C. Singleton.
Company G — Captain, A. N. Proctor; Lieutenants, A. E. Proctor and Charles Jarvis.

Considerable time elapsed before the regiment was full. The system adopted by the Governor, of assigning quotas to cities and towns, was found to work to the disadvantage of the seven original companies comprising the regiment in gaining recruits, as such quotas preferred to enlist in a regiment, as a body, under officers of their own choice, whenever the quotas were sufficient to form a company, or companies. It became evident, early in September, that the Forty-Second Regiment could not be filled to ten full companies unless some of the original companies gave way to such city or town companies as could be secured. Colonel Burrell, with his officers and their friends, spent time and money, visiting various cities and towns endeavoring to have them join the Forty-Second.

There being a vacancy of three companies in the regiment, Colonel Burrell, although having offers of five full companies to join at one time, thought he could conscientiously accept of only three, viz., one from Weymouth, one from Medway, and one from Dorchester, preferring to let the other two join some other regiment, and to wait a short time longer, in hope that officers recruiting for the original seven companies would have full commands in a short time, although recruiting was very, very dull at the time for four of those companies. When two of the old companies, D and G, were full to the maximum, and the third, Company C, was progressing favorably, it was evident Companies A, B, E and F could not be recruited, and were delaying formation of the regiment.

Company H, recruited by Captain Bailey, was about full. This company was not in the old Second Regiment. Bailey had some sort of authority to recruit a company, and expressed a desire to become a part of the Forty-Second. He made his headquarters at Readville, and sent men into camp often. There was a great deal of bounty jumping in this company before it was mustered in. The keeping of a correct list of men sent to camp by the captain was a tough job, as the adjutant and sergeant-major well remember. What blunders were made, or obstacles met and overcome by Captain Bailey, no one can tell, for the captain kept his own counsel.

In Company B, Captain Townsend was very troublesome. In September he carried his supposed grievances so far as to remain away from camp, and order his men to keep away also. This culminated on the eighteenth, when Colonel Burrell requested the adjutant-general to discharge him; also recommended that Companies B and C be consolidated, and that Company C be the nucleus and letter of the new company. Orders were issued by the Governor disbanding A, B, E and F, transferring the men to other companies. The Weymouth company was designated Company A; Medway company, Company B; Dorchester company, Company I; and steps were taken to try and secure town quotas to fill the three companies required to complete the regiment.

During October the Governor decided to consolidate certain regiments, in order to remedy an apparent evil, and get the troops into the field as soon as possible. More regiments were being recruited in the State than could be filled by the State quota of nine months volunteers. The Forty-Second and Fifty-Fourth regiments had the smallest number of men mustered into service; the Forty-Second having seven companies, the Fifty-Fourth, six companies. Three companies from Worcester County, viz., from Leicester, Captain Cogswell, Worcester, Captain Stiles, Ware, Captain Davis, of the Fifty-Fourth, were transferred to the Forty-Second regiment. One company of the Fifty-Fourth was transferred to the Fiftieth Regiment, two companies of the Fifty-Fourth to the Fifty-First Regiment, and the Fifty-Fourth Regiment was disbanded.

All through the attempt to recruit the regiment to its maximum strength, Lieutenant-Colonel Perkins and Major Beach, instead of rendering any valuable service in that direction, were hampering the efforts of others. A jealousy sprang up in the breasts of these two officers against the colonel, born from what no one seems to know, and it is doubtful if they knew themselves. This jealous feeling was intensified when Companies A, B, E and F were disbanded, opening the way for three new companies from city and town quotas to take their places. With only three companies remaining of the old Second Regiment, a triangular fight sprang up for the positions of colonel, lieutenant-colonel and major; elective in all nine months troops from Massachusetts, line officers casting the ballots. Officers of the three Worcester County companies held the balance of power. They were desirous of obtaining for field officers the best men they could find in the regiment. A council was held one evening, seated in a circle upon the grass some distance from quarters, where the matter was fully discussed. It was finally decided to vote for Isaac S. Burrell for colonel, as he was well known to most of them as an old militia officer; for Captain Stedman, Company B, to be lieutenant-colonel, as he had been highly recommended to them by officials connected with the Norwich, Vermont, Military Academy (where Stedman formerly held a position as instructor in military tactics), with whom a correspondence was carried on without the knowledge of Captain Stedman; for Captain Stiles, Company E, to be major, as they all knew him to be an excellent officer. The question of proportioning the field positions so as to recognize the new companies that had joined the regiment did not enter into their discussions at all.

The election occurred on Thursday afternoon, November 6th, at regimental headquarters. Every line officer was present. Brigadier-General Peirce was presiding officer, with acting Post-Adjutant Lieutenant Partridge, Company

B, recording officer. The vote for colonel stood twenty-eight for I. S. Burrell and two for T. L. D. Perkins. The vote for lieutenant-colonel stood sixteen for Captain Joseph Stedman, ten for Lieutenant-Colonel T. L. D. Perkins, two for Major George W. Beach, and two for Captain A. N. Proctor. The vote for major stood seventeen for Captain F. G. Stiles, three for Major George W. Beach, and ten for Captain A. N. Proctor.

Friends of Captain Proctor based his claim for the positions of lieutenant-colonel and major on the fact that he was the senior captain, a valid claim, which would have had weight with officers holding the balance of power if they had known more of his military history at that time. His friends did not press his claim until it was evident Perkins and Beach could not be elected.*

The dates of muster into the United States service are as follows:

Company A — September 13, 1862.
" B — " 13, "
" C — October 11, "
" D — September 19, "
" E — " 30, "
" F — " 30, "
" G — " 16, "
" H — " 24, "
" I — " 16, "
" K — October 14, "

The field and staff were commissioned November 6th, 1862, and mustered in November 11th, 1862. The time of the regiment commenced from October 14th, 1862.

* The wounds of disappointment inflicted by this election were never fully healed, but did not interfere with all of the officers doing their duty as they understood it. In very small things did any feeling show itself afterwards, and not then until the lieutenant-colonel was in command, while the colonel was a prisoner.

It would be a hard task to pick out a finer body of men than composed the rank and file of the Forty-Second Regiment as it now stood, containing men from all ranks of life and all grades of society. A few bad men were enlisted, 't is true, but less than the usual proportion found in regiments formed and enlisted as this was. About one-tenth, or say nearly one hundred men, were of that disposition and temperament, in case of going into action the very best thing to be done with them, for the safety of the regiment, would be to hurl them into a ditch with orders to stay there until the fighting was over. That the record of the regiment does not equal the best from Massachusetts was due to events over which it had no control. The material was there, the courage was there; it needed merely a baptism fire to fully acquaint the rank and file with the smell of powder, and then opportunities to prove their metal.

Life in camp at Readville was by no means monotonous. During August, September, and part of October, the men were under canvas. Regular routine duties of camp were performed, and the hours after duty were passed in social pleasures, which only those who have a natural taste for the life of a soldier, or young novices in camp life, know how to enjoy. The weather, for a large portion of the time, was glorious. The surrounding scenery at Readville is very fine, as any person who has visited the ground can testify. As the facilities for visiting from Boston were very good, *via* the Boston and Providence Railroad, also by splendid drives over excellent roads, all of the troops concentrated there, over three thousand men, had many visitors to while away the time when off duty, causing the various camps to have a gala appearance at all parades of ceremony, such as guard mounting, dress parades and reviews. Bands of music were specially engaged at various times to assist in these parades, much to the gratification of the men. All day long the rat-a-tap of the drums was to be heard, as the newly-organized drum corps attached to the regiments went on with their practice. It was a continual scene of excitement, without danger, until orders came for the various bodies to move. Between other regiments and the Forty-Second there was not much social intercourse, except in a few instances. There appeared to exist a feeling that the Forty-Second did not amount to much.*

Surgeon Cummings, appointed *vice* Lamson resigned, commenced his duties and reports September 6th, at once taking hold of matters with a will and devotion to the interests of men in camp characteristic of him.† With a sharp eye kept on the rations, cooking, sanitary condition of grounds and quarters, hardly a day passed without his embodying some suggestion of importance in his daily reports to the colonel. At first he had great difficulty in getting first-sergeants of companies to answer properly the surgeon's call at his quarters in the morning, whereby some men were neglected who were sick in quarters and were not reported. He maintained his right, by virtue of the army regulations then in force, demanding that the first-sergeants, or those acting in their stead, attend the call punctually, report in writing all on sick furlough, all sick in quarters and unable to attend, and cause all who were sick so as to incapacitate them from duty, or claimed to be so, to appear at his quarters, where each company

---

*Among the members of a band occasionally engaged for duty on Sundays at Readville Camp was Mariani, the old drum-major of Gilmore's Band when at the zenith of its fame in Boston. Signior (as he was called) Mariani was a man of commanding presence, very tall and very heavy in build. He was a jolly companion, full of anecdote regarding his native land, Italy. His one time, two time, three time story has never been forgotten by those who had the pleasure of hearing it.

†Cummings served in the Army of the Potomac, between Yorktown and Richmond; also did duty in the Yorktown and Portsmouth Grove general hospitals.

would be called in turn, prescribed for, and the men sent to quarters, to hospital, on furlough, to easy duty or full duty; and if after the morning call any were taken sick, a sergeant or corporal in all cases be sent with them to his quarters, or to summon him to see them at their own quarters when too sick to go to his tent. By hammering away he finally got this system at work to his satisfaction. He calculated to keep the run of all sick men in the regiment, as was his duty, and did not want any one to say he had been neglected. Companies C and H gave the surgeon much trouble, and ruffled his temper, because not able to obtain any report from them, day after day, even after they were mustered into service.

The regimental hospital tent was one of the first things to occupy his attention. By constant efforts on his part and of Colonel Burrell, he was able to report on the twentieth of September that he was supplied with all the medicines needed; on the eighteenth of October that the hospital tent was ready for such patients as needed treatment there, with accommodations for ten patients — in his opinion the best at the post. On the second of October, and up to that date, accommodations in regimental hospital had been such, and those unfit in the estimation of the surgeon, that only two men could be received. Until the hospital was ready, the practice was to allow sick men to go home on furlough if unfit for duty. A few of the men attempted to play "old soldier," but very soon exposed themselves in some way, and had to do double duty as the penalty. Surgeon Cummings could not be fooled very long.

In the matter of police duty in the camp, he kept a careful watch to see whether the officer of the day had sinks properly attended to. Cook houses, cooking utensils and their care were often inspected by him; also the cooking and food for rations. The guard quarters frequently had his inspection, nor was he forgetful of the sentries on night duty, many times recommending that hot coffee be served to them when the nights were cold. With constant persevering efforts and rigid rules the camp was kept very free from filth and vermin, that curse of military camps in general.

Most of the sick cases were from slight ailments. All serious cases were furloughed home, and for a greater part of the time the average sick was quite small; the camp continued to remain in a healthy condition. Some cases of scarlet fever appeared in October and November. Prompt isolation of persons affected prevented any spread of this disease. One fatal case occurred in the regiment previous to leaving the State — Private Robert T. Morse, of Company B, died October 4th, 1862. While in regimental hospital his symptoms not being favorable he was taken home by relatives and died there. In October the surgeon discovered that Private Warren J. Partridge, Company B, twenty-three years old, had an aneurism of the right subclavian artery, liable to burst and destroy his life at any moment, and recommended a discharge from the service. Private Partridge was discharged October 22d. The surgeon also reported on October 22d that one of the cases in hospital he believed to be feigned, Private Abner Ward, of Company C. He had learned Ward was determined to get a discharge at all hazards, and was fifty-two years old. Ward enlisted as forty-four years of age, never went with the regiment, and did obtain a discharge for disability March 12th, 1863.

Assistant-Surgeon Hitchcock was appointed and assigned to the regiment by the surgeon-general of the State, reporting for duty in September. Before leaving the State there were no opportunities to judge of his capacity. He made a favorable impression on some and was not liked by others. His appearance and conversation was that of a young graduate from college. The reason he failed to satisfy men of the regiment while in the field may partially be traced to early impressions he made upon them at Readville.

The rations furnished while in camp were good, and could not cause complaint. So near home, with many friends, pocket money plenty, the regular rations were supplemented by extras to such an extent that it may be said most of the men fared sumptuously. Notwithstanding all this, the natural instinct of a soldier in camp or on active service, to forage, would make itself manifest in spite of extra precautions taken to prevent it. A supper, participated in by a favored few one evening, was one of the pleasant events of this camp. Those invited were pledged not to ask questions. As chicken after chicken was brought forth from a ground-hole inside of the tent, the reason was obvious. It would have been awkward for some persons present to have asked questions and been told the truth, for frequent complaints of despoiled hen-roosts had been made by residents in adjacent farm-houses, and all officers, commissioned and non-commissioned, were ordered to keep a sharp lookout for chickens served as rations, and to follow up the clue so obtained.

The non-commissioned staff made an attempt to form a mess, with an arrangement made with one of the company cooks to attend to the cooking. The plan worked well for a short time. The sharp appetites of all who composed that mess got the better of their willingness to allow fair play and a fair chance for all to sit down and have a proper share of what was on the mess table, so the unlucky member who was late would find nothing to eat. Dissatisfaction was expressed by the unlucky member at such times, which was to be expected, but precious little satisfaction could he get. One after another withdrew until there was not enough left to stand the expense, when the non-commissioned staff mess became a thing of the past. No attempt was ever made to revive it.

To vary the monotony of company and battalion drills, that had been pushed ever since camp was located, short practice marches were made from camp in different directions over the various roads in the vicinity. The day after a march made October 9th, Surgeon Cummings, in his morning report, commented as follows: "The march of yesterday had its usual effect upon those not in perfect health, of which class there are always more or less in every regiment. A larger proportion, however, than usual, will, I believe, be found in this regiment capable of enduring severe and exhausting hardships, which are unavoidable in the field." Throughout October the weather could not have been better. What with the bracing air, constant out-door exercise, plain food, strict regularity of meals and good hours for sleep, it was astonishing to see how tough and hardy those men became who had heretofore led a sedentary and confined life in counting-rooms. The greater number of this class of men afterwards stood fatigue of campaign service much better than those who appeared to be healthier and stronger. In fact, the men who were strong, from having out-door occupations, were among the first to break down when hot weather set in, while serving in the Nineteenth Corps.

On the departure of the Forty-Fourth Regiment for North Carolina, October 22d, the Forty-Second struck its camp, occupied the barracks vacated by that regiment, and rapidly improved in discipline and drill. On going into the barracks of the Forty-Fourth they were found to be in a dirty and filthy condition. It was hard work policing the grounds and cleaning up quarters before the surgeon would be satisfied with the sanitary condition of grounds and barracks. The regimental camp hospital was removed to the barrack hospital on the twenty-third, much against the judgment of Surgeon Cummings, who expressed a preference for his tent as long as the weather was not too cold. In his morning report of October 23d, Cummings says, "The removing of the camp from its present site to that lately occupied by the Forty-Fourth Regiment in this weather will, I fear, cause more or less sickness from exposure; but the men stand camp life remarkably well — much better than we had any reason to expect. The field, barracks, cook-houses, hospital, wells, and especially the sinks, lately occupied and used by the Forty-Fourth Regiment were left in the most dirty and filthy condition imaginable. I was astonished to find a camp which had been reported to the surgeon-general as a pattern of neatness and excellent sanitary regulation in such an exceedingly filthy condition, especially the sinks. They evidently have not been filled in for more than a week, to say the least. I shall report to the surgeon-general the exact state, as near as possible, in which the camp was left for us."

November was a cold month. On the seventh a severe north-east snow-storm was experienced, causing much inconvenience and suffering, as stoves had not been placed in the barracks. The next day this was remedied by obtaining stoves from the Forty-Fifth Regiment barracks.

Orders were originally prepared for the regiment to proceed to Newbern, N. C., but Colonel Sprague, Fifty-First, who had served under General Foster, wishing to do so again, an interview was held with Adjutant-General Schouler by the two colonels, and as Colonel Burrell expressed a preference to serve under General Banks, the original orders were destroyed; orders were then issued to report to Major-General N. P. Banks in New York, to form a part of his expedition, or "Banks' expedition" as it was publicly known.

The regiment left Readville at one o'clock in the afternoon, Friday, November 21st, in a heavy rain-storm, *via* Boston and Providence Railroad, by cars to Groton, Conn., thence by steamer *Commodore* to New York.

The original mustered strength of the regiment was as follows:

Field and Staff,	9 officers,		. . . . . .	9	total.
Non-Commissioned Staff,		5 enlisted men,		5	"
Company A,	3 officers,	94	"	97	"
" B,	3 "	92	"	95	"
" C,	3 "	88	"	91	"
" D,	3 "	86	"	89	"
" E,	3 "	79	"	82	"
" F,	3 "	88	"	91	"
" G,	3 "	96	"	99	"
" H,	3 "	88	"	91	"
" I,	3 "	92	"	95	"
" K,	3 "	86	"	89	"

The following men had been discharged for disability before leaving the State:

Company A,	Private	Joseph Viger,	November	18,	1862.
" A,	"	Bernard Doherty,	"	18,	"
" A,	"	James C. Wendall,	"	18,	"
" B,	"	Warren J. Partridge,	October	22,	"
" F,	"	James O. Boyd,	November	19,	"
" F,	"	Henry W. Pratt,	"	19,	"
" F,	"	Anthony Sherman,	"	19,	"
" K,	"	William B. Gould,	"	18,	"

There were left behind, in the State, the following

officer and enlisted men, on detached service, sick, or in jail:

Lieutenant D. A. Partridge, Company B — Remained at Readville camp by orders of Colonel Day, issued October 27th, 1862, on detached duty, looking out for deserters; six men were returned to the regiment through him. There was some difficulty and correspondence relating to his rejoining the regiment. A feud existed between Lieutenant-Colonel Stedman and Partridge, occasioned by the election for captain in Company B, when Partridge was jumped over by Cook, through interference of Stedman, so Partridge claims. Stedman lost friends in the regiment by his action. Lieutenant Partridge was mustered out of service March 5th, 1863, to accept a commission in the Fifty-Fifth Regiment.

Private Newman B. Luce, Company E — Sick in hospital at Camp Wool, Worcester, since October 2d, 1862. Rejoined his company April 9th, 1863.

Private Frederick A. Mahan, Company E — Sick in hospital at Camp Wool, since October 10th, 1862. Rejoined his company April 9th, 1863.

Private Asa Breckenridge, Company K — Sick in hospital at Readville. Sent home to Worcester, November 12th, 1862. Did not rejoin the regiment.

Private John W. Sheppard, Company K — Sick in hospital at Readville. Sent home to Warren, Mass., November 12th, 1862. Discharged for disability April 8th, 1863.

Private Abner C. Ward, Company C — Shot himself to escape duty. Left at Hopkinton, Mass. Discharged for disability March 12th, 1863.

Private George A. Davis, Company D — Sick at home in Roxbury, Mass., since November 21st, 1862. Rejoined his company May 16th, 1863.

Private John O'Harran, Company D — Confined in

Dedham jail on sentence for manslaughter; killing a citizen in a drunken brawl at Mill Village, Dedham, Mass. Never rejoined his company.

Private John Nolan, Company D — Confined in Dedham jail as a witness in O'Harran's case. Released and joined the regiment February 4th, 1863.

Private Thomas H. Rillian, Company D — At home sick. Discharged for disability March 7th, 1863.

Private John A. Pierce, Company H — At home sick. Discharged for disability March 5th, 1863.

Private Charles H. Hill, Company I — Sick in hospital at Readville, November 22d, 1862. Discharged for disability March 28th, 1863.

Others were also left, but they reported in camp at East New York before the regiment sailed for New Orleans.

The roster of the regiment was as follows:

Colonel — Isaac S. Burrell.
Lieutenant-Colonel — Joseph Stedman.
Major — Frederick G. Stiles.
Adjutant — Charles A. Davis.
Quartermaster — Charles B. Burrell.
Surgeon — Arial I. Cummings.
Assistant-Surgeon — Thomas B. Hitchcock.
Assistant-Surgeon — Rush B. Heintzelman.
Chaplain — George J. Sanger.
Sergeant-Major — Charles P. Bosson, Jr.
Quartermaster-Sergeant — Henry C. Foster.
Commissary-Sergeant — William H. Hutchinson.
Hospital-Steward — Charles J. Wood.
Drum-Major — Richard A. Neuert.
Company A — Captain, Hiram S. Coburn; Lieutenants, Martin Burrell, Jr. and John P. Burrell.

Company B — Captain, Ira B. Cook; Lieutenants, David A. Partridge and Joseph C. Clifford.

Company C — Captain, Orville W. Leonard; Lieutenants, Isaac B. White and Joseph Sanderson, Jr.

Company D — Captain, George Sherive; Lieutenants, William H. Cowdin and Darius F. Eddy.

Company E — Captain, Charles A. Pratt; Lieutenants, John W. Emerson and Brown P. Stowell.

Company F — Captain, John D. Cogswell; Lieutenants, Timothy M. Duncan and Lyman A. Powers.

Company G — Captain, Alfred N. Proctor; Lieutenants, Albert E. Proctor and Thaddeus H. Newcomb.

Company H — Captain, Davis W. Bailey; Lieutenants, Charles C. Phillips and Augustus L. Gould.

Company I — Captain, Cyrus Savage; Lieutenants, Samuel F. White and Benjamin F. Bartlett.

Company K — Captain, George P. Davis; Lieutenants, Henry A. Harding and J. Martin Gorham.

CHAPTER II.

EN ROUTE—CAMP AT EAST NEW YORK—ON TRANSPORTS.

ON arrival at Groton, the men were immediately marched aboard the steamer *Commodore*, owned by Commodore Vanderbilt, exclusively used for transport service since the war commenced. Owing to a dense fog which prevailed and stormy character of the weather, it was near two o'clock Saturday morning before the boat left her pier.

At this place the regiment came near losing the sergeant-major. After the men had filed aboard and been assigned positions upon the boat, he went ashore to take a look around the wharf, to ascertain if all stragglers had reported on board; while doing so, the darkness causing all lights to be very indistinct, he was about to walk off the dock when a friendly voice of caution was heard just in the nick of time. Dressed in a great coat, with belt and sword, and heavy knapsack strapped upon his back, to have dropped into the chilly water on that cold night was almost certain to have ended his life.

Only those who have participated in like occasions can imagine the scene that presented itself on board the *Commodore*. One would think this body of over nine hundred men were bound on a picnic rather than a duty which involved life or death. No one could foretell what the future had in store for him, whether a victim to disease, maimed or diseased for life, death upon the field, temporary sufferings from curable wounds, or a return home in as good health and spirits as when he left. They took the risk. They should have credit for the courage to do so.

A trip through the cars while *en route* from Readville Camp showed the men to be in rather a sober state of mind. Nothing gloomy about them, but very thoughtful. The car containing the field, staff and line officers, had the appearance of a silent prayer meeting. The colonel was quite meditative. Parting with wife and children was no easy matter to a man of his noble disposition. Many men had been married only a few weeks or months, and to them the enforced separation was keenly felt. As the day was rainy a very limited number of friends were present in camp to say good-by, and affecting parting incidents were not so many as they otherwise would have been. All homesick feelings passed away when the regiment reached Groton, and each man was himself again.

The quartermaster and commissary stores, ammunition and horses were in cars on the fore part of the train, in charge of detailed men. The jolliest crowd upon the train was in the ammunition car, composed of Sam Hersey, the colonel's clerk, Sergeant Courtney, Sergeant-Major Bosson, and Sergeant Wentworth.

With singing, dancing, card playing, frollicking, and cutting up pranks of various sorts, time passed rapidly. There were parties who did not sleep at all that night. Those who have ever been on excursions such as used to be indulged in by the old militia organizations, can form some idea of the manner in which the night was passed.

Owing to the late hour of leaving Groton the *Commodore* did not arrive at New York until noon of Saturday. Rations had been issued, to be carried in haversacks, sufficient to last three meals to each man; but with that carelessness so habitual to a raw soldier the rations lasted a majority of them for one meal; the consequence was, that on arrival at New York, the men were tired, very hungry, and very cross. About dusk orders were received to proceed to the Union Race Course at East New York, and report to Colonel Chickering, Forty-First Massachusetts Volunteers, commanding the post. The steamer *Commodore* was then lying at Williamsburg. The baggage wanted immediately was packed and sent forward; the troops filed out of the steamer, forming regimental line in South Second Street. The citizens (noble hearted people) furnished the entire regiment with hot coffee, crackers, fresh bread, cheese and cold meats. Some ladies went so far as to furnish hot pies, baking and dealing them out while the men were halted, refreshing themselves in their neighborhood. By eight o'clock the entire body was amply refreshed and ready to commence the ten-mile march which was before them. All through the City of Williamsburg the regiment was greeted with cheers, wavings of handkerchiefs, expressions of good-will, and all those demonstrations which proved a people's interest in the cause for which the men were enlisted. While this excitement continued the column was steady enough, but after the populous part of the city was passed and the muddy road was reached, with all quiet outside of the column, straggling commenced. The weight of knapsack, gun and ammunition pouch began to be felt; feet became sore; silence reigned in the ranks, and nought could be heard save the rattling of the drums at the head of the column, the solid tramp, splash, tramp, splash, or words of command from officers.

The night was dark as black pitch, the road rapidly became worse as the regiment advanced, the weather became very cold, with strong, chilly, wintry blasts, so that by the time Hiram Woodruff's hotel and stables was reached the men were not in the best of spirits to receive the intelligence imparted to them. It was here Colonel Chickering had his headquarters. When Colonel Burrell reported himself and command for instructions, he was ordered to the race-course to feed the men, and procure the best quarters possible. There were some four thousand men already in camp and bivouac. No ground had been allotted the regiment, and no tents were to be had, so that soon after reaching the race-course the regiment countermarched back to Woodruff's stables, and the men were ordered to find shelter for the night in the horse-stalls, hen-houses, etc., to the best of their ability. The One Hundred and Sixty First New York Infantry had arrived but a short time previous, and were placed in a similar position. How the various companies of the regiment passed the night would be an interesting history by itself, suffice it to record every man survived, and in the morning, on forming regimental line, none seemed the worse for a little hard experience so early in his military career. On arrival at New York the colonel, quartermaster, and adjutant, reported to General Banks. Requisition was made at once on Post-Quartermaster Colonel Van Vliet for camp equipage. Adjutant Davis was left to get this camp equipage *en route* for the camp-ground, and had a tough time to obtain drays and induce the drivers to start for East New York. The late hour when all was ready made it necessary to persistently stick to the work, or else it would not have been accomplished. This camp equipage arrived during the night, ready for use the next morning.

 Camp was pitched on Sunday, a bitter cold day, and from this time until the day it was vacated the regular routine of camp life was done. At first the cold weather occasioned much distress, but moderating in a few days comparative comfort was experienced. Most of the men, with "Yankee" ingenuity, built underground ovens in their tents with a passage to the outside for escape of smoke. Towards night these ovens were filled with wood and a fire started, which generally would last all night, enabling occupants, with the aid of straw bedding, to keep tolerably warm. Every night huge bonfires were made at the head of each company street, and around them the men would cluster and discuss their treatment, talk of those at home, crack jokes, sing songs, tell stories (some of them good, others not good), while few of a philosophical turn of mind indulged in speculations as to the future. The poor fellows on sentry duty had a hard time; the guard reliefs would gather about a bonfire in front of the guard tents roasting the side of their bodies nearest the fire while the other side was freezing, then reverse this position and thaw out one side while the other froze again. During the eleven days in camp here a large amount of wood was consumed, in order to keep warm. Many trees in rear of the camp were cut down and burned, besides the amount of wood allowed by Government and drawn through the quartermaster, for the nights would be cold even when the days were comfortable.

There were two evils under which the troops suffered while at this post: rations, and officers on leave of absence. Instead of allowing rations to be drawn in kind, a post-kitchen had been established; somebody having contracted with some United States official to furnish cooked rations at so much a ration. This somebody must have realized a very large amount of greenbacks by the operation. Frequently the food was not fit for dogs to eat. Not once could the coffee be drank without creating a nausea. This necessary article would be drawn by the company cooks from the post-kitchen in pails, and then thrown away, alleging, as a reason for doing so, that so much was stopped from delivery to the rest of the troops in camp. At times the meat served out was eatable, but often better fitted to be used as manure than to sustain life in a human being. The bread was good, and on this, with clear, cold water, most of the men subsisted. Some companies did manage to obtain a little good coffee and cheese, from New York City, on their private account. To such a pitch had the feelings of men been wrought by this one item of bad rations, when the post commissary building caught fire one day, not a soldier would lend a helping hand to quench the flames until it was announced that the post hospital was over the cook-house. They then worked with a will to stop the fire. In the month of December, a few weeks after the regiment had left, this same cook-house caught fire again, and was burnt to the ground. It is supposed to have been designedly set on fire by soldiers then in camp. After this was done Government rations were issued according to army regulations. When the Forty-Second got orders to leave camp, Colonel Burrell had a wordy fight with the contractor who furnished rations, as he refused to sign a receipt for full rations, telling him the whole scheme was a fraud. Time was precious, and a compromise was arrived at by Burrell consenting to sign a receipt for one-third the number of rations claimed to have been issued.

All furloughs or leaves of absence had to be granted by Colonel Chickering. Battalion commanders had no right to grant them. Field officers were obliged to be absent more or less on business. Line officers of the regiment were continually away on furlough, to visit New York City, often without leave, taking the liberty without applying for it in the regular way. At this time the discipline of the enlisted men was far ahead of that shown by their officers. Orders were frequently received from post headquarters when no commissioned officer could be found in camp to take them. The regular drills would, in most cases, have to be conducted by non-commissioned officers, in the absence of those in commission. Is it to be wondered at, with such a state of things existing among the officers, that the men should adopt the same policy? If a furlough was not granted run the guard and be absent on " French leave," as it was termed. There were some forty cases, on an average, each day, of men absent without leave.

True to his duty and profession, Surgeon Cummings had the hospital tent put up and placed in order immediately after the camp-ground was selected. Those who were under his treatment can testify to his care of them, and the amount of work he did to keep the sick in good spirits. He labored under extraordinary difficulties at this particular time, with several serious cases on his hands. Four of them had to be left in hospital when the regiment proceeded to embark on transports, viz., Private Abijah S. Tainter, Company E, Private Charles S. Knight, Company F, Private Paschal E. Burnham, Company G, and Private George A. Cushing, Company A.

Cushing, Knight and Burnham did not rejoin the regiment, being discharged and mustered out of service during the Spring of 1863. Tainter never rejoined his company, and was not mustered out until the expiration of service by the regiment.

One peculiar case under the surgeon's care deserves mention. A private from one of the companies was in hospital sick. It was difficult to diagnosis his case. There was no trace of disease except his complaint of being sick. He was in the hospital about two days, eating heartily, sleeping soundly, generally enjoying the snug place like an epicure. The surgeon got mad. It is usual to make convalescents in camp hospitals do some light work when there is any to do and they are capable of doing it. He set this fellow to do some light chores in the tent, when his peculiar disease developed itself suddenly. It was laziness. To square accounts with the impostor, Cummings pronounced him cured, but, before discharging him from the sick-list to duty, said he must take a bath; upon disrobing himself his shirt and flannels were found literally alive with vermin; they could not be cleaned; a hole was dug in the ground, a fire made, when the clothing, with vermin, was burned. The fellow was too lazy to keep himself clean.

Cummings enjoyed a good smoke before going to sleep. A look into his tent any night after he had retired would show him to be covered up to his chin with coverlids, a night-cap on almost covering his eyes, and from the small exposed part of his face volumes of smoke would be rolling upward from an old clay pipe seen in his mouth. Those who were aware of this habit used to think it a good joke to invite anybody to take a peep into the tent and see the surgeon at his devotions.

Thanksgiving Day found most of the companies with enough turkey and chicken to go around. Where they came from is not a mystery. Some from home, but not all. The complaints of farmers near by, who had poultry to lose, destroys all mystery about it. To the credit of the regiment be it said that this was the only time when any foraging was done clandestinely while at East New York. The justification must rest on the ground of neglect by proper officers to furnish proper food.

The City Government of Boston having generously furnished the regiment with a complete set of band instruments, which were received December 1st, while at

East New York, a band was organized from the rank and file, consisting of the following members, viz.:

1. Bugler Joseph R. Parks, Company D, Leader.
2. Drummer Frederick L. Bowditch, Company A.
3. Private George A. Morse, Company B.
4. Private Joseph Clark, Company B.
5. Bugler Bernard McKenna, Company C — in February, 1863, gave up his connection with the band and joined his company at Camp Parapet, La.
6. Corporal Frederick S. McIntosh, Company D — was completely prostrated by long sickness, and discharged from the service in June, 1863, for disability.
7. Private Edmund L. Chenery, Company D.
8. Private Francis L. Howard, Company E.
9. Drummer Frank Lamb, Company F.
10. Corporal Charles H. Woodcock, Company F — gave up his warrant in March, to join the band.
11. Corporal Edward A. Spooner, Company F — attached in March.
12. Private Orrin F. Bacon, Company I.
13. Fifer Thomas Bowe, Company I.
14. Bugler Henry B. Sargent, Company I.
15. Corporal William A. Cowles, Company I.
16. Bugler Cyrus S. Loud, Company K.

The places of sick members were temporarily filled by others from the ranks. A queer compound of human flesh, Sergeant Charles A. Attwell, Company G, was made band-major March 2d, magnifying his position and duties to such an extent that his appointment was revoked July 18th. Parks, the leader, was another queer fish. He worked hard in his own way, ably seconded by Tom Bowe, to improve the band. The talent could not be called first-class, while his own ability to instruct members was limited. He should be congratulated for such a tolerable degree of proficiency as was attained. Notwithstanding the band did not have a good selection of band music for a long time, it was a source of pleasure while in service. Old Parks, as he was called, was a great tobacco chewer, with a cud in his mouth at all hours. One afternoon he forgot to remove this article from his mouth while on regimental dress parade in New Orleans, and blew the same into his instrument when the band commenced to sound off down the line. He played, or tried to play away, without success, and set the boys laughing by his look of wonder, and attempts to remedy the evil. Not until this parade was over, amid bantering by his comrades, did he discover what was the source of trouble.

Long since has it been demonstrated that regimental bands are not desirable during active service. The attention, the accommodations and privileges they require, are not commensurate with the service they render. Field music, where there is in addition a band, is sure to be neglected. Out of fourteen to twenty drums in the Forty-Second Regiment that should always have been in good working order, from two to five only were usually found fit for use, while the band was kept supplied with everything it required. The long roll has been beaten by one drum because all other drums were without drum-heads. Often the same drummer has had to first beat drummers call at guard quarters, then beat the stated signals in front of the camp.

Drum-Major Neuert must have been very much disgusted with his position and duties while at Bayou Gentilly Camp in Louisiana, to have devoted so much of his spare time in teaching some of the young darkies who hung around the camp how to drum. These youngsters learned very rapidly how to beat a drum, using a piece of board to practise upon. An excellent drum corps of from twelve to fifteen drummers could easily have been formed from these camp followers, who, in a short time, would be almost as proficient as the regular drummers.

At noon, on the second day of December, orders were received from General Banks directing the regiment to proceed at once to Brooklyn and embark upon transports, that were to be in readiness. Camp was struck at once, baggage packed and sent forward, cooked rations for twenty-four hours issued, or supposed to have been, for what was received from the post-kitchen was not reliable, and by three o'clock in the afternoon the regiment was *en route*. Just before leaving the camp-ground to take the road the Twenty-Eighth Connecticut Infantry Regiment passed by, on the way also to take transports. From the music given by the Twenty-Eighth regimental musicians, that could be distinctly heard for some minutes as the regiment came along the road hid by the woods, it was supposed they had a very fine band. Great was the surprise to those who were near enough the road to see when the head of the column came in sight, that the music was rendered by drummers, fifers and buglers only. With those who were interested in such matters it was the opinion, that the music rendered by these field musicians equalled, and in some selections of pieces played surpassed, anything the band of the Forty-Second ever did.

Passing through Brooklyn, a similar demonstration greeted the regiment as when passing through Williamsburg. It was a fine evening, about dark, as the men marched upon the sidewalks (the streets were quite muddy) along some of the most pleasant thoroughfares of Brooklyn. Houses appeared to be in a blaze of light, the people crowded at windows, on door-steps and sidewalks, full of enthusiasm. Many requests were made by young ladies to be favored with a letter after taking the field; many little necessaries were given to the men; neatly folded within the packages were found *billet-doux*, with the name and address of the writer, saying the donor expected to hear again from the recipient. Some of these notes fell into rather queer hands. So far as could be ascertained, no undue advantage was ever taken by the men of the Forty-Second from this epidemic of nonsense.

On arrival at the South Ferry, foot of Atlantic Avenue, at seven o'clock, one transport was found at the designated pier, accommodating two companies, and she was not ready to embark men. Quarters for the night were generously tendered Lieutenant-Colonel Stedman, for the regiment, by the Thirteenth and Fourteenth Regiments, N. Y. National Guard, in their armory. The colonel, major, and quartermaster went to New York on business at General Banks' headquarters. Refreshments were furnished by the same regiments, and by citizens. Many of the men were entertained in private residences with supper, lodging and breakfast. To the postmaster, and Mayor of Brooklyn the regiment was especially indebted for favors extended. State Agent Colonel Tufts, in charge of the New England rooms in New York, supposing the Forty-Second would embark at foot of Canal Street in that city, had provided a full supply of hot coffee, sandwiches, crackers and cheese, at that point. On learning this fact the sergeant-major was dispatched to have the food brought over to Brooklyn, which was done late in the evening, arriving after the men were all fed. The supply thus obtained was dealt out in the morning to those who needed it.*

---

* After sentinels were posted, to prevent men from straggling away from quarters, many ludicrous scenes occurred in attempts made to get out. The most ingenious contrivances were adopted; some men even risked their lives in these attempts to evade the guard, by windows, and from the armory roof. They tried to crawl through ventilators, and to tunnel into the street from the cellar. Nearly all these devices

The greater part of the regiment behaved finely on this occasion. There was some straggling and some desertions. The worst case of neglect of duty that occurred was Color-Sergeants Vialle, Company G, and Humphrey, Company D, who had in their charge the State and United States colors. Instead of leaving them in the armory where the regiment was quartered, they were left in a low groggery on Atlantic Avenue, and found by the sergeant-major, by the merest accident, late in the evening, taken to the armory, and placed in charge of the color company. It was the intention of Colonel Burrell to have had an inquiry into this case of neglect, when circumstances would permit. The separation of the companies and his being retained a prisoner of war for a long time alone prevented.

Early on the morning of December third the embarkation commenced, transports having arrived. Owing to the large number of stragglers during the day it was dark before all were got aboard, and the vessels hauled into the river.* It was now evident that the three steamers upon which the regiment was embarked were not sufficient for the purpose. Upon the *Charles Osgood*, *Shetucket*, and *Saxon*, at least one hundred men upon each vessel were

failed, and by midnight all were fast asleep. Private Gusebio, Company C, was caught by a police officer, as he emerged from a coal-hole in the sidewalk, and beaten with a club until the guard took charge of him. These policemen on duty did not exercise any judgment whatever. They were finally taken away from the neighborhood to prevent a collision with the men, who were enraged at their bullying behavior.

*Among these stragglers was Private Wilson Curtis, an *alias*, of Company C, a professional bounty jumper, who had deserted from Readville Camp, a tough customer every way. He was spotted in New York by Lieutenant White, over there for the purpose of picking up stray men from his company, as he was on his way to board the *Shetucket*. Lieutenant White accosted him, and expected to have a fight before he could get him on board, but Curtis, who at first denied his identity, soon deemed it best to rejoin his company, as White covered him with his pistol besides using an argument on him, the substance of which was, that his life was not worth a cent if he was handed over to the military authorities. Curtis served faithfully with his company to the end.

obliged to sleep on deck. Proper representations were made to General Banks the next day, who placed a fourth transport, the *Quincy*, at the colonel's disposal, when three companies were transferred to that vessel.

Perhaps those men who on the night of the third of December were so loud in their denunciations of the colonel and his staff, laying all the blame for the hardships then suffered on those who strove in every way, and used every means within their power, to benefit their condition; perhaps those men, when time had given them a chance to reflect and compare their whole experience with what it was that night, would acknowledge that they were wrong in their snap judgment. If they could have seen the work done that night, and heard the opinions of their officers, they would then have known that the colonel and staff had their welfare and good condition at heart.

Shame on all men who will endeavor to foment a mutiny on the strength of fancied wrong, or incompetency of those in command, on such occasions as the one in point presented. There were men on board the transports that night who should hang their heads in shame.

The regiment was finally distributed as follows:

On the *Saxon*—Colonel Burrell, Adjutant Davis, Quartermaster Burrell, Surgeon Cummings, Chaplain Sanger, Quartermaster-Sergeant Foster, and Companies D, G and I. On the *Quincy*—Lieutenant-Colonel Stedman, Sergeant-Major Bosson, Commissary-Sergeant Friend S. Courtney, who had been promoted from a private in Company D, *vice* Hutchinson, discharged at East New York on account of sickness, Drum-Major Neuert, Assistant-Surgeon Hitchcock, the band, and Companies A, B and F, with fifty men of Company C, Twenty-Eighth Connecticut Volunteers. Upon the *Charles Osgood*—Companies E and K, and Hospital-Steward Wood. Upon the *Shetucket*—

Major Stiles, Ward-Master Lewis, of Company D, Ordnance-Sergeant Wentworth, Company G, and Companies C and H. A few officers and men were detached for special duty on transports *Quinnebaug* and *Eastern Queen*.

The regiment departed South in these transports, leaving behind the enlisted men named in the following table, who straggled from their colors or deserted them while in camp at Readville and East New York, and while embarking for the South : a mere handful ever returned.

There may have been some excuse for the desertion of a few of the younger men. Often a young man, after enlisting, has had such a pressure put upon him by family relations as to cause his desertion. In other cases cowardice was the true reason. While in a camp of instruction, and in no danger, all is well; when marching orders are received and preparations made to reach the seat of war, then weak-hearted young or old men are apt to desert. The greater portion of deserters from the Forty-Second Regiment were professional bounty jumpers under assumed names.

NAME.	RANK.	CO.	DATE.	REMARKS.
William Hoes,	Private.	C.	October 15.	Deserted from Readville Camp.
George Gray,	"	"	" 16.	"
William Nickerson,	"	"	" 18.	"
John Osborne,	"	"	" 18.	"
Henry Phillips,	"	"	" 20.	Deserted from Readville Camp, and also was a deserter from the First Mass.
James Boyd,	"	"	" 20.	Deserted from Readville Camp.
David Coleman,	"	"	" 20.	"
Herman Hemming,	"	"	" 28.	"
John Single,	"	"	November 2.	"
John Gordon,	"	"	" 2.	"
Edward Harrison,	"	"	" 15.	"
John Isensee,	"	"	" 15.	"
Patrick Murphy,	"	"	" 15.	"
John Stevens,	"	"	" 17.	"
James Haley,	"	"	" 17.	"
Hugh Cameron,	"	"	" 29.	Deserted from camp at East New York.
Thomas F. McKenna,	"	"	December 2.	Deserted at Brooklyn, N. Y.
Alexander Campbell,	"	D.	Time not known.	Deserted.
Henry Doyle,	"	"	December 4.	Deserted at Brooklyn, N. Y.
William H. Ellis,	"	"	Time not known.	Deserted.
Michael Hagan,	"	"	December 4.	Deserted at Brooklyn, N. Y.
John Hathon,	"	"	" 4.	"
Samuel Holmes,	"	"	" 4.	"
James Johnson,	"	"	" 4.	"
James Long,	"	"	" 4.	"

MASSACHUSETTS VOLUNTEERS.   35

Name	Rank	Co.	Date	Remarks
Trueworthy L. Moulton,	"	"	"	"
Henry Morrill,	"	"	"	"
Henry O. Williams,	"	"	Time not known.	Deserted.
Christopher Smith,	"	"	"	"
Thomas Burns,	"	"	December 4.	Straggler at Brooklyn, N. Y.; rejoined Feb. 4, 1863.
John Nolan,	"	"	" 4.	Straggler at Brooklyn, N. Y.; rejoined Feb 4, 1863.
Thomas Mathews,	"	"	" 4.	Straggler at Brooklyn, N. Y.; rejoined Feb. 4, 1863.
Patrick Goughan,	"	E.	October 4.	Deserted from Camp Wool, Worcester, Mass.
Samuel E. Lull,	"	G.	" 1.	Deserted from Readville Camp.
William Mullen,	"	"	" 12.	"
Robert Cunningham,	"	"	November 10.	"
Joseph Reed,	"	"	" 18.	"
Henry Bridges,	"	"	December 3.	"
James M. Marston,	"	"	" 3.	Deserted at Brooklyn, N.Y.; apprehended at Albany; sent to regiment Dec. 31, by Major I. T. Sprague, 1st Inf., U. S. A., Supt. Recruiting N.Y. Vols., but never joined; deserted again.
Joseph V. Colson,	"	"	" 3.	Deserted at Brooklyn, N. Y.
Rufus C. Greene,	1st Sergeant.	"	" 3.	Straggler at Brooklyn, N. Y.; reported himself to the proper officer, and rejoined the regiment Feb. 18, 1863.
John Luzardo,	2d "	"	" 3.	Came to New Orleans on the transport *Quinnebaug*; rejoined the regiment Feb. 3, 1863.
George G. Nichols,		"	" 3.	"
James L. Vialle,		"	" 3.	"
Charles A. Atwell,	4th "	"	" 3.	"

Name.	Rank.	Co.	Date.	Remarks.
Edward Bliss,	Private.	H.	September 25.	Deserted from Readville Camp.
John Fitzsimmons,	"	"	" 25.	"
John Flanigan,	"	"	" 30.	"
William Gorman,	"	"	" 25.	"
Joseph W. McLaughlin,	"	"	" 26.	"
John Quinn,	"	"	" 30.	"
William Thompson,	"	"	" 30.	"
Charles Stewart,	"	"	October 1.	"
Henry Canivan,	"	"	" 1.	"
George Cook,	"	"	" 1.	"
Francis Curly,	"	"	" 20.	"
Samuel D. Gregory,	"	"	" 1.	"
Charles Kenney,	"	"	" 18.	"
Timothy Linehan,	"	"	" 18.	"
Patrick Maline,	"	"	" 10.	"
Patrick McNally,	"	"	November 5.	"
John C. Anels,	"	"	" 29.	Deserted from camp at East New York.
Thomas Cahill,	"	"	" 18.	Deserted from Readville Camp.
Joseph H. Gleason,	"	"	" 14.	"
John Higgins,	"	"	" 1.	"
Florence Crowley,	"	"	" 24.	Deserted from camp at East New York.
John McCarty,	"	"	" 1.	Deserted from Readville Camp.
Dennis O'Connors,	"	"	" 17.	"
Thomas H. Ryan,	"	"	" 17.	"
Benjamin F. Wilde,	"	"	" 25.	Deserted from camp at East New York.
Hans F. Hansen,	"	"	" 29.	"

Alonzo Jones,	"	"	December 4.	Deserted at Brooklyn, N. Y.
James Baxter,	"	I.	September 24.	Deserted from Readville Camp.
Nathan Green,	"	"	" 25.	" " " "
James Gorman,	"	"	" 25.	" " " "
David Gracy,	"	"	" 25.	" " " "
Frederick Ernell,	"	"	November 18.	" " " "
John Snier,	"	"	" 18.	" " " "
Levi Elmer,	"	"	December 3.	Deserted at Brooklyn, N. Y.
Edward Fisher,	"	K.	" 2.	Straggler at Brooklyn; was sick, and discharged the service March 12, 1863.
George A. Whitney,	"	"	" 2.	Straggler at Brooklyn; was sick, and discharged the service March 5, 1863.
Dennis O'Mara,	"	"	" 3.	Deserted at Brooklyn, N. Y.
Andrew J. Horton,	"	"	" 3.	Straggler at Brooklyn, N. Y.; rejoined the regiment February 3, 1863.

CHAPTER III.

ON BOARD TRANSPORTS—THE SAXON—QUINCY—CHARLES OSGOOD—SHETUCKET—QUINNEBAUG.

"HEADQUARTERS" transport *Saxon*, so called because the colonel with a majority of his staff were on board, was commanded by Captain Lavender, and remained in the harbor until the morning of Friday, December 5th, the men subsisting on crackers and cold water. At eight o'clock she proceeded to sea, the boys giving a round of cheers to a lady upon the ramparts of Fort Columbus, who waved a United States flag as they passed. All arrangements were promptly made for the voyage: cooks detailed to cook rations, and men assigned to bunks below deck.

Rough weather experienced the first night out soon became a gale, which lasted for two days, playing the deuse with company cooks, and prevented any use of the galley situated between decks. Those who could eat at all had to subsist on hard bread and raw, salt pork. Nearly all of the men and all of the officers were very sea-sick. The galley fire was started several times, but rolling of the steamer would cause fat in the pans to run over upon the galley stove, and blazing up quick would set fire to the deck. Quick work with buckets of water would put the fire out and prevent any serious damage.

The gale moderated during the night of December 7th. On Monday, December 8th, after passing Cape Hatteras during Sunday night, the sea became smooth, when men began to show themselves on deck. Somewhat hungry, and not liking the regular allotted fare, on Monday night a few men broke open the ice-chest and stole some fresh beef, cooking it at the galley. Next morning the culprits were picked out. Corporal Sanford Wood, Company I, was broke, had his chevrons stripped from his uniform, and was put in irons by order of the colonel, as he was ringleader in the affair. Privates J. Colson, Company I, Frank McConlow and Fitzallen Gourley, both of Company D, detailed cooks at the time, were also put in irons for not revealing the thieves names.

The *Saxon* proved to be the safest and fastest boat of the four vessels. She made a fine run to Key West, where anchor was cast at six o'clock December 11th, without anything of an exciting nature to enliven the trip except striking a school of finback whales about ten o'clock on the morning of the tenth. The orders to transport-captains were, to sail forty-eight hours out to sea and then open their sealed orders, which were to rendezvous at Ship Island, Gulf of Mexico, with permission, in case of distress, want of coal, water or provisions, to stop at Port Royal, Tortugas or Key West. Taking in a supply of fresh water and coal the steamer left Key West at six o'clock on the morning of December 12th, bound for Ship Island direct; but early on the morning of December 15th, which was very dark, the mate in charge of the deck lost his course, and at full speed almost ran by the blockading fleet off Mobile Bay. The gunboat *R. R. Cuyler* hailed them at two A.M., and was answered, when a blank shot followed by a cannon-ball from the gunboat *Montgomery* caused the mate to slow up and heave to. Not provided with a steam whistle there was nothing to do but to wait for something to develop, and soon the *Saxon* was boarded by naval officers, who gave the unwelcome intelligence that the transport was off her course, heading direct for Mobile, and was then past the inner line of picket boats, about one and a half miles from Mobile Bar.

The *Saxon* then proceeded on the correct course for Ship Island, arriving there at nine o'clock A. M. About twenty-five tons of coal was taken aboard from coal vessel *General Berry*, that had lain at Ship Island for four months without a bushel of coal being removed until the *Saxon* took her small supply. After receiving orders and coaling, at five o'clock in the afternoon a start was made for New Orleans, encountering a severe northerly gale during the night, which caused the vessel to roll worse than at any time previous on the voyage. At seven o'clock, December 16th, the bar at South-West Pass of the Mississippi River was in sight, and at nine o'clock she was on her way up river, passing Forts Jackson and St. Philip at noon, tieing up at the left bank at nine o'clock for the night; two sentinels were placed upon the river bank as a protection from any possible guerilla attack.

Early on the morning of December 17th, say about three o'clock, the vessel proceeded to New Orleans, arriving at seven o'clock, after a trip of twelve days from Sandy Hook, New York harbor. At four o'clock in the afternoon the *Saxon* steamed up river to Carrollton, arriving at seven o'clock, and anchored for the night, the men landing to go into camp late in the afternoon of next day, eighteenth.

The *Quincy* was the first transport to get away, passing Sandy Hook at night December 4th, in face of a threatening gale that lasted about three days. While passing Cape Hatteras the gale became so severe that the vessel was in great danger of not being able to weather it, as Captain George W. Clapp, an old and experienced navigator, afterward acknowledged. Had she foundered, few, if any, could have survived to tell the tale. Except the crew and Captain Cogswell, all hands were in that state of sea-sickness they did not care whether they lived or died. The *Quincy* was an old freight propeller with two light masts, and one small upright boiler to work her machinery, previously in the merchant marine on one of the western lakes. She was lost December 12th, 1863, while making the voyage from New York to New Orleans, having sprung a leak during a violent gale, going down in sight of Hatteras Light. Out of twenty-five persons aboard nine were saved. Captain Clapp was lost.

On the evening of December 8th a leak in the boiler was discovered. The fire was put out to admit of repairs being made; the steamer drifting through the night. Fortunately the weather was all that could be desired, and no bad results from the accident were to be feared. Steam was got up on the morning of the ninth, but the same evening another and worse leak in the boiler was discovered. At a council of officers convened it was decided to instruct the captain to put into Port Royal for repairs. The weather continued magnificent, with a smooth sea. Port Royal was reached at noon on the eleventh under circumstances which did not admit of a doubt that had the steamer been delayed twelve hours longer her engine could not have been used at all. A Board of Survey, granted by Brigadier-General Brannan, U. S. A., commanding the District, and Commodore Dupont, pronounced the vessel sea-worthy, while the boiler and engine were altogether too small for ocean service, besides being very much out of order.

The troops were landed and quartered at Hilton Head while repairs were made. Lieutenant Powers was sea-sick from the start, refusing nourishment part of the time, and not able to retain any on his stomach when he attempted to take it; wrapped in his blanket he lay a picture of helplessness, losing strength day by day until it became a question whether he would survive to reach Ship Island. The landings at Hilton Head and Tortugas enabled him to recuperate sufficient strength to stand the strain while upon the water, for when going to sea after each landing he was flat on his back again the moment the long ocean swell was reached. While the gale lasted for the first days out from New York, sick as they were between decks, in an atmosphere almost stifling from combined effects of stench from the cooking-range and stench of another character, the men did not miss the funny scenes that constantly occurred, causing laughter from men too sick to raise their heads. One of these scenes was when the vessel gave a lurch, that came near putting her upon her beam ends and threw the men below promiscuously out of their berths, when one of them scrambled to the other side, clung to a bunk and shouted, "for God's sake, boys, all on this side and right her!"

Buckets of water were kept in readiness for use in case of fire, because in a heavy sea fat in stew-pans on the galley would be thrown out and flash up in a blaze, causing danger to constantly exist of a fire breaking out among inflammable material. This was so in all transports conveying the Forty-Second, notwithstanding every precaution was taken to guard against such a danger when cooking ranges were placed on board.

Surgeon Hitchcock had a few severe cases of fever under his care, attending to them faithfully, with a loss of one man by death. To his care and attention many men owe a debt of gratitude, and for assistance he rendered in placing them on their sea-legs; dealing out nourishment suited to the debilitated condition they were in until sufficient strength and appetite was gained to go on with the army ration. When fairly over their sea-sick attack appetites of men became voracious.

On shore at Hilton Head the men were allowed to roam at will, an opportunity they exercised to the utmost,— visiting other troops in camp; taking daily baths at the sand beach, where they also washed their under-clothing; feasted on fresh bread from the post-bakery, equal to any furnished by the best of hotels in Boston; stole apples at night from under the noses of a guard posted upon the wharf where the barrels lay; sight-seeing upon the island like school-boys on a vacation. The quarters were in some empty barracks near a sluggish bayou, upon whose bank was a small graveyard, covered with ashes, with a neglected appearance in general, where were interred the remains of a few sailors who lost their lives at the capture of Forts Beauregard and Walker by the Federal Navy in November, 1861.

Everything wore a quaint look, not only here but at every stopping place *en route* to New Orleans, exercising a peculiar charm over men from the North who had never visited the South, experienced by all travellers to parts of this world remote from their own residences, regardless of any facts bearing on the climatic influences on unacclimated beings. Until the stern reality of war was forced upon them, it seemed to each and every man as though he was travelling for pleasure at the Government expense. The first agreeable impressions of localities visited on the voyage from New York to New Orleans cannot be eradicated from minds of men belonging to the Forty-Second Regiment.

After repairs were finished the men reëmbarked December 16th, proceeding at once to sea, and made a fine run to Tortugas, arriving at Fort Jefferson on the twentieth, at nine o'clock A. M., to take in coal. While coasting in sight of Florida Keys the steamer *Memenon Sanford*, that formerly ran between Boston and Bangor, was seen upon the reefs with wreckers around her. The *Sanford* had the One Hundred and Fifty-Sixth New York Infantry Regiment on board; every man was saved and taken to Key West, December 11th, with nothing but what they carried in their hands. The baggage and stores were afterwards obtained, but the steamer could not be saved.

In Fort Jefferson was a garrison of four companies, Ninetieth New York Infantry, weak in numbers from heavy losses by yellow fever during the summer months. There was a large number of military and civilian prisoners kept at work upon the fort, not then in a finished state. Occupying a part of the parade within the walls were several three-story brick dwelling houses with gardens attached, and trees of large growth under whose sheltering branches several head of cattle, belonging to the Commissary Department, would collect to escape the hot sun at mid-day.

As another instance of danger that existed during the transportation of Banks' expeditionary corps to New Orleans, while the *Quincy* was at Tortugas an old rat-trap steamer came into port in a leaky condition with New York troops on board. The pumps were kept constantly at work since leaving New York, so the men stated. How the unseaworthy transports managed to carry their human freights without loss of life from dangers of the sea is one of those curious mysteries of God's providence.

After coaling and starting again seaward a collision occurred in the channel with a Government schooner, carrying away the after part of the steamer's deck cabin, which caused a detention of several days to repair damages. At dusk, on the twenty-second, the *Quincy* put to sea, arriving at Ship Island on the twenty-fifth, at nine o'clock P. M. Early on the morning of the twenty-fifth Private

W. H. Young, Company C, Twenty-Eighth Connecticut Volunteers, died of fever, and was committed to the deep at eleven A. M. with appropriate services. Before the death of Young was announced, scattered on deck and below, were knots of men engaged in the pastime of cards. Lounging around, fishing and card playing were what the men did to kill time since leaving Hilton Head; a book of any sort in their hands was not to be noticed. On the announcement — presto — a sudden change; cards were put away; nearly every man had his Bible, and was intently engaged in its contents for the balance of the day. A death at sea with solemn funeral rites was not without effect.

Receiving his orders, Lieutenant-Colonel Stedman had the *Quincy* sail for New Orleans on the twenty-sixth, arriving late at night on the twenty-ninth, after a passage of twenty-five days from Sandy Hook. The South-West Pass was reached at nightfall; a thick curtain of mist preventing an entrance then. In company with several other transports the *Quincy* lay outside the bar until morning; a continual noise from fog-whistles causing one to think he was in New York harbor. In the morning, as the heavy fog lifted, a beautiful mirage was seen in the sky, showing a brig ashore on a mud bank of the Delta. A perfect representation of what was soon seen to be actually the case.

The *Quincy* disembarked her troops at Carrollton, who went into camp at Camp Mansfield.

The *Charles Osgood* was an unfortunate vessel. An old propeller used on Long Island Sound, she was in every respect consort of the *Shetucket;* each fitted up in the same manner to convey troops, *i.e.*, with a false deck to cover bunks and cooking apparatus. In a serious blow, with heavy sea running, this deck was liable to be swept away at any moment. The steamer anchored in the river after all hands were on board, proceeding to Sandy Hook on the fifth; there remained until she put to sea at half past five o'clock A.M. December 6th. Captain Geer never was beyond Fortress Munroe, and knew little about ocean navigation. He put to sea with one small compass, no charts, no chronometer, no life preservers on board, and with two small boats. With clear, cold weather, a high wind and rough sea, the *Osgood* ran down the coast and into Cape May harbor during the night of the seventh, for refuge. While in Delaware Bay a severe blow split sails and caused a slight displacement of the boiler, causing the captain to run into Delaware River and anchor off Delaware City at six o'clock, eighth, then to Philadelphia next day for repairs. She remained at Philadelphia for five days, to obtain new sails, new boat oars, life preservers, charts, and repairs on the boiler. The captain secured the services of an old and experienced navigator, Captain Sears.

As the men were afraid to continue the voyage on the steamer they were not allowed to go ashore, for fear none would return when all was ready to start. They grumbled considerably, and when the vessel ran aground on League Island, about half past seven A.M. on the fourteenth, some men improved the opportunity to run ashore upon the ice. They went to Philadelphia, got drunk, but all came back before she got afloat at the next full tide except Private Chauncey Converse, Company K. Private Converse did not rejoin his regiment until April 11th, 1863. He surrendered himself to United States officers, taking the benefit of general orders No. 58, War Department, series of 1863, granting pardon to all deserters who did so. Regarding this case of apparent desertion Adjutant-General Schouler wrote Lieutenant-Colonel Stedman, under date of February 21st, that Converse reported he was left sick at Philadelphia, and said he had tried and wished to rejoin his regiment.

At half past eight o'clock A.M. on the sixteenth this transport got a fair start, after remaining over night inside the breakwater at Cape Henlopen, proceeding down the coast in sight of land during the day and running out to sea at night until Key West was reached at two o'clock on the afternoon of the twenty-third. The vessel struck on Fernandina Shoals, on the twentieth, about four o'clock in the morning; fortunately no damage was done, although boats were got ready to cast off in case of necessity. Leaving Key West at nine o'clock A.M. on the twenty-sixth, bound direct for Ship Island for orders, the transport arrived there at seven o'clock P.M., December 29th, proceeding to New Orleans early next morning (four o'clock), two hours later running aground and remaining for a few minutes, off Chandeleur Light; made Pass L'Outre, mouth of the Mississippi, at four o'clock in the afternoon, arriving at New Orleans at two o'clock A.M., January 1st.

Ordered forthwith to Galveston, the transport left New Orleans at four o'clock in the morning, January 2d, and anchored at South-West Pass for the night, about five o'clock in the afternoon. On the third, at six o'clock A.M., the voyage was continued, but after a five hours run gunboat *Clifton* hailed the *Charles Osgood* and ordered her back to New Orleans, because Galveston was lost. She again reached that city at three o'clock P.M. on the fourth.

Companies E and K were disembarked at Carrollton on the afternoon of January 5th, and reported to Lieutenant-Colonel Stedman, in command of Companies A, B and F, in camp at Camp Mansfield. Five companies of the regiment were now united after a month's separation by the sea. Greetings were cordial and heartfelt. The

Charles Osgood was twenty-six days making the voyage from Sandy Hook to New Orleans, although the men had to live on board for thirty-three days.

The *Shetucket* was another unfortunate transport, with a tedious passage. She went to sea on the morning of December 6th. The men had embarked during the day of December 3d, proceeding down the bay to Sandy Hook on the morning of the fifth, when Captain Philo B. Huntley, in command of the steamer, was obliged to seek shelter until a snow-storm, then raging, had somewhat abated.

The officers on board were: Major Stiles in command; Captain Leonard, Lieutenants White and Sanderson, of Company C; Lieutenants Phillips and Gould, of Company H; and Lieutenant Duncan, Company F, detailed to act as commissary. Captain Bailey, Company H, had been granted a two hours furlough on shore for the express purpose of obtaining oil to counteract the effect of salt water upon the muskets, and taken with him acting Commissary-Sergeant Wentworth, Company G. They failed to report on board at the limitation of time, but took passage for New Orleans on the *North Star*, conveying the Forty-First Massachusetts Infantry, General Banks and staff. The *North Star* left New York December 4th, before the *Shetucket* left her anchorage in the river. Captain Bailey did not assume command of his company until January 12th. He and Wentworth arrived in New Orleans December 15th. Wentworth was ordered to join his company on the *Saxon*. No hospital accommodations was upon the transport, and no medicines, except what meagre supplies were obtained by Major Stiles at Fortress Munroe and Hilton Head. Private Thomas M. Lewis, Company D, enlisted from Roxbury, a man forty-five years old, and a friend of Surgeon Cummings, was

detailed to act as surgeon. He was familiarly known as
"old salts," a nickname given by the men, suggested by a
rule he invariably followed of prescribing a dose of salts
to about every man who complained of sickness.

The *Shetucket* was an old two-masted propeller freight
boat, plying between New York and New London. A
false deck-house of unsound lumber had been built upon
her main deck, covering the whole vessel from bow to
stern; in this deck-house bunks were built to accommodate near two hundred men, and cooking apparatus
placed. In a rough sea every wave that struck her sides
would send salt water into the bunks, so much so that
when the water was rough very few men would occupy
them; those that did arranged rubber blankets for what
protection they would afford. All of the accommodations
were extremely poor. Sailing orders were the same as on
other transports; no one on board knew their destination
until after leaving Key West, except Major Stiles, Captain
Huntley, and Captain Leonard. This commendable
secrecy was observed upon all four of the transports
that conveyed the Forty-Second.

Slow progress was made by this vessel when at sea.
On the third night, December 8th, Major Stiles retired
early, worn out with loss of sleep, leaving the command
with Captain Leonard, and Lieutenant White on duty as
officer of the guard. About eight o'clock Lieutenant Gould,
conversing with Lieutenant White, remarked that if the
captain kept on in the direction he was going the vessel
would be ashore, as he knew the course steered was wrong
from his experience and knowledge, obtained while serving
upon a Baltimore steamer. White paid no special attention to what Gould said, and it does not appear that the
attention of Major Stiles was called to the matter. Lieutenants White and Phillips were engaged in a game of

cards in the cabin about nine o'clock when a sudden shock was felt, bringing them to their feet in an instant. Another shock followed immediately, and on the deck they went, when another was felt, each one shaking the vessel from bow to stern. The sky was clear, the sea tolerably smooth, and the shore could be seen distinctly about one-half a mile away. There were two boats (one large and one small) upon the *Shetucket;* the large boat was not sea-worthy, while the small boat was capable of carrying three men. The old sailors (there were many in Companies C and H) were sharp at work trying to launch them. Captain Leonard sought the major, who sprang from his berth on the grating sound awakening him, and was dressing, and said: "The men have mutinied, and are all on deck. The officers of the boat up in the rigging assailed by the men and dare not come down, and the boat is aground; for God's sake, come on deck."

There was the usual commotion and confusion incident to such occasions, and the major, half-dressed, was met by Lieutenant Phillips at the head of the companion-way, who handed him a rope saying: "Make yourself fast major, or you will be washed overboard."

Lieutenant White drove men away from the boats, not until Sergeant Henry Mann kicked a hole in one of them, and remarked as he did so: "Only the officers can use it." They then went for the hatchway, broke it open, and commenced work on what little cargo there was aboard; for what reason it is difficult to understand, unless to obtain material to float upon in case it was necessary to take to the water as the only means of escape, or to lighten the vessel. This was soon stopped. Major Stiles ordered the men to their quarters below, answered by a chorus of voices shouting: "We will be d—d if we will." A persuader in shape of a couple of cocked revolvers, with a determination to shoot the first man who refused to obey his order, settled the business in a very short time, and they went below.

Captain Huntley came down from aloft and informed the officers his vessel was on Hog Island Shoals. For half an hour all attempts to back off ended in failure, until a long, ocean swell lifted her bow, when she floated into deep water. An examination of the hold proved that the ship was making water slowly — not enough to be dangerous, as the pumps, when set to work, were found able to control it. Her rudder was sprung, two flukes were gone from the propeller, and two of her keel planks had been smashed. The *Shetucket* proceeded on, and reached Fortress Munroe next day.

One of the funny incidents of this adventure was Lieutenant Sanderson appearing on deck with a patent rubber pillow, for use in case of shipwreck, at that period sold extensively in New York City, so fixed about his body near the hips that if he should have been washed overboard it would be difficult, if not impossible, to keep either head or feet above water. The lieutenant was obliged to hear many sharp jokes on this account the remainder of the trip.

At Fortress Munroe the vessel was ordered to Norfolk for necessary repairs, arriving in the evening at six o'clock. In passing Craney Island on the way to Norfolk they came to a blockade of piles with bare room enough for a vessel to pass through, and a gunboat on guard. In answer to a hail from this gunboat a dare-devil in Company H shouted in reply: "Go to h—ll!" an answer that aroused the anger of Mr. gunboat commander, who threatened to blow them to pieces. Apologies were of no avail; a demand was made for the man who made the insulting reply, but no one would point him out. The affair calmed down and the *Shetucket* went on her way.

The men disembarked, quartered in the Seamen's Bethel on West Wide Water Street, and gave their officers considerable trouble by pranks they carried on while in the city. General Vialle at one time threatened to send a battery and fire into them; they made so much disturbance ringing the church bell. During their stay Privates Luke Armstrong and Alexander B. Ralsea, Company H, were taken sick and placed in the general hospital; neither men rejoined the regiment during its term of service. Private Ralsea was mustered out of service at Fortress Munroe, for disability, May 27th.

Repairs finished, on the afternoon of December 21st the *Shetucket* proceeded to sea, making very slow time, and ran short of coal and water, causing Captain Huntley to bear up for Hilton Head. In the attempt to make that port he ran into the blockading squadron off Charleston, S. C., at three A.M. on the twenty-fifth, sailing a direct course for Fort Sumter, when hailed by war-vessel *Powhattan*, whose crew were beat to quarters, with a command: "Stop, or I will sink you!" The naval officers were out of temper, and used strong language to Captain Huntley for his stupidity, intimating that he deserved sinking, and would have got it but for the troops on board. Anchor was dropped at Hilton Head in the afternoon at half-past five o'clock.

The next day, twenty-sixth, an affair happened that threatened serious consequences to one of the participators. Coal schooner *J. G. Babcock* was alongside coaling the steamer. For some time the men had been chaffing the schooner's crew in a good-natured manner, and when a drummer-boy of Company H began to climb the rigging he was ordered down by the sailing-master, who was in an angry mood. This drummer paid no attention to the order until the master sprang into the rigging to force the boy back. He was coming down as the officer passed up, and was kicked by the latter a few times in the head. That was enough to make the men furious. Seizing lumps of coal they began to hurl the missiles into the rigging, uttering threats to kick him overboard if he came down, and frightened the officer to such an extent that he dare not do so, but kept on going up to the crosstrees with an intention of coming down on the other side of the mast. Privates John Davis, Company H, Con. Dougherty, William Cook and Joseph Cole, Company C, and others, all rough fighters, jumped on board the schooner and were in the rigging on that side to get at him, when Lieutenant White, whose personal courage no one ever had occasion to doubt, sprang to the schooner's deck ordering them down. All of the company officers then got these men aboard the *Shetucket*, and the *Babcock's* crew cut the ropes, letting her drift away to a safe distance. On the twenty-seventh another schooner finished coaling.

As water was scarce at Hilton Head, the *Shetucket* was ordered to Beaufort to replenish water casks, doing so on Sunday, the twenty-eighth. With a few hours to spare while at Beaufort, Major Stiles decided to give the men leave of absence on shore until five o'clock P.M., for at that hour the tide would serve to proceed to sea. Thoroughly disgusted with the *Shetucket*, the men held a mass meeting in a square of the town during the day and voted not to go on board the old boat again. A committee was appointed to notify Major Stiles of their decision; this committee attending to that duty between two and three o'clock in the afternoon. No time was to be lost if the men were to be got aboard that day in season to sail. The quality and temper of the men was such, that any attempt to persuade them was useless and merely involved loss of valuable time. Major Stiles called upon the provost-marshal, informed him of the situation and asked his assistance, which he was willing to give if the major would assume all responsibility if trouble ensued. Of course this was done.

With about one hundred cavalry-men and seventy-five infantry the provost-marshal, almost at the point of the bayonet and sabre, it might be said, drove the men slowly toward the wharf, and every man but one (a member of Company H) was got aboard at the appointed time. The missing man was asleep in a house and overlooked, but found next morning, brought down to Hilton Head and put aboard. On casting off and reaching the channel, the provost-guard was saluted with many forcible compliments, such as can only be given by men in a like situation.

It is not surprising such an incipient mutiny should have occurred when all the circumstances of the case are considered: an old, unseaworthy boat; indifferently officered, manned and equipped; consuming days of valuable time to make a comparatively short voyage; liable to founder, if caught in a heavy gale; not able to make over four knots an hour at her best speed. The regimental officers consider it creditable that the men bore their hardships patiently so long as they did.

Sailing from Hilton Head on the twenty-ninth, the steamer arrived at Key West January 2d, 1863, for provisions. There was much amusement on board when the U. S. gunboat *Sagamore* hailed them in the afternoon of the day they went into Key West, and the officer in charge of her deck, when informed what day the vessel left New York, replied: "Where in h—ll have you been all this time?"

Lieutenant Duncan, who was sea-sick whenever at sea,

had a penchant for collecting leaves and flowers wherever a landing was made, placing them between leaves of books to press, and thus preserve them. While at Key West some wags among the officers, who were ashore strolling around, conceived the idea of carrying on board an appropriate sample of the product of the soil. A huge cactus plant was obtained, taken aboard, and presented to Lieutenant Duncan to press and preserve. He had to stand many a joke about that cactus for a long time.

After obtaining a supply of repacked beef, that tasted well enough when cooked and cold, but during the process of cooking made such a stench the men could not remain below, the *Shetucket*, on the fourth day of January, sailed for Ship Island, encountering a rough gale on the sixth, that made things lively on board, and blew them fifty miles from their course. Late in the afternoon on the seventh two steam vessels were seen, or rather, the smoke they made was sighted on the horizon. There was some commotion on board, and speculation was rife as to their identity. The Confederate war vessel *Alabama* was a nightmare that haunted the minds of all upon transports conveying troops to the Gulf Department. The following morning a vessel was in sight giving chase. Rapidly gaining upon the *Shetucket*, a blank shot, then two solid shots were fired, the last striking water about two hundred yards away from the transport, when she was hove to. The vessel in pursuit was the gunboat *R. R. Cuyler*, who had sighted the afternoon before, the transport and another steamer, giving chase first to the *Shetucket*, until finding her to be a slow sailer had gone in pursuit of the other vessel, overhauling her during the night, capturing a good prize in an English iron-built blockade runner, and then started for the transport again, confident she could be found at any time.

This was on the morning of the eighth, and in the evening, at nine o'clock, they arrived at Ship Island. Receiving orders to proceed to New Orleans, a start was made at noon the next day, entering the Mississippi River by Pass L'Outre early on the morning of the tenth, arriving at New Orleans in the afternoon of Sunday, January 11th, with only three men sick after such a trip.

The regiment was in camp at Carrollton, and Companies C and H proceeded next day to that place, disembarked, and joined Companies A, B, E, F and K, having been thirty-six days on the trip from Sandy Hook to New Orleans.

The transport *Quinnebaug* was in charge of Lieutenant Proctor, Company G. Corporal Hodsdon, Company D, was detailed to report to Colonel Beckwith, chief commissary, and by him assigned to the vessel. It was intended at one time to send some horses upon her, but the accommodations were such that none would have lived, and it was abandoned. This transport was like the *Charles Osgood* and *Shetucket*, fitted up with bunks to accommodate troops. After some changes of mind in regard to this vessel, she was loaded with stores, sufficient for twenty-four thousand army rations.

Lieutenant Proctor, while on the way to go aboard his steamer in the river, ready to proceed, was hailed on Broadway by Sergeants Nichols, Vialle and Atwell, who said they had been left, together with Private Greene, all of them members of Company G. Proctor told them to find Greene and go on board the *Quinnebaug*, which they did.

One of the ridiculous things done in loading this vessel was to put in a large refrigerator built next to the engine boilers, against remonstrances of men who knew this would not do, packing it with ice and fresh beef. As was to be expected, heat from the boilers melted the ice fast, and by the time they went into Tortugas the beef was spoilt. The *Quincy* was there at the same time, but her troops could not, or would not, eat the meat which Lieutenant Proctor sent on board to the extent of several tons. The balance he threw overboad after leaving Tortugas.

This vessel sailed December 6th, proceeding to Fortress Munroe for orders, as directed, remaining there two days; also touched at Hilton Head for one day, Tortugas for one day and a half and Ship Island for one day, arriving at New Orleans December 29th, having been twenty-three days on the trip from Sandy Hook.

When Captain Beckley, commanding vessel, heard the sailing orders read at sea, which directed them to Ship Island, he was mad, and said his boat was unseaworthy and in no condition to go over the Bahama Banks; he was also without charts for a voyage beyond Charleston, S. C., and was obliged to send to Baltimore for them, from Fortress Munroe, where they were obtained with difficulty. The *Quinnebaug*, in July, 1864, while conveying from Morehead City to Baltimore about two hundred and eighty discharged soldiers, was driven ashore when off Cape Lookout, the machinery refusing to work, and became a total wreck. Between eighty and ninety soldiers were lost.

Other detailed men from the regiment for detached duty were: Corporal Alfred Thayer, Company I, Wagoners John Willy, Company B, Joseph B. Ford, Company A, Chauncey K. Bullock, Company D, Nelson Wright, Company E, Porter Carter, Company K, in charge of horses upon the transport-ship *Wizard King*. This ship sailed from New York December 8th, and arrived at New Orleans December 31st. Besides a large amount of stores, about one hundred and sixty horses were on board, belonging to field officers of various regiments in the expedition. Each regiment detailed men to care for its own horses. Twenty-five horses were lost on the trip, among them Surgeon Hitchcock's horse.

The experience of other Massachusetts troops on the voyage to New Orleans was varied, as the following condensed statement will show:

Fourth Regiment Infantry — Seven companies and a portion of another sailed from New York January 3d in the transport-ship *Geo. Peabody;* arrived February 7th, not landing until the thirteenth; forty-seven days on board; balance of regiment arrived about the same time.

Forty-Seventh Regiment Infantry — Entire regiment sailed from New York December 22d on steamer *Mississippi;* had a pleasant voyage of eight days to Ship Island; arrived at New Orleans December 31st.

Forty-Eighth Regiment Infantry — Embarked December 29th on steamer *Constellation,* sailing from New York for Fortress Munroe January 4th; after detention of seven days sailed for New Orleans, and arrived February 1st.

Forty-Ninth Regiment Infantry — Left New York January 24th on the steamer *Illinois;* arrived at New Orleans February 7th.

Fiftieth Regiment Infantry — Three companies were on steamer *Jersey Blue,* one company on steamer *New Brunswick,* five companies on steamer *Niagara,* one company on ship *Jenny Lind.* The *Jersey Blue* sailed from New York about December 11th, became unmanageable at sea and was obliged to put into Hilton Head in distress; troops were landed and remained on shore about three weeks, then embarked on bark *Guerrilla,* and arrived at New Orleans January 20th. The *New Brunswick* sailed December 1st; arrived at New Orleans December 16th. The *Niagara* sailed December 13th, sprang a leak first night out, machinery became disabled, and it was necessary to put in at Delaware Breakwater; arrived at Philadelphia sixteenth, where the steamer was condemned by a Board of Survey as unfit for transport service. Ship *Jenny Lind* arrived at Philadelphia January 1st, took the five companies on board, and on the ninth sailed for Fortress Munroe, arriving on the thirteenth. As the *Jenny Lind* was not capable of accommodating all the troops, three companies were transferred to ship *Montebello*—she sailed sixteenth; arrived at New Orleans January 27th. The *Jenny Lind* arrived at New Orleans February 9th.

Fifty-Third Regiment Infantry—Embarked on steamer *Continental* January 17th, and after a stormy passage of twelve days reached New Orleans January 30th.

Thirty-Eighth Regiment Infantry — Left Baltimore November 10th on steamer *Baltic;* arrived at Fortress Munroe November 12th; left Fortress Munroe December 4th; after a smooth and pleasant passage arrived at Ship Island December 13th; went into camp on the island until the twenty-ninth; embarked on steamer *Northern Light*, and arrived at New Orleans December 31st.

Forty-First Regiment Infantry—Sailed from New York December 4th in steamer *North Star*, and after a remarkable pleasant passage arrived at New Orleans, *via* Ship Island, December 15th.

Twelfth Light Battery—Sailed from Boston January 3d in ship *E. W. Farley;* arrived at New Orleans February 3d, after a very rough passage.

Thirteenth Light Battery—Sailed from Boston January 20th in ship *De Witt Clinton;* arrived at Fortress Munroe February 11th, after a very stormy passage and loss of fifty-seven horses; after a long, tedious voyage from Fortress Munroe arrived at New Orleans May 10th:

becalmed off the Florida coast, steamer *Geo. Peabody* towed the ship to Key West; from Key West the steamer *St. Mary's* towed the ship to within one day's sail of the Mississippi River.

Fifteenth Light Battery — Sailed from Boston March 9th in ship *Zouave;* touched at Fortress Munroe, and arrived at New Orleans April 9th.

CHAPTER IV.

GALVESTON.

OFF FOR GALVESTON — LANDING — OCCUPATION OF THE CITY — ACTION OF JANUARY FIRST — LOSS OF THE "HARRIET LANE" — DESERTED BY THE NAVY — SURRENDER.

COMPANIES D, G and I went into camp at Carrollton on the afternoon of December 18th, 1862. A telegraphic order was received from New Orleans on the nineteenth, sent by General Banks, which read as follows: "Colonel Burrell, with his three companies of the Forty-Second Massachusetts Volunteers, will proceed to Galveston forthwith." Supposing execution of this order was urgent, preparations to move were at once made. At three o'clock in the afternoon camp was struck and the companies ready to move; but, as the transport *Saxon*, at New Orleans for repairs, did not arrive, tents were again pitched and occupied until the twenty-first. Next day, twentieth, written special orders from General Banks were handed to Colonel Burrell by General Sherman, commanding the post, and read: "Colonel Burrell, with the three companies of the Forty-Second Regiment, Massachusetts Volunteers, will proceed to Galveston, land and take post."

Colonel Burrell decided to execute his orders promptly. On the twenty-first the *Saxon* was ready to embark his men. Camp was struck early in the morning. At eight o'clock men, baggage and equipage were all on board, and the steamer proceeded down river until eight o'clock in the evening, having anchored opposite New Orleans for about two hours, while the colonel, accompanied by Chaplain Sanger, went ashore for an interview with General Banks at his headquarters, to obtain definite instructions. The only officer to be found at headquarters was Colonel S. B. Holabird, chief-quartermaster of the Department, who said full instructions in writing had been prepared, but he could not find them; during the conversation carefully looking over documents in the office. Colonel Holabird suggested to Colonel Burrell not to be in a hurry in proceeding to Galveston, and having heard the subject talked over in consultations that had taken place among other staff-officers and General Banks, advised him, on arrival at Galveston, to consult with Commodore Renshaw, commander of the fleet, in reference to his course of action; that instructions would be forwarded very soon, as the balance of the regiment on arrival from New York would be promptly sent to him. The intention of General Banks, Holabird stated, was to send there an additional regiment of infantry, a regiment of cavalry, and a light artillery battery, as soon as it could possibly be done; that General Banks' idea was, for the three companies to remain under protection of the navy guns until reünforcements arrived. Colonel Holabird cautioned Colonel Burrell, not to be drawn into any scrapes by Confederate General Magruder, who had lately assumed command of all forces in Texas.

After lying alongside the river bank until half-past one o'clock next morning, the transport proceeded on her way. Passing out of the Mississippi River by the South West Pass into the Gulf of Mexico at eleven o'clock in the morning, the course was taken for Galveston.

The troops on board the *Saxon* consisted of:

Colonel — Isaac S. Burrell.
Adjutant — Charles A. Davis.
Quartermaster — Charles B. Burrell.
Surgeon — Ariel I. Cummings.
Chaplain — George J. Sanger.
Quartermaster-Sergeant — Henry C. Foster.

A young volunteer in the engineer corps named W. S. Long, who reported on board at New Orleans.

Lieutenant Brown P. Stowell, Company E, who was sick when the regiment left New York, and embarked on the *Saxon*, instead of remaining with his company.

Private Samuel R. Hersey, Company C, acting as clerk to the colonel. Frank Veazie, cook to officers' mess, not an enlisted man. Two colored boys, Charles L. Amos of Dedham, Mass., servant of Quartermaster Burrell, and Charles F. Revaleon of Boylston, Mass., servant of Surgeon Cummings.

The following officers and men of Company D:

1. Captain George Sherive.
2. First Lieutenant Wm. H. Cowdin.
3. Second Lieutenant Darius F. Eddy.
4. First Sergeant Samuel A. Waterman.
5. Second Sergeant Charles D. Frye.
6. Third Sergeant Charles R. Todd.
7. Fourth Sergeant Wm. E. Humphrey (color bearer).
8. Fifth Sergeant John W. Davis.
9. First Corporal Chas. C. Richards.
10. Second Corporal Benjamin Noyes.
11. Third Corporal Wm. H. Tileston.
12. Fourth Corporal Chas. J. Oldham.
13. Fifth Corporal Benjamin F. Bean.
14. Sixth Corporal Lewis M. Calhoun.
15. Corporal Henry W. McIntosh.
16. Drummer Lewis Eddy.

17. Private Albert S. Allen.
18. " William H. Brown.
19. " William H. Bullard.
20. " William H. Batson.
21. " Charles Brown.
22. " Charles W. Bailey.
23. " John Barnes.
24. " Edward Boardman.
25. " William Burke.
26. " Major Bacon.
27. " Michael Buckmaster.
28. " John Burns.
29. " Charles H. Cushman.
30. " George T. Clinton.
31. " Dennis Dailey.
32. " John Drury.
33. " Peter Durnam.
34. " Tobias Enslee.
35. " George M. Fisk.
36. " Henry Fisk.
37. " John Fay.
38. " Fitzallen Gourley.
39. " Charles J. Grinnell.
40. " Amos B Howard.
41. " Thomas C. Houghton.
42. " David Howe.
43. " Wallace A. Josselyn.
44. " Edwin F. Josselyn.
45. " Jacob Kopf.
46. " William B. Larrabee.
47. " Fred. Lamote.
48. Private Thomas Londergan.
49. " Frank McConlow.
50. " Randolph P. Mosely.
51. " John V. McIlroy.
52. " James Moore.
53. " Francis L. Morrill.
54. " Angus G. Nicholson.
55. " James O'Shaughnessy.
56. " Benjamin Pratt.
57. " George Powers.
58. " Louis Preami.
59. " Gustavus Raymond.
60. " Cornelius Ryan.
61. " Jerry S. Russell.
62. " William Rigby.
63. " Jeremiah Quinn.
64. " Henry C. Sellea.
65. " Joseph H. Stowell.
66. " Sargent L. Stoddard.
67. " Daniel J. Sullivan.
68. " Laban Thaxter.
69. " Josiah Thompson.
70. " James Thomaston.
71. " Daniel H. Vining.
72. " Charles G. Weymouth.
73. " Daniel L. Weymouth.
74. " George S. Walls.
75. " George H. Wight.
76. " Jonathan G. Wight.
77. " Albert P. Wright.
78. " Nathaniel White.

The following officers and men of Company G:

1. Captain Alfred N. Proctor.
2. 2d Lieutenant Thaddeus H. Newcomb.
3. Sergeant Levi W. Goodrich.
4. " Philip P. Hackett.
5. Corporal John W. Buttrick.
6. " Seth E. Clapp.
7. " John C. Bishop.

MASSACHUSETTS VOLUNTEERS.

    8. Corporal George W. Griggs.
    9.   "   Moses Lincoln, Jr.
  10.   "   Robert G. Thompson.
  11.   "   George G. Morrison.
  12.   "   David L. Wentworth, acting as ordnance-sergeant.
  13. Drummer Horace W. Chandler.
  14.   "   David A. Ireson.
  15. Wagoner Roland C. Judkins.

16.	Private	Obed F. Allen.	49.	Private John W. Gordon.
17.	"	Joseph Brownlow.	50.	" George S. Hyde.
18.	"	Charles A. Bailey.	51.	" Albert A. Hayden.
19.	"	John Brown.	52.	" John Harmon.
20.	"	William H. Bickers.	53.	" Henry T. Horn.
21.	"	Charles L. Barrett.	54.	" Albert A. Holt.
22.	"	Charles Barrett.	55.	" Lucius Higgins.
23.	"	Charles Boardman.	56.	" Charles Hilger.
24.	"	John M. Barnard, Jr.	57.	" Alonzo D. Ireson.
25.	"	William M. Bird.	58.	" Eli P. Johnson.
26.	"	Gilbert F. Blaisdell.	59.	" Francis Knight.
27.	"	John H. Cary.	60.	" George W. Kibbey.
28.	"	Thomas O. Bryant.	61.	" Arthur Kelley.
29.	"	John Carvey.	62.	" Charles B. Lynde.
30.	"	John T. Cook.	63.	" Amos W. Lynde.
31.	"	Lemuel S. Copeland.	64.	" William Logan.
32.	"	Frank Covell.	65.	" Samuel Marshall.
33.	"	Frederick Corson.	66.	" Joseph Mullen.
34.	"	Gilbert Crocker.	67.	" James H. McAllister.
35.	"	Fred T. Clark.	68.	" Francis L. Nott.
36.	"	William Carter.	69.	" Joseph W. D. Parker.
37.	"	George H. Davis.	70.	" Charles Paine.
38.	"	John E. Davis.	71.	" Daniel D. Penney.
39.	"	James L. Davis.	72.	" John F. Parrott.
40.	"	George R. Dary.	73.	" Benjamin R. Pierce.
41.	"	Edmund B. Doubel.	74.	" Diomede Roseline.
42.	"	Daniel Dinnegan.	75.	" Martin W. Roberts.
43.	"	James G. Emerson.	76.	" Chas. W. H. Sanborn.
44.	"	John Eaton.	77.	" Albert I. Smart.
45.	"	John Eastman.	78.	" Thomas T. Sweetser.
46.	"	Richard Ellis.	79.	" Henry O. Studley.
47.	"	Thomas Field.	80.	" William Stiles.
48.	"	Benjamin Gould.	81.	" Charles H. Upham.

82. Private Edwin A. Vinton.
83. " Levi Vincent.
84. " James W. Vinal.
85. " James Vance.
86. Private Abiel F. White.
87. " Henry J. Wethern.
88. " William B. York.
89. " Josiah R. York.

And the following officers and men of Company I:

1. Captain Cyrus Savage.
2. First Lieutenant Samuel F. White.
3. Second Lieutenant Benjamin F. Bartlett.
4. First Sergeant Wm. H. Hunt.
5. Second Sergeant John F. Hewins.
6. Third Sergeant Chauncy B. Sawyer.
7. Fourth Sergeant Edward Merrill, Jr.
8. Fifth Sergeant Cornelius G. Kenney.
9. First Corporal Frank M. Adams.
10. Second Corporal Nathaniel H. Bird.
11. Third Corporal Sanford H. Brigham.
12. Fourth Corporal David F. Sloan.
13. Fifth Corporal Daniel H. Walker.
14. Drummer Albert Schneider.

15. Private Moses Averill.
16. " Edward F. Bryant.
17. " Jonathan Baker.
18. " Edward J. Baker.
19. " Edward K. Baker.
20. " John K. Clements.
21. " Samuel Crowell.
22. " Jefferson W. Cheney.
23. " Peter Cuddy.
24. " Thomas P. Contillon.
25. " James G. Colson.
26. " David Chapin.
27. " Timothy Dolan.
28. " Thomas Dellanty.
29. " Charles H. Dodge.
30. " Wm. C. Elder.
31. " Horace W. Eaton.
32. " John Elliott.
33. " George K. Farnum.
34. " Willard S. Farrington.
35. Private Henry E. Farrington.
36. " James F. Floyd.
37. " George T. Fernald.
38. " Edward S. Gray.
39. " Thomas V. Gleason.
40. " Charles Gleason.
41. " William F. Gardner.
42. " George Glover, Jr.
43. " Charles E. Hewins.
44. " John A. Hodgkins.
45. " Frederick Huggins.
46. " Elijah Hunt.
47. " Lewis A. Hunt.
48. " Alexander Hobbs.
49. " Thomas F. Igo.
50. " Ambrose A. Knight.
51. " Charles Littlefield.
52. " William B. Lambert.
53. " Frank B. Laury.
54. " David W. Lannergan.

55. Private James Mulry.
56. " Thomas Morris.
57. " William Morgan.
58. " Dennis Mahoney.
59. " Nathaniel McCreary.
60. " Lawrence Mannix.
61. " James McGee.
62. " Jos. W. McLaughlin.
63. " Thomas A. Noyes.
64. " Solomon Nordlinger.
65. " Albert H. Plummer.
66. " Porter Plummer.
67. " George L. Pitman.
68. " George B. Proctor, Jr.
69. " John B. Pratt.
70. " Charles H. Poole.
71. " Joseph T. Paget.
72. Private Evelyn Ransom.
73. " Asa Robbins.
74. " Geo. W. Richardson.
75. " Edwin Smith.
76. " Joseph Scaff.
77. " Charles J. Sumner, Jr.
78. " George W. Sloan.
79. " James E. Stanley.
80. " William Spargo.
81. " John Taylor.
82. " Jacob H. Taylor.
83. " Joseph A. Teeling.
84. " Wm. H. H. Weeman.
85. " George W. Wescott.
86. " Ozias Willis.
87. " Joel F. Williams
88. " Sanford Woods.

The total force amounting to 15 officers, 249 enlisted men, 1 white citizen, and 2 colored boys.

The instructions Colonel Holabird could not find were handed to Lieutenant-Colonel Stedman as the steamer *Che-Kiang* was about to leave New Orleans for Galveston. They never reached Colonel Burrell. They were as follows: —

"HEADQUARTERS DEPT. OF THE GULF,
"NEW ORLEANS, LA., January 3d, 1863.
"LIEUT.-COL. STEDMAN, 42d Reg't Mass. Vols. :

"*Colonel*, — I am directed by the Commanding General to enclose you instructions, which he requests you to hand Colonel Isaac S. Burrell.

"Very respectfully, your obedient servant,
"W. L. G. GREEN,
"*Aid-de-Camp.*"

"HEADQUARTERS DEPT. OF THE GULF,
"NEW ORLEANS, LA., January 3d, 1863.

"COLONEL:

"Your regiment having been ordered to Galveston, you are hereby placed in command of that post. You will execute such orders as you may receive from these headquarters. My instructions from the Department of War forbid me at present to make any extended military movements in Texas. The situation of the people of Galveston makes it expedient to send a small force there for the purpose of their protection, and also to afford such facilities as may be possible for recruiting soldiers for the military service of the United States. Every assistance in your power will be afforded for the complete attainment of these objects.

"General Hamilton is appointed Military Governor of the State of Texas, and will be recognized by you in that capacity, but your orders you will receive from these headquarters.

"Until the port of Galveston is regularly opened by the Government of the United States, no trade can be carried on, and no attempt for that purpose will be recognized, or countenanced by you.

"I rely fully upon your energy, vigilance and capacity, for the performance of the important duties intrusted to you. Do not fail to make frequent reports of all that transpires within your command, and of whatever important facts you may learn from the enemy in Texas, or from its people.

"It is not probable that any successful movement can be made upon the main-land until our force shall be considerably strengthened; and you will take care not to involve yourself in such difficulty as to endanger the safety of your command.

"Other instructions will be sent to you from time to time, as occasion may require and opportunity offer.

"N. P. BANKS,
"*Major-General commanding.*

"COLONEL ISAAC S. BURRELL,
"42d Regiment Mass. Vols."

"HEADQUARTERS DEPT. OF THE GULF,
"NEW ORLEANS, LA., January 3d, 1863.
"COLONEL:

"You will immediately cause to be constructed a *tete-du-pont*, to command the bridge which connects Galveston Island with the main-land.

"I directed an engineer officer to go there some time since, and I suppose he is there. If so, he will give suitable directions for the work.

"Very respectfully yours,
"N. P. BANKS,
"*Major-General commanding.*

"COLONEL ISAAC S. BURRELL,
"commanding U. S. Forces at Galveston."

The trip to Galveston was devoid of interest. The weather was fine and the sea moderately smooth. Few were sea-sick. At half past eleven on the morning of the twenty-fourth land was sighted; at noon, the gunboat *Tennessee* fired a shot across the bow of the *Saxon*, and she hove too, off Galveston Bar, for about two hours, when a pilot was taken. The navy had been expecting troops to arrive for some days. Commander Law, of the *Clifton*, when he ascertained what troops were on board the *Saxon* and their purpose, sent a boat to bring the colonel over the bar, and on board his vessel, which then proceeded up the channel a short distance. As the *Saxon* would not be able to get over the bar at once, an offer from Law, to take Burrell in his gig to see Commander Renshaw, was accepted. Upon reaching the flag-ship *Westfield*, Renshaw, who was entertaining Confederate officers in the cabin under a flag of truce, met the colonel at the gangway, extending a hearty welcome. He suggested the postponement of a conference at that time, not wishing the Confederate officers to see Colonel Burrell, and would meet him on board the *Clifton* with all commanding officers of gunboats then in the harbor, viz.: —

Westfield—A ferry-boat; eight guns; Commander W. B. Renshaw.

Clifton—A Staten Island ferry-boat; seven guns; Lieutenant-Commander R. L. Law.

Harriet Lane—Formerly a United States revenue cutter; eight guns; Commander J. M. Wainwright.

Owasco—Screw propeller; regular war vessel; six guns; Lieutenant-Commander H. Wilson.

Commander Renshaw, as agreed, met Colonel Burrell on board the *Clifton*. The situation was explained and discussed. Renshaw strongly urged landing the troops in the city, and was supported in this advice by all of his officers. Burrell suggested landing on Pelican Spit, an island near the harbor entrance, with plenty of space, and buildings that could be occupied until more troops arrived. Great stress was placed on the difficulty of obtaining water upon the spit, while abundance was to be had in the city. Renshaw scouted the idea of danger to so small a force in the city. A decision was finally made to land on Kuhn's Wharf, occupy for barracks the wooden storehouse upon it, and fully understood by all officers present, that the troops would be under protection of the navy guns. They were to be protected or removed. In case an attack was threatened, the *Owasco* was to take position on the right, the *Clifton* on the left of Kuhn's Wharf, and these vessels were accustomed to occupy those positions every night. Assurance was also given that the troops could be taken from the wharf in five minutes time if it became necessary to do so.

Galveston City in 1861 was a port of entry and capital of Galveston County. It is situated near the east end of Galveston Island, with the best and least difficult harbor on the whole Texas coast. It was the commercial emporium of Texas, with the bulk of its commerce coastwise with New Orleans and New York. The former port connected with it by regular steamship lines. The city contained the court-house, a jail, and other county buildings, several churches, numerous warehouses, wholesale and retail stores, and hotels; and published several newspapers. The island in which the city stands, is about thirty-six miles long, with an average width of two miles. The soil is good, being a black mould, about a foot deep, resting on sand and shells, and it has several ponds of good water. Separated from the main-land by West Bay, it was connected by a wooden railroad bridge, two miles in length, used by the Galveston and Houston Railroad. No portion of the surface is more than twenty feet above the level of the Gulf of Mexico, and with the exception of several groves of live oak, the whole is open prairie. Before the war the land was said to have been in a state of excellent cultivation, and the city the residence of many wealthy farmers. Very few slaves were held on the island, and the population was about seven thousand.

Federal naval forces had virtually been in possession of Galveston since October 8th, 1862, in full control of the harbor, but lacking adequate force to land and occupy permanently the city. Besides the four gunboats in the harbor when the detachment first arrived, the gunboat *Sachem*, an altered merchant screw propeller steamer, five guns, Acting Master Amos Johnson, came in December 29th with her boilers out of repair, and, securing the services of two boiler makers from the city, anchored in the channel on the city front to have them patched up. The small Government schooner *Corypheus*, Acting Master A. T. Spear, with one gun, and manned by fifteen men, also came into port with the *Sachem*.

The sailing barks *Arthur*, *Cavallo*, and *Elias Pike*, loaded with coal for the fleet; the transport steamer *Mary Boardman*, loaded with hay and horses; and the transport steamer *Saxon*, was all the shipping that was in Galveston Harbor, January 1st, 1863.

At two o'clock the *Saxon* passed over the bar, her keel striking bottom a few times, and at half-past four came to anchor in the harbor channel.

The troops made a landing December 25th, at ten o'clock in the morning. The two-story storehouse was occupied on the upper floor for sleeping, the lower floor to store quartermaster and commissary stores, ammunition, and intrenching tools, which were removed from the *Saxon* that day and next. A partitioned room on the lower floor was fitted up by Surgeon Cummings for a hospital. The commissary supplies consisted of coffee, hard bread, beans, salt pork, and molasses, sufficient to last about thirty days for three hundred men. The intrenching tools were spades, picks and axes, for five hundred men. Three months medical supplies and about twenty-five thousand rounds fixed ammunition for infantry was also landed.

Kuhn's Wharf was the largest on the harbor front, the storehouse end large and roomy, connected with the land by a bridge-like wharf some four hundred feet long, about twenty feet wide, built on piling. The water was quite shallow at any tide almost to the end. Tides in Galveston harbor and bay ebb and flow very little; the depth of water is greatly influenced by heavy northerly winds, which blow the water over the bar out to sea. Heavy draft vessels at such times must keep to the narrow channel.

A flag-pole was found which belonged on the storehouse, and being placed in position upon the cupola, the old garrison flag, used by the regiment at Readville, was run up about eleven o'clock and greeted with cheers. Sentries were at once posted in the city as far as Market Square, one of the principal places with all of the main streets leading into it. They were also posted on the streets to the right and left, communicating directly with the wharf. At night these posts were reënforced in such a manner as to constitute picket-posts.

Immediately upon landing and taking post, Colonel Burrell adopted such measures to secure all the protection possible that in his judgment the situation demanded. From this time until the morning of January 1st it was *work, work, work.* Fatigue and working parties were constantly employed. Guards and pickets were on duty day and night. Reconnoitring detachments were on duty by day and squads scouting at night. The Forty-Second Infantry, posted upon Kuhn's Wharf, were very active during their short stay, occupying the city so far as the small force and prudence would allow, and exercising proper surveillance. The men were barely allowed sufficient time to obtain needed sleep.

Among the first things done was to barricade the interior of the storehouse facing the city, by placing against that side, on each floor, barrels of whiting, plaster and hair, found on the premises. For a temporary shelter to men on picket at night, if forced to seek it, it was decided to build a breastwork upon the wharf by tearing up and utilizing the planks. Volunteer Engineer Long saw no use or necessity for this, not exercising any supervision over the work until operations had commenced and he saw that the colonel was determined about it. Commencing at a point some fifty feet from the shore end, the hard pine planks were removed to make a gap in the wharf for the space of about another fifty feet, and the first breastwork was erected on the edge of this gap the day of landing. Fortunately Quartermaster Burrell, in looking around the city in the morning, had found a keg of large-sized spikes and ordered them taken to the wharf where they might be found useful. They were very useful in building this work.

An examination of the ammunition, ordered in a few days after landing when it was evident the enemy meant mischief, was not a welcome surprise. Company G was armed with Springfield rifles, and Companies D and I had Springfield smooth-bore muskets. The bulk of ammunition landed was found to be for rifles, with only a small supply of ball and buckshot cartridges for smooth-bores. There was also found to be a scarcity of caps. This is accounted for by the confused manner in which the regiment was embarked at Brooklyn on the different transports — a proper apportionment of the ammunition was not possible under the circumstances. Sending Adjutant Davis to the fleet for any surplus caps they had to spare added very little to the supply, as they were short also. It was found that cartridges and caps sufficient to give each man eighteen rounds in his cartridge box was all the ammunition that could be made serviceable when a distribution was made to the men on the thirty-first. This was kept a secret from the command. The men were cautioned to husband their ammunition until it could be used to effect at close quarters, in case of an action. No man was to fire his musket unless so ordered by an officer.

Commander Wainwright, with a few sailors armed with cutlasses and pistols, visited the wharf on the twenty-sixth. After a conference with Colonel Burrell, a *reconnoissance* through Galveston and its suburbs was determined upon. Captain Sherive, with about one hundred men, including the sailors, accompanied by the colonel, adjutant, quartermaster and chaplain, with Wainwright, started about nine o'clock in the morning to reconnoitre, proceeding as far as the brick kilns, some two miles outside of the city. It was not deemed advisable to go further in the direction of Eagle Grove, about three miles, but a circuit of the outskirts was made and the city looked over. The inhabitants had fled. It was almost entirely deserted. Unlike many other cities and towns occupied by Federal troops, very few colored people were to be seen. A lookout was established in a four-story brick building on the Strand near Market Square and within the guard lines, where all that was going on at Eagle Grove on the island, and Virginia Point on the main-land, was distinctly visible in the daytime by the aid of a field-glass. This lookout was constantly maintained.

In the afternoon Colonel Burrell, accompanied by Volunteer Engineer Long, proceeded in the *Harriet Lane* towards West Bay as far as the channel would allow. A good view of Eagle Grove and Virginia Point was obtained. The earthwork, mounting three guns, thrown up at Eagle Grove by Confederates, to protect the railroad bridge, was abandoned. The end of the bridge at Virginia Point was protected by extensive works with heavy guns in position, and here the enemy appeared to be in force. Their camps could be plainly seen.

It was while on this trip in the *Harriet Lane* that

Colonel Burrell made up his mind to destroy the railroad bridge. None of the naval vessels could get near enough to do any permanent damage, on account of the narrow, tortuous and shallow channel. The distance from the fleet anchorage by way of the channel was about four and one-half miles. Heavy naval guns, fired from a point of anchorage where it would have been safe to try it, would not have reached the bridge with any accuracy, the gun-carriages not admitting a sufficient elevation of the guns to carry shot or shell that distance, while such heavy charges of powder would be required for the distance that the concussion upon the gun-decks of such vessels as were then at Galveston would have caused serious damage to the vessels, had everything been favorable in other particulars for attempting the destruction of the bridge in this manner. The bridge could not be effectually severed by the navy except by sending up armed launches prepared for such duty. These the gunboats did not have; all of their row-boats were small, not capable of carrying light guns, even if they had them. This would have been hazardous service, as the enemy were vigilant and brave. That the navy could have sent up boat crews and destroyed it when the vessels first entered the harbor in October, was admitted by a number of naval officers, because the enemy had precipitately taken flight, abandoning everything. The Confederate military commander at that time was a weak-kneed sort of man. In a very short time the Confederate troops rallied, removed all of their guns on the island, and built the works at Eagle Grove rendering the attempt hazardous. Destroying the bridge would not have prevented all communication between the island and the main-land, only rendered it difficult, as the enemy had plenty of boats hid in the creeks and bayous adjacent that could be used for ferry purposes.

But no attempt of any sort had been made by the navy since first entering Galveston Bay to damage or sever this bridge.

Collecting barrels of tar pitch, with other combustible material, and confiscating a dray (all horses had been run out of town), the colonel ordered them stored ready for use, intending to move up immediately on the landing of the balance of his regiment, occupy the works at Eagle Grove, destroy the bridge as far as possible, mount some heavy guns, and shell the enemy from his works on the main-land. Those naval officers who talked the matter over with officers of the Forty-Second agreed that it ought to be done. Commander Wainwright was especially in favor of severing this means of communication. Had the seven companies of the regiment arrived on or before the twenty-eighth of December, it was thought not much difficulty would have been experienced. The enemy soon ascertained the small strength of the detachment landed, and on the twenty-ninth reoccupied the earthworks at Eagle Grove, and mounted heavy cannon to protect the bridge and approaches. Colonel Burrell then requested Commander Renshaw to go up the bay as far as possible with two of his lightest draft vessels, and shell the enemy from the island, which he refused to do. After the twenty-eighth December, the destruction of this bridge could not have been accomplished without an action with the enemy in force at Eagle Grove, but an attempt would have been made had not the event of January 1st occurred.

During the afternoon of the twenty-sixth, while Captain Sherive with a small force of men was out on a foraging expedition, to see what could be found for cooking-stoves, eight Confederate cavalry-men appeared under a flag of truce, with a request to see the British consul. No flag-of-truce trick could be played on Captain Sherive. He promptly halted the party, and notified his commanding officer. One man, under guard, was allowed to see the consul, and the Confederate captain in charge was ordered to leave by six o'clock, as after that hour they would be fired upon. For weeks had the enemy enjoyed the hospitality of Commander Renshaw under these convenient flags of truce, used freely for the most trivial reasons; but the military commander stopped all such nonsense at once. This truce flag was the only one recognized until the day of surrender.

Supplies of food were not plenty in the city. The Confederates would not allow any to be brought from the main-land, consequently, what few inhabitants remained in Galveston, mostly women, found it hard work to subsist. In a small way, rations were given to them by Colonel Burrell. Not much could be done in this direction, owing to the small supply on hand for the troops, who must be fed and kept in fighting condition. There were quite a number of German women with gold and silver coin, who wished to purchase provisions from the quartermaster. Their husbands were serving in the Confederate army, and much valuable information was obtained from them.

Confederate cavalry commenced to infest the city and suburbs at night, about three days after a landing was made; but did not attempt to molest the pickets. These cavalry-men came along the beach, concealed by a range of sand hills on the Gulf shore; on reaching the outskirts they would separate to go through the city in squads of two and three. Before daylight these squads would rendezvous at a place called Schmidt's Garden, and return to Eagle Grove by the same route they came. They easily obtained, during these nocturnal trips, all information they required, for the men talked freely with such of the inhabitants as wished to converse. While there were a handful of Union men, or refugees as they were termed by the enemy, who sought protection under the Federal flag, the bulk of the small population, men, women and children, were secessionists to the core.

Lieutenant Eddy and Private Hersey must have had this fact very forcibly impressed upon their minds when they were *entertained* by some Galveston ladies at a house on the Strand, some two miles from quarters, on the afternoon of Sunday, December 28th. The ladies sang all of the latest Confederate songs, Eddy and Hersey in return singing the latest from the North. The conversation was bitter disunion on the female side, and well calculated to draw out information on military affairs. On bidding them good afternoon as they left, several young men were seen loitering in the vicinity, who had undoubtedly been listeners to the conversation.

While the enemy easily obtained information of the Federal strength, position and purposes, the men of the Forty-Second as easily secured definite information of the Confederate strength and intentions. At this game of cards honors were easy.

On the night of the twenty-seventh a report was brought in that a force of Confederate cavalry was in the city. Captain Sherive with fifty men and Captain Savage with fifty men received separate orders to drive them out. Taking different directions, a thorough scout failed to discover any traces of this cavalry until Captain Sherive arrived at the beach road leading to Fort Point, when fresh horse-shoe prints in the sand were discovered, showing that a force of mounted men had gone in the direction of Fort Point, where there was an abandoned earthwork thrown up to command the harbor entrance. Captain Savage came up soon after, joined forces with Sherive, and was directed to place his men on the sand ridge of the beach, lying down, while Sherive with his men covered the beach, and all awaited developments. About midnight Captain Savage became impatient, if not a little timid, as signal rockets were seen sent up in the city, and he declined to remain longer, proceeding back to the wharf. This forced Captain Sherive to retire also, as he doubted his ability to meet the supposed force of the enemy with the men left. It was afterwards ascertained that the party was General Magruder, reconnoitring the entrance to the bay with some eighty of his officers and men, who would certainly have been captured, killed, or wounded, if the detachments had remained where Captain Sherive had them posted. There was no escape, except by breaking through the detachments, and the enemy could not successfully do that while Captain Sherive was around. Captain Savage destroyed the telegraph lines connecting Galveston with the main-land, that had remained intact up to this time, as part of the night's operations.

There was a lull in the preparations and rounds of duty on Sunday, the twenty-eighth, giving the men that rest they sorely needed. Only two civilians were molested by the troops during their short stay in Galveston. A German was arrested on this day for uttering seditious language. He was confined at guard quarters in the wharf storehouse, remaining there during the action of January 1st, almost forgotten, but miraculously escaped without a wound. The other was a citizen caught hanging around the head of the wharf in a suspicious manner, and was arrested for a spy, retained in confinement some six hours, and then released. This arrest occurred on the ———th.

Sunday afternoon Colonel Burrell, in a row-boat, proceeded to Fort Point to inspect a 100 Pr. gun, dismounted in the fort, with the intention of removing

KUHN'S WHARF, GALVESTON, TEXAS.

it to the earthwork at Eagle Grove when his force was increased. The gun was found to be sound, not spiked, and ready for immediate service, when mounted on a gun-carriage. The story of the dismounting of this heavy gun, as told by naval officers and sailors, is said to be true.

It seems that when the fleet was sailing towards Galveston Bar the orders were not to fire, even if fired upon, until the signal was displayed from the flag-ship. A gunner on the *Clifton*, standing by his gun, with lanyard in hand, accidentally slipped when the vessel lurched, causing him to pull the lanyard with a sudden jerk and fire the gun. Without being trained on the fort, the solid shot took effect on the gun-carriage of this 100 Pr., near the stanchions, shattering the carriage, heaving the gun up in the air, tumbling it over backward in the sand. The garrison became panic struck at the effect of this chance shot and fled. The fleet then entered the harbor without another gun being fired.

The situation looked serious, and with a doubt in his mind about the loyalty of the naval commander, and no news from his expected reënforcements, Colonel Burrell decided on the twenty-ninth to send Quartermaster Burrell to New Orleans on the *Saxon*, with despatches for General Banks. The commissary supplies had dwindled down to fifteen days rations for three hundred men, and the ammunition was not available. Engineer Long decided to go also, not being under the orders of Colonel Burrell, and took passage on the *Saxon*. Much to the transport captain's relief, for he had been in a highly nervous state while lying at the wharf, the *Saxon* left, proceeding as far as Pelican Spit, where she had to remain until January 1st. A strong northerly wind, that continued on the thirtieth and thirty-first, had blown the water from Galveston Bar so that only three feet of water covered it, rendering proceeding to sea impossible.

LETTER CARRIED TO GENERAL BANKS, BY QUARTERMASTER BURRELL.

"HEADQUARTERS,
"GALVESTON, TEXAS, December 29th, 1862.

"*Sir:* In obedience to orders, upon arriving at this place on the evening of the twenty-fourth instant, after consulting with the commander of the blockading fleet, I landed the three companies of my command, which were with me upon the transport *Saxon*, on the end of Kuhn's Wharf, and quartered them in the warehouse there. I have taken possession of the city as boldly as I could with the small force at my command, and have thoroughly reconnoitred the built-upon portions of the city up to within range of their battery at Eagle Grove, which is apparently well built, mounting three guns. They have also one gun at the draw, which is about midway of the bridge. Upon Virginia Point they have a strong battery, mounted with heavy guns. From the best information obtainable, I judge their force in this immediate vicinity to be about two thousand strong.

"During the day we control the city, but at night, owing to our small force (as the balance of my regiment has not yet arrived), I am obliged to draw in the pickets to the wharf on which we are quartered. I think there are still living upon the island about three thousand persons, a large proportion of whom are women and children. A great many of these people are almost entirely destitute of the means of subsistence, as the enemy will not allow anything to be brought over from the main-land, thinking, doubtless, to make them disloyal by starvation. The naval officer in command has contributed all he could spare from his stores, and my men have shared their bread rations with them. I believe the larger part of the residents now here to be loyal and really desire to remain in the city, and that common humanity calls upon us to render them assistance. This, in my judgment, can best be done by placing the city under martial law as soon as my force is large enough, and forcing the rich, who are mainly the secessionists, to feed the poor. I would most respectfully urge upon your consideration the necessity of sending provisions for immediate relief. These can be sold to them at Government prices, thus conferring a real charity, without subjecting them to the mortification of being beggars. Under the existing circumstances I have thought it best to send one of my staff, Quartermaster Burrell, and Mr. Long, the engineer, who accompanied us here, to report to you in person. These gentlemen will explain in detail the state of affairs, and the importance of the knowledge which they can convey to you has, in my judgment, authorized me in ordering the *Saxon* back to New Orleans, which I humbly trust will meet your approbation.

"I have the honor to be, your obedient servant,

"ISAAC S. BURRELL,

"*Colonel commanding 42d regiment Mass. Vols.*"

The small schooner *Corypheus* had lying useless upon her deck two captured 12 Pr. Howitzer field-guns, with over three hundred rounds of ammunition for them. Adjutant Davis was sent on the night of the twenty-ninth to Commander Renshaw, with a request for the guns to be landed upon the wharf. Colonel Burrell intended to place them in position in the storehouse, opening port-holes on the land side. Company D (the old Roxbury Artillery) had many Roxbury men who knew how to handle such guns, besides having in the ranks a dozen man-of-wars men, who had enlisted in Boston shortly after their discharge from a war-vessel, that had arrived from a long cruise. The idea was ridiculed by Renshaw, who flatly refused the request.

General Magruder, when he assumed command in December of the Confederate forces in Texas, immediately set about perfecting plans to recover possession of Galveston, and to capture or cripple the fleet. These plans were so far matured that he intended to attack on the twenty-seventh, but was obliged to postpone it until the morning of January 1st from delay in fitting out his river steamers.

The naval commander heard of these steamers being got in readiness to attack him, but did not think he would have much difficulty in blowing them to pieces with his guns; in fact, affected to look upon such preparations of the enemy as futile. As for the information of Magruder's plan of action on land, obtained by the military force, none of the naval officers, with the exception of Wainwright, placed much reliance upon it until the thirty-first, as they had heard every day since they had been there reports of an attack to be made.

Definite news was obtained on the thirtieth that the enemy would make an attack that day or next. Commander Renshaw had not at any time since the troops landed been very communicative, or evince any desire to consult over the situation, although an occasional visitor to the military headquarters. Determined to protect the men as far as possible, a second breastwork, close to the storehouse, was commenced in the afternoon and finished by midnight, tearing up the wharf in front and opening another gap for fifty feet.

The two breastworks were strong enough to resist infantry-fire, but not artillery. Composed of two and two and one-half inch planking laid one upon the other, two planks deep, so that the faces were composed of the edges only, they were some thirty inches in thickness, built shoulder high. On this last work the entrance port was protected by a cotton bale. Not satisfied with this, a raft lying at the wharf, such as is used by caulkers in working on vessels' seams near the water line, was raised from the water by hard labor, and securely placed in position on the right of the second breastwork, to protect as far as it would a fire from the next wharf on that flank, one-eighth of a mile distant. The storehouse protected the left flank from infantry-fire from the wharf on that side, also about one-eighth of a mile distant.

That night a false alarm, about ten o'clock, brought the entire force to arms behind the breastworks, and gunboats took positions near the wharf as agreed — one on the left and one on the right.

While the city was apparently deserted for some days after landing, on the thirtieth and thirty-first of December it was noticed that many men in citizen's attire had returned and were strolling around. It was believed then, by the officers of the Forty-Second, that these men were in the Confederate service. No attempt was made to interfere with them so long as they remained civil, committing no overt wrong. With the small force on hand, no decisive measures concerning the inhabitants could be adopted, or any attempt made to govern the city.

During the day of the thirty-first, in company with Commander Wainwright, Colonel Burrell with a guard patrolled some of the streets, and noticed many of these strange faces, who seemed to shun them. From the lookout station the enemy were seen assembling on the plain near Eagle Grove, horse, foot and artillery. Wainwright remarked: "Active operations going on, colonel; things look squally, and we had better not remain here. I will go up to-morrow and feel of them." He intended to go up in his vessel as far as the channel would permit, and endeavor to shell them from the island.

Between these two officers a friendship for each other existed from their first meeting. They were frequently together, strollers around the city and suburbs, consulting the STATUS of affairs. Many of the other naval officers were frequent visitors, very courteous and obliging, but none appeared to take the same interest in matters that Wainwright did. The Forty-Second officers thought he was the only live man in the fleet.

In none of their perambulations and confidential talks did Wainwright breathe a word against his superior officer, although the colonel, after a few days on shore, could not remain quiet with the conviction forced upon his mind that Renshaw was not acting in such a manner as to warrant confidence, and bluntly told Wainwright only a day or two before the final events took place he thought Renshaw was a traitor. To this plain and straightforward expression of opinion the naval captain made no reply. Not so with the sailors; they, coming in contact with the enlisted men, frequently expressed their suspicion of the "commodore."

On the morning of the thirty-first of December the *Owasco* went down to the coal bark *Arthur*, lying in the channel near the harbor entrance, about a mile and one-half from the wharf, for a supply of coal. Contrary to her usual custom she did not return to her position near the wharf when night came. The *Westfield* lay near Pelican Spit, on guard at the harbor entrance, and covering the Bolivar channel of the bay. She had lately received a new heavy gun, brought by the *Tennessee* to replace one disabled while on the coast some time previous. Up to midnight the balance of the fleet were distributed along the water front of Galveston, in the channel, which averaged at any point only a little less than two hundred and twenty yards in width. The *Clifton* was at the right of Kuhn's Wharf, about one hundred yards distant; then came the *Sachem*, still at work on repairs to her boilers; then the small schooner *Corypheus*; and up the channel, a mile away, nearly opposite the depot wharf, was stationed the *Harriet Lane*.

At night a conference was held by officers of the Forty-Second. Positions were assigned for the companies in case of attack. Companies D and I remained upon the wharf, in the building, to snatch what sleep they could, while Company G, Captain Proctor in command, was on picket during the night. The three companies had been held in readiness every night since landing. Those not on duty slept on their arms. On the thirtieth and thirty-first only one company at a time was allowed to sleep. The men were informed of what was expected, their courage and manhood appealed to, with every point emphasized, that would naturally tend to inspire them with confidence. Not a word was uttered that could possibly convey any idea foreign to the fact, that fight was a duty they were to perform.

Burrell did not like the outlook, nor his position upon the wharf. Commodore Renshaw had failed to inspire him with any confidence in his integrity. Seated in his quarters that evening to muse over his situation, without allowing his officers or men to know his thoughts for fear of disheartening them, the colonel fully determined to order the *Saxon* up to the wharf next morning, embark his men, and remain on board in the harbor until reënforcements arrived.

About midnight Colonel Burrell, Captain Sherive, and

Chaplain Sanger, visited the picket sentinel posts in the city, finding the men were drawn in from their original positions, and did not occupy the usual ground. The original posts were reëstablished. Rumbling noise of artillery wheels was heard distinctly through the night, together with the sound of moving railroad cars accompanied by the locomotive whistles. Captain Proctor had reported in person to inform Colonel Burrell, "there was trouble ahead"; so when the *Harriet Lane*, in the moonlight, discovered black smoke from smoke-stacks of Confederate vessels across the bay, some two miles away, and signaled with rockets, Lieutenant Stowell, placed in charge of the fireworks signals, burned some lights for the purpose of giving information to the navy that the military force was wide awake and ready. Every man on the wharf was ordered to man the breastworks.

It was at this time the colonel noticed that the *Clifton* had left her position. She was signaled by Renshaw from the *Westfield* that he was aground, and gone to her assistance between twelve and one o'clock. The *Westfield* discovered these Confederate steamers about the same time as the *Harriet Lane* and got under way, but very soon was hard and fast ashore at high water. The absence of both the *Owasco* and *Clifton* left the military upon the wharf unprotected on the flanks for some hours.

The *Bayou City* had left Choppers Bar, at Morgan's Point, between nine and ten o'clock Wednesday night, December 31st, with the *Royal Yacht* and *J. F. Carr* in tow. The *Royal Yacht* got aground at Redfish Bar and had to be left behind. The Confederate boats being light draft steamers could navigate the shoal waters of the bay, and were not obliged, on arriving opposite the city, to keep to the ship channel. Upon being discovered these steamers withdrew out of sight to Half Moon Shoals, six miles distant. The military force went into their barracks again to sleep on their arms.

Captain Sherive, with the chaplain, made a second visit to the city, by a mistake getting outside of the lines; they had been drawn in once more without any notification to the rest of the command. They found the city full of people; and had the enemy been ready then for operations, both officers would have been killed, or wounded and taken prisoners. Not ready to act, the Confederates kept in hiding as much as possible.

About half-past three o'clock in the morning, masses of moving men in the streets were discovered by the picket sentries, who fired at them and slowly fell back toward the wharf, without eliciting a fire in return. The troops asleep in the barracks, equipments and overcoats on, for the night was cold, and guns by their side, were immediately ordered up, and to line the work built on the thirtieth. The order was promptly obeyed: Company I upon the right; Company G upon the left; while Company D was to be stationed in line, with its left resting at the breastwork, the right prolonged towards the harbor, ready to wheel either to the right or left up to the work. As the picket detail came in over the single plank left upon the openings in the wharf for that purpose, they took position with Company G. Lieutenant Newcomb was the last man in. Up to between one and two o'clock a bright moonlight enabled objects to be distinguished for some distance, but after two o'clock darkness had shut in to such a degree that objects ten feet off could not be seen. A few cheering words were rapidly addressed to his men by the colonel, who cautioned them not to forget the State they represented, and to reserve their fire until orders were given to commence. The enemy lost no time in getting into position. Magruder must have expected to be able to cut off the whole or part of the picket from reaching the wharf by placing his first gun at the large open door of the Star Foundry, a building at the head of the next wharf to the right of Kuhn's Wharf, for the position gave him a chance to rake the wharf. It was this gun that was first fired, having been rapidly placed in the foundry after the pickets gave warning he was at hand.

A city clock had a few minutes previous struck four o'clock when this gun was fired by General Magruder in person, the ball glancing over the edge of the breastwork, crashing through the storehouse, and the action opened. All of the enemy's artillery opened fire shortly after with solid shot, shell and canister. Before he fired the first gun, Magruder remarked: "Boys, now we will give them hell," and after firing left for his headquarters, established on Broadway, saying, "Now boys, I have done my part as private, I will go and attend to that of general."

A number of men not exactly sick, but worn out and tired from continued hard work, together with a few lazy fellows, remained in the building when the rest filed out. They did not stay long. Private Mosely, Company D, who was lying down when told by Sergeant Waterman to get up and come along, said it was "d——d nonsense," and proposed to have some sleep. The cannon ball crashing and smashing things over his head sent Mose rolling down the run that lead to the second story. Private Dave Howe, Company D, who claimed to be sick, climbed out of a window to a pitch roof, that covered the water tank, straddling along until the end was reached, when he found himself looking down into the water; a shell over his head just then sent him wriggling back and through the window again, and down he tumbled over the run to the wharf. One of the incidents the men can never forget was the chaplain finding Privates Thompson and Vining had got into a large iron tank, used to catch rain-water from the storehouse roofs, that was set upon its side close to the building, drove them out and got in himself. Not a very safe place to take shelter if a solid shot happened to strike it.

The Confederate land force under General Magruder, consisted of infantry commands of Colonels Green, Bagby and Reily, Lieutenant-Colonel L. A. Abercrombie and Major Griffin; Colonel Pyron's regiment dismounted dragoons; Colonel X. B. Debray's cavalry regiment; and cavalry companies of Captain Bowles, Atkins, Andrews, and Durant; Colonel J. J. Cook's regiment artillery; and Wilson's six-gun light battery. The country for miles around was thoroughly scoured for volunteers, who flocked to Magruder's force, in this way swelled to about five or six thousand men of all arms. The brigade commanders were Brigadier-General W. R. Scurry and Colonel Reily. General Scurry had command in the immediate vicinity of the wharf. Besides Wilson's light battery the enemy had six siege guns, fourteen field pieces — some of them rifled — and a railroad ram, armed with an eight-inch Dahlgren mounted on a railroad flat car. Most of this artillery arrived from the Mississippi River a week before. In regard to the numbers of his men General Magruder, in conversation with the officers some time after they were prisoners of war, admitted he had no means of officially knowing the strength of his force, and then placed it as

---

Daniel Harvey Vining, of Weymouth, an odd character, was sixty-five years old. He tried to get mustered with Company A, but the mustering officer rejected him as too old. When Company D was mustered into service Vining dyed his hair, fixed up to look young, and tried it again with that company. The officer knew him however, and asked: "How old are you to-day?" Vining answered promptly, "Forty-four years old." No further questions were put and he was mustered in, to his delight.

about five or six thousand men because such large numbers of volunteers joined him.

Details of the attack were made at Pyron's camp. Three heavy guns were ordered to Fort Point in charge of Captain S. T. Fontaine, of Cook's artillery regiment, supported by six companies dismounted dragoons, under Colonel Pyron. Major Wilson was to open fire on the wharf with his battery. The railroad ram was to take position on railroad wharf to fire at the *Harriet Lane.* The remainder of the artillery, manned by Cook's regiment, was to be posted in eligible positions on the Strand and water front, and warehouses along the edge. Artillery was hauled by mules and by hand half way to the city from the railroad bridge, at one o'clock that night. A large quantity of cotton was also carried by rail to railroad wharf for use in building a breastwork, besides a large quantity of intrenching tools, for the purpose of Magruder was to throw up intrenchments at the ends of streets leading to the water if his plan of action did not succeed before daylight. Signals agreed upon were: white light — enemy in sight; blue light — order to prepare; red light — make ready for action; at twenty minutes intervals.

General Magruder is credited with sending this dispatch to Major Leon Smith from Summit Station, thirty-five miles from Galveston, on the Galveston and Houston Railroad, as his soldiers commenced the march to take positions assigned them: "I am off, and will make the attack as agreed, whether you come up or not. The rangers of the prairie send greeting to the rangers of the sea."

Upon reaching the city, shortly before four o'clock, the Confederates placed a 32 Pr. gun at the cotton press near McKinney's Wharf, to engage the *Harriet Lane.* This point was the left of the Confederate battle line. A 42 Pr. gun was placed at the head of Kuhn's Wharf, near Social Hall, and a section of Wilson's battery was near Hendleir's Wharf. Why they did not attempt to place guns upon ends of the wharves on each side of Kuhn's Wharf, where an enfilading fire upon the soldiers of the Forty-Second could have been obtained, is a mystery, unless they feared the positions too much exposed.

Of the navy, the *Sachem* was first to open fire, followed by the *Corypheus* and the *Harriet Lane*. For an hour did shot and shell fly all around the troops upon the wharf, accompanied with musket balls, causing them to think they were to get "h—ll" sure, as Magruder said, and to hug the planks and huddle close to the breastwork in such a manner that the original position planned for them to take at that work was lost. After a few rounds had been fired at them with no wholesale slaughter occurring, many of the men began to gain that confidence old soldiers possess, and to note progress of the action.

The navy fired high and made hot work in the city, but did not for some time do any execution among the enemy's guns. Seeing this, Captain Sherive shouted to them: "Fire lower, and not so high." In spite of the distance, sailors of the *Sachem*, who were afterwards taken prisoners at Sabine Pass, said they distinctly heard the warning, and then depressed their guns as much as possible. The Confederates admitted that the firing from heavy guns on the naval vessels was hard to stand. The crashing of walls and falling timbers, and a constant rain of bricks, mortar and roofing, as the shot and shell plunged through buildings, added to the crash of many hundreds of window panes, assisted to make the night hideous.

At the first shot from the enemy Colonel Burrell ordered

every man to lie down. During the first hour the colonel walked the wharf, taking careful notice of all that occurred. Many shells would drop upon the wharf and explode, or burst overhead, pieces flying forward and overboard, yet he did not receive a scratch. A shell exploded in the storehouse and, seeing flame and smoke, he ran in, but a wooden partition prevented his reaching the fire. He shouted: "Is any one in there?" Private Hersey, with a few others, was lying down close to one of the rain-water hogsheads in the building when the fire started among the tents stored there, and at once endeavored to put it out. Hersey answered that HE was and that the tents were on fire, when Colonel Burrell ordered them thrown into the water by a back door, that could be easily reached. Part of the burning tents were soon floating in the harbor; but finding an empty pail, and drawing water from the hogshead, Hersey soon extinguished the fire. The ammunition that lay in dangerous proximity to the tents was at once attended to. A call for men to "come in here and rout out this ammunition" was promptly obeyed by a squad of men, who soon placed the boxes near the end of the wharf where they could easily be pitched overboard in case of necessity.

It was still dark at five o'clock when the enemy suddenly ceased their artillery fire. This was ominous; everybody felt an assault was premeditated. Not a shot had been fired from the wharf, which must have deceived the enemy as to the condition the Forty-Second detachment was in to repel an assault. They supposed many were killed or wounded. A sharp lookout from the breastwork was ordered. Somebody sung out that they were coming in boats to the left of the wharf. Colonel Burrell called for men, and ran to where the storehouse abuts the wharf-edge, but could not see or hear anything. Leaving the men to watch, he rapidly passed back to the breastwork to see that the men there took position ready to open fire, and again ran back to the left. He was there when the first fire was opened to repel the assault.

The assaulting column (about five hundred men) under Colonel Cook, said to have been composed of two small regiments, could be heard splashing in the water as they waded out. The understanding among the officers was, in case of an assault they were to wait until the enemy came within easy range before firing.

Adjutant Davis, Captains Proctor and Sherive, and Lieutenant Newcomb, were anxiously looking over the breastwork into the darkness to catch a glimpse of where the enemy were. Captain Proctor sang out that he could see moving objects in the water, when Adjutant Davis gave the order to fire. A volley was given, followed up by some rapid firing at will, as fast as the men could load. Those in the front ranks had to look out, for in the excitement men from the rear would crowd up and blaze away regardless of friend or foe. As the line of fire was mostly straight away from the shoulder, very few firing downwards into the water, the casualties to the attacking force was not heavy. Some of them attempted to come out upon the wharf, by placing planks over the openings where they had been torn up. They did get to the first breastwork, and showed their heads above it, as the musketry flashes lit up the scene, but no further.

The *Sachem* and *Corypheus*, attracted by this fight, sent shot and shells toward the head of the wharf among the enemy in such a manner that they were glad to fall back, with such scaling ladders as they carried, taking most of the dead and wounded ashore. A few bodies were floating in the water during the morning hours.

After this repulse the enemy retired behind the protection of buildings and side streets, out of musket range. The combined fire of the three gunboats, who continued to send their compliments among the enemy's artillery placed to cover Kuhn's Wharf, prevented the Confederates from anything more than random artillery firing after this assault. Some of their batteries they had previously found great difficulty in keeping manned; the gunners were forced to return to their pieces many times by cavalry patrols stationed in the rear.

As daylight dawned, a scattered musketry-fire was opened on both sides. The Confederate riflemen took positions in windows, and upon the flat roofs of such warehouses as overlooked the wharf within range. The small field-gun, stationed at the Star Foundry, was sending some shells which exploded underneath the wharf, making it a question whether the piling would not eventually be severed and destroy the wharf. The gunners had also got the range where the men lay, and by a little elevation they could sweep them. Hastily calling for some good rifle shots, Colonel Burrell posted them near the flanking raft, with orders to prevent that gun from being served. This detail did the duty well, effectually putting a stop to the Confederates dodging from around the street corner to load and fire. Major Dickinson, General Magruder's assistant adjutant-general, lost an eye while gallantry trying to attach a drag-rope to the gun in order to draw it away, when they found it dangerous to keep at work; a nephew of the general, Lieutenant George A. Magruder, aide-de-camp, also made the attempt after Dickinson was wounded — all of no avail, the gun had to be abandoned by them.

An attempt was made about seven o'clock to launch a boat that was upon the wharf for repairs, and then supposed to be in condition for use, in order to send Captain Sherive, who volunteered to go, on board one of the vessels with a request that they come up and take the troops off. Colonel Burrell, Captain Sherive, Adjutant Davis, Lieutenant Cowdin and Private Morrill, Company D, had got the boat launched from the end of the wharf, but it filled with water and sank at once, because some bullet holes had not been noticed, when the riflemen from a brick building at the head of the next wharf commenced to fire at them. As the bullets began to whistle over their heads the men shouted: "Look out, colonel, they are firing at you!" Private Morrill was severely wounded in a hand, Captain Sherive and Adjutant Davis dodged behind hawser posts, Lieutenant Cowdin jumped for shelter, and the colonel disappeared in a hurry down a sloping freight gangway that was handy. The men thought he was shot until he called to them : "I am all right."

In a few moments the *Owasco* was seen in the slight foggy mist of the morning coming along from the coal bark, and when off the wharf sent a few shells into the building, driving the annoying riflemen out. The *Clifton*, ordered by Renshaw to return to the city when the action opened, with difficulty kept the channel, and returned from Pelican Spit soon after daylight, opening fire upon the enemy's guns placed in position on the sand beach near Fort Point by Captain Fontaine, driving the gunners away, and continued on past the wharf a short distance, taking position near the *Sachem*. In passing, a solid shot was fired over the wharf obliquely, into the brick building used for a lookout station, one quarter of a mile distant, tearing a corner out and making a bad wreck of the building.

With the exception of a few shot and shell fired into the city by the gunboats nearly all firing had ceased when it was about broad daylight. The enemy had removed most of their artillery; only a few pieces remained that they could not and dare not persist in attempting to take away: the rifles of Company G could reach them and prevented it. Captain Sherive asked permission to take his company out and secure them, but the colonel would not allow it, fearing an ambuscade. Volunteers were called for, to go out and ascertain the position of the enemy. Several volunteered, but the selection fell upon Private Colson, Company I, a rather tough customer, who had been put in irons for misbehavior and confined in the guard-house for some time, but been released. He went out, soon returned, and reported the enemy hid behind buildings and massed in the yards not far away.

The naval force, excepting the *Westfield*, all assembled on the harbor front, daylight to assist them in discovering the enemy's position; the front of Kuhn's Wharf cleared of their presence, it did seem for a short time that a victory would eventually be won.

In less than fifteen minutes the whole aspect of affairs was changed. The State authorities had taken the *Bayou City*, a Houston and Galveston packet steamer, made bulwarks of cotton bales upon her sides and armed her with a 68 Pr. rifled gun, placed in the bow. The river steamer *Neptune* was also fitted out in the same manner and carried two Howitzer guns. Steamers *Lucy Govirn* and *Royal Yacht* were used as tenders to collect wood for the gunboats, and steamer *John F. Carr* was fitted up for a hospital boat.

The *Bayou City* was commanded by Captain Henry Lubbock, with Captain M. McCormick for pilot. Colonel Green had command of troops on board, about one hundred and fifty men. Captain A. R. Wier, Cook's regiment artillery, was in charge of her artillery. Captain Martin, of the cavalry, was a volunteer on board. The *Neptune* was commanded by Captain Sangster, with Captains Swift and McGovern for pilots. Colonel Bagby had command of troops on board, about one hundred men. Lieutenant Harby, in command of a company infantry acting as artillery, was in charge of her artillery. The *John F. Carr* was commanded by Major A. W. McKee. General Magruder called for three hundred volunteers from Sibley's brigade, armed with Enfield rifles and double-barrel shot-guns, to man this flotilla.

The entire flotilla was under command of Captain Leon Smith, a man of great experience in steamboat management, who was employed by Magruder in the Quartermaster Department, made a volunteer aide on his staff with rank of major, and afterwards called *commodore* by the general. Major Smith had charge of all work in preparing these steamers for action. He had orders to be ready to attack the Federal vessels at midnight.

At half-past four o'clock the Confederate flotilla, at Half Moon Shoals, fired up with rosin and proceeded towards Galveston, arriving within a mile of the Federal gunboats at daylight.

When a lookout on the *Harriet Lane* soon after midnight first discovered the Confederate flotilla, Wainwright, asleep in his stateroom, was notified and assumed charge of the deck. After this flotilla disappeared the *Harriet Lane* retained her position, with steam on, while her officers, on the watch for further developments, leaned over her rails listening to sounds from on shore, that indicated some movement there by the enemy, until the first gun was fired at the wharf. Her anchor was then raised to the cathead, but not secured, and attempts made to turn around for the purpose of proceeding towards Kuhn's Wharf to occupy the place made vacant by the *Clifton*, gone to Renshaw's assistance. To do this without getting aground necessitated a use of great skill and consumed much time, for the vessel had to forward and back to gradually swing her bow around. Why she should have been stationed at this point—head of the ship channel where it was impossible to manœuvre her—when the *Westfield* or *Clifton* (old ferry-boats) were better adapted for the position, had often been discussed by naval officers at Galveston.

While working his vessel around Wainwright opened fire on the city. Her bow was headed towards the wharf when signs of an approach by the flotilla were again seen, which caused him to abandon proceeding down the channel and to work his vessel around again in order to present her bow to the enemy. Fairly around she steamed up to meet the *Bayou City* and *Neptune*, who showed a disposition to attack, other cotton boats keeping out of harm's way. A fire was opened upon them with shells from her eight-inch forward gun, sending three shells and a cannon shot into the *Bayou City;* the shells passed through her engineer's room, one exploding near the engineer, doing some damage; the cannon shot passed through her messroom and pantry.

Within one-half a mile the *Bayou City* opened fire. Her second shot struck the *Lane* plumb behind a wheel, close to the magazine, making a hole large enough for a man to crawl through; when fired a fourth time the gun exploded, killing Captain Wier, with others, and wounding Captain Schneider, with other men.

As it was plain that the enemy's intention was to close with him, Wainwright backed his vessel some distance in order to get a good headway, for it was understood on board, the *Lane* was to try and ram her bow into the *Bayou City*, cut her down even if it crippled the *Lane*, then reach the *Neptune* and capture her by boarding. This was not to be, because just before reaching the *Bayou City* her bow ran aground, barely allowing the Confederate pilot time to put his helm hard around in season to prevent his boat going on to the *Lane's* bow in a strong ebb tide, which also prevented his running against the *Lane* so as to strike forward of the port or left wheel-house, which was his purpose to enable the Confederates to board. He did carry away the *Lane's* port cathead, whereby an anchor was let go, and ran out fifteen fathom of chain attached. The *Harriet Lane* was now at an anchor and also aground.

Wainwright, from his position upon the bridge with Third Assistant Engineer Mullen by his side, ordered the crew forward upon the forecastle ready to repel boarders. As the *Bayou City* struck a glancing blow in passing, about twenty of her men jumped for the forecastle deck. Many fell into the water, and those that reached the deck were met by sailors armed with pistols, cutlasses and boarding pikes, to be hurled overboard. One colored sailor, Nick Wheeler, caught a man upon a pike, which entered his body near the stomach and came out between his shoulders, and had to shake him off into the water. All this occupied very few minutes.

As the *Bayou City* passed to shoal water off in the harbor beyond the channel, with her outside planking of port wheel-house and sides torn off from contact with the *Lane's* strong upper works, her men from behind cotton bales opened a scattering musketry-fire upon the blue-jackets. The blue-jackets trained a gun upon her, and at a favorable moment Acting Master Hamilton pulled the lanyard, which broke; he reached for a hatchet that had lain beside the gun-carriage a few moments before, intending to strike the percussion-cap to fire the gun, but it was gone; some one had seized that hatchet for a weapon when Wainwright called for boarders to be repelled.

It was then thought she would be taken in hand by

other naval vessels, and attention was given to the *Neptune*, that came up immediately afterwards and struck the *Harriet Lane* upon the starboard (or right) side, intending to board, but did not succeed, and passed by, her men firing from their rifles. At this time Commander Wainwright was killed upon the bridge where he had remained a mark for the enemy, paying no attention to suggestions from his officers not to expose himself. He received one ball in the forehead, that went out back of his head, and four balls in the body. Lieutenant Lea was also mortally wounded in the abdomen and carried below, and Acting Master Hamilton was wounded in the arm. Fire was returned by the *Lane's* crew as fast as they could load their small-arms.

The *Neptune* passed astern, turned, and came back making for the port side, with a brisk musketry-fire maintained by her men, when a shot or shell from one of the *Lane's* nine-inch port guns, fired by Engineer Mullen (who broke the lanyard on the first pull, quickly tied it together and tried a second time with success), smashed the *Neptune's* bow, causing her to take water fast. She got on to the channel's edge, and soon sank in about eight feet of water. Many of her men jumped overboard to reach land, and for a time the Confederate riflemen on shore opened a fire upon their own men escaping from one of their own vessels.

When it was seen that the *Neptune* was out of the fight a round of cheers went up on board the *Harriet Lane*, and her men threw their caps in the air with joy, supposing all was ended. But the vessels below had not attended to the *Bayou City*, and she had rounded and again approached the *Lane*, swung diagonally across the channel, aground, with her anchor out, for sufficient time had not elapsed to remedy either mishap. As she came along evidently intending to board, the pivot gun forward was trained upon her and fired; the shot struck her wheel-house without inflicting any perceptible damage, and before another gun could be brought to bear she struck the *Lane* abaft the port wheel-house, running her bow so far under the gunwale and wheel that both vessels were stuck fast.

After a short exchange of shots with small-arms the enemy, headed by Major Leon Smith, Colonel Tom Green and Captain Martin, commenced to jump into the boarding nettings that were up in place, cutting them apart with their long knives. They got aboard in three places, on the wheel-house and aft; met with a gallant resistance by the *Lane's* crew, who fought upon deck until driven under the gangway, forecastle and hurricane decks by superior numbers, where they still kept it up, and hurled at the enemy their pistols, boarding pikes, and whatever they could find suitable for such a purpose after their small-arm ammunition had been expended.

No formal surrender of the *Harriet Lane* was made, and no man can tell just when her capture could be considered complete. It is said that her pennant was hauled down by James Dowland, Jr., clerk to Captain Wharton, assistant quartermaster, and it is a settled fact, the claim made by Major Leon Smith that he killed with his own hands Commander Wainwright is not true, and could not be, as Wainwright was dead some time before.

Why the casualties upon the *Harriet Lane* and *Bayou City* were so light as they proved to be, is one of those rare circumstances impossible to explain. While it lasted the fighting had been of a desperate character on both sides; shot and dangerous missives of destruction flew in all directions. Upon a comparison of notes afterwards, officers of both sides considered it a miracle so few were seriously injured. Many men suffered from bruises and light wounds, easily healed, who are not mentioned in the official report of killed and wounded.

Like their companions on shore the Confederates upon the *Bayou City* were without discipline, and for a time after they had obtained control of the *Harriet Lane* her officers and crew were in danger of being shot down in cold blood. Sailing Master Munroe, as he came down from the hurricane-deck to surrender, had a shot-gun levelled at him, and was shot in the face by a drunken Confederate loafer. He could not be called a soldier, for soldiers do not act in such a cowardly manner. This loafer met his deserved punishment then and there, by being instantly shot through the head by Engineer Mullen.

Among the *Lane's* crew were several colored sailors who fought nobly; and little Robert Cummings, a second-class white boy, with two revolvers in his hands danced about the deck, continually yelling at the top of his voice and sending a shot at the enemy every opportunity he got, full of fight as any man aboard.

Beside the crew, made prisoners, were the following officers: Commander Wainwright, killed; Lieutenant-Commander Edward Lea, mortally wounded in bowels; Acting Master Charles H. Hamilton, wounded in arm; Acting Master Josiah A. Hannum; Acting Master W. F. Munroe, seriously wounded; Second Assistant Engineers M. H. Plunkett (in charge) and Charles H. Stone; Third Assistant Engineers A. T. E. Mullen, Robert N. Ellis and John E. Cooper; Assistant Surgeon Thomas N. Penroes; Paymaster R. Julius Richardson.

When it was seen that the *Harriet Lane* had been captured, the *Clifton* and *Owasco* tried to get near enough to so disable her as to be unfitted for use to the enemy. One of the eleven-inch shells, fired while on the way, struck close to her stern-post, and opened a hole in her hull large enough for a man to walk in. When this shell from the *Owasco* went into the stern, Paymaster Richardson was about to open his stateroom door to obtain his watch. The entire shell passed crashing through his room, while he was turning the door handle; a moment sooner and he would have been killed or wounded.

The Confederates then placed the captured officers upon the hurricane-deck, with a threat to shoot them down if another gun was fired by the *Owasco*, an act of barbarism they would have carried out in their state of excitement. The *Owasco* got too close and within easy range of the Confederate riflemen, who fired a volley that killed and wounded several of the crew, including every man serving the rifled gun. In consequence of this loss, all of her guns could not afterwards be manned. The gunboats were short of a full complement of men; none of them could suffer much loss without being seriously crippled.

None of the Confederate steamers were a match for any United States vessel present. They were considered mere playthings by naval officers, upon which an officer of sound judgment and discretion would not have risked his life or reputation in attacking the Federal navy. An ordinary man-of-war steam launch, armed with a light bow gun, could have coped successfully with them. They took the chances, and by nothing but good luck were saved from an ignominious defeat. Look and see how this luck favored them: first, the *Harriet Lane* should not have been placed where she was, while two other vessels were present who could have been more easily handled at this point of the channel; second, she ran aground when on the verge of ramming the *Bayou City*, and that steamer barely had time to save herself; third, the gun missing fire that Hamilton had trained upon the *Bayou City*, which undoubtedly would have sent that steamer where the *Neptune* went. Everything favored the Confederates at critical moments during the engagement, and they had nothing to brag about, except good fortune, for their dare-devil bravery.

After the volley had been fired the *Owasco* fell back, opening fire upon the city. In passing Kuhn's Wharf, within thirty feet, she was hailed by Colonel Burrell, to take his men off. This request was heard on board, but no response given. The *Owasco* kept on.

The *Bayou City* and *Harriet Lane*, entangled and aground, disabled for any service they could render in this fight, with the *Neptune* sunk, were at the mercy of the Federal vessels if they acted promptly. The *Lucy Govirn* and *John F. Carr* remained out of danger. In this emergency Major Leon Smith ordered a white flag run up at 8 A. M., and adopted bluff tactics. Captain Lubbock was sent on board the *Clifton* and *Owasco* to demand an immediate surrender of the fleet. This demand was made of Lieutenant-Commander Law, who asked what terms of surrender were offered, and received for a reply "that he would be allowed a ship to remove his people, the balance of the public property to be surrendered." Law was also informed by Captain Lubbock, that Wainwright and Lea were killed, with two-thirds of the crew killed and wounded, a statement Acting Master Hannum, who was with Lubbock, confirmed. The truth was, only ten out of a crew of one hundred and twenty men were seriously injured. Hannum had lost his head and did not know what he was about.

Commander Law asked for three hours' time to consult with Commander Renshaw, still aground near Pelican Spit, and a three hours' truce was then agreed upon at about eight o'clock. Law proposed to go with his vessel, but Lubbock insisted he should go in his gig, anchoring the *Clifton* exactly where she was until the truce was over. Law thought it was rather rough, but agreed. The senior officer of the *Harriet Lane* fit for duty, Acting Master Hannum, was allowed to go with Law, on his parole of honor to return. All of the gunboats then displayed white flags.

Renshaw refused to accede to the Confederate proposition, and ordered Law to get every vessel out of port with despatch while he blew up the *Westfield*, as all attempts to float her had failed.

Not receiving any communication from the navy, and at a loss to understand what was going on, while the *Clifton* and *Owasco* had dropped down the channel far enough to be out of direct range of the enemy's desultory musketry-fire which was kept up on the troops upon the wharf, Colonel Burrell ordered Corporal Henry W. McIntosh, Company D, to stand up upon the breastwork, with a piece of sail-cloth attached to an oar-blade. Several handkerchiefs were also attached to bayonets and raised in the air.

Corporal McIntosh was fired at several times, the bullets whizzing very close, before the truce flag was acknowledged. General Magruder afterwards apologized for this breach of the usages of war, explaining the difficulty of managing the unruly men that formed his command, and the personal exertions made by himself and staff-officers to stop the firing. Magruder was called to account, for this action of his men, by the Confederate War Department at Richmond. He had a personal interview with Colonel Burrell, while a prisoner at Houston, and produced an order calling upon him to report forthwith to the War Department, and requested a signed document from the colonel stating the facts.

A cessation of hostilities for half an hour was asked, for the express purpose of communicating with the fleet. This was granted with the understanding that only one man was to leave the wharf. The intention of Colonel Burrell was to prevail upon the naval commander to send a gunboat to the wharf, embark his men at the expiration of the half-hour, and assist the navy with his men if the fight was to continue. No idea of a surrender entered his head at this time.

Selecting Adjutant Davis to see the naval commander, a difficulty presented itself in obtaining a boat, as the one held at the wharf was sunk. The Confederates had managed quietly to remove from the neighborhood all of the row-boats without attracting any attention. Fortunately two refugees just then passed towards the gunboats, were hailed, ordered to the wharf, and took the adjutant into their boat, proceeding towards the *Clifton*. While on the way a row-boat, containing some Confederate officers and flying a flag of truce, tried to overtake them. One of the officers ordered them to stop, when the adjutant shouted: "I will see you d——d first," and with his revolver in hand ordered the refugees to row for all they were worth to the *Owasco*, the nearest vessel, fearing some treachery.

On reaching the *Owasco* he found that Commander Law, the ranking officer, had gone to see Renshaw. Commander Wilson refused to do anything until Law's return, as the truce flags were up. No amount of entreaty was of avail. Wilson's attention was called to the fact that the Confederates on shore had again manned their guns and moved others into position, even while truce flags were up on shore — a violation of the truce on their part. It was of no use, Adjutant Davis had to remain until Commander Law should return.

The time agreed upon for cessation of hostilities expired.

The Confederates had replaced their artillery in favorable positions to fully command the wharf. No reply had been received to the request sent the naval commander, and the naval vessels had left the troops without protection. Thus abandoned by his only support, not a sign of succor from any source, his position completely at the mercy of the enemy's artillery, with riflemen posted in commanding and covered places, when the Confederate truce flag came to the wharf, at the expiration of the time agreed upon, Colonel Burrell proceeded to meet it. After a discussion of terms of surrender, it was agreed that upon an unconditional surrender the officers and men were to retain all of their personal effects and all private baggage. Only property of the United States, except knapsacks, haversacks and canteens, was to be delivered up. The very best terms the enemy would concede.

Colonel Burrell then offered General Scurry his sword, which that officer refused, saying: "Keep your sword colonel, a man's done what you have deserves to wear it." The Confederate troops came down yelling like mad people when the surrender was completed, and soon swarmed upon the wharf. When Major-General Magruder, in a gorgeous uniform, met Colonel Burrell, he remarked: "Don't be cast down colonel, it is the fortune of war; you will soon be paroled." On his appearance upon the wharf, Surgeon Cummings courteously offered him a glass of whiskey, but Magruder declined with thanks. The numerous "colonels" and "majors," who seemed to be thick as bees, were not so backward, for they sampled a case of fine liquors, the private property of the officers, in such a manner that it was never seen afterwards.

To their anxious inquiries about the killed and wounded, when informed none were killed with but few wounded they expressed great surprise, expecting to find a heavy loss had been sustained. Magruder remarked that they would probably never again be subjected to such a heavy fire and suffer so small a loss.

An inspection of the breastwork disclosed that it was marked in hundreds of places by bullets, while the storehouse looked like a sieve. The officers occupied quarters in the storehouse on and after the twenty-ninth. Previous to this time they had lived aboard the *Saxon*, while she lay at the wharf. The enlisted men were in the building. Some cooking was done on the *Saxon* at the cooking-range; but stoves having been procured on the twenty-seventh they were set up, but not fully protected so as to prevent setting fire to the building until the thirty-first, when they were ready for use. A pot of beans was being baked in one of the stoves for the officers, who expected next day to have a royal meal; a shot cut the stove funnel in two; the stove sustained no damage; the next day Confederates enjoyed that royal meal with the savory dish of New England.

The regimental flags were placed in the barracks between two heavy beams. Lieutenant Cowdin received instructions, when landing, to keep a sharp eye on the colors, and in no event allow them to be lost. Why Lieutenant Cowdin at this period did not think of some way in which to avoid their capture is excusable only on the ground that he was severely wounded in the back and under the surgeon's care. Why other officers, or men, did not arrange to save them is a puzzle. To be sure it was a time of intense anxiety and excitement; but the colors should not have been forgotten. It was an easy matter to take them from the staffs and either placed in somebody's knapsack or have been wound around the body of some man, under his clothing, and the staffs destroyed, or, what would have been better, the flags could have been torn into pieces and distributed amongst the men for keepsakes. The enemy did not know so small a force had colors with them until they were found after the action.

Confederate Major Shannon, who had been a prisoner of war in the Federal hands and received kind treatment, as a mark of his gratitude for that treatment, asked for and received permission to take care of private baggage of the command, and prevent unruly men of Magruder's force from despoiling it. This was not an easy matter to do, but the major succeeded in his purpose; the baggage was properly delivered in a few days to the prisoners at Houston. The officers' swords were passed over to the provost-marshal at Houston, properly marked, to be returned when the owners were paroled or exchanged. They never were seen again.

About nine o'clock arms had been stacked, knapsacks slung, and the Forty-Second detachment marched from the wharf, passing between lines of General Magruder's force drawn up in the streets of Galveston, and proceeded to some empty houses in the suburbs, where the men remained until one o'clock in the afternoon. The captured crew of the *Harriet Lane* joined them during the forenoon.

As the troops marched from the wharf Commander Law returned. When Adjutant Davis asked him what was going to be done, he replied: "The *Harriet Lane* is captured, Wainwright dead, and the fleet will proceed to sea immediately." Orders were sent to the little schooner *Corypheus* for the captain to scuttle her and take his men on board some of the remaining vessels; but he asked permission to set sail, and did so, saving her. With truce flags flying, the gunboats proceeded to sea. The *Clifton* lead, followed by the *Owasco*, then the *Corypheus*, and last was the *Sachem,* whose commander, by diligent work during the action, had patched up her boilers and got steam started.

Renshaw sent the *Westfield's* crew on board transports *Saxon* and *Mary Boardman,* and a slow-match was applied to a train of powder leading to her magazine. As no explosion took place at the expected time, he went back in a row-boat with Lieutenant Zimmerman, Engineer Green, two quartermasters, four firemen and five sailors. As Renshaw was about coming over her side into the row-boat again, a premature explosion took place. The *Westfield* fell to pieces, and not a vestige of the boat's occupants was ever seen again. This was about ten o'clock A.M. Her guns were afterwards recovered by the enemy, and placed in battery to protect the harbor from another visit by Federal vessels. News of Renshaw's death reached Law when the *Clifton* was half-way towards the bar, placing him in command of the navy, and that officer concluded to proceed at once to New Orleans, abandoning the blockade from fear of an attack by the *Harriet Lane,* although an officer on board the *Mary Boardman* informed him another transport-vessel would be down in forty-eight hours, and ought to be warned. In the race for New Orleans the *Mary Boardman* reached the city first, followed next day by the *Clifton,* and afterwards the *Saxon* and *Honduras.*

The following account of how the *Westfield* was destroyed is taken from a letter written by William L. Burt, aide-de-camp to General Hamilton, to Major-General Banks. Major Burt was on board transport *Mary A. Boardman,* lying at anchor near the flag-ship *Westfield:*
"Captain Law had an interview with Commander Renshaw. Our vessel, the *Mary Boardman,* was then alongside the *Westfield,* having endeavored to haul her off. As soon as

Captain Law left for his own vessel Commander Renshaw sent an officer to us saying, that he was going to blow up the *Westfield*, and requesting us to assist in taking off her men and whatever could be saved. I remonstrated with this officer, that it was unnecessary, and that the whole force could lie by and protect the *Westfield* until the tide turned (which was then running out), when she would float, and we could save her, and as she was heavily armed and of light draught she was invaluable. I also requested the commander to come on board. This remonstrance was repeated to every officer that came to my vessel with men. We received on board the men and their baggage, with property of the ship, until our decks would hold no more, and the rest was placed on the transport *Saxon*.

"At about ten A.M., while the commander's boat and crew and second cutter and crew were at the *Westfield* to receive the last men, the commander, having poured turpentine over the forward magazine and just over where she was aground, set her on fire with his own hand. He stepped down into his boat, in which were Lieutenant Zimmerman, Chief-Engineer Green, and two oarsmen. The magazine immediately exploded, tearing the bow of the vessel open and blowing her to pieces to the water's edge and back to the smoke-stack. After the explosion no living thing could be seen. She did not sink, being aground; her guns aft, which were double-shotted and run out, as the flames should reach them, threatened us, at the short distance we were from her, with destruction, which might have been foreseen when she was fired.

"Acting Sailing-Master Smalley took charge of us as pilot, and we started for the bar. It was evident that we could not get over with what we had on board, and we threw overboard everything on deck except what belonged to the men of the *Westfield*. We went over the bar, striking very heavily, followed by the *Saxon*, two small schooners, the *Clifton*, *Owasco* and *Sachem*, gunboats, leaving the *Harriet Lane* in the hands of the rebels, with two barks loaded with coal, and one small schooner."

The behavior of Colonel Burrell is spoken of in the highest terms by officers and men who were under him. He walked the wharf during the entire time the action continued, with shot and shell flying around in unpleasant proximity. While risking his own life in this manner, in order to be able to observe all that was taking place, he kept his men under shelter as much as possible. They rose to their feet from behind the breastwork only when ready to fire on the enemy.

All of the officers are entitled to credit for their gallant conduct under the trying circumstances of this their first fight. Gallant Captain Sherive especially showed marked courage and bravery.

The men, as a whole, behaved like veterans; not that there was no quivering — there was; but no display of childish fear took place. Every order given was obeyed with marked promptitude, and in such a manner to show that they stood to their duty like men.

Many comical incidents happened during the engagement, and if all could be remembered they would make a respectable-sized chapter. A few, that the men often talked and laughed about, are here given: Frank Veazie, officers' cook, during the hot firing, kept up a promenade inside the storehouse with his coat collar up and bent over as if rain was falling upon him. Private Billy Burt, Company D, when all hands were crowded for shelter near the breastwork, during the first hour, shouted: "For God's sake, get where the sergeants are and we will be safe!" The quartermaster's colored boy, Charlie Amos, fell asleep early in the evening, sleeping through all the uproar, and did not awake until it was over.

The loss by the United States naval squadron was:

Clifton—One wounded.

Owasco—One killed; fifteen wounded, including Comnander Wilson.

Harriet Lane—Five killed; five wounded; exclusive of officers, one hundred and ten sailors were made prisoners.

Westfield—Fourteen killed.

The Confederate loss is hard to ascertain. From the character of their raw volunteers many men slightly wounded must have never been reported, besides, their administration department was too loose for an exact official report of casualties. While not so heavy as would be supposed from the naval cannonade of the city, it is officially reported by General Magruder to have been about twenty-six killed and one hundred and seventeen wounded, but Surgeon Cummings, who had excellent opportunities for knowing, places it at about three hundred killed and wounded.* A part of the Confederate loss was known at the time to be as follows:

Colonel Pyron's regiment—Two killed; six wounded.
Captain Wilson's battery—— killed; four wounded.
On steamer *Bayou City*—Five killed; two wounded.
On steamer *Neptune*—Seven killed; twenty-eight wounded.

Among the Confederate officers placed *hors-de-combat* were:

Surgeon Fisher, Colonel Cook's regiment, killed.
Captain Weir, Company B, Texas artillery, killed on *Bayou City*.

* Andrew Parish, a lad of fourteen or fifteen years, Magruder's colored servant, who was with the general in Virginia and Texas, says he saw at Galveston from fifty to seventy-five Confederate dead after the action was over. With the usual proportion of wounded to killed, Mr. Parish almost corroborates Surgeon Cummings.

Lieutenant Sidney W. Sherman, Texas artillery, killed.

Lieutenant Harvey Clark, Colonel Cook's regiment, mortally wounded.

Major Dickinson, wounded in eye badly.

Major A. M. Lea, C. S. engineers, wounded.

Captain Schneider, slightly wounded.

Lieutenant Madden, slightly wounded.

Captain McMahan, slightly wounded.

Property captured by the enemy was as follows: the *Harriet Lane* with her fine battery, the guns on the *Westfield*, three sailing vessels loaded with coal, viz., *Arthur, Cavallo* and *Elias Pike* — these vessels were said to have been burned by the navy, or set on fire — one set regimental colors, one garrison flag, arms and ammunition, tents, intrenching tools, commissary supplies, and quartermaster stores of clothing, etc., etc., that the detachment carried to Galveston.

The garrison flag was afterwards found upon a Confederate Texan soldier, made prisoner at Thibodeaux by Lieutenant Alf. Halstead, Company K, One Hundred and Seventy-Sixth New York Infantry, on the twenty-third June, 1863, a few days after the action at La-Fourche Crossing, in which a detachment of the Forty-Second Regiment took part. This soldier had got possession of the flag, and carefully preserved it. By request of Lieutenant Halstead the flag was forwarded to Governor John A. Andrew, to be placed among other State *mementos* of the war.

On the day of surrender the following vessels, with reënforcements and military stores, were on the way to Galveston. Had the action been delayed one week quite a respectable military force would have been assembled upon the island.

Transport steamer *Cambria*, with Governor Hamilton and troops.

Transport steamer *Honduras*, with detachment First Vermont Battery, Captain Hibbard.

Transport steamer *Charles Osgood*, with two companies Forty-Second Regiment.

Transport steamer *Che-Kiang*, with three companies Forty-Second Regiment, one company Texas cavalry, and a number of Texas refugees.

The *Honduras* and *Charles Osgood* were spoken in the Gulf by gunboat *Clifton*, and returned to New Orleans. The *Che-Kiang* lay at the United States Barracks below New Orleans January 3d, ready to proceed the next day, when the news was telegraphed from the Passes, and her orders were countermanded. The *Cambria* arrived off Galveston January 2d, and was fortunate to escape capture from well-laid plans of General Magruder.

The following accounts were given by Sergeant Nichols, Company G, Forty-Second Regiment, and by Purser Bach, steamer *Cambria*, before it was known what steps were taken by the Confederates to catch the transport steamer:

STATEMENT OF SERGEANT NICHOLS.

"The *Cambria*, Captain Sumner, arrived off Galveston Bar at three o'clock P.M. January 2d. On board were three hundred men First Texas Cavalry, Colonel Davis, recruited in New Orleans from Texas refugees, and equipments for a full cavalry regiment; a detachment First Vermont Battery with guns; Sergeants Nichols, Vialle, Attwell, and Private Greene, all of Company G, Forty-Second Regiment, *en route* to join their company. A small brass cannon on deck was fired several times to signal a pilot and notify the navy, without attracting attention. Several refugees, 'Nicaragua' Smith, Foley, big 'Jack' and others, volunteered and went in a row-boat to notify the fleet. As his volunteers did not return, Captain Sumner remained off the bar until morning without suspicion of any danger. About ten o'clock A.M. next day a sloop, pilot flag up, with three or four men aboard, approached and made an attempt to entice the steamer on the bar, reporting she could follow, and they would take soundings. There was ten and one-half feet of water on the bar, and the *Cambria* drew eleven feet. Not one of the men would come on board. After some talk Captain Sumner became suspicious, and, in a loud voice, ordered: 'Men, stand by the ports!' although the steamer was not armed. Just then a few refugees on board recognized Confederate Captain Payne on the sloop, told Sumner of the fact, who ordered him to come on board the *Cambria* or the sloop would be blown to pieces. Captain Payne came aboard, and, in answer to questions, said, Captain Wainwright was in command of the fleet, with several other false stories, playing his part well until he, in turn, recognized several faces on board. He then knew he was trapped, and said: 'The game is up, I am lying; the Confederates are in possession of the city and harbor.' The whole story of what had occurred was then told, including a tale of the capture of Smith and his comrades. Payne reported that the *Harriet Lane* was about ready to come out after the *Cambria*, so Captain Sumner allowed the other men on the sloop to get away, while he made haste to reach New Orleans. This Captain Payne was placed in confinement on a war-vessel at New Orleans. He was afterwards seen on the streets of that city apparently a free man."

"Nicaragua" Smith was tried by a court-martial, declared a traitor, and shot January 8th, game to the last. Six balls entered his body. A characteristic speech made by him when face to face with the firing party would not bear repetition here. Two of his comrades escaped, but Foley and big "Jack" managed to be paroled when the enlisted men were sent to the Federal lines.

STATEMENT OF PURSER BACH.

"ON BOARD STEAMER CAMBRIA,
"January 7th, 1863.

"MAJOR-GENERAL BANKS,
"Commanding Department of the Gulf:

"The steamer *Cambria*, with two companies First Texas Cavalry, horses of the Second Vermont Battery, and a great number of men, women and children (refugees), left New Orleans for Galveston December 31st, 1862, at 9 P.M. Arrived outside the island January 2d, at 7 P.M. Strong wind and high sea running. No sign of pilot, consequently came to anchor.

"Next morning, third instant, weather very hazy and high sea. We commenced beating about, in the hope of a pilot coming to us, up to 12 M. No such success, during which time several of the refugees, being well acquainted with the bar, were desirous of piloting us in. The captain would not listen to any such suggestions. They then offered to take one of the life-boats and go for a pilot, to which he also dissented; but, upon the earnest solicitations of officers and refugees, amounting almost to a demand, he reluctantly consented, and the boat left, manned by six men, two of whom were soldiers and four refugees. This was about 12.30 P.M. The colonel sent a pressing letter to the officer in command, stating that we were in distress, the horses on board suffering from the rough weather, and demanding assistance.

"About 7 P.M. the weather cleared to bright moonlight; sea more calm. The boat did not return, and hopes for her safety were given up, as it was supposed she might have swamped in crossing the bar. At this time three shells were plainly visible as having been fired from near the city, which was the first cause of uneasiness on the part of our captain. On the supposed warning the colonel had his men called together and put in readiness in case of emergency. Nothing further transpired, however, during the night.

"The next morning the day broke clear, the sun shining bright, with the city and its surroundings in full view. We hoisted pilot-jack and blew the whistle about eight o'clock, which signal was answered by pilot-boat inside the bar, near a schooner, and a bark with American colors flying, which proved to be the bark *Cavallo*. After the boat came toward us she tacked, apparently running and sounding the bar. She then went toward the bark and lowered her jack, signifying that she had put the pilot on board. In the meantime the pilot-boat shot up alongside and asked: 'How much water do you draw, captain?' To which he replied: 'Nine and a half to ten feet.' The answer then was: 'You can go in; there is plenty of water on the bar.' 'Are you a pilot?' was then demanded. *Reply.*—'No, but you can follow us in.' *Question.*—'Where is the pilot?' *Answer.*—'On the bark.' *Question.*—'Why does he not come out for us?' *Answer.*—'Because he had special orders to take the bark out first.' In the meantime we separated some distance. Again the pilot-boat shot up alongside, when the captain ordered the pilot on board, when he replied: 'There are too many men there for me.' He then immediately hauled jib-sheet to windward, slacked off the main-sheet, and put his helm hard to port, with the intention of getting clear. Seeing this, the captain ordered the steamer backed, which placed the steamer between the pilot-boat and the bar. The captain then called out: 'Stand by your guns, fore and aft, and be ready to fire. Do not open your port-holes before the colonel gives the word.' The pilot-boat then came to, and the pilot said he would come on board. The colonel asked him who was in command. His immediate reply was: 'Captain Wainwright.' After several unimportant questions and answers he was recognized and called by name by one of the refugees, by which he was apparently confused and lost his presence of mind. Seeing that the captain looked upon him with marked suspicion, he said: 'Gentlemen, I cannot lie any longer; Galveston is in the hands of the Confederacy.' The captain, hearing that the *Harriet Lane* was in their hands and as she was reported uninjured, immediately put the steamer to sea. The counterfeit pilot, T. W. Paine, was, of course, detained on board as prisoner. The pilot-boat and crew were permitted to depart, as the colonel thought by their returning it would give us more time to escape.

"About nine o'clock on the evening of the fifth instant we met the United States sloop-of-war *Brooklyn*, and was boarded by an officer from her, to whom we gave the foregoing information. We afterward learned that the boat sent ashore with the six men was detained and the men taken prisoners.

"Respectfully submitted,
"LEWIS BACH,
"*Acting-Purser Steamer Cambria.*"

What steps were taken to entrap the *Cambria*, or any transports unlucky enough to arrive while the United States gunboats fled to New Orleans, is described by General Magruder in his official report of the action. He says: "Having buried the dead, taken care of the wounded, and secured the captured property, my exertions were directed to getting the *Harriet Lane* to sea. The enemy's ships fled to New Orleans, to which place one of their steam transports was dispatched during the action. I knew that a large naval force might be expected to return in a few days. I therefore ordered the employment at high wages of all the available mechanics to repair the *Harriet Lane*, her main shaft having been dislocated and her iron wheel greatly disabled, so that the engine could not work. The United States flags were ordered to remain flying on the custom-house and at the mast-heads of the ships, so as to attract into the harbor any of the enemy's vessels which might be bound for the port of Galveston. A line of iron buoys, which we had established for the guidance of his ships in the harbor, were displaced and so arranged as to insure their getting aground.

"On the third of January, I being then on board of the *Harriet Lane*, a yawl-boat, containing several men, in command of a person named Thomas Smith, recently a citizen of Galveston, and who had deserted from our army, was reported alongside. He informed me he was sent from the United States transport-steamship *Cambria*, then off the bar, for a pilot, and that they had no idea of the occupation of the city by us. I forthwith ordered a pilot-boat, under command of Captain Johnson, to bring in this ship, but, through a most extraordinary combination of circumstances, the vessel which contained E. J. Davis and many other apostate Texans, besides several hundred troops and 2,500 saddles for the use of native sympathizers, succeeded in making her escape. The man Smith, who had, it is said, several times set fire to the city of Galveston before he deserted, had been known as Nicaragua Smith, and was dreaded by every one. He returned to Galveston in order to act as Federal provost-marshal. His arrival produced much excitement, during which some one without orders sent a sail-boat to Pelican Spit, now occupied by our troops, to direct the commanding officer there not fire on our pilot-boat, although she was under Yankee colors. The sail-boat thus sent was at once supposed to be destined for the Yankee transport. The pilot-boat gave chase to her, and the guns from the shore opened on her within hearing of the ship.

"Night coming on, I thought it surer, as the alarm might be taken, to capture her at sea before morning; but the *Harriet Lane* could not move, and our cotton gunboats could not live on the rough sea on the bar. Therefore one of the barks, the *Royal Yacht*, a schooner of ours, the pilot-boat and the *Leader*, a schooner loaded with cotton, which I had ordered to be sent to a foreign port, with a proclamation of the raising of the blockade at Galveston, were directed to be prepared and armed with light artillery. This was done by two o'clock the same night, our little fleet being manned by volunteers, under the command of Captain Mason, of Cook's regiment of artillery.

"Unfortunately the wind lulled, and none but the pilot-boat could reach the enemy's ship. The pilot-boat went out under the command of a gallant sailor, Captain Payne, of Galveston. The enemy's ship proved to be a splendid iron steamer, built in the Clyde. I had ascertained from her men taken ashore that she had only two guns, and they were packed on deck under a large quantity of hay, and I anticipated an easy conquest and one of great political importance, as this ship contained almost all the Texans out of the State who had proved recreant to their duty to the Confederacy and to Texas. The pilot-boat was allowed to get close to the ship, when the boat was hailed and the pilot ordered to come on board. Captain Payne answered that he thought there were rather too many men to trust himself to; whereupon he was directed to come on board, or he would be fired into. He went on board as ordered, and soon after the steamer sailed in all haste seaward, leaving the pilot-boat and hands to return to us.

"I am thus particular in this narration as the friends of Captain Payne fear that he may meet with foul play from the enemy. I shall ascertain, through Commodore Bell, his fate, and act accordingly. Smith, the deserter, was tried regularly the next day before a general court-martial, and, being convicted of deserting to the enemy, was publicly shot in Galveston, in accordance with his sentence. The proceedings, which were formal in all respects, legal and regular, are forwarded."

The following papers, connected with this action, are here given. The first, a dispatch from William L. Burt, was the first news sent North of the action, and naturally caused many a heart to ache for relatives and friends supposed to be at Galveston:

"SOUTHWEST PASS, LA.,
"January 3d, 1863, 1.45 P.M.

"MAJOR-GENERAL BANKS:

"I have received the following dispatch, which I hasten to communicate:

"'ON BOARD MARY BOARDMAN,
"'January 3d, 1863, 12 noon.

"'N. P. BANKS,

"'Commanding Department of the Gulf:

"'Galveston was attacked by land and water on the morning of January 1st. Colonel Burrell and his men were all killed or taken prisoners. Four rebel rams made an attack on the *Harriet Lane*, and carried her by boarding. Captain Wainwright and Lieutenant Lee killed, and all the men killed or prisoners. The captain of the *Owasco* (Wilson) was killed. Commander Renshaw blew up the flag-ship *Westfield* to prevent her from falling into the hands of the enemy. He was killed, and also First-Lieutenant Zimmerman. Two barks loaded with coal fell into the hands of the rebels. We have some seventy men from the *Westfield* on board. They must have some arrangements for taking charge of them immediately on our arrival, as we have only our own crew.

"'WM. L. BURT,

"'*Major and Aide-de-Camp, Staff of General Hamilton.*'
"C. HUGGINS."

General Banks, in a letter to Major-General Halleck, gives as his reason for sending Colonel Burrell to Galveston, the following:

"HEADQUARTERS DEPT. OF THE GULF,
"NEW ORLEANS, LA., January 7th, 1863.
(*Extract.*)

"*Sir:* The detachment of troops was sent to Galveston upon the suggestion of Admiral Farragut, and upon the statement of General Butler, that he had contemplated ordering a small force there to assist in recruiting Texas refugees. It was supposed that the fleet made the occupation of the part of the island adjacent to the gunboats perfectly secure. It would not, however, have been sent forward so soon after my arrival had it not been for the impatience of General Hamilton. When it became known that our destination was New Orleans and not Texas, which was not until our arrival here, those connected with him became very violent, and denounced unsparingly the Government and all connected with the expedition for what was called bad faith in its management.

"General Hamilton is not a bad man, but he does not manifest great force of character, and is surrounded by men who came here on the Government transports, unbeknown to me, for base, speculative purposes, and nothing else. I notified him of the conduct of these men, and he promised to correct it, but has not yet done so. He explains their presence by saying, that in the North he became indebted to them for pecuniary assistance. I sent him notice that they would be required to leave the Department if their course was approved by him.

"It was mainly the impatience of these people that prompted me to forward the detachment to Galveston; but only upon the concurrence of Admiral Farragut and General Butler as to its expediency and safety. Such is a full statement of my participation in this affair.

"I have the honor to be, with much respect,

"your obedient servant,

N. P. BANKS,

"*Major-General commanding.*

"MAJOR-GENERAL HALLECK,
 "*Commander-in-Chief U. S. Army.*"

The flag-of-truce scheme, so fortunately put into use by Major Smith, led to some correspondence on the subject between General Magruder and Commodore Bell, commanding United States forces off Galveston. None of this correspondence is of material interest to the Forty-Second Regiment, except the following extract from a letter by Colonel Debray to Commodore Bell, January 22d, viz.: "As to your complaint of a breach of truce in connection with the Forty-Second Massachusetts, I would respectfully state that the land troops were not embraced in the terms of truce on the 1st instant, either directly or indirectly. As soon as daylight came they could have been destroyed by our guns and musketry in five minutes. To avert a misunderstanding on this subject with you, which Major-General Magruder would much regret, he will send a full statement by to-morrow morning."

The full statement of Magruder to Bell is embraced in the following papers sent to the Confederate War Department in Richmond, Va., by Major-General Magruder, in justification of himself. It is proper to state that the statement signed by Colonel Burrell, was drafted after a long consultation between his officers, and, while not correct in every respect, the officers felt under obligations to Generals Magruder and Scurry, for favors granted and expected, and were disposed to help Magruder out of his muddle with the Confederate War Department. The documents were:

"The following document is not to be considered or used as official in any way, but as strictly personal.

"ISAAC S. BURRELL,
"*Colonel 42d Regt. Mass. Vols.*

"*Statement in relation to the surrender of a portion of the Forty-Second Regiment, Massachusetts Volunteers, at Galveston, Texas, on the morning of January 1st, A.D. 1863, to the Confederate forces under the command of Major-General J. B. Magruder, with the circumstances attending the surrender:*

"After the steamer *Harriet Lane* had raised the white flag in token of surrender, the white flag was also raised by the Forty-Second Regiment by order of the colonel commanding; but the fire continuing for ten or fifteen minutes from the wharf, and the brick building above Kuhn's Wharf, where the said Forty-Second Regiment was stationed, when Brigadier-General Scurry came down to Kuhn's Wharf and demanded the unconditional surrender of the troops on the wharf the firing ceased and was not resumed so far as the wharf is concerned.

"The surrender was made immediately, and the battle terminated, so far as said Forty-Second Regiment was concerned. Between the time the white flag was raised on the wharf and the cessation of the firing only one man was wounded and none killed.

"This statement is made in justice to Brigadier-General Scurry, who, by his gentlemanly conduct and uniform kindness to officers and privates, is entitled to the grateful remembrance of the whole command. We believe that the firing after the white flag was raised was unknown to him and against his will or orders.

"The flag of truce was not raised on the wharf by the Forty-Second Regiment until every vessel in the harbor had raised one.

"When the demand for surrender was made by Brigadier-General Scurry, the colonel of the Forty-Second Regiment asked to be allowed the same time given to the fleet for consideration (three hours), but his request was refused.

"Having carefully examined the above statement, I believe it to be true in every point, and accordingly I have affixed my signature thereto.

"ISAAC S. BURRELL,

"*Colonel 42d Regt. Mass. Vols.*"

this was enclosed in a letter sent to Richmond, Va., by General Magruder, of which the following is an extract:

"Houston, Texas, January 23d, 1863.

"This statement made by Colonel Burrell, commanding the detachment of the Forty-Second Massachusetts Regiment Volunteers, captured at Galveston on the 1st instant, it will be seen agrees in every important particular with the statement furnished by me in my communication to Commodore Bell. Our naval officers distinctly state that the white flag hoisted on board the ship did not apply to the land force. Captain Lubbock, the commander of one of our gunboats, who arranged with the senior officer in command of the Federal fleet the terms of the truce, stated, on his return from the Federal flag-ship, to Brigadier-General Scurry, in the presence of Colonel Burrell, that the land troops were not embraced in these terms, directly or indirectly, he having been sent by Captain Leon Smith, commanding our fleet of gunboats, to demand the surrender of the rest of the Federal fleet, and to give the Federal commander three hours' time to accept or decline his demand, during which time the fire was to cease between the ships. I knew nothing of the arrangements, nor did any officer ashore, and when Captain Lubbock, on his return, touched at Kuhn's Wharf, where the Forty-Second Massachusetts Regiment was stationed, he gave the above information to Brigadier-General Scurry in the presence of Colonel Burrell, and the latter surrendered unconditionally, after his request to be allowed the same time given the ships was refused. Had the Federal commander of the land forces been in superior force to myself and engaged in battle ashore he would certainly have prosecuted his advantage to the utmost, regardless of a truce between two fleets, which he had not authorized. If necessary, I think it can be fully established also that the Federal troops ashore were ready to surrender the moment daylight gave them an opportunity of doing so, and would have done it even before daylight had it been possible.

"I have also to state that I am informed by Brigadier-General Scurry, who was in that portion of the battle, that the white flag displayed from Kuhn's Wharf was respected the moment it was seen."

With the exception of Private Hersey, left to help take care of baggage, wounded men taken to hospital, Surgeon Cummings, left to attend them, and naval officers to attend the funeral of Wainwright and Lea, all of the prisoners marched to Virginia Point in the afternoon, where they were obliged to wait until half-past one o'clock A. M. next day, January 2d, for cars to transport them to Houston.

On arrival at that city, about noon, the depot was reported to be crowded with people, and the train was stopped half a mile out. The men then marched, under guard, through Houston to their quarters in a cotton warehouse near Buffalo Bayou. The officers were confined in Kennedy's building, corner of Travis and Congress Streets.

On the march through crowded streets, many bantering remarks were made, mostly by women, who were exceedingly bitter and sarcastic. The men had been cautioned by their colonel not to pay any attention to insults, which they must expect to receive, but carry themselves as if on parade. They did march through the City of Houston as if on parade, giving the people a sight of good marching, military bearing and good manners such as they had not seen before.

In passing the *Houston Telegraph* newspaper office, where from the windows was displayed the captured regimental colors underneath the Texas Lone Star Flag, the men got mad, some of them threatening to "go for them." Cool counsel prevailed, and no trouble occurred.

The *Houston Telegraph*, in giving an account of the arrival of the prisoners, said they were acknowledged Americans, with an occasional foreigner to be seen among them, either Irish or Dutch. Gave them credit for being well dressed and good looking. Spoke of Colonel Burrell as a tall, slim specimen of a man, who was much stared at by the people, but he never lifted his eyes from the ground during the march. As the prisoners of war marched up Main Street they were well treated, and received from the Houstonites the compliment of being a fine-looking body of men, who ought to be ashamed of themselves for volunteering their services in the villainy of trying to subjugate a chivalrous people.

At the hospitals in Galveston Surgeon Cummings remained until the eighteenth of January, attending Federal wounded, also assisting the Confederate surgeons. Sisters of Mercy, attached to the Convent of St. Leon, rendered service to the wounded of both sides impartially. On the tenth, while a gunboat was shelling the city from the Gulf side, some shells exploded in the convent yard, necessitating removal of patients to a small, wooden school-house, when a hospital flag was raised, which stopped further mischief.

Commander Wainwright and Lieutenant Lea, of the *Harriet Lane*, were buried with Masonic and military honors on the second. Major Lea, C. S. A., father of the lieutenant, officiated at the grave, reading the Episcopal Church burial service in a firm, unfaltering voice to the end, when he gave way to his feelings and wept like a child. The rest of the killed were buried on the third.

Surgeon Cummings, on the twentieth of January, found

time to make the following official report of the killed and wounded:

"HOUSTON, TEXAS, January 20th, 1863.
"COLONEL I. S. BURRELL,
 "42d Regt. Mass. Vols.:

"*Sir*,— The following is a correct list of the wounded of said Forty-Second Regiment at the battle of Galveston, January 1st, 1863:

NAME.	Co.	RANK.	How Wounded.	Result.
Francis L. Nott.	G.	Private.	Shell in left side of bowels.	Died in 17 hours.
Jos. W. D. Parker.	G.	"	Ball in arm.	Recovering.
Edmund B. Doubel.	G.	"	Ball in left hand, severe.	"
George R. Dary.	G.	"	Ball in left arm, above elbow.	"
Thos. T. Sweetser.	G.	"	Buckshot in chin, slight.	"
James L. Davis.	G.	"	Splinter in face, slight.	"
John M. Barnard, Jr.	G.	"	Spent ball in left leg, slight.	"
John T. Cook.	G.	"	Splinter in leg, slight.	"
David L. Wentworth		Act-Ord. Sergt. of regt.	Shell in leg.	"
Wm. H. Cowdin.	D.	1st Lieut.	Ball in back.	"
Francis L. Morrill.	D.	Private.	Minnie ball in hand, severe.	I fear loss of arm.
Tobias Enslee.	D.	"	Splinter in head, slight.	Recovering.
Edwin F. Josselyn.	D.	"	Shell in head, severe.	"
Daniel J. Sullivan.	D.	"	Minnie ball in hand, severe.	"
Jas. O'Shaughnessy.	D.	"	Shell in both legs, right leg amputated.	"

"These are all the casualties in our regiment in the late severe battle, in which the only wonder is that one of us lived to tell the story. It seems indeed providential that so few are wounded and none killed on the spot. We have to mourn the loss of one noble fellow, Nott of Company G, a brave soldier and an excellent man, and to regret the loss of a leg of Company D, O'Shaughnessy, who is recovering rapidly. I amputated his leg just below the knee, in order to give him the benefit of the joint, which was not injured.

"I have the honor to be, dear sir,

"Yours faithfully,

"A. I. CUMMINGS,

"*Surgeon 42d Mass. Regt. Vols.*"

Besides the above, there were wounded, who did not report to the surgeon: Private John Barnes, Company D, slightly in leg; and Private James W. Vinal, Company G, slightly in hip.

Quartermaster-Sergeant Foster was standing by the breastwork in conversation with Private Hersey when the first shot was fired, glanced on the breastwork and passed into the building. In a moment of excitement Foster fell wounded, so Hersey thought, but on an examination of a wound he received, a bad cut of a thumb, it proved to have been made by oyster shells upon which he had fallen. It was jocularly reported Foster had received a shell wound in the action.

Private Nott was wounded during the first hour. He had got behind a hawser-post, where Colonel Burrell found him moaning faintly, with a terrible wound in the side and bowels. He was not apparently suffering any intense pain. To the question, if he was badly hurt, he replied, "Yes, in the side," and begged for water. Private Hersey went into the building and got it, which appeared to revive him somewhat from a state of apathy. When the surgeon got an opportunity to examine his case, Nott was told he could not live many hours, as he was bleeding internally, and any message for home had better be given then.

Private O'Shaughnessy was wounded during the first half hour. He yelled like an Indian on the war-path, and was carried into the hospital-room, where the surgeon remained at his post the entire time that the enemy's fire was concentrated upon it.

Privates Enslee and Josselyn were wounded at the commencement, while standing ready to fire before the order was heard to lie down. A solid shot, or a shell, struck and crashed through the breastwork, splinters wounding Enslee in the head. A fragment of shell ruined Josselyn's musket, knocked it overboard, then glanced to his head. The wound bled profusely, but Josselyn did not know he was hit until blood was running down his face. Upon reporting at the hospital he was so covered with blood Surgeon Cummings was unable to recognize him. Binding his head up with a handkerchief, Josselyn returned to his post.

Private Morrill, when wounded, tied a handkerchief around his hand and kept his place in the ranks until the action was over before reporting to the surgeon.

Lieutenant Cowdin was wounded while lying down, during the first hour. A canister shot struck the storehouse brick chimney, knocking it to pieces, the debris flying in all directions. Supposing he had been wounded by a falling brick, on standing up he was surprised to find several small shot ran down his clothing into a boot; they had struck him in the back, low down, going through coat, shirt, pants and under-drawers.

Company I, from its sheltered position, had no casualties. Private Eaton had his bayonet cut in halves, another man received a ball in his hat, and Private Paget had a ball cut his haversack straps.

An official report of the action was not made to General Banks, until July, 1864, when Colonel Burrell arrived in New Orleans, paroled and exchanged.

"NEW ORLEANS, July 27th, 1864.
"To MAJOR GEORGE B. DRAKE,
"*Assistant Adjutant-General:*

"*Major,*— Pursuant to orders, I proceeded with my command to Galveston, Texas, and took post. I arrived there December 24th, 1862, landed next day on Kuhn's Wharf, and fortified by building barricades, and tearing up the bridge, making my position as strong as possible.

"I took possession of the city as far as my small force would allow; my scouts destroyed the telegraph running to Houston; and I took such precautions as I thought necessary for holding the place. Commander Renshaw, who had command of the fleet, laid four months within musket shot of this telegraph and had allowed it to remain in working order. We found the railroad in good condition. Signals were thrown up every night, giving the enemy all the information they wanted.

"I requested Commander Renshaw to go up the bay with two of his lightest draft steamers and dislodge the enemy. I also requested the use of two howitzers, which were on board of a schooner, and of no use to the schooner. Both requests he refused to grant.

"I landed my command on the wharf with the distinct understanding that I was to be supported by the steamer *Harriet Lane* on my right and the steamer *Clifton* on my left. On the morning of the first January, 1863, about four o'clock, I was attacked by a force of infantry and cavalry, amounting to over six thousand men, with thirty-two pieces of artillery. The only support I received was from the steamer *Sachem*, and the schooner *Corypheus* manned with fifteen men and one gun. The steamer *Sachem* was out of order, with her fires out to repair boilers. The *Harriet Lane* laid so far up the stream she was unable to retreat, and became easy prey. The steamer *Owasco* was two miles below the city, with little or no steam up. The steamer *Westfield*, with Commander Renshaw aboard, managed to get aground three miles below the city, and signaled for the *Clifton* to come and get her off. At this time the enemy opened their heavy guns upon me from the head of the wharf, and continued to throw shot and shell for one hour, when they made an assault with two of their regiments to drive me from my position. We repulsed them, and they retreated with severe loss. My officers and men fought with great gallantry. Being without artillery I had to rely upon the *Sachem* and a little schooner for support.

"At this time two cotton boats attacked the *Harriet Lane*, driving the men from their guns, killing Captain Wainwright. The steamer *Owasco* came up and fired a few shots, also the *Clifton*, who had fired but seven or eight shots when a flag of truce was entertained, and they agreed to cease hostilities for three hours, and immediately dropped down stream without consulting me at all in the matter. At this time the enemy were in full retreat from the wharf; the artillery had limbered up and withdrawn.

"In a short time they returned, and immediately put their guns in position and opened fire. I had no alternative but to surrender after the fleet had left. Entirely deserted by the navy in a cowardly manner. They had agreed to take my command off the wharf if we were hard pressed. The steamers *Clifton* and *Owasco* passed by, but refused to render any assistance. After receiving the fire of the enemy for a half-hour, and receiving no assistance, I was compelled to surrender myself and my command.

"The fleet, at the expiration of the three hours agreed upon by flag of truce (except the *Westfield*, which was blown up), ran out of the harbor without firing a shot.

"It is my opinion and belief that Commander Renshaw was a traitor, he being in constant communication with the enemy. Commander Law proved himself unworthy of his command. In not holding Galveston we lost the key to Texas.

"Enclosed please find the report of my excellent and lamented surgeon, Dr. A. I. Cummings.

"The following is a list of the amount of property lost and surrendered: two hundred and seventy small-arms, (one hundred and eighty Springfield smooth-bores and ninety Springfield rifles); equipments for two hundred and sixty men; medical stores to the amount of $1,000; one set of surgical instruments; twenty A tents and three wall tents; five boxes of ammunition; twenty days' rations for two hundred and sixty men.

"I remain, major,

"Very respectfully,

"I. S. BURRELL,

"*Colonel 42d Regt. Mass. Vols.*"

Admiral Farragut severely censured the naval officers for their conduct in this action, and would not listen to any explanations. He was chagrined at the capture of the *Harriet Lane*. When her crew, under parole, reported to him, on their return to the Federal lines, he gave them a severe lecture, and accused each and every man of cowardice, threatening to punish those who tried to offer an excuse. The sailors said they had never seen the "old man" so mad. A bitter feeling existed among the *Harriet Lane's* crew against the *Clifton's* crew, which led to several fistic encounters in New Orleans, when they met each other.

A full inquiry into the cause of the disaster had been made by Admiral Farragut. A court-martial, held on board the flag-ship *Hartford*, had resulted in condemning Commanders Law and Wilson. The blame for this defeat had been placed where it belonged, and when the exchanged officers of the regiment left New Orleans for New York, General Banks placed in the colonel's hands the following letter:

"HEADQUARTERS DEPT. OF THE GULF,

"NEW ORLEANS, August 5th, 1864.

"To HIS EXCELLENCY GOVERNOR ANDREW,

"Of Massachusetts:

"*Sir*,— Colonel Isaac S. Burrell, of the Forty-Second Massachusetts Volunteers, left New York with the troops under my command at the time I entered service in this Department. Two days after I assumed command here he was sent with his regiment to protect the island of Galveston, which had been for three months in the possession of the naval authorities of the United States. Two companies of his regiment, under his own command, arrived there on the twenty-fourth of December, 1862. The plans of the rebels for the recapture of the island had been so far matured that before the balance of his regiment could reach the island (a large part of which was within sight at the time the recapture occurred), it was impossible for him, with his small force, to defend the post or effect a retreat with his men. By an arrangement with the commanding officer of the naval squadron the rebels had maintained a railway communication from the main-land to the island, and upon the night of the attack they ran their forces of five or six thousand, with heavy artillery, to within a quarter of a mile of the position occupied by Colonel Burrell. It is unnecessary for me to recount the facts connected with this disaster to our arms, but it is just to Colonel Burrell, to say, that it is in no wise attributable to him, but that his conduct and that of his men, from the testimony of all parties, was highly creditable to the service.

"He has been held prisoner of war by the enemy from the first of January, 1863, until recently exchanged. He has suffered greatly in health, and is entitled to consideration from the officers of the general government, as from the officers of the State of Massachusetts. I commend him to the favor of your Excellency, as in all respects worthy of favorable consideration.

"I have the honor to be

"Very respectfully, your obedient servant,

"N. P. BANKS,

"*Major-General commanding.*"

CHAPTER V.

AT CARROLLTON — BOUND FOR GALVESTON — ARRIVAL OF COMPANIES — CAMP MANSFIELD — DETAILS.

BRIGADIER-GENERAL T. W. SHERMAN was in command of all United States forces assembled at several camps in and about Carrollton, a suburb of New Orleans, distant a few miles north of that city. The town did not contain many houses or white inhabitants, and was situated on low, wet, swampy ground. The vacant squares of building lots was ground on which the troops pitched their tents. Camp Mansfield contained the One Hundred and Tenth New York Infantry, One Hundred and Fifty-Sixth New York Infantry, One Hundred and Sixty-First New York Infantry, Third New Hampshire Infantry, Twenty-Fifth Connecticut Infantry, detachment Forty-Second Massachusetts Infantry, Twenty-Fifth New York Light Battery, Reed's Massachusetts Rifle Rangers — in all about four thousand men; Colonel Littlejohn, ——th New York, commanding the post.

The release from close confinement on board transports was, for a time, enjoyed by everybody, regardless of weather changes. The days were warm and pleasant, but the nights freezing cold, causing much suffering, as no boards could be obtained for tent floors, or firewood to build bonfires. Why diarrhœa and dysentery did not attack more men while at this camp, than was the case, is surprising. Camp regulations in regard to men being out of quarters after taps had to be set aside, for, finding it impossible to sleep without getting chilled, many of them would cluster around the cooking-stoves, that were kept heated, and endeavor to keep warm until day, with its bright, southern sunshine and warmth, should dawn, when they could be comfortable. The rattling of drums beating reveille in the various camps caused many a man of that four thousand to feel thankful.

According to orders received the evening of January 2d, 1863, the detachment (Companies A, B and F) struck camp on the morning of January 3d, went to the river levee and embarked on board steamer *Che-Kiang*, at nine o'clock, *en route* for Galveston, Texas, to join Companies D, G and I. While lying at the United States Barracks at night on the third, where most of the day was passed in taking aboard stores, ammunition, horses, and a detachment First Texas Cavalry, recruited from Texas refugees, a furious thunder-storm occurred. Rain fell in torrents; the lightning seemed to be everywhere and constant, with deafening peals of thunder. It was a scene not to be forgotten, and although showers of the same magnitude were afterwards experienced, none made so vivid an impression on the memory as this first thunder-storm witnessed in the sunny South.

During Sunday, the fourth, there seemed to be a strange foreboding in the minds of a great many that some unfortunate occurrence had taken place. The transport was not in a hurry to proceed on the voyage, and there was an ominous silence among officers who were supposed to know the cause of delay. At noon the truth became known. Galveston had been captured by Confederates, with Companies D, G and I, and the regimental colors. All the mad projects, which found vent in words, that started in the brains of men on board the *Che-Kiang* would not be believed if they were given here. A dare-devil spirit to do something that would recapture their comrades, restore their colors, and wipe out the stigma which they felt would be against the regiment, animated every breast.

When Lieutenant M. Burrell, Jr. with First-Sergeant Henry White, of Company A, came on board and recited their story of the affair, although not very elaborate or satisfactory, it was listened to with marked attention. They had started a few days before in the transport *Honduras* for Galveston, with the First Vermont Battery on board, arriving off the harbor on the morning of the capture, and been ordered back to New Orleans by a naval officer commanding a gunboat that was in the action. The companies disembarked a second time at Carrollton in the afternoon of January 4th, and went into camp at Camp Mansfield on worse ground than before.

Next day Companies E and K, from the *Charles Osgood*, reported for duty and pitched their tents. Quartermaster Burrell and Adjutant Davis also came into camp, having just arrived from Galveston after escaping capture. They were received with cheers and congratulations.

This camp was situated on very swampy ground with two ravines running lengthwise through it, made to drain the water during rainy seasons. The arrangement of tents was made as symmetrical as possible, but formation of the ground completely spoiled its beauty. To reach the color-line a deep water gully had to be passed, marring the good appearance of a dress parade. The hospital was located in a vacated school-house, distant half a mile from camp, because it was impossible to accommodate patients in the hospital tent. Assistant-Surgeon Hitchcock was quite sick with typhoid fever soon after reaching Carrollton, and Assistant-Surgeon George C. Smith, One Hundred and Fifty-Sixth New York Infantry, was detailed to occupy his position temporarily, serving the regiment from January 17th to 27th.*

On the twelfth, Major Stiles, with Companies C and H, reported for duty at camp, receiving a warm reception. The men were as much pleased to tread dry land once more as their comrades were to see them. The day and night was occupied by the men in reciting each other's adventures since they parted in New York.

An aggravating case of desertion occurred January 2d, when Private Lewis Buffum, Company B, deserted the service and his regiment under circumstances proving him to be an arrant coward. Placed in a position as acting-engineer on board the transport *Quincy*, while on her trip from New York with the three companies, he received the best of treatment, lived in the same manner as the officers, at no cost to himself, and on arrival at New Orleans received extra pay from Captain Clapp of the *Quincy*, for his services on the voyage; this Buffum, regardless of all feelings of honor and duty, improved the opportunity thus given him, detached and away from his company for a few days after landing, to procure a change of clothing and bribe the first-engineer on the *Quincy* to conceal him on board upon her return trip to New York.

Several orders sent him to report for duty with his company and not obeyed caused a search to be made, when his desertion was discovered. An overhauling of the *Quincy* failed to find him. It was ascertained some months afterward (April 24th), when he came into the hands of provost-marshal Captain John Pickering of New

---

* While at Carrollton the average daily sick in the regiment was: taken sick, five; returned to duty, five; sick in hospital, twelve; sick in quarters, eighteen; an average of thirty men each day under a surgeon's care.

Orleans, having surrendered himself at Fort Columbus, New York harbor, March 31st, under the promise of pardon made by President Lincoln in General Orders No. 58, War Department, issued March 11th, 1863, to all deserters who returned to duty, that Buffum was on board the *Quincy* during the search, stowed away on the top of her boiler. As the searching party passed one side of it he would slide down the opposite side until they had passed, and then return to the top.

There are no extenuating circumstances connected with Buffum's desertion. He was a married man, with wife and children living. As a man he should have had some respect for their feelings, even though he was without honor himself. He never was ill-treated by his officers. His profession placed him in a position to be of great service to the Government, by performing detached duty as engineer on some of the railroads and steamers controlled by United States officers in Louisiana. Private Buffum was so detailed by orders from Department headquarters, to which detail answer had to be returned: "Deserted in New Orleans, January 2d, 1863, and has not since been apprehended."

In connection with this case of desertion may properly be stated the three cases of enlisted men who were disciplined at this camp. Corporal Denny, Company E, was, January 22d, ordered to be placed in arrest by Lieutenant-Colonel Stedman. A captain objected to some statements that had appeared in a communication sent home by the corporal for publication, and preferred charges against him. Denny remained in arrest until after his trial by a division court-martial held January 27th, in New Orleans, and the proceedings of the court could be passed upon by General Sherman. The charge and specification was as follows:

CHARGE.

"Conduct to the prejudice of Good Order and Military Discipline."

Specification — In this: that he, Corporal Denny, was author of, did write and cause to be published in the *Worcester Daily Spy*, on the morning of December 29th, 1862, an article containing sentiments false and calculated to mislead the public with reference to the acts of Captain George P. Davis, then commanding troops on board the *Charles Osgood*, and reflecting censure on his (Corporal Denny's) superior officer, which article was, in form and substance, as follows:

"Considerable feeling was created by the refusal of the privilege, but a quantity of *whiskey* provided by the officers allayed the feeling with some, while it only added intensity with others. It was looked at by many as a kind of *bribe*, while others were conscientiously opposed to the indiscriminate distribution of whiskey by even superior officers. It is to the credit of a large number that they threw the stuff overboard as soon as received. There is a general feeling that whiskey drinking is already too prevalent to have it so openly countenanced, and all well-wishers of the Union army hope the practice may soon be abandoned."

Said article, of which the above is only an extract, was written after the departure of the steamer *Charles Osgood* from New York and before her arrival at New Orleans.

To which charge and specification the accused pleaded as follows:

To the specification — Not guilty.
To the charge — Not guilty.

FINDING OF THE COURT.

The Court, after mature deliberation on the evidence adduced, finds the accused, Corporal Everett A. Denny of Company E, Forty-Second Regiment Massachusetts Volunteers, as follows :

Of the specification — Guilty.
Of the charge — Guilty.

SENTENCE.

And the Court does therefore sentence him, Corporal Everett A. Denny, Company E, Forty-Second Regiment Massachusetts Volunteers, to be reduced to the ranks, to forfeit ten dollars of his pay, and to be publicly reprimanded by the commanding officer of his regiment.

The sentence was approved in General Orders No. 16, Defences New Orleans, March 7th, 1863, and Corporal Denny released from arrest and returned to duty with his company March 17th.

Whether the offence was worth the trouble and expense of a trial is a debatable question. Corporal Denny was young and inexperienced at the time; with more years upon his shoulders he would probably have been more discreet. There were many young correspondents with the army who did not always confine their letters to matters of public interest, but dabbled with surmises of probable movements by the troops, their strength, positions occupied, and *morale* of officers and men. This is against army rules, and not to be tolerated. It is indirectly furnishing information of value to the enemy.

Private James White, of Company A, while at Carrollton, disobeyed orders, using disrespectful language towards his superior officer. A regimental court-martial convicted and sentenced him to forfeit one month's pay and to walk six hours a day for fourteen days — three in the morning and three in the afternoon — with a log of wood tied across his back, weighing not more than fifty pounds and not less than twenty-five pounds, and to do fatigue duty every morning. As provided in orders for regimental courts-martial, the sentence was approved by the brigade commander.

Private Jotham E. Bigelow, of Company K, was placed in arrest for sleeping on his sentry post. By regimental General Orders No. 11, issued January 30th, he was released from arrest and ordered to duty, because, "from his previous good conduct as a soldier in all matters, and being the first case of the kind in the regiment." A warning was issued in the orders that future cases would not be dealt with so leniently.

All proceedings in cases proper for a regimental court-martial had to be before a field-officer of the regiment, by General Orders No. 91, issued July 29th, 1862, from the War Department. Major Stiles was in every case detailed to hear the evidence.

At Carrollton several heavy details were made of working parties to unload vessels at the levee, besides attending to a regular routine of camp duty. Short marches were taken out on the shell road to accustom the troops to that exercise. When Brigadier-General Emory assumed the command he watched sharply these marching drills, also the company and battalion drills of each organization. As some field-officers were inclined to consume time in executing fancy tactical movements when they had their regiments on drill, a general order was issued indicating a more rapid mode of instruction for the field. The following points were enjoined as of the first importance:

1st. The firings — to be executed with facility, promptness, and good order.

2d. Rapid ployments and deployments while marching as well as from a halt.

3d. Sudden and rapid formations of squares against cavalry.

With these instructions carefully and faithfully carried out, any troops could soon be made fairly efficient for field service, with discipline also enforced.

Lieutenant-Colonel Stedman, on several occasions, as field-officer of the day, had to make the grand rounds. The start was usually made between eleven and twelve o'clock at night. Considerable ground had to be covered to reach various bodies of troops occupying scattered camps, while the outpost stations would consume much time. Acting under verbal orders to thoroughly do this duty, numerous attempts were made to catch sentries off their guard; in some cases quite successfully, but it resulted in creating bad feeling between the organization so caught, and the regiment from which the field-officer of the day belonged. One of the most notable cases was a surprise of the Fifteenth New Hampshire camp. Upon approaching a sentry he failed to challenge, and seemed glad to take part in a casual conversation, which was commenced, when it was seen the man was not reliable in his duty. Finally, he was seized without resistance and his musket taken away, frightening the poor fellow to such an extent it was with difficulty the grand rounds' party could remain by him while proceeding towards the guard quarters, where everything was found to be all right, with the men alert.

The One Hundred and Tenth New York camp was entered one night without a challenge, or being seen by any sentinels; on stealthily approaching the guard quarters, where a log fire was burning, no sign of life was seen excepting a solitary sentinel pacing to and fro before a line of stacked muskets. Watching a favorable opportunity he was made a quasi-prisoner, much to his chagrin, and on inspecting the guard tents a few men were found sound asleep, with no officer of the guard present. Routing out the regimental officer of the day to investigate the matter, it appeared that the reliefs, together with officers of the guard, had gone to their quarters for sleep.

After a few incidents like these were reported to post headquarters, it was not long before sentries were wide awake for surprises. It became dangerous business to attempt any fooling with sentries, and such attempts were abandoned. Whenever a field-officer of the Fifteenth New Hampshire or One Hundred and Tenth New York had the grand rounds, in retaliation, they tried various ways to catch the Forty-Second guard napping, but never succeeded.

On one of these grand rounds' tour of duty, while proceeding along the levee road towards outpost stations, the road was found to be in an impassable condition, owing to a small break in the levee, not known to exist, as during the early afternoon one of the officers had found the road in good condition. An occupant of a house near at hand was awakened to obtain directions how to proceed: the man either intentionally or by mistake directed the party to take the levee embankment, his reasons for the bad condition of the road not creating any suspicion that a crevasse existed in the levee. Proceeding along the embankment with Sergeant-Major Bosson leading the mounted party, his horse suddenly stopped, and no amount of urging could induce the animal to move forward. In the pitchy darkness it was impossible to see what was the matter, so the party with difficulty (the embankment top was very narrow) turned about, going back, finally reaching another road leading to the outposts. The next morning, upon examining the road at this point, there was found a small break in the levee. Had the horse kept on for a few feet, both horse and rider would have been in the Mississippi River.

A sharp report from several muskets, fired by sentinels, followed with a cry of fire, roused the camp at two o'clock on the morning of January 26th. Not far from the camp lines was a small frame house, used by officers of the Forty-Second for messing. This had caught fire, burning to the ground. The primitive fire department of Carrollton rallied, consisting of several white men, a gang of negroes with an old worn out double-deck hand fire-engine, requiring not over ten men to man the brakes, without suction hose, water being furnished the engine by hand buckets, and a small hose carriage. A detail of men from the regiment soon took possession of this fire apparatus, relieving the local firemen of any responsibility, and earnestly endeavored to stop the flames. What was in rain water cisterns attached to the nearest houses was all the water that could be used. There was great sport in fighting this fire, as well as some sharp and brave work in saving what was in the house. For the purpose of obtaining indemnity from the Government, the owner implicated officers of the regiment with this fire. A council of investigation was ordered by Brigadier-General Emory into the circumstances; the detail consisted of Captains Cogswell and Cook and Lieutenant Gorham, who found that the fire was accidental.

Lieutenant Proctor was without a command, as his company were prisoners of war. Upon landing, with men of Company G who were with him, he met Colonel N. A. M. Dudley, an old friend, in the city, who requested him to join his brigade, then at Baton Rouge, as he wanted a brigade quartermaster, and wished to appoint the lieutenant to that position. Although attached to another brigade and division, Colonel Dudley thought he could arrange the matter with his division general, Grover, and the Department headquarters. Lieutenant Proctor proceeded to Baton Rouge, but Dudley could not carry out his plan, as Adjutant-General Irwin stated it was against the rules of the service. This was true. Lieutenant Proctor and his men reported back to the regiment February 3d.

First Sergeant Nichols, Company G, was detailed acting lieutenant of Company E, *vice* Stowell, a prisoner of war.

Sergeant Attwell, Company G, remained unattached.

Private H. C. Green, Company G, was attached to Company K for duty.

Private John Luzardo, Company G, was attached to Company K for duty.

Sergeant Vialle, Company G, remained unattached.

War Department General Orders No. 5, issued January 5th, 1863, had made the troops in the Gulf Department to constitute the Nineteenth Army Corps, to date from December 14th, 1862. Orders were issued from Department headquarters on the thirteenth of January attaching the Forty-Second to the Second Brigade, Second Division, Nineteenth Army Corps. In the brigade were the Twenty-Sixth Massachusetts Infantry, three years men; Forty-Second Massachusetts Infantry, nine months men; Forty-Seventh Massachusetts Infantry, nine months men; Ninth Connecticut Infantry, three years men; Twenty-Eighth Maine Infantry, nine months men. The brigade was then under command of Colonel Farr, Twenty-Sixth Massachusetts Volunteers, and constituted part of the garrison in the Defences of New Orleans.

The regiment remained in camp at Carrollton until January 28th, receiving marching orders for five companies to take post at Bayou Gentilly, on the Ponchartrain Railroad crossing, on the twenty-seventh.

Up to this date the following changes by detail and sickness had occurred:

January 17th — Companies C and H left for duty in engineer service.

January 25th — Quartermaster Burrell was detailed by brigade orders as acting brigade quartermaster. Lieutenant Albert E. Proctor, Company G, by regimental orders, was detailed as acting regimental quartermaster, on the twenty-sixth.

Assistant Surgeon Isaac Smith, Jr., Twenty-Sixth Massachusetts Volunteers, was detailed to act as surgeon during Surgeon Hitchcock's sickness, relieving Surgeon Smith, One Hundred and Fifty-Sixth New York Volunteers, and joined the regiment for duty on the twenty-ninth, at Bayou Gentilly.

Captain George P. Davis, Company K, and Lieutenant T. M. Duncan, Company F, by department orders, were detailed for duty in the provost-marshal general's office, on the twenty-first.

Captain Charles A. Pratt, Company E, had been absent from camp on sick leave, and not on duty since his company landed from the *Charles Osgood*. Captain Pratt did not see any service with his company. He resigned, and was discharged for ill health by Special Orders No. —, Gulf Department, March 28th, 1863.

January 3d — Corporal Alonzo I. Hodsdon, Company D, was appointed acting quartermaster-sergeant, in place of Foster, taken prisoner at Galveston. Hodsdon, with the pay of his rank as corporal to July 12th, performed the arduous duty of the position in a most admirable manner during the term of the regiment. Special mention is made in his case over that of other non-commissioned staff-officers, because of his devoted attention to the duties with no prospect before him of any promotion to the position. While Foster lived, Corporal Hodsdon remained a corporal. Foster's parole, when released by the Confederates, did not allow him to take his position until exchanged, which did not occur during the term of service.

January 1st — Private Eldridge G. Harwood, Company B, was appointed regimental carpenter.

January 15th — Private Clark K. Denny, Company F, was detailed as orderly and clerk at regimental headquarters.

January 15th — Private Leavitt Bates, Company A, was detailed as clerk to headquarters of General Emory, at Carrollton. Relieved February 3d.

January 15th — Private John A. Loud, Company A, was made regimental armorer.

January 30th — Private Winfield B. Tirrell, Company A, was detailed as orderly at brigade headquarters, by brigade orders.

The Quartermaster Department was advanced a stage in its appointments, by organizing the wagon train, as follows: Private John Willy, Company B, chief wagoner; Private Porter Carter, Company K, Corporal Alfred Thayer, Company I, Privates Chauncey K. Bullock, Company D, G. G. Belcher, Company F, Joseph B. Ford, Company A, as wagoners.

On moving to Bayou Gentilly the following sick men were left in general hospital at Carrollton: Privates Adin P. Blake, Company B, George E. Pond, Company B, Lucius M. Turner, Company B, and Surgeon Hitchcock.

CHAPTER VI.

FEBRUARY — AT BAYOU GENTILLY — MORE DETAILS.

THAT part of Bayou Gentilly where a portion of the Forty-Second was to remain in camp for nearly five months was, at the time of arrival, a most desolate looking place. The Gentilly road passed the camp ground, leading to Fort Macomb, on Lake Ponchartrain, and at this point, at this time, was in a wretched condition. Each side of the road was lined by small plantations and pasture lands, extending back for a short distance to swamps. Most of the plantations were uninhabited, the land covered with rank vegetation, and showed every sign of abandonment. Occasionally some hut or rude cabin would give signs of life — occupied by charcoal burners, who carried on their vocation in the swamps. The Ponchartrain Railroad, from New Orleans to Lakeport, on Lake Ponchartrain, five miles long, in a direct line through the swamp to the lake, ran only two trains a day. Save the regiment, scarcely a person would be seen for days.

A sugar-cane plantation near the camp, belonging to a Mr. Lee, was used to pasture private and Government cattle, and recruit the strength of horses and mules run down by hard service in the army. The private residence, negro cabins, stables and work houses remained in very good order. The sugar-house was a mass of ruins. An extensive grove of plum trees was in good condition.

Pent up in this flat spot of land, with nothing to relieve the eye but a mass of trees situated in the swamp, their limbs covered with light-colored moss, had a depressing effect on the spirits of some men, who began early to show signs of home-sickness.

The ground selected for the camp was upon the old Louisiana race-course, the best to be found in the neighborhood. This race-course had been surrounded by a high board fence, such as enclose similar grounds, but had disappeared, leaving the ground as open as the land about it. Adjoining the Gentilly road and Ponchartrain Railroad, the side towards New Orleans was on the border of a swamp. This ground was formerly occupied for a camp by Confederate troops. The famous Washington Artillery, of New Orleans, first went into camp at this place at the commencement of hostilities. A portion of the Confederate garrison of New Orleans, when General Butler landed, were also encamped here. What few inhabitants were to be seen said that a large number of men had at various times been in camp at this point, and was a general rendezvous for many of the Louisiana troops when organizing for the war. Many an hour has been pleasantly passed inspecting the writings and pictures upon the walls of a building used by them as a hospital, placed there by men from the Thirtieth and Thirty-First Louisiana regiments.

By railroad the distance from New Orleans to Gentilly Station was three miles, and from Gentilly Station to the Lake End, or Lakeport, was two miles. A short distance up the track towards Lakeport and back from the Gentilly road, which the railroad crosses at grade, was an earthwork mounting four heavy guns, called Battery Gentilly, flanked by extensive breastworks for infantry, with wide and deep ditches in front filled with water. Trees in the swamp in front had been cut down for a considerable distance to give good range to the guns. Another earthwork, mounting nine guns, was situated on the Gentilly road, towards Fort Macomb, some two and one-half miles from the railroad track, and was in all its surroundings similar to Battery Gentilly.

On the twenty-eighth of January, when the regiment changed camps, the roads were in very good condition in spite of cold weather, and rain falling for two days previous. Great coats were worn; the men were in excellent spirits, and the distance, about three miles, was accomplished early in the afternoon. Very few men straggled; most of those that did were suffering from diarrhœa. The line of march embraced a circuit of New Orleans on its immediate outskirts, affording few opportunities to see subjects of interest to strangers in a new land. A greater part of the houses were either deserted or occupied by the poorer class of people; only a few were evidently the property of wealthy individuals. Some handsome residences were seen, but their occupants were decidedly unfriendly. They could be seen looking slyly through blinds and from door corners, but none threw their windows open in a bold manner to look out of them, as the regiment marched past.

The houses were generally in good repair, many of one or two stories in height, with large windows and doors; nearly one-half had a veranda in front of each story. The gardens were in a deplorable condition. Few people were seen on the roads, and they, except the negroes, evinced no interest in the regiment. There was one knot of women collected together who would frequently hiss: "d——d Yankees," "ain't you ashamed," "hope you will all die," and similar words of welcome. None of the men paid any attention to them. Coffee houses and apologies for restaurants, located on the route, were generally closed for want of business; their signs were retained, put up when the secession excitement was in full blaze. *Beauregard* was the favorite name for use on these signs.

Having arrived at Bayou Gentilly, by night-time camp was pitched and everything made as comfortable as possible. The hospital was located in a wide and long one-story wooden building, formerly used for a liquor and refreshment saloon, attached to the race-course. Headquarters was also established in the building. The quartermaster and commissary stores, and the horses, occupied a similar building, which had been built or refitted for the purpose, a short distance away towards the railroad crossing

General Banks, having issued a general order calling for volunteers to fill the Second Vermont Battery, Captain Holcomb, the next day, twenty-ninth, Corporal Thomas Hanson White, Company K, Private John B. Williams, Company K, Private Addison J. Williams, Company K, Private William F. Howard, Company K, Private Horace M. Cowles, Company K, Private Oscar J. Stockwell, Company E, and Private Oliver King, Company E, who had volunteered, received their descriptive lists, final orders, and left camp to join the battery then stationed at Donaldsonville, to remain until their term of service expired. This battery was in the army before Port Hudson, and the men saw some hard service. None of them died from disease, or were wounded or killed. They rejoined the regiment at Algiers, July 23d.

The month of January closed with five companies on duty at Bayou Gentilly, showing a strength of sixteen officers and four hundred and forty-nine men present, with sixteen of the men sick in hospital.

In February the regiment was still further scattered by several details. Cold and rainy weather, combined with these continual details, rather dispirited for awhile both officers and men, who gradually became convinced that as a body the regiment was not destined during its service to perform any gallant deeds, or be placed in a position to try and do so.

A detachment of one sergeant, three corporals and twenty-five privates from Company A, under command of Lieutenant Martin Burrell, Jr., was ordered February 3d to take charge and guard the battery situated on the Gentilly road, towards Fort Macomb. At the time of taking charge of this battery it mounted nine guns. Battery Gentilly did not have an armament. During the month, as nothing was to be feared from the enemy in this direction, and the Confederates could attempt a demonstration against New Orleans from the direction of the lake in the neighborhood of Lakeport, Bayou St. John and Hickok's Landing, General Sherman, commanding Defences New Orleans, had his ordnance officer, Captain Pease, Forty-Seventh Massachusetts Volunteers, remove the guns from this battery and use them to equip Battery Gentilly on the railroad track and Battery St. John on St. John Bayou. Removal of these guns and putting them into their new positions occupied about one month. On the eighteenth the transfer had so far advanced that the detachment under Lieutenant Burrell was ordered to the battery on the Ponchartrain Road. It was not until March 10th that Battery St. John was occupied and taken in charge by the remaining men of Company A, under command of Captain Coburn.

Pay day were talismanic words to the soldier. Visions of a pocket full of "Uncle Sam's" greenbacks float before the eyes of those men who had not allotted their money. Depending altogether on his frugality, for days or weeks after being paid off a soldier can visit the sutler, and at enormous prices buy little delicacies and necessaries to go with his Government rations, to make them more palatable. Tobacco and pipes were the most popular articles of purchase. Liquor had peculiar charms for a great many.

The first muster for pay of the regiment took place at Carrollton on the twenty-seventh of January, when the troops at that place were mustered to December 31st, 1862. Government always has its troops in arrears two months at least, to cover any overdrafts on clothing account, or fines charged them by sentence of courts-martial for misdemeanors. The troops are mustered for pay on the last day of the month every two months during the year, when all men present are reported on the muster and pay rolls, who draw their pay when the paymaster makes his appearance. Absent men, except on detached service by orders, do not get mustered, but have to wait until the next muster and payment before obtaining any money; this, to most men, is sufficient punishment for their absence without leave.

Companies A, B, E, F and K were paid off at Bayou Gentilly on February 2d, by a major in the Paymasters' Department attached to the Department of the Gulf. Companies C and H were paid a few days later at Camp Parapet. Payments to all companies of the regiment (except Company K) were made with regularity and promptness during the term of service, because, stationed in close proximity to New Orleans most of the time afforded paymasters easy access to them. Company K, while on duty with the army in the field, was not so fortunate. The paroled men of Companies D, G and I were first mustered for pay on the regular muster day, February 28th, and first paid April 27th, when they were paid from the date of their enlistment to March 1st.

Those who did not allot any of their pay, received what

seemed to be at that time large sums of money. The nine months troops were allowed regular pay from time of signing the enlistment rolls, and a large number had done so early in August and September, 1862; they had, therefore, some six and seven months pay due them. The allotment system never found much favor with men of the Forty-Second, so that nearly every soldier received the full amount due him without any deductions. Many men, with families at home, availed themselves of an express arrangement at low rates with the Adams & Co. Express, to forward most of their pay, every pay day, to those in need of it.

The unmarried men, with those of a spendthrift character, retained their money, spending the larger part of it in a bar-room, otherwise called a sutler's shop, situated in the same building used for headquarters and for a hospital, kept by a man called Charley Ellis. This man Ellis, in all outward appearances a well-meaning man, was at heart a perfect rogue. Formerly lessee of the New Orleans race-course (the grounds occupied by the regiment for a camp), at the time Louisiana seceded he was a professed Union man, suffering a short imprisonment in the Parish jail, and was treated to a coat of tar and feathers for his sentiments. Nothing definite is known of his former history except that he was a professional horse jockey, an admirer of sports of the turf, and a regular sporting man. As lessee of the race-course he ran in debt, and was unable to pay. Upon the occupation of New Orleans by troops under General Butler, he enlisted the sympathies of that general. He kept a regular drinking saloon in the city, and whenever troops occupied the race-course for a camp opened a branch establishment on the ground, if he was lucky enough to hoodwink the commanding officer, nominally to furnish sutlers' stores, but practically as a drinking saloon.

Ellis, by his plausible stories and seductive manners, completely blindfolded the eyes of officers in the Forty-Second at first, and was allowed to open his saloon. By rendering little favors and trifling services to the officers he managed to keep in their good graces, and became intimate enough to borrow considerable sums of money from them, much of which was never repaid. He once got a loan from the hospital fund that created some trouble in the hospital by his not paying back the money at the stipulated time, thereby preventing the surgeons from obtaining those little extras they were in the habit of furnishing to their patients, until, by threats, Ellis was made to pay this borrowed amount.

The building occupied for headquarters and hospital Ellis endeavored to make the officers believe belonged to him, as lessee of the grounds, although it was known his lease was void from non-fulfilment of its conditions on his part. On the departure of the regiment from Bayou Gentilly he presented a bill for rent of the building, at the rate of five hundred dollars a month, for the length of time it was occupied by the regiment, to Lieutenant-Colonel Stedman, for his approval. It was never approved. Why Ellis was allowed to remain inside of the regimental lines with his stock of bad liquors for sale was a mystery to those who had learned his character and saw what mischief he was doing. The surgeons were opposed to his being allowed there, and remonstrated against it, and Chaplain Sanger, who could not help seeing that not alone disease of the body but disease of the mind was one of the results sure to accrue from this sutler's shop, joined in the remonstrance.

Two other liquor saloons on the road, in close proximity to the camp, were also doing mischief. Verbal orders were at one time given their proprietors not to sell liquor to a soldier, on pain of having their stock demolished; but as no extra vigilance was exercised in detecting offences against the orders, they were not considered as of any account.

February 4th, Privates Thomas Burns, John Nolan and Thomas Mathews, stragglers in New York from Company D, returned and were assigned to duty with Company E. On the eighteenth, Privates Greene and Luzardo, of Company G, on duty with Company K, were detached and assigned to duty with Company E, and Private Joseph V. Colson, Company G, was assigned to Company E. Private Colson was a straggler in New York from the regiment. He had a varied experience on his trip to New Orleans. Reporting to the proper officer in New York, he was put aboard the ship *Planter*, with some two hundred other men belonging to various regiments of the Nineteenth Corps. The ship went upon the reefs at Grand Abeco Island, in the Bahama Channel, during good weather, about four o'clock in the morning. All hands were saved by the ship's boats, landing them upon the island, where they remained seventeen days, subsisting on pork and water saved from the wreck and shell fish obtained on the island. Finally a few wrecking schooners carried the troops to Key West, and from there they were sent to New Orleans to rejoin their several commands. Of the two hundred and fifty horses aboard, all were lost. The vast amount of medical stores and other property was mostly saved by wreckers; some fifty wrecker sail were counted by Colson hovering about the ship in three days after going upon the reef. What was saved by these wreckers was taken to Nassau. Aboard the ship it was believed that the captain, a Southerner, purposely wrecked the vessel. Colson reported having a good time on the trip, but it seemed like home to him when he reached the regiment.

The only case in February before Major Stiles, for discipline, was that of Private James Minz, Company K, for disobedience of orders and using disrespectful language to his superior officer. Conviction and sentence followed, the sentence meeting the approval of the brigade commander, which was, to forfeit eight dollars a month of his pay to the United States for two months and to remain a prisoner at the guard tent for seven days, doing fatigue duty each day.

A system of rocket signals was arranged between the brigade headquarters in New Orleans, the Gentilly Station and Lakeport. In case the enemy appeared at night upon the lake, three rockets at Lakeport, or in the city, was the signal for the regiment to get under arms and await orders from the general commanding Defences of New Orleans. Several times the sentries mistook shooting stars for rockets, and raised alarms in the camp; even the officers have been led at times to think these stars were signal rockets. They certainly did have that appearance when seen for a moment in the remarkable clear atmosphere prevailing during the early part of the night, just above tall trees of the swamp, and would be apt to mislead any person who was on the lookout for such signals.

Among the several *new sensations* experienced at Bayou Gentilly were a few night alarms. Only those who have for the first time in a hostile country heard the drums beat to arms near the midnight hour can form any idea of the sensation it gives to a raw soldier. The heart beats quick; he can feel his blood warming up; every nerve is strung to the highest tension in anticipation of stirring events about to happen.

The regiment, for several nights in succession, during February, was under arms for what, at the time, were thought to be good causes, but at a later period partook of the ludicrous and provoked a smile. The first alarm was started one night by Lieutenant-Colonel Stedman, for the purpose of testing the guard in a knowledge of its duty. At a distance of about one-quarter of a mile from camp he fired his pistol some three or four times towards the camp and then quickly returned to his headquarters. The officer of the guard aroused the camp at once by causing the long roll to be beaten, and reported the circumstances to the officer of the day, who proceeded to report to Lieutenant-Colonel Stedman, and entered headquarters a moment after his return. The regiment was always in line from five to ten minutes after a call to arms, ready to obey orders.

On the occasion narrated a detachment of thirty men was sent down the road leading toward Fort Macomb, with orders to scour the plantations upon each side and ascertain the cause of firing. Sergeant-Major Bosson was fond of giving his experience on this, his first night on a scout. In detail he gave the *peculiar* feelings that came over him when prowling around and looking into every nook and corner of a ruined sugar-house, accompanied by two men, expecting to find a body of armed men secreted there; how he afterwards joined the detachment on the road, and then with another detail of two men searched plantations upon the left of the road as far down as the battery, where Lieutenant Burrell with his detachment was stationed, saving the life of a cow one of his companions mistook for a man dodging around among the swamp trees and made ready to fire at.

A number of officers had with them patent-armored vests, that were sold extensively when the nine months troops were enlisting. Those iron-clad arrangements were put on with such alacrity at every night alarm that the officers who unfortunately owned them must have laughed when, at home safe and sound after their term of service expired, they thought over the *dangers* they passed through in Louisiana, especially at Bayou Gentilly. Some of the officers have slept at night with these iron cases on, and it came to be a fixed custom until the hot weather set in for owners of iron vests to don them when the regiment was under arms for any supposable emerg ncy, more for the purpose of making some use of them, or, as they jocosely remarked, "get their money's worth out of them at any rate." Officers who were in the Galveston action also had these iron vests. They were forgotten when trouble was expected and no use made of them.

A private in Company F, a troublesome fellow and great shirk, endeavored to pass a sentinel without giving the countersign on the night of February 14th. He was properly challenged but paid no attention to the call, "Who goes there!" repeated a number of times, when the sentry, also a private of Company F, aimed his musket and fired at him for his temerity. The ball whistled by his head and passed through the hospital without damage. The fellow did not receive any sympathy, nor did he deserve any, and the fright given him was deemed sufficient punishment and warning not to repeat the blunder.*

Quite a number of men in Company F were sick. Two of the cases baffled the surgeon's skill until it was decided, after an inspection of company quarters, that in these two cases signs and symptoms of scurvy was manifested, and

---

* Adjutant Davis had a similar adventure at this camp. A sentry challenged him without receiving a reply, made ready and levelled his gun at him. The click of the trigger woke Davis from a reverie to instantly comprehend his situation and answer the challenge. This sentry acknowledged he recognized the adjutant, and yet maintained he should have fired at him in a moment after taking aim. As Davis was inside the camp on official business, such action on the sentinel's part would not have been humane or proper, while it might have been justified. As he recognized his officer and thought, as he admits, that his challenge was not heard, to have stopped the adjutant at the point of his bayonet was sufficient.

fresh meat in place of "salt horse" ought to be provided. The brigade quartermaster was unable to fill a requisition for fresh meat, while the camp was serenaded night and day by constant tinkling of a hundred cow-bells, attached to as many cows. The idea of going without fresh meat when it was needed, with a herd of cattle within reach, was more than the officers could stand, and a council was held at regimental headquarters. The result was, Captain Cogswell received authority to take some of his men, who understood how to slaughter and dress cattle, and go to work that night.

The party consisted of Major Stiles, Captain Cogswell, Sergeant-Major Bosson, Sergeant B. A. Bottomley, Corporal Sylvander Bothwell, Privates Harvey Allen (company cook), George Mann and Charles Sanderson, of Company F. They selected a fine animal, placed a rope around her horns with difficulty, and dragged the cow towards a grove of trees, selected as a proper place to dress her. Everything was done in a workmanlike manner, as the butchers knew their business, and after the fresh beef was carried upon a confiscated ladder to the regimental quartermaster's depot all hands returned to Company F's quarters, to partake of broiled steak and liver, cooked by Harvey Allen about one o'clock in the morning.

Not satisfied with this supply of beef, Lieutenant Harding and men from his company (Company K) again made a raid on the herd of cattle shortly after and slaughtered cow number two, without authority. In this case the hide and entrails were buried in the swamp, while Captain Cogswell's butchers threw the head, hide and entrails into a well of water used by the cattle, near the paroled camp. No one supposed these cows would be missed, until the owner appeared and made inquiries about them. He was not satisfied with his reception in the camp, proceeding to prowl around to ascertain where they were. His attention was attracted to the well of water, where all that remained of cow number one had been placed, by the moaning of several head of cattle that stood near smelling of the water and tearing up the turf with their feet, when a hundred men of the regiment, who had been watching him with curiosity from the camp line, saw the owner fish out the head and hide with a long pole.

He then made complaint to the provost-marshal in New Orleans, who invited the regimental officers to explain. In order to prevent an unpleasant inquiry the affair was settled by the officers making up a purse of about three hundred dollars to pay the owner's claim; this fresh meat costing them dear in the end. No cattle were molested afterwards.

Before Assistant-Surgeon Smith, Twenty-Sixth Massachusetts, was relieved from charge of the hospital a curious case came under his care, ending in a manner discreditable to him. Private Francis N. Prouty, Company F, was sick in hospital with malarial fever. No one thought the case serious until, one morning, Surgeon Smith came into the headquarters office excited and breathless, reporting Prouty as dying. Word was sent to Captain Cogswell and his company officers, who at once repaired to the sick-room, accompanied by Chaplain Sanger and several others, to witness the dying scene. There Prouty lay upon his cot, with head and shoulders bolstered up by pillows, breathing short and quick, no sign of death in his face, that had an intelligent look, and his eyes their natural appearance. The other patients in the room were resting upon elbows on their cots watching Prouty with wondering eyes, as the solemn procession filed in and took positions near the supposed dying man. While the surgeon kept one hand upon the patient's pulse, Chaplain Sanger offered a fervent prayer in his behalf that only served to produce a look of wonder in Prouty's eyes, that appeared to say, what in the devil is this all about? He did not die, and afterwards said, had no intention of doing so, to please any one. The whole scene ended, after waiting about half an hour, in the solemn procession retiring from his side, pleased to find that the end was not to come, and somewhat mad with the surgeon for his opinion on the case. Smith had not been considered a surgeon of any skill before this event, and this case served to deepen the distrust of his ability.

During February New Orleans was alive with army officers and men, on furlough and without leave, indulging in all sorts of wild dissipation. The evil became so great that special orders were issued by General Banks to General Sherman to stop it. Stringent orders relative to passes, rigidly enforced, soon put an end to this demoralizing conduct. Another source of trouble was the presence of large negro contraband camps in the vicinity of the city, requiring other stringent orders to be issued for their government, and regulating the behavior of soldiers towards them. In January the ladies in New Orleans had shown a disposition to indulge in petty insults to soldiers whom they met on the streets, and caused a circular, dated January 13th, to be issued, which put a stop to much of this silly nonsense, but did not do away with it entirely. The circular read as follows:

"HEADQUARTERS DEPT. OF THE GULF,
"NEW ORLEANS, January 13th, 1863.

"Notice is hereby given by the commanding general of this Department that offensive personal demonstrations, by language or conduct of any character, by persons of any class whatever, with the intention of giving personal offence, or tending to disturb the public peace, are forbidden, and will be punished with relentless severity. Parents will be held responsible for the respectful conduct of their children, and prompt measures will be taken to fasten upon the proper parties any act of this character. All persons who may be witnesses to such conduct, are directed, as a measure of public peace, to give information thereof to the provost-marshal, or at these headquarters.

"By command of

"MAJOR-GENERAL BANKS.

"RICHARD B. IRWIN,

"*Lieut-Col., Assistant Adjutant-General.*"

Brigade drills under Colonel Farr, and a brigade review and inspection, by Brigadier-General Sherman, commanding division, were had while at Gentilly Bayou. The brigade drills were interesting, and considering the short time most of the regiments had been in service were quite satisfactory. Three drills were all this brigade ever had, on account of its being posted over a large extent of ground, and at posts that could not be left exposed by gathering the men together for such a purpose.

It was the custom to leave camp at eight A.M. on brigade drill days, in light marching order, as a march had to be made of about three miles to the drill ground. The weather would be hot and sun very scorching; on one drill only did the weather prove treacherous, and then the regiment was caught in a thunder shower. After several hours devoted to drill, and then a march back to camp with but short intervals for rest during the time, no rations in haversacks to make a dinner from, when the regiment arrived in camp, usually about half-past three to four o'clock in the afternoon, the men would be thirsty, hungry, hot and dusty. While such service may not be equal to a day's march in an active campaign, yet for the regiment to perform it with so few men falling out of the ranks from fatigue, as was the case, shows what good material for service composed the regiment.

These drills were not without their attendant scenes and excitements. Crowds of negroes, of both sexes, would hover around the ground to hear the bands of music and witness the evolutions. Colonel Farr would frequently lose his temper and damn both officers and men; Colonel Marsh, Forty-Seventh Massachusetts Volunteers, particularly meriting the displeasure of the brigade commander, and received many of that officer's choice remarks. Colonel Marsh was not a military man. The way in which he managed to twist his regiment around, mix the companies up and the brigade also, caused more laughter among the men than any other incident. It was amusing to see the expression of wonder on the face of Colonel Marsh when his regiment would be out of place, with the brigade standing at ease, waiting for him to place the regiment where it belonged, and Colonel Farr, accompanied by his entire staff, coming up at a full gallop to know "What in h—ll is the matter now?" Captain "Ned" Bird, Company I, Forty-Seventh Massachusetts, acting as major, would always have to give the correct orders that brought his regiment into proper position.

At a brigade drill which took place on the twenty-sixth of February, the new colors, which had been sent to the regiment by Governor Andrew, to replace those lost at Galveston, were unfurled and carried in the ranks for the first time. This second set of regimental colors never trembled from the whistle of bullets or fluttered amid smoke from powder during the term of service. They were seldom used, consequently on the return home of the regiment they looked new, bright colored and clean, as though fresh from the designer's hand.

Brigadier-General Sherman impressed an observer very favorably. He was a regular army officer, familiar with all details of the service, courteous in manner towards all officers — a thorough soldier and gentleman. When inspecting the brigade assembled for a drill, February 19th, on reaching the Forty-Second, in position for inspection, he noticed the regimental colors were missing. He sharply called the attention of Lieutenant-Colonel Stedman to the fact, and when informed they had been lost at Galveston his tone of voice quickly changed; lifting his hat he replied: "I beg your pardon, colonel." There is no importance attached to this incident, except that it showed the thoroughbred officer, and made quite an impression on those near enough to hear the conversation, engendering a feeling that here was an officer to be trusted, and his orders could be obeyed with confidence. Not many volunteer officers display such tact and discrimination.

During February the following additional changes by detail occurred: Private Martin Proctor, Company F, was made steward for the field and staff officers' mess at regimental headquarters; on that duty until relieved in July in consequence of sickness.

February 2nd — Private Henry E. Putnam, Company E, was detailed as clerk at brigade headquarters by brigade orders, where he remained until July, and then returned to his company.

February 18th — Private Edward J. Worcester, Company E, was made regimental armorer, a position he held until his term of service expired, *vice* Private Loud, detailed to assist Lieutenant Pease.

February 18th — Company K left the regiment to act as pontoniers to the Nineteenth Army Corps.

February 25th — Captain Cogswell, Company F, appointed as corporals George L. Stone and Sylvander Bothwell, in place of C. H. Woodcock and E. A. Spooner, who preferred to join the regimental band.

At the close of February there were present for duty in the four companies at Gentilly Bayou, and Company K, in New Orleans, twenty officers and four hundred and twenty-five men. Present sick in hospital, seventeen men. The average sick per day of the regiment during February was: taken sick, five; returned to duty, five; in hospital, fourteen; in quarters, eleven. Two men were sent to general hospitals in New Orleans. Surgeon Hitchcock returned to duty on the twenty-fourth, relieving Surgeon Smith, and Surgeon Heintzelman reported for duty March 1st.

CHAPTER VII.

ENLISTED MEN PRISONERS AT HOUSTON — MARCH FOR THE FEDERAL LINES — ARRIVAL AT NEW ORLEANS.

THE rank and file of the Forty-Second, with captured sailors of the *Harriet Lane*, were confined in a cotton press, situated in close proximity to Buffalo Bayou. The officers were quartered in the third story of Kennedy's brick building, upon one of the streets not far from the cotton press.

While in Houston the men received good treatment and were allowed a furlough in the city every day, four men at a time, under guard. Their officers were allowed to visit them frequently, and cheering words, coupled with good advice, was not wanting. The food furnished was the same as issued to Confederate soldiers, consisting of corn meal, rice, sugar, dried and fresh beef, corn coffee, and occasionally a small supply of salt. The coarse ground corn meal was baked and made into what was called corn-dodger, to take the place of the Federal ration of hard bread. Until General Magruder left Houston, when the ration was taken away, the officers were favored with extra rations of flour. A German baker, formerly of Roxbury, Mass., was found, who took this flour in exchange for bread. Diarrhœa and dysentery were quite prevalent under this diet and a change of water, with sudden, sharp changes of weather that occurred, from warm to cold, and *vice versa*.

Surgeon Cummings, whose ability was acknowledged at

all times by the Confederate officers, was, for a time, given his parole of honor, and assisted in taking care of the wounded and sick, Federals and Confederates. It was asserted that many of the Confederate wounded would not allow their own surgeons to attend them, preferring the care of Surgeon Cummings, in whose honor be it said, friend or foe, who needed his services, shared alike.

A jolly, social set of men, who made everything pleasant as possible, composed the guard — a dismounted company of cavalry, known as Captain Clipper's company. Their discipline and drill was very, *very* crude, and often a subject of comment and amusement to the prisoners, who heartily enjoyed the ceremony of guard-mounting as done by this company; soldiers continually chewing tobacco, spitting the juice freely, talking with each other, and laughing all through the parade. The unsoldier-like conduct and poor quality of Sibley's men, and the entire Confederate force under General Magruder, was a noted fact throughout the State: poorly armed and equipped, indifferently officered, without honor, discipline, or *esprit de corps*. After the fight at Galveston, Magruder issued an order to his command calling attention to these facts, entreating them to reform and be true soldiers, reciting, as an example of what well-disciplined, efficient troops could accomplish, the stubborn defence of Kuhn's Wharf by the Forty-Second Massachusetts Volunteers.

The prisoners busied themselves with card playing, singing, making little trinkets from bones left from their meat, and in various other ways; selling their bone trinkets in large numbers to the ladies and others of Houston at good prices in Confederate money, which was used to buy what extras for food they could purchase. Many of the inhabitants would gather in the vicinity of the cotton press to obtain a glimpse at the northern barbarians, as the prisoners were termed; people from the country for miles around came to Houston for this purpose. It is related for a fact, by a sergeant who overheard the conversation, that a little girl who had been brought by her mother to see them, said to her: "Why, mother, they haven't got any horns; you said they had!" This was about the idea Texan people had of northern troops at the time.

Previous to leaving Houston positive information was obtained relative to the fate of Amos and Revaleon. They had been sold as slaves to Texan planters, bringing somewhere near five hundred dollars each. They were bright, intelligent colored lads, cousins, fascinated with camp life, and notwithstanding the bitter opposition of their parents were determined to see service in the army in some capacity, finally prevailing upon the surgeon and quartermaster to take them as servants. Revaleon was owned by several masters, receiving good treatment, until at last he was taken for a servant by Major Leon Smith, who intended to send him into the Federal lines if he ever got near enough to do so. A few colored men that were in the *Harriet Lane* crew did not fare so well, suffering harsh treatment by being treated as convicts, with incarceration in the State Prison at Huntsville. All were released at the close of the war and came home in the summer of 1865.

Orders were issued at five o'clock on the morning of January 22d for the men to be ready to move at ten o'clock. Permission was given the captains to visit their companies and bid them good-by. Captains Savage and Sherive did so. Captain Savage said a few words of regret at the necessary separation, and was expressing his fervent wishes for their future safety and prosperity when obliged to stop short, his feelings having completely unmanned him. Captain Sherive was full of fight, and exhorted them to pitch in and "give them h—ll" whenever exchanged and again armed. Colonel Burrell (who was refused the privilege of seeing his men) and the other officers, after an interview with the orderly-sergeants at officers' quarters, sent by them a farewell to the companies.

Delays occurred in the preparations, and it was two o'clock in the afternoon before the men fell into line for roll-call, proceeding at once, after repeated cheers for the officers were given, to the depot, where platform cars with seats built upon them were in readiness. With a good-by to the guard a start was made about six o'clock for Beaumont.

The following sick and wounded men were left behind, not able to stand the fatigue and exposure of the journey: Private Edwin F. Josselyn, Company D, wounded; Private Francis L. Morrill, Company D, wounded; Private James O'Shaughnessy, Company D, wounded; Corporal Henry W. McIntosh, Company D, sick; Private Dennis Dailey, Company D, sick; Sergeant David L. Wentworth, Company G, wounded; Private Joseph W. D. Parker, Company G, wounded; Private Joseph W. McLaughlin, Company I, sick, returned to Houston from Beaumont; Private Samuel R. Hersey, Company C, remained with the colonel; Citizen Frank Veazie, cook to officers' mess, remained with the colonel.

Corporal McIntosh, suffering with diarrhœa, was so weak he had to be supported by two soldiers when led out to say good-by to his comrades he never expected to see again, and never did.

At first General Magruder intimated his intention to march the men across Texas to the Red or Mississippi Rivers. Such a march was condemned by prominent officers in his Department as certain death to a large number, and transportation was furnished for part of the way. It was stated in a boastful manner by the guards and citizens, that few would live to reach the Federal lines. This may have been mere boasting and only an expression of what they wished would occur, for the condition of the country passed over, and hardships endured by the men, were in no measure to be compared to what they had been led to expect by the representations of these parties, and it may safely be said their enemies were ignorant of what would have to be encountered.

With enlisted men and Chaplain Sanger, of the Forty-Second Regiment, were the sailors of the *Harriet Lane*, Assistant-Surgeon Thomas N. Penrose, Paymaster R. Julius Richardson, and the third assistant-engineers of that vessel, who had been allowed to go upon a claim made by all the captured officers, that these officers were non-combatants and could not be classed as commissioned officers. Considerable argument had to be used before the Confederate officials were made to acknowledge the point and let them go.

There was one smart affair managed successfully by a few warrant officers of the Forty-Second that saved the life of Andrew Romain, a Texan refugee, who was smuggled through as a member of the regiment with great difficulty, and when detection was almost certain. Romain, who formerly had lived in one of the New England States, was at the head of a little band of refugees who quartered on Kuhn's Wharf under protection of the naval guns, and was of great benefit to the fleet before land forces arrived as a spy, from his intimate acquaintance with the inhabitants and country in the immediate vicinity of Galveston. His person, character, and the service he rendered United States officers was well known to the Confederate leaders, hence he was a marked man. Of medium size, he wore an immense black beard of great length, almost covering his face to the eyes, and up to the time of surrender wore citizen's clothes.

After the surrender, and when names of prisoners were taken by the Confederate officers, Romain was not to be seen, and it was surmised by the boys he had escaped to the fleet. By some lucky chance he had safely hid away, until, at a favorable moment, he joined the ranks on the march through Galveston towards Virginia Point, clad in a blue army blouse, buttoned close to the neck, covering the long, flowing part of his beard, wearing a fatigue cap, and with knapsack upon his shoulders. On arrival at Houston he was partly shaved by Sergeant Frye, Company D, who left him with whiskers of the mutton-chop style. Each successive shave was improved to alter the style of cut to the hair upon his face. A sailor from the *Harriet Lane* assisted at times in these tonsorial duties.

Shortly after arriving in Houston the Confederate officers began to inquire after Romain, their actions indicating they suspected he was among the prisoners.

A great difficulty to overcome was passing him through the roll-calls, as Confederate officers attended these calls of names, which were made one company at a time. Romain would dodge from one company in line, ready for roll-call, to the ranks of a company whose roll-call was over, assisted in this by various devices of those most active in getting him through, and managed with success for some time in this way. Feeling confident he was among the prisoners, a last effort was made to detect him when the men were ready to march for the depot.

The companies were separately ordered into line, outside of quarters; as each name was called the man stepped to the front and had his name checked. Romain, who saw that his chances to get off with the rest were very slim, prudently remained in the building, and the rolls were found correct. Company G had passed out of the gate, leaving the other companies inside, when Sergeant Phil. Hackett obtained permission to go into the quarters for some few things he stated were left there, and in a short time came out followed by Romain, whom he rated soundly with abuse and curses for having left the ranks to go back to quarters without leave. On his approach towards Confederate Lieutenant Todd, who stood at the gate, Romain was the picture of a devil-may-care sort of man, puffing away at a large pipe, with a broom thrown over his shoulder. Lieutenant Todd sharply asked why he was there, and Romain replied that Sergeant Goodrich had sent him back to get a broom to sweep the cars, because they were covered with charcoal dust. Todd asked his name, and Romain gave one suggested to him by Hackett. Calling for Sergeant Goodrich, Todd inquired who he had sent back, the Sergeant answering with the same name that Romain used, for Hackett and Goodrich were acting in concert. Examining the roll of Company G the name was found, and Romain was ordered to "get out of here."

The whole thing was so neatly planned and carried out by the two sergeants that the Confederates were completely hoodwinked, and Romain got off with the prisoners. After leaving Houston it was easy work to pass him along.

He left a wife and child at Galveston, who probably thought him dead. He was able to give valuable information to General Banks regarding Texas, and Andrew Romain was afterwards in the secret service corps of the Gulf Department. He was a brave man. It required uncommon fortitude to bear up under the constant dread of capture which must have haunted him, as death was certain were he discovered. From the fact that Romain was armed with a revolver, furnished by some friendly hand, it is surmised, if discovered, he would have sold his life dearly, if not contemplating suicide rather than fall into Confederate hands. A man of quiet reserve, seldom making any conversation with others, it was thought by the paroled men he had no gratitude for the assistance rendered by them, because he never expressed any. When Phil. Hackett was buried at Gentilly Camp, Romain was present, and his presence at those last sad rites is good proof he was grateful for what had been done to save him.

The train left Houston with a speed of about four miles an hour, crossing San Jacinto Bayou at midnight, not reaching Beaumont until four o'clock in the afternoon next day — distance eighty-three miles by rail. This was a tiresome ride for it rained all night, rendering sleep impossible, besides the charcoal dust upon the cars became wet, and in the shifting and turning about hands would get covered with it; these same hands were often applied to faces, and in the morning the men were a sight to behold. As the locomotive could not draw the entire train at once, sections were taken and run until a siding was reached, when the engine would go back for the remaining cars. There appeared to be plenty of cattle in sight grazing on the prairie lands through which the railroad ran, and this was also noticed to be the case on the trip from Galveston to Houston.

At Beaumont the men remained until the twenty-ninth, awaiting the return of a steamboat that had preceded them with baggage, horses, beef cattle, commissary stores, and wagons brought from Houston, to be used on the march to Alexandria. Occupying several abandoned shanties near Drake's Bayou, the time was made to pass quickly by various expedients. Pigs were plenty in the neighborhood, so that pork was not a luxury, four or five being killed each day, the owners not missing them. They were caught by the lassoing process from a trap-door in an old blacksmith shop, underneath which they congregated. Wild mules were also plenty, whose backs the soldiers and sailors did not miss any opportunity to ride, affording great amusement to spectators by their antics.

Finally the steamer *Roe Buck* arrived, and a start was made at half-past one o'clock in the afternoon down the narrow Neches River to Sabine Bay; proceeding up the Sabine River, at daylight on the thirtieth, the steamer tied up at Novell's Bluff, Louisiana, for a short time, and then proceeded to Morgan's Bluff to remain over night, arriving there at half-past six o'clock in the afternoon.

After wooding-up the trip was resumed early next morning on the crooked and narrow river, lined with forests upon either bank, causing the boys to keep a sharp lookout, as the boat would often snap limbs off the trees to fall upon the deck. At six o'clock in the afternoon a stop was made at Possum Bluff for the night. Here the men had to use fence rails, near at hand, for fuel to cook rations, as all of the cut wood was required for the boat.

The boat steamed along, with occasional stops to take in wood and tie up each night, until half-past four o'clock in the afternoon, February 4th, when the journey by boat was over, on arriving at Burr's Ferry Landing. The weather had been cloudy, rainy and cold almost the entire trip, creating great inconvenience to the men, who were obliged to use rubber and woollen blankets to stop rain-water leaks in their sleeping-places. Several were quite sick. Private David Chapin, Company I, nineteen years old, died at night, February 2d, at quarter-past eleven, when the boat was stopped at Starks' Ferry Landing, Newton County, Texas. Chapin was not well when he left Houston, and was down with intermittent fever in a few days. After breakfast, on the third, a beautiful spot in the woods, under cypress and pine trees, was selected for a grave. The funeral took place at half-past nine o'clock in the morning, with three volleys fired over the remains by the guard, as poor Chapin, in a rough-made coffin, the best his comrades could make, was lowered into the grave.

At Burr's Landing the prisoners went into bivouac in a pine grove about one-half a mile from the river. To make a shelter from the cold, northerly winds, some men made tents with rubber blankets; others built shanties made of bushes, pine boughs and such other material as they could gather, in a manner peculiar only to the "Yankee" soldier. All hands had washed their flannels during the fifth, leaving them out over night to dry, to find them frozen stiff the next morning, and a white frost covering the ground.

Private Henry C. Sellea, Company D, had been sick on board the boat for four days with intermittent fever, and, as his case seemed hopeless, arrangements were made by his comrades to remove him to a farm house owned and occupied by Mrs. Burr, who came from Springfield, Mass., where he would be sure to receive the best of care. This was accomplished at two o'clock on the afternoon of the sixth; but poor Sellea, only nineteen years old, died at five o'clock P.M. the next day.

As in the case of Private Chapin, a rough coffin was made by his comrades, the burial services taking place at eleven o'clock A.M. on the eighth, with Privates Charles G. Weymouth, Daniel L. Weymouth, R. P. Mosely and Henry Fisk acting as pall bearers. The grave was in Mrs. Burr's private burying ground, where the boys sang "There will be no more sorrow there," and the guard fired the customary volleys. A neat head-board, with name, age, company and regiment inscribed thereon, was placed on both graves.

Chapin and Sellea were delirious the last days of their life, not recognizing anybody. Every attention possible was paid to them by the members of their companies, and if the sympathy of their fellow soldiers could have saved them they would not have died. These two deaths were the only losses suffered on the trip, but several laid the foundation for diseases, which subsequently carried them to their graves.

Orders were issued on the eighth to be ready to commence the march for Alexandria at four o'clock A.M. on the ninth. Extra rations were given out to the cooks, who were at work all night attending to cooking. Mess kettles were few in number, and the practice on the entire trip, either on board boat or on the march, was to detail each night four men to cook until midnight, relieved by four men from that hour until daylight. The rations consisted of corn meal, pork, and fresh beef killed about every day, with such vegetables as the boys could forage, or buy from the few inhabitants living near the route of march.

The Confederate guard consisted of thirty men from the Fourth Texas Cavalry, commanded by Lieutenant W. J. Howerton, a pompous, overbearing individual, without military knowledge or manners. On the march the enlisted men were mounted upon Texas mustang ponies, tolerably well armed and equipped, but without drill or discipline. At any time they could have been overpowered by the prisoners. The guard were well disposed and well behaved towards their prisoners with a few exceptions; one private, a large, fat, red-headed man, whose looks was enough to condemn him to be a coward, was very bitter in speech and treatment of the men. In turn, the prisoners neglected no opportunity to work him up by badinage, partaking more of a sacrilegious tone than the chaplain thought was proper.

With the exception of a few fights among themselves to settle old scores, and retaliating in kind for any taunts made by members of the guard, the conduct of the prisoners was good. Lieutenant Howerton had his good and ill-natured days. At one place where a halt was made for the night some of the prisoners obtained permission to get food and lodging in a so-called tavern, neglecting in the morning to pay for the accommodation. This neglect put the lieutenant in a rage, when the landlord complained about it. Previous to this occurrence the men had been allowed to march in disorder, but on forming column that morning the lieutenant ordered column of fours, and made a speech from his saddle, the substance being, that a citizen of the Confederate States, whom one of his own men would not dare to wrong, had been grossly insulted by some "scabs" of Northern soldiers. He had given orders that the march that day would be in column of fours, and any man who straggled from that formation of column would be shot down or cut down, "by G—d." One of the sailors slyly shouted s-h-o-w, when the enraged lieutenant rose in his stirrups and yelled: "I'll show yer!" swinging his sabre over his head to suit action to his words. Several men did get struck for not obeying the orders, although none were seriously hurt. This did not help Howerton, in the estimation of the boys.

No tents were carried, and the men were obliged to sleep in the open air, through fair or foul weather. No rivers were in their path, but several swamps had to be passed, one of them while a heavy rain-storm was in progress. The train, in charge of a wagoner, consisted of four wagons, each drawn by six mule teams. The feed for horses and mules was chiefly wild sugar-cane.

Doctor Penroes acted as surgeon for everybody when he could obtain medicines, for the escort carried none. He attended Chapin and Sellea, doing the best in his power, travelling some miles to obtain a supply of medicine to treat their cases. The sick had to suffer and get along as best they could; those very sick were taken in the wagons, while the men who did not feel strong enough to be encumbered by the weight of a knapsack, but able to march when not encumbered, could purchase from the guard the privilege of stowing away what they wished in the wagons. Frequently a ride upon the ponies belonging to good-natured men of the guard was to be had by parting with some article of value to them, as the Texans were always ready to trade or steal when they could. A Sergeant Bradford is said by the boys to have been a "tip-top fellow."

The story of the march cannot be described in a more interesting manner than is given by Sergeant Waterman, Company D, in his diary, and the same is presented here:

"February 9th — Breakfast at five A.M. At six o'clock formed line, and one half an hour later commenced the march for the day from Burr's Ferry. The first eight miles were done without a halt, over a good road, through a heavily-timbered country. Hard pine, very large and tall, some one hundred feet high to the limbs. After we started again from a rest, we went through a swamp about three miles in length, timbered with beach, magnolia and other trees, and at noon halted, after making eleven miles. On this halt killed and dressed two beeves. Marched again about two miles through swamps and then came to higher ground with pine trees again, large and straight, as before. At six o'clock P.M. arrived at a place called

Huddleston and went into bivouac for the night, with the boys about played out after marching eighteen miles, and after lying still about two months.

"February 10th — Started at seven o'clock A.M. footsore and weary, with the sky looking like rain. At noon had marched seven miles. Dined on corn-dodger and beef; some of the boys felt as if they had eaten so much beef they were ashamed to look a cow in the face. Weather became warm and pleasant. At half-past five o'clock P.M. halted for the night in a pine grove with a brook near by, at a little place with two houses and one cotton press, called Fifteen Mile Mill.

"February 11th — Started at half-past six A.M. and at eight o'clock met the mail — a man on horseback with a mail bag. It is trying to rain, but cannot make out very well. At noon it cleared off and a halt was made for dinner in a pine forest. Has been nearly all pine woods so far. Passed over a sandstone ledge this morning so soft that it could easily be broken in the hand. At three o'clock P. M. we were halted once more to rest and remain over night, as the march has badly blistered the feet of the boys.

"February 12th — Rain commenced to fall at four o'clock A.M., raining hard until seven o'clock, when, slacking up some, we started again through a swamp seven miles long, with the water knee deep all the way. Had to stop in the rain for a bridge to be repaired, so that the wagons could pass. Passed Hineston, a village of three shanties and a pig-stye, at quarter-past ten, and at noon halted to cook a pot of mush for dinner, the rain spoiling all of the corn bread and meat. The mush tasted good, as we had very little breakfast. Are on high pine land with wild flowers in bloom. Put up for the night in a very pretty place with enough old shanties to hold all the men. Had to sit up until eleven o'clock trying to dry our clothes.

"February 13th — Started at eight in the morning over a very good road for about three miles, and then came down on to what they call Red River bottom, composed of a red sand, clay and glue. Such walking was never seen. Passed by some very fine plantations, where the negroes were as happy as clams at high water, lining the fences and grinning like so many Cheshire cats. Halted near a bayou for dinner, where, upon the opposite side, the mocking birds were singing. Sun came out and it is warm. The grass is green and looks like the last of May at home. Plenty of sheep and lambs all around. Passed through a hedge of rose bushes at least twenty feet high. We are in sight of Alexandria, and at seven P. M. went aboard the roomy steamer *New Falls City*, in time to escape the rain.

"February 14th — A pleasant day. Boys feel somewhat sore. Heard yesterday that we might have to march two hundred miles more, but I told Lieutenant Howerton to-day that we could not do it any way, and he says we may not have to march more than twenty-five or thirty miles — perhaps none at all. At three P. M. it looks like a heavy shower; the clouds are black and threatening, with heavy thunder. The river is high and roily; as we use it to cook with, the corn-dodger looks like a red sweet cake."

Marching was over when the Red River was reached. The men had done well, bearing sickness, suffering and fatigue without a murmur; obeying the orders of Sergeants Waterman, Goodrich and Hunt (who were in command of Companies D, G and I, respectively), with commendable zeal, excepting in one instance when Private Fitzallen Gourley, Company D, defied the authority of Sergeant

Waterman, who had placed him upon a working detail of men while at Beaumont, and obliged the sergeant to report the case to the Confederate lieutenant, who threatened to return Gourley to Houston, and place him in jail, before he would yield.

That part of the country covered by the line of march was generally admired by the men, so different from anything to be seen at home, and their first sight at pine woods. Small villages on the route, considerable distance apart, with very few houses intervening, made it seem as though they were passing through a wilderness. The dense woods furnished an abundance of wood for cooking purposes, and torches for light at night. The few inhabitants to be met were well-disposed, simple-minded, honest people.

It was on Sunday, February 15th, that the Federal war steamer *Queen of the West*, an inferior looking craft, having safely passed the Vicksburg batteries to play a flying-devil upon the Red River, gave the Confederates a great scare at Alexandria. The prisoners were ashore, when word came at four o'clock A. M. to be ready to start at any moment as the Federals were coming up river. After breakfast, at half-past six o'clock, all hands were hurried on board the steamer *General Quitman*, and a race was run for about five miles, with the river behind them full of boats skedaddling in a perfect panic. In the afternoon the panic subsided, and at four o'clock, after news had been received that two Federal gunboats had been taken — the *Queen of the West* captured, and the *De Soto* abandoned and burnt — all speed was made for Alexandria again, where mules and wagons were taken aboard.

After starting down the river at daylight next day, the *Queen* was met during the morning in tow of a river steamer on her way to Alexandria for repairs. The crew of the

Queen had escaped to the gunboat *De Soto* by floating upon cotton bales, except five men who were noticed on shore, where a fire was started to obtain warmth, and were made prisoners. Everything went on quiet and smooth until passing three small one-gun batteries upon the right bank; at half-past two o'clock P. M., because a signal to stop was not noticed, two rounds of grape-shot were fired at and almost into them. Shot flew thick all around the boat, fortunately hitting no one. Turning back, despatches for the Confederate officer in command were sent on board, causing a delay of half an hour before the trip was resumed, and continued until dark. About midnight, orders came from the lieutenant of the guard for all hands to turn out and help wood-up ship; but his unbearable manner in giving his order roused the devil in them and they refused to do so. He threatened and swore, to no purpose, for the men remained obdurate. He had his revenge, however, in not allowing the prisoners to draw rations next day until late in the afternoon, thus allowing them only one meal in twenty-four hours.

On the seventeenth, early in the morning, while proceeding up river again in wake of three other steamers, all making fast time, the subject of seizing the transport-boat was again broached by sailors anxious and ready to try it. While on their way down the Neches River to Sabine Lake, a seizure of the boat then was talked over by the warrant officers in command of companies, but was abandoned from a want of knowledge where to go after obtaining possession. Upon the Red River there did not exist so favorable circumstances for success as there was at Sabine Lake. At the latter place they would have had to pass down the lake to Sabine Pass, and by a fort commanding the channel, before reaching the blockading vessels. Stratagem could have effected this purpose, but upon the Red River Confederate gunboats held the river to the Mississippi after the *Queen of the West* and *De Soto* were lost by the Federals. To have passed the enemy's boats by deceit, or otherwise, would have been impossible. Frequent consultations of the men concerned in the plot failed to develop any plan of action all would give coöperation, and the attempt was wisely abandoned.

After remaining over night above the three batteries before mentioned waiting the return of a courier, sent to Alexandria early in the evening for orders, at noon a transport-boat came alongside with a detachment of two hundred and seventy-eight men, Eighth Infantry, United States Regulars, who had been basely surrendered in Texas, by General Twiggs, May 9th, 1861, on the commencement of hostilities between the North and South, and been retained in close confinement up to this time. Five or six of the men had their wives with them; one with a family of two children.

A day or two after these prisoners arrived on board, one of the women got into a wordy warfare with a private of the guard, who was abusive in speech and manner. The Confederate soldier had said to the woman that if she was only a man he would shoot her, when a private of the Eighth Regulars, who could stand it no longer, made the quarrel a personal one with himself, calling the Confederate a d——n coward, and offered to go ashore for a fight with any weapon he would name. To this bold challenge the Confederate interposed an objection, that he could not fight with a prisoner of war. Our "bold soger boy" said: "That need not interfere; I will fight you with pistols, ten paces apart, right here." Nothing but sneers were given in reply by the soldier and his comrades of the guard, who had clustered around. In return the United States soldier taunted them all with being cowards, offering to fight the crowd in any fashion they chose, without effect; they finally slunk away. The women were not molested afterwards.

All of the prisoners were conditionally paroled on the eighteenth and nineteenth, and a flag of truce raised upon the boat, with the intention of proceeding to Vicksburg. Horses, mules and wagons were sent ashore, but a start was not made until the twenty-third, on account of trouble experienced in obtaining wood. There was a dispute on the twenty-first, between the officer of the prisoners' guard and officers upon the steamer *Grand Era*, in regard to wood that had been supplied the flag of truce boat by the steamer *La-Fourche* in the morning, resulting finally in a compromise, allowing the *Grand Era* to have one-half of what was on board. Pistols were drawn amid a general cursing match in the altercation, and at one time a fight was imminent between the two factions. Just as the wood was gone the *Grand Duke* came alongside searching for the same article, but left without obtaining any.

At last, during the evening of the twenty-second, a boat load of sixty cords was received, about half enough for one day's consumption, for the *General Quitman* used from ninety to one hundred and ten cords each twenty-four hours, when the boat steamed down river at daylight next day. After stopping at a wood pile to take on about one hundred cords more, a final start was made for Port Hudson, instead of Vicksburg as first intended, passing Fort De Russy during the day, when Romain was able to rough sketch the work. The Mississippi River was reached at half-past two P. M., and at the sunset hour a high bluff, lined with cannon and men, was dimly discernible, on account of the thick misty rain storm prevailing, which the guard called Port Hudson.

Early on the morning of the twenty-fourth the prisoners

were turned over to Federal naval officers, who sent them and the *General Quitman* to Baton Rouge, where they landed and were made comfortable, glad to be once more within the Federal lines. Lieutenant Howerton received a torrent of abuse as the paroled men left his boat, after revenge prompted them to throw overboard all movable property they could find upon the steamer, without any attention to Howerton's request: "Now, gentlemen, please stop." The red-headed soldier of his command did not dare to show his ugly face, for the prisoners wanted to thrash him. Several negroes were on the river shores, above Alexandria, when the sight of blue-coated soldiers upon the *Quitman* conveyed an idea to them that the Federals occupied the river. They shouted and sang for "Massa Linkum's sogers" — "take us wid yer" — in a manner that upset the temper of Lieutenant Howerton, who ordered his men ashore to capture them. They were brought aboard and made to attend boiler fires until reaching Port Hudson, when they stole a boat belonging to the *Quitman* and made their escape.

Cloudy, or rainy and cold weather had been experienced about every day since their arrival at Alexandria. Cooped on board river steamers most of the time, using Red River water for cooking and drinking, with the depressing effect of bad weather, caused a great deal of sickness among the men, chiefly diarrhœa. On the march, or on board river steamers, through sickness, suffering and fatigue, the men kept up their spirits wonderfully. Very little recreation in the way of foraging for food could be done upon the march, although every opportunity that presented itself was improved to the utmost, many a "porker" falling victim to their snares. Pigs appeared to be the only animal available when a foraging party went to work.

Embarking upon the *Iberville*, at nine o'clock on the

evening of the twenty-fourth, the prisoners arrived at New Orleans about daylight on the twenty-fifth. Through some negligence they were not reported at general headquarters until the twenty-sixth, when special orders were issued, stating that "two hundred and forty men of the Forty-Second Regiment, Massachusetts Volunteers, paroled prisoners, not having been reported to the headquarters, and on the *Iberville* unattended to and in a starving condition, will be taken charge of by Lieutenant Farnsworth, Fourth Wisconsin Volunteers, and conducted to the camp at Gentilly Crossing, and turned over and kept as paroled men under proper officers."

They disembarked on the twenty-sixth, and marched to camp under escort of Companies A, B, E and F, after attending a brigade drill. Many were the heartfelt greetings exchanged all around, and for days afterwards the boys were occupied in reciting their adventures and trials.

A communication from General Sherman, commanding Defences of New Orleans, gives the status of the prisoners as follows:

"The Forty-Second Regiment on the *Iberville*, with the exception of the chaplain, are paroled but not exchanged; the chaplain is unconditionally released. The conditions of the parole are thus stated in the fourth article of the cartel between the United States and the enemy, promulgated in General Orders No. 146 of 1862 from the War Department, adjutant-general's office: 'The surplus prisoners not exchanged shall not be permitted to take up arms again, nor to serve as military police or constabulary force in any fort, garrison or field work held by either of the respective parties, nor as guards of prisons, depots, or stores, nor to discharge any duty usually performed by soldiers, until exchanged under the provisions of this cartel.'"

A reply was made March 6th, which elicited from General Sherman a response that everything was satisfactory.

"HEADQUARTERS, 42ND MASS. VOLS.,

"CAMP FARR, BAYOU GENTILLY, LA., March 6th, 1863.

"*Sir*,— I have the honor to state that your communication of the third inst., enclosing a copy of letter of instructions from headquarters, Department of the Gulf, and inquiring whether special orders from these headquarters, No. 73, current series, February 26th, have been fully carried out, is just received.

"In reply, I would respectfully state, that the two hundred and forty men of this regiment, paroled prisoners, were reported to me by Lieutenant Farnsworth, as ordered; and that I have placed them in a separate camp, at a distance of three hundred and eighty paces, or seventy-six rods, from the camp of the men under my command. That I have placed Captain J. D. Cogswell, a competent and efficient officer, at the camp to take charge of them, with instructions to treat them as paroled but unexchanged prisoners of war, and to make such rules and regulations, subject to my approval, as shall conduce to their comfort and welfare.

"I have also given instructions to Lieutenant A. E. Proctor, acting regimental quartermaster, to furnish for them proper rations and such articles of clothing as they are in need of, some of them being quite destitute of clothing. I would also respectfully add, that I have required nothing whatever that shall in the least manner effect their parole, or cause a violation of the 'cartel' alluded to.

"I have the honor to remain,

"Very respectfully, your obedient servant,

"J. STEDMAN,

"*Lieut-Colonel commanding.*

"To CAPTAIN WICKHAM HOFFMAN,

"*A. A. General Defences New Orleans.*"

Had the men at Galveston been captured prior to January 1st, 1863, they would have been declared duly exchanged and ordered to report for duty immediately, February 9th, 1863; a general order issued that day from Department headquarters required all officers, enlisted men and camp followers captured in the States of Texas and Louisiana up to January 1st, 1863, to return to duty at once, as they are declared duly exchanged prisoners of war by General Orders No. 10, dated January 10th, 1863, from the War Department, adjutant-general's office. The men of the Eighth Regiment, United States Regulars, were exchanged and organized into a battalion for duty with the army. A portion of them under command of Lieutenant Copley Amory, Fourth Cavalry, arrived at Opelousas April 23d to join in the campaign then under way by the Nineteenth Corps. On the twenty-fifth, they were relieved from this service and ordered to return North, as an act of justice to those gallant men. A national salute was fired when leaving Opelousas, and a similar honor was paid them on their departure from New Orleans; General Orders No. 34, Nineteenth Army Corps, made honorable mention of their record, accompanied by a full roster of the men.

The trouble between Federal and Confederate War Departments over the exchange of prisoners commenced in 1863, so all attempts to effect an exchange for the men of the Forty-Second failed. At Gentilly Crossing they remained, until about the time the regiment embarked for home, in a camp laid out very neat, kept in good order, with ovens and fire-places for cooking purposes, built of brick obtained from the ruins of an old sugar house across the Gentilly road, opposite their camp.

Familiarly nicknamed the "pet lambs," their military life was one of inglorious ease, much to their disgust.

CHAPTER VIII.

At Bayou Gentilly — March — April.

THE month of March was dull enough to suit an epicure or sluggard. Additional details from the regiment for service elsewhere was the order of the day. In response to a call by special orders from headquarters, Defences of New Orleans, the following men were detailed from Company E, March 1st, for service in the Fourth Massachusetts Battery, in need of men:

Privates Alender E. Dorman, Henry C. Tyler, George H. Hathorn, Lyman Hathorn, Leonard Mahon and Michael Nedow.

On the tenth, Captain Coburn and Lieutenant John P. Burrell, Company A, with three sergeants, five corporals and forty-eight privates, left camp to take post at Battery St. John, situated on the Bayou St. John.

The monotony of camp life was relieved by a brigade drill held on the third. On this occasion Sergeant Charles A. Attwell, Company G, who had been detailed March 2d to act as band-major, made his first effort in that line of business. Attwell was a stout, pompous appearing man, well calculated to deceive anybody on a slight acquaintance, and he made out of his position all that any man could possibly squeeze. On the march to and from the drill ground he made love to all the women, who followed the regiment with pies and cakes for sale. Dropping to the rear of the column, when a route step was taken, Attwell would be found, escorted by these women, liberally helping himself to their goods. There was a reason for all this on his part; a perfect specimen of a "dead beat," he never paid for anything, except in compliments.

A ripple of excitement was created on the eighth, when a letter from Colonel Farr was received, with orders to hold the men in readiness for marching orders at a moment's notice. On the thirteenth, when the paroled men were ordered to get ready for transfer to the United States Barracks and there quartered, it looked like a general breaking up of camp at Gentilly Bayou, and the men were in fine spirits again. The latter orders were immediately countermanded, and the camp soon settled down to the old state of things.

There existed, among regiments that arrived in January and February, a heavy sick list, accompanied with a loss of many men by death. An inquiry into the cause, ordered by General Sherman, produced the following interesting circular, issued to all commanding officers under his orders. One reason for incorporating this circular as a part of the regimental record, is to show certain officers and men of the regiment, who were accustomed to disregard nearly all of the recommendations contained therein, what results will follow from not performing one of the highest duties that belong to an officer on active service, viz., personal attention to the health of his men.

"CIRCULAR.
"HEADQUARTERS DEFENCES NEW ORLEANS,
"NEW ORLEANS, March 7th, 1863.

"Upon the following report of the medical director of this command of February 21st, ult., the brigadier-general commanding has made this indorsement:

"'It is believed that a publication of Surgeon Sanger's report, to the troops of this command, fully approved as it is by me, will be sufficient to awaken a greater spirit of pride and vigor in attention to duty.

"'There is no doubt but that a want of attention to personal cleanliness, of proper police, and of vigorous, hearty, and interested attention to duty, is the cause of most sickness now prevalent.

"'I call upon all commanding officers to look carefully into this matter, and endeavor to prevent not only all unnecessary mortality, but that continued reduction of the duty list, which so much enfeebles the efficiency of the command.

"'Commanding officers must not take upon themselves to excuse men and officers from duty on the plea of sickness. The medical officers alone are to decide who are fit or unfit for duty.'

"WICKHAM HOFFMAN,
"*Assistant Adjutant-General.*

"NEW ORLEANS, March 5th, 1863.

"CAPTAIN W. HOFFMAN,
"*Assistant Adjutant-General:*

"In obedience to your instructions, I have examined with care and interest the various hospitals and regiments in this command, to ascertain the cause of so much sickness. My investigations have been thorough, having visited nearly every cook-house, street, and tent, observing drainage, etc., in this command.

"The results of my investigations are not altogether satisfactory, and in some instances contradictory. The special cause of disease in individual regiments is hard to arrive at, because what seems to predispose to disease in one case is harmless in another, and results are so dependent upon the mental and moral influences exerted over the men, their special predisposition and resistance to disease, and their idiosyncracies, and previous habits. I have, however, arrived at certain general conclusions of importance.

"*First.* There is but little, if any, malarious poison generated at present. I did not see a characteristic case of intermittent fever, and but one case of remittent. In many cases where malarial fever was reported, it was either initiative fever, or one of the species of the continued form, or the regiments had been previously exposed to malaria, and the damp weather, or other untoward circumstances had developed or reproduced it. In confirmation of this may be instanced the Twenty-Sixth Massachusetts, now suffering from intermittent. This regiment had fever and ague severely at Forts Philip and Jackson last June and July, but after being ordered to the Custom House, beyond malarious influences, recovered. Since the rainy season set in, their quarters have been dark and damp, and this fever has been reproduced.

"*Second.* The camping ground outside the city is very similar in character; there is but little choice of grounds, most of the camps are susceptible of pretty good drainage, and the difference of altitude does not vary more than twelve to seventeen inches. Some camps are more accessible to certain conveniences, such as drinking water, sinks and places for the disposal of slops, and those on the immediate banks of the river are more exempt from whatever malaria exists at the present time, yet these differences do not account for the disparities in the sick reports.

"*Third.* Neatness in cooking and person, and cleanliness of camps, are powerful agents in preserving health, and in proportion to the observance of Heaven's first law, did I see exemption from disease. It is not sufficient, however, that soldiers should be passive agents in the accomplishment of this, but their pride and ambition should be aroused, they should be made to feel that it was not only *necessary for the preservation of health*, but *laudable*.

"Wherever I found officers who had inspired spirit in their men, and had taken a personal interest in keeping their soldiers and camps clean, and where soldiers had been made to feel that excellence in these points was meritorious, and that a deviation would not only not be *permitted* but surely *punished;* and where I found men were convinced that to complain was unmanly and nursing not the privilege of the soldier, there I found a healthy regiment.

"The One Hundred and Tenth New York had the largest sick list, two hundred and ninety-two; this regiment was on shipboard fifty-three days; after landing had some ship fever and about one hundred cases of measles; lost fifteen men. The voyage, measles and deaths depressed the men somewhat, besides men from agricultural districts do not seem to be so hardy and stand campaigning as well as city soldiers. The camp was neat, tents floored and cooking good; men looked pretty vigorous; think the surgeon too lenient, but he said if he did not excuse the men the colonel would. Should say the sick report might be reduced one-third with impunity.

"The Sixteenth New Hampshire was encamped near the One Hundred and Tenth New York, had one hundred and seventy-three sick; only fifteen days on shipboard; lost ten men; principal disease, diarrhœa; camp was not so well drained as the One Hundred and Tenth New York. Tents and streets were very dirty and the men unwashed, some had not washed for four weeks and the most not for two weeks.

"The One Hundred and Sixty-Second New York, camping on the same ground, had very few sick. This regiment was enlisted in New York City; were forty-one days on shipboard, and, I believe, had not lost a man in camp. The surgeon attended personally to the cooking, drainage and cleanliness of camp, and the commanding officer had his suggestions rigorously enforced.

"The Thirty-Eighth Massachusetts had one hundred and fifty-five sick; tents provided with floors; streets pretty neat, and the facilities for drainage good; cook tents too much crowded, and cooking not attended to as it ought to be; principal disease, diarrhœa; think the surgeon a little too lenient; says there were forty chronic cases, which never ought to have been enlisted; attributes diarrhœa to sour bread.

"The Fifty-Third Massachusetts had one hundred and thirty-six sick; sick list swelled by a number of cases of scarlet and lung fever; lung fever caused by sleeping on the damp ground for the first fortnight after their arrival. The hospital was not neat; sick were not provided with comforts, and the surgeon complains that he could not make his hospital fund available. Both assistant-surgeons sick. Cooking done in the open air, without shelter from the heavy rains.

"The One Hundred and Twenty-Eighth New York had one hundred and twenty-three sick; were on shipboard forty-two days; did not pay the same attention to cleanliness and fumigation that the One Hundred and Sixty-Second New York did; have had a large number of cases of ship fever, nearly one hundred; lost thirty-nine men. Principal cause of disease at present, diarrhœa. Neither the camp nor hospital are in good condition. The soldiers don't take pride in grading their streets and keeping their tents clean. Counted beef bones by the dozen about their tents. Many of their patients are treated in hospital tents and on the floor. Suggested to the colonel to take a confiscated house within his regimental lines, now occupied by the One Hundred and Sixty-Second New York. A vacant house can be found near the camp of the One Hundred and Sixty-Second New York, quite as convenient for the latter.

"The Twenty-Sixth Connecticut has one hundred and fifty sick. Diseases, typhoid fever and diarrhœa. Number of deaths, nine. I think the cause of so much disease, and *kind*, can be traced to want of cleanliness. The tents were all disorderly and dirty. Attention was not paid to keeping the drains and streets free from mouldy bread, meat bones and orange peel. The men had a listless and indifferent look, as if waiting the expiration of their term of service.

"The Fourth Massachusetts had one hundred and fourteen sick; on shipboard forty-eight days; no deaths; diarrhœa prevailing. Through the energy and attention of their commander, this regiment has escaped serious disease. Did not see any very sick in hospital or quarters. The men were enjoying a little respite after long confinement on shipboard.

"The Sixth Michigan is improving; still show the effects of the malaria of last summer.

"The Fifteenth New Hampshire are rapidly improving; officers and men becoming very much interested in improving their camp.

"The Twenty-Sixth Massachusetts has a large number in general hospital. The inclement weather and dark, gloomy and damp quarters give them a sickly look. I think they would rapidly improve if the regiment was removed to drier and more airy quarters.

"The One Hundred and Sixty-Fifth New York and Thirty-First Massachusetts are very free from disease. Much is due in both these regiments to the spirit, energy and attention of their commanders and surgeons. The camp of the One Hundred and Sixty-Fifth New York is scrupulously neat, clean and well drained — best camp in this command; and personal attention seems to be paid by the officers to everything conducive to health and comfort. The other regiments of your command are in very good condition, and present very small sick reports.

"I found very few of the regimental cooks furnished with the little cook books issued by the Commissaries. Either the Commissaries have failed to furnish them, or the company to distribute them. Most of the cooks seemed anxious to be supplied with them.

"The use of mixed vegetables is almost universally neglected. It is important to accustom the regiments to the use of them, at least once a week, in soups, as fresh potatoes will soon fail, and the habitual use of some succulent vegetable is essential to health, as well as to prevent the cravings of a ravenous appetite, produced by a want of that variety to which soldiers have been accustomed in private life. A morbid appetite is created by this neglect, and when soldiers get access to such food they invariably overload their stomachs.

"Respectfully, your obedient servant,

"EUGENE F. SANGER,

"*Medical Director, General Sherman's Command.*"

The first vacancy among commissioned officers of the regiment was caused by the resignation of First-Lieutenant David A. Partridge, of Company B, who remained in Massachusetts to look after deserters when the regiment left the State, and was granted a discharge by War Department Special Orders No. 105, dated March 5th, to enable him to accept a commission and recruit for the Fifty-Fourth Massachusetts Colored Volunteers. The vacancy was filled March 24th by the *election* of Second-Sergeant Benjamin C. Tinkham, Company B, jumping Second-Lieutenant J. C. Clifford and the first-sergeant, who were in the line of promotion.

The second vacancy was caused by the resignation of Captain Charles A. Pratt, Company E. This vacancy was also filled by an *election* by the company, April 2d. First-Lieutenant John W. Emerson was made captain, and Second-Sergeant Augustus Ford, Company E, was elected a first-lieutenant, *vice* Emerson, promoted (if this can be called promotion), jumping Second-Lieutenant Brown P. Stowell, a prisoner of war in Texas, and the first-sergeant, who were in the line of promotion.

This *elective* system of filling vacancies, one of the inducements held out to attract men to enlist in the nine months' troops from Massachusetts, was a ridiculous system; one of caucus politics in the army. It was the cause of considerable ill feeling and much trouble in nine months' organizations from the State. To allow the rank and file to choose by an election their company officers was entirely wrong. Under it any man in the company, no matter what his qualifications may be, stands a chance, by electioneering, to win an officer's position that is vacant. Merit in that officer who has a right to expect the promotion is overlooked, if that officer has been so unlucky as to incur the displeasure of a few prominent men in his company, and they proceed to spread the dissatisfaction to others, and take their revenge by electing another over him not entitled to the vacancy. What is the consequence? The officer so jumped forthwith loses the interest he formerly had in the command, and does not exert himself to work for the good of the men under him.

It is just to say that in the above cases the selections were good. Perhaps could not be better.

With the exception of a slight clashing of authority between Captain Coburn, in command at Battery St. John, and Lieutenant-Colonel Stedman, concerning some captures of prisoners and seizures of contraband goods on the night of the fourteenth, which required two peremptory letters to be sent Captain Coburn before it was straightened out, everything worked smooth with the command. This was a case where four citizens were arrested near Bayou St. John in the act of smuggling contraband goods across Lake Ponchartrain; three of them were sent to New Orleans March 17th by orders, and one was discharged March 16th by Lieutenant-Colonel Stedman.

The City of New Orleans so near to many camps, full of enticements of a varied character, was the place to tempt many a soldier who was disposed to evade duty and absent himself without leave. Stragglers from these camps without passes gave provost-guards so much trouble and the evil grew to such proportions every day, Department Special Orders No. 61 were issued March 2d to put a stop to it. There were five hundred men in the city without passes and in confinement reported to the provost-marshal-general March 2d. In one day the provost-guard found nineteen men from one company without a pass; but one man from the Forty-Second is known to have visited the city in this way during March, and he, Private Owen Fox,

Company A, was promptly arrested by the guard and sent back to the regiment.

Besides the details already mentioned, the following details were made and changes occurred during the month:

March 4th — Corporal John C. Yeaton, Company E, was reduced to the ranks by regimental special orders as unfit for the position.

March 4th — Private G. G. Belcher, Company F, was relieved as a wagoner and ordered to duty in the ranks, and the captain ordered to appoint a trustworthy person to fill the position of wagoner.

March 5th — Privates Thomas H. Sawyer, Company B, and Joseph V. Colson, Company G, were detailed as markers.

March 5th — Private John A. Loud, Company A, was ordered to report to Lieutenant Pease, division ordnance-officer, to do duty as a mechanic in unspiking guns at Chalmette. He returned to duty in the regiment June 13th.

March 7th — Private J. Augustus Fitts, Company B, was detailed as orderly at regimental headquarters.

March 7th — Private William H. Haven was transferred from Company E to Company F, to date from March 1st.

March 8th — Private Clark K. Denny was relieved from duty as orderly and made a clerk at regimental headquarters.

March 9th — Special Orders, Defences New Orleans, appointed Corporal Uriel Josephs and Sergeant Eben Tirrell, Jr., of Company A, as ordnance-sergeants at Batteries Gentilly and St. John, reporting to the division ordnance-officer.

March 9th — Private Elbridge G. Harwood, Company B, was made regimental carpenter, serving in that capacity until relieved in July.

March 9th — Private George H. Greenwood, Company

B, was made cook for the wagoner's mess, serving as such until relieved in July.

March 31st — Major Stiles and Lieutenant Duncan, Company F, were detailed on court-martial duty by general orders, Defences New Orleans, to serve when such court was held. They were not relieved until July 30th.

In addition to these details the chief-quartermaster asked for names of such men in the regiment as were qualified to act as superintendent of machine works, and in the manufacture and preparation of lumber. Upon inquiry there were found quite a number, who were recommended accordingly, but no detail was made from the regiment.

In this month (March) a few unimportant incidents occurred worth notice because a few members, who are aware of the facts, cannot forget them. One was a hunt after dogs, on the night of March 31st, by a few wild, restless spirits, with a view to exterminate all they could from the neighborhood infested with them. Another was an old negro who could not tell his age, but, from facts gleaned in conversation with him, must have been over one hundred years old. Bent over with age, trembling with weakness, without a home or friends, this old man was a wanderer from camp to camp for food and shelter. On a bitter cold night he struck the Forty-Second camp, and was provided with lodging in the guard-house. None of his kind would care for him, so he said, "since old massa had dun gon' away."

Sergeant-Major Bosson, and Sergeant Phil. Hackett, Company G, had an adventure on the Gentilly road on the night of March 10th. A beautiful moonlight evening it was. As they strolled along the road songs were heard, sung by a party of men evidently in liquor. To hide and listen, under the shadow of a board fence, was suggested by Hackett. No sooner done than a few snatches of a secession refrain raised Hackett's anger to such a point that he was ready to whip the entire party. Bosson advised no interference, as the men had a perfect right to sing. Hackett's blood was up, however, and when a citizen (the party separated a few moments before) arrived opposite their hiding place, Phil. jumped for him, when the man showed fight. Hackett threw him into a ditch, alongside the road, and by the time he got out, swearing vengeance, Bosson was on hand. The two confronted him. He raised one arm to the back of his neck, when stories, often read in books, of Southerners with bowie knives carried in that spot flashed across the minds of both men, and simultaneously they seized him. Hackett held his arms while Bosson placed a pistol to his head. Frenchman as he was, excited with anger and liquor, the cold muzzle against his temple completely cowed the fellow. A search was made for the suspected bowie knife, but none was found. The man, who gave his name as citizen Ambrose Leonard, was marched into camp a prisoner. As nothing could be charged against him, he was released from arrest March 12th by Lieutenant-Colonel Stedman. There was no good cause for this arrest; the affair sprang from a spirit of mischief and from ignorance of what they had a right to do.

On March 21st occurred the first loss by death the regiment sustained at Bayou Gentilly. Private Obed F. Allen, Company G, a paroled prisoner of war, died in the regimental hospital of typhoid fever. The disease was contracted on the march from Houston. His body was embalmed by a city undertaker at the expense of his comrades in Company G, and sent to his home in Quincy, Massachusetts.

At the close of March there were present for duty in

the four companies at Gentilly Bayou and vicinity, seventeen officers and three hundred and fifty-five men.

Present sick in hospital, thirty-six. The average sick per day of the regiment during March was: taken sick, two; returned to duty, two; in hospital, twenty; in quarters, three.

In April the companies attached to regimental headquarters had some work to perform. Brigade special orders, issued on the fourth, placed Lieutenant-Colonel Stedman in command of the stations Bayou Gentilly, Bayou St. John, Lakeport, and the bayous dependent upon the same, with headquarters at Gentilly Bayou, and he was ordered to relieve two companies of the Ninth Connecticut Infantry, then stationed at Lake-end of Bayou St. John and at Lakeport, with two companies from the Forty-Second.

On the fifth, a fine Sunday morning, about ten o'clock, Captain Cogswell (who had been relieved from command of the paroled camp by Lieutenant Powers, Company F) proceeded with his company to Lakeport and relieved Company E, Ninth Connecticut, Captain Wright, then on picket duty from Lakeport to Point aux Herbes, fifteen miles. On the same day thirty-five men of Company A, under Captain Coburn, proceeded to Lake-end of Bayou St. John and relieved Company G, Ninth Connecticut. The Ninth Connecticut men behaved in a most unsoldierlike manner, causing Lieutenant-Colonel Stedman to state the facts to brigade headquarters in the accompanying letter:

"HEADQUARTERS FORTY-SECOND REGT., MASS. VOLS.,

"CAMP FARR, BAYOU GENTILLY, LA., April 6th, 1863.

"*Sir*,— I have the honor to report that I proceeded yesterday, according to Special Orders No. 54, and moved

Company F of this regiment to Lakeport, and there relieved the Ninth Connecticut, Captain Wright, who turned over the public property in his possession to Captain J. D. Cogswell, commanding Company F. The pickets were taken from Company F for Lakeport and all stations below that point.

"At the Lake-end of Bayou St. John I placed thirty men and four non-commissioned officers from Company A, leaving thirty men of the same company at Battery St. John; the whole under command of Captain Coburn, of Company A.

"I have remaining of Company A, nineteen men, four non-commissioned officers and one lieutenant, who are now stationed at Battery Gentilly on the Ponchartrain Railroad, thus making all the stations and pickets outside of this immediate camp under charge of Companies A and F.

"In connection with the relieving of the companies of the Ninth Connecticut Volunteers, I am sorry to be obliged to report the ill-will manifested by many of them at their removal from the lake.

"At Lakeport they broke up and destroyed all the bunks in the building they occupied as quarters and sold all the boards they could remove from the building. Several of them were badly intoxicated, and one drew a knife and another a club on one of the members of Company F for refusing to allow them to pull out the faucets of the water tanks and waste all the water at the quarters.

"At the Lake-end of Bayou St. John the Government schooner *Hortense* was lying, and the crew of that boat managed, before my men took possession of her, to damage her in several ways. Twelve lights of glass were broken of the cabin windows, and the cabin furniture considerably damaged. They sold the hawser, also the launch, or tender, of the schooner, and many of the cooking utensils were thrown overboard and lost. The water cask and a few of the ropes have been recovered from parties who bought them, but the launch and other things, which they sold, we have not found as yet.

"I would respectfully submit this report as a simple statement of facts which have come under my observation since relieving the companies named.

"I have the honor to remain,

"Your most obedient servant,

"J. STEDMAN,

"*Lieutenant-Colonel commanding.*

"To LIEUTENANT GEORGE E. DAVIS, *A. A. A. General,*
"*Second Brigade, Second Division, New Orleans.*"

The boat of the *Hortense* was found May 2d at Hickok's Landing in the possession of a coffee house proprietor. There was some correspondence with the brigade commander about this affair, but it was allowed to blow over, and no steps were taken to punish the ringleaders. The Connecticut men were very angry, because taken from a post where they enjoyed themselves to the neglect of duty.

Captain Cogswell soon found there was business to occupy his attention. Within two hours after his arrival a man representing himself as J. D. O'Connell, special detective in Government employ, with a companion, requested assistance in a case they were engaged in working up. Not producing any proof, as requested, that they were in the Government service, a special messenger was sent to the provost-marshal of New Orleans, who returned with the information O'Connell was "all right." While not fully satisfied in his own mind, the captain concluded to join in the game, intending to arrest them if they did not prove "all right."

The case was one in which a party of Confederates wished to get across the lake. A sail-boat was furnished by Captain Cogswell with one man disguised as a fisherman, who was to have the boat ready at a certain lonely spot on the road leading to Bayou St. John where it ran close to the water. The party of Confederates were to be ready to cross on the eighth, but did not make the attempt until the night of the tenth. Requesting assistance from the lieutenant-colonel, eight men from Company B, under Lieutenant Tinkham, were sent to Lakeport on the eighth.

A detail of twelve men, divided into two squads, under the commands of Lieutenant Tinkham and Orderly-Sergeant J. A. Titus, Company F, were secreted among bushes that bordered upon the road. Accompanied by the two detectives, who pretended to be Confederates, the party appeared about nine o'clock P.M. The detectives waited until their companions had reached the boat, when they gave a pre-arranged signal, responded to by Lieutenant Tinkham shouting the agreed-on command, "Rally on centre," fired his pistol, and the squads dashed out from their hiding-places with a shout. One detective pretended to be killed, the other was made a prisoner; all in the plan. It was supposed the men who reached the boat would make a hot fight, but they shouted not to fire and they would agree to come in; as there was some delay in doing so, Sergeant Ballou, Company B, asked and received permission to wade out and hurry them up, taking possession and remaining upon the boat until relieved.

Under guard, the prisoners were marched to Captain Cogswell's headquarters for examination. They proved to be Major Breedlove, a Confederate spy within the lines for nearly three months, Captain Switzer, a Confederate steamboat man, on his way to take command of a gunboat, and three other men. On the person of Captain Switzer was found $3,098.00; $2,800.00 was in one-hundred-dollar Confederate bills, the balance in notes of Louisiana State Banks, located in New Orleans. Relieved of their personal effects, the prisoners were turned over to the provost-marshal of New Orleans, and the property also. They were confined in the Parish prison for several weeks, and then released. Breedlove and Switzer afterwards visited Captain Cogswell to obtain their property.

Later, on the same night, a negro reported men loading a boat on the lake near the "White House." Sergeant Ballou was sent with a detail of men to the spot, but did not capture any prisoners. The boat was secured, and found to contain boots, shoes, cards for carding cotton, pipes, matches and sundries.

A schooner, under a Confederate flag of truce, conveying one hundred and thirty-three United States soldiers, sailors and marines, captured at Vicksburg, paroled for exchange, arrived on the sixth, accompanied by Confederate Commissioner of Exchange, Colonel Zyminsky. The men were in a sad condition from detention upon the lake by a severe storm, three days without food or water. They were supplied with all of the food at the post, not enough to go around, and some of the men ate raw potatoes, preferring to do so instead of waiting to have them cooked. After a few hours delay sufficient supply for their immediate wants was obtained.

Colonel Zyminsky, a Pole by birth, resided in New Orleans when the war commenced. His wife was then residing in the city, and came out to the post to see him. Captain Cogswell allowed her five minutes to exchange compliments, but that was all the colonel desired, and, in fact, said he did not want to see her anyhow. Zyminsky was a giant, six feet four inches in height, as large everyway in proportion. Such a nose! A pickled blood-beet was pale beside it. He wanted a twelve-gallon demijohn of Louisiana rum more than he did a visit from his wife. He got the visit, but did not get the rum, although he clandestinely ordered it. The demijohn was brought to the wharf, where Cogswell would not allow it to pass, so Colonel Zyminsky went back across the lake very dry.

To northern soldiers all southern scenery, cities and towns, so different in character to what they were accustomed to see North, charmed the eye and senses of those men who had not travelled far away from home, until a thorough acquaintance with any locality where they were stationed produced a desire to get away. After the novelty of being in a new section of country wore off, the men were unanimous in praise of their own sections as the proper place to live, enjoy life while living, and be laid away when dead.

Lakeport was no exception to this first seductive influence. A small village, with a few one-story houses, two hotels that entertained dinner parties from New Orleans, repair shops for the Ponchartrain Railroad, and a schoolhouse was about all there was to it. On Sundays there were many visitors from the city bent on pleasure, as though no war was in progress. The hotels for dinners and bath houses to sport in the lake water were objective points. Occasionally, large numbers of colored men and women came out early on Sunday mornings to witness ceremonies of baptism to a score of both sexes who had joined a church. The religious fervor was always great on such occasions, coupled with antics of voice and body that cannot be described. White-robed negro women would become unmanageable when *ducked under*, as the boys termed it; if two stout assistants did not lead their religious sisters to where the minister stood and be ready to seize them after baptism for conveyance on shore they would drown. An exhibition of this character once seen can never be forgotten. While on duty at Lakeport, Company F could not complain of a monotonous existence.

Picket duty at the lake-end Bayou St. John requiring extra attention, ten privates were sent from Gentilly Battery, on the sixth, to reënforce Captain Coburn, and on the ninth, Lieutenant Clifford, Company B, was ordered there to assist the captain, remaining at the post until the twenty-first.

The schooner *Hortense* was repaired under supervision of Corporal Croome, Company F (an old sailor), who was detailed to command her, with the following crew: Kirkland A. Hawes (an old sailor) was mate; Privates John J. Upham, cook; George M. Roberts, Thomas H. Robinson, George Adams, all of Company F, and Rufus C. Greene, Company G, were seamen. Two picket-boats for night duty were respectively in charge of Corporal George L. Stone, assisted by Privates Charles M. Marsh and John Kraft; Sergeant Hiram Cowan, assisted by Privates Albert W. Cargell and James F. Harlow. These small boats captured many prisoners with contraband goods, in their attempts to cross the lake. The schooner was used for picket duty and to carry supplies to such picket-posts as were stationed on the bayou outlets.

On the fifth, Corporal Rhodes and three privates of Company B, with rations for one week, were detailed to proceed as a guard, on the schooner *Concordia*, carrying stores and property to Fort Pike and Fort Macomb.

When the steamer *N. P. Banks* was loaded at Lakeport with supplies for Pensacola, and ready to sail on the twenty-first, Captain A. N. Shipley, A. Q. M. in New Orleans, called for a detail. Sergeant Ballou, Corporal Fales and twelve privates from Company B composed the detail, with rations for one week. The instructions

Ballou received from Shipley were, to go aboard the *Banks* as a guard, watch the captain, a southerner, and see that he stopped at all forts on the lake to leave provisions and various stores, then to proceed to Fort Pickens, and Pensacola. If the steamboat captain showed any disposition to do otherwise, then he was to arrest all of the officers and run the steamer into the blockading fleet off Mobile and report. The transport vessel that made a similar trip, a short time previous, had been run through the blockaders into Mobile by her officers, and the cargo passed into Confederate hands. The round trip was made in five days, without any event of importance.

These duties of detailed men, with constant activity at the lake posts to prevent smuggling across to the enemy, gave many men a taste of active duty that was fatiguing, if it was without glory.

It was hard work to get rolls, returns and statements, required by army regulations, made correctly and promptly by company officers of the regiment. A few officers appeared to think these documents were unnecessary, a species of red tape to be fought down. Still it was said they averaged as good as any organization in the Gulf Department, if not better. In the army, among those who knew nothing about it, a great deal of talk was constantly made about red tape. Among business men the wonder was, that the vast machinery of an army could be successfully kept going with such simple returns. There was nothing about them a school-boy of ordinary ability could fail to understand in a short time of study. To understand the nature and use of these documents was as much the duty of an officer as to know how to drill his men. His duty to the men demanded it. Without them payments could not be made, either bounties or wages, rations provided, clothing held in readiness for issue, pensions granted for disability or to the proper relatives of deceased soldiers. Many a large corporation or business house, in their method of conducting business, requires a system much more complicated than the Government has in use for administration of the army. When delays and trouble occurred in the rolls, returns, etc., it was usually traced to the inability of some officer to understand them.

The company returns required were: morning reports, company muster rolls, company muster and pay rolls, company monthly return, returns of men joined company, descriptive lists, quarterly company returns deceased soldiers, muster-in rolls, muster-out rolls, enlistments, re-enlistments, furloughs, discharges, final statements, rolls of prisoners of war, ordnance returns.

All very simple to fill up properly; each return so printed that there was no excuse for not understanding how it was to be done.

The regimental returns required were: consolidated morning reports, field and staff muster rolls, field and staff muster and pay rolls, muster rolls of hospital, muster and pay rolls of hospital, regimental monthly returns, lists of officers, alterations in officers, quarterly regimental returns of deceased soldiers, annual return of casualties.

Careful supervision at regimental headquarters was necessary of company pay rolls, in order to have them correct before forwarding to proper officers.

The regimental books were lost at Galveston; it became necessary to make out a new descriptive book, and could only be done by obtaining the company descriptive books to copy. Captain Bailey, Company H, had peculiar ideas of his own in regard to making proper company returns to regimental headquarters, and when he refused to obey an order from Lieutenant-Colonel Stedman, to forward his company book, it was proper to discipline him.

On the thirteenth a regimental order to Captain Leonard, Company C, in command of Companies C and H, contained the following: "You will also forward to these headquarters the descriptive books of both companies C and H of the regiment, for copying in the regimental records." What followed is explained in a letter written to the brigade-commander next day: —

"HEADQUARTERS FORTY-SECOND REGT., MASS. VOLS.,

"CAMP FARR, GENTILLY STATION, LA., April 14th, 1863.

"*Sir*, — I would respectfully report that the enclosed is a copy of an order sent to Camp Parapet yesterday, by my orderly, and that Captain Leonard complied with the order at once. Captain D. W. Bailey, of Company H, absolutely refused to send his descriptive book, saying that 'the colonel or no other man should have his company books.' If he was under my immediate command here at the camp, it would be clear to my mind how I should act in this case. In the present instance I am not sufficiently informed what my action should be in the premises, not knowing fully how the commanding general considers their relations to this regiment, and more particularly to the commanding officer of the same.

"I would respectfully refer the case to Colonel Farr, for advice and information.

"I have the honor to remain,

"Your obedient servant,.

"J. STEDMAN,
"*Lieutenant-Colonel, 42nd Mass. Vols.*

"To LIEUT. GEO. E. DAVIS, *A. A. A. General,*
"*Second Brigade, Second Division, New Orleans.*"

By orders of General Sherman, Captain Bailey was placed in arrest on the sixteenth, sent to Gentilly Station the next day, an orderly bringing the descriptive book that caused the trouble. Under orders from brigade headquarters, charges and specification of charges were forwarded on the sixteenth. The assignment to quarters, while in arrest, was as follows: ·

"HEADQUARTERS FORTY-SECOND REGT., MASS. VOLS.,

"CAMP FARR, BAYOU GENTILLY, LA., April 17th, 1863.

"*Captain*,— You having been reported at these headquarters in arrest by orders of Brigadier-General Sherman, you are hereby assigned quarters in the large tent to the left of these headquarters, and you will hold yourself within the following limits, viz.: On the right, on a line with the guard line and the right flank of this camp. In front, on a line with the woods in front of the camp. On the left, on a line with the tents on the left flank of the camp of paroled prisoners. In the rear, on a line with the road extending along the rear of this camp.

"You are also referred to the Army Regulations in relation to officers in arrest, in relation to communications, etc.

"By command of

"LIEUTENANT-COLONEL J. STEDMAN,

"CHARLES A. DAVIS, *Adjutant*.

"To CAPTAIN DAVIS W. BAILEY,

"*Company H, 42d Regt., Mass. Vols.*"

Until May 14th the captain remained at Gentilly Bayou, when he was allowed the limits of New Orleans, until the findings in his case were promulgated.

The charges and specifications in this case, and findings of the Court, were as follows — copied from General Orders, No. 48, Nineteenth Army Corps:

CHARGE FIRST.

"Disobedience of Orders."

Specification — "In this: that he, Captain Davis W. Bailey, Company H, Forty-Second Regiment, Massachusetts Volunteers, when ordered by Lieutenant-Colonel J. Stedman, in the execution of his office, and through Captain O. W. Leonard, senior captain of Companies C and H, Forty-Second Regiment, Massachusetts Volunteers, and to whom the order was addressed, to send to the regimental headquarters his company Descriptive Book, did absolutely refuse and fail so to do. All this at Camp Parapet, Louisiana, on or about the thirteenth day of April, 1863."

CHARGE SECOND.

"Conduct unbecoming an Officer and Gentleman."

Specification First — "In this: that he, Captain Davis W. Bailey, Forty-Second Regiment, Massachusetts Volunteers, when notified by Captain O. W. Leonard, senior captain of Companies C and H, Forty-Second Regiment, Massachusetts Volunteers, that he (Captain Leonard) had received an order from Lieutenant-Colonel Stedman (commanding Forty-Second Regiment, Massachusetts Volunteers), to send to the regimental headquarters the Descriptive Books of said Companies C and H, did then and there use disrespectful language of his superior officer, saying in substance as follows: 'the colonel or no other man can have my company books.' All this at Camp Parapet, Louisiana, on or about the thirteenth day of April, 1863."

Specification Second — "In this: that he, Captain Davis W. Bailey, Company H, Forty-Second Regiment, Massachusetts Volunteers, did, on or about the thirteenth day of April, 1863, at or near his quarters at Camp Parapet, Louisiana, when waited on by an orderly from the regimental headquarters of the Forty-Second Regiment, Massachusetts Volunteers, which orderly was sent by Lieutenant-Colonel J. Stedman, in the execution of his office, with a written order to Companies C and H, Forty-Second Regiment, Massachusetts Volunteers, to forward their company Descriptive Books for copying on the regimental records, did refuse to send his Descriptive Book, and neglect so to do. All this at Camp Parapet, Louisiana, on or about the thirteenth day of April, 1863."

CHARGE THIRD.

"Conduct to the prejudice of Good Order and Military Discipline."

Specification — "In this: that he, Captain Davis W. Bailey, Company H, Forty-Second Regiment, Massachusetts Volunteers, when informed by Captain Leonard, senior captain of Companies C and H, Forty-Second Regiment, Massachusetts Volunteers, that the lieutenant-colonel had sent an order for the Descriptive Books of said companies, did, then and there, at or near his quarters at Camp Parapet, Louisiana, and in the presence of Captain Leonard and at least two enlisted men of the Forty-Second Regiment, Massachusetts Volunteers, refuse to send his Descriptive Book, averring in substance as follows: 'Lieutenant-Colonel Stedman or no other man can have my company books.' All this at Camp Parapet, Louisiana, on or about the thirteenth day of April, 1863."

To all of which charges and specifications the accused pleaded "not guilty."

The Court, after mature deliberation on the evidence adduced, finds the accused as follows:

Of the specification, first charge — "Not guilty."
Of the first charge — "Not guilty."
Of the first specification, second charge —" Not guilty."
Of the second specification, second charge—"Not guilty."
Of the second charge — "Not guilty."
Of the specification, third charge — "Not guilty."
Of the third charge — "Not guilty."

And does therefore acquit him.

The case was clear and charges filed correctly, but, on his trial before a general court-martial, held in New Orleans, March 25th, the charges were not sustained; a material witness failed to remember anything.

The proceedings of this court-martial were approved by General Banks in General Orders of June 9th, when Captain Bailey was acquitted, released from arrest and returned to duty; the orders did not take effect until July 20th, when they reached the regiment.

At a general court-martial convened in New Orleans, January 27th, 1863, of which Major F. Frye, Ninth Connecticut Volunteers, was president, the following enlisted men of the Forty-Second were tried, in addition to the case of Private Denny, Company E, already mentioned:

Private William H. Thomas, Company B, for "sleeping on post."

Private Frank L. Fisher, Company B, for "sleeping on post."

Privates Thomas and Fisher when found asleep, were awakened and cautioned by the officer of the guard as to the penalty they would incur by going to sleep while on sentry duty. Notwithstanding the caution they allowed themselves to fall asleep again while on guard, and in the same relief.

The findings of this Court were not promulgated in General Orders until March 7th. In the case of Thomas, he was found asleep on post 13, in front of regimental headquarters at Gentilly Bayou, between the hours of one and half-past one o'clock on the morning of February 12th. He pleaded "guilty" to the charge and specification. His plea was accepted, and, as it appeared that he was sick at the time and excused from duty by the surgeon, it was recommended that he be returned to duty.

Private Fisher was found asleep on post 15, at the stable and quartermasters' department at Gentilly Bayou, between the hours of one and two o'clock on the morning of February 10th. He pleaded "not guilty" to both charge and specification, and the Court on the evidence adduced found him "not guilty," and recommended that he be returned to duty. Fisher and Thomas, confined since February 12th, were released from confinement in the guard-house March 18th.

Private Freeman Doane, Company F, was also found asleep on post at Lakeport on the twenty-ninth of April, and placed in arrest. Upon examination of the case Captain Cogswell was so well satisfied that Doane was sick and not fit to have been placed on sentry duty, being under the surgeon's care, that he asked for and obtained his release the next day.

Lieutenant Albert E. Proctor, Company G, acting regimental quartermaster, met with a very serious accident on the morning of the twentieth by being thrown from his horse, in front of headquarters, immediately after mounting, preparatory to proceeding to the city on official business, sustaining a fracture of the right arm near the socket of the shoulder, which incapacitated him from further duty with the regiment during its term of service.

A moment before he left headquarters in fine spirits,

and when brought in looking deathly pale everybody present was dumfounded. Luckily, Assistant - Surgeon Heintzelman was present on duty with the regiment, having reported at camp March 1st. He immediately made a careful examination of the fracture, properly bandaged it, and prepared everything to make Proctor comfortable until he arrived at the hospital in New Orleans, where he was sent the same day and had his arm reset. Lieutenant Proctor showed true fortitude throughout the day. Not a groan escaped his lips, although the pain he suffered was excruciating. He gave proper directions for the continued performance of his duties and what disposition to make of unfinished business he had on hand with utmost *sang-froid*.

Lieutenant Proctor was a twin brother of Captain Alfred N. Proctor, Company G, then a prisoner of war in Texas. It was difficult to say who was who, even when seen together. The lieutenant remarked, soon after the accident to himself, that his brother Alfred had met with an accident also. His reason for thinking so was because a sympathetic feeling had always existed between them. As a matter of fact, Captain Proctor did have one of the bones of an ankle broken while wrestling with Sergeant Wentworth, March 27th.

Until May 20th, when Quartermaster Burrell reported back for duty, having been relieved as acting brigade-quartermaster, when Colonel Cahill, Ninth Connecticut Volunteers, superseded Colonel Farr, the active duties of the position were well performed by Acting Quartermaster-Sergeant Alonzo I. Hodsdon, corporal in Company D.

The regiment was fortunate in having good quartermasters during the term of service, and in obtaining supplies of proper food. The salt meats, coffee, potatoes, bread, etc., were of excellent quality. It was necessary only once (May 15th) during the entire term of service to call for a Board of Survey to examine into the quality of subsistence stores received from the Commissary Department. Quartermaster Burrell was socially one of the best of men, with business qualifications for his duty of a high order. Acting-Quartermaster Proctor was also adapted to fill the position, and was a jovial man. Corporal Hodsdon, without a business training to fit him to hold such a position at once, had mastered the details to such extent from his connection with the department that during the time he performed the duties everything went along smoothly.

At the close of April there were present for duty in the four companies at Gentilly Bayou and vicinity, thirteen officers and three hundred and fifty-six men. Sick in regimental hospital: one officer (Lieutenant Harding, Company K, who arrived April 27th, sick with fever), and twenty-one men. Thirteen men were sick in quarters. The average sick per day for the month had been: taken sick, four; returned to duty, four; in hospital, twenty; in quarters, fourteen. One man died at the camp hospital of typhoid fever, Private Frank Covell, Company G, a paroled prisoner, April 22d. The body was embalmed and sent home. Private Covell, quite young in years, was careless of his health. He would insist on sleeping at night in the open air instead of under tent cover, exposed unprotected to change in the atmosphere, usually very rapid after nine o'clock. Repeated cautions not to do so were given him. Company G was unfortunate at this camp in the loss of men by death from disease. The other companies of paroled men, D and I, did not lose a man.

At Bayou Gentilly the night air was treacherous and dangerous. In good weather the days, at this season of the year, would be hot and sultry up to about ten o'clock in the night, when changes would commence to occur, becoming damp and hazy. About midnight sentinels were obliged to wear their great-coats. Many men would persist in sleeping upon the ground in the open air, regardless of repeated warnings not to do so. When the midnight change took place, if they by chance awoke, they would occupy their tents. This careless habit caused much sickness in the regiment from bowel complaints and fevers, that was charged by the sufferers to bad quality of rations issued.

Discipline of the camp continued good, and the paroled men behaved well under their enforced idleness. Very few men absented themselves without leave. Corporal Clapp, Privates Holt, Barnard and Davis, all from Company G, tried it on and were picked up by the patrol in New Orleans, April 4th. Privates Dolan, Dellanty, Contillon and Morgan, all from Company I, were bagged by the patrol on the fifth, and Private Marshall, Company G, was arrested by the police of New Orleans, April 12th. These men were returned to camp by the provost-marshal in one or two days after their arrest.

Two deserters reported back to the regiment this month: Private Chauncy Converse, Company K, on the eleventh; Private Lewis Buffum, Company B, on the twenty-fifth.

While able to furnish details of skilled mechanics, if wanted, on a call for telegraph operators, made on the twenty-ninth, to do duty in the Defences of New Orleans, a careful inquiry failed to find any — the only request ever made by a general officer, either of brigade or division, that the Forty-Second Regiment was not able to meet.

CHAPTER IX.

AT BAYOU GENTILLY — MAY.

AFTER hot weather fairly set in not much time was occupied in drill at Gentilly Camp. When the many details for regular camp and extra duty had been provided, there were few men left to go on drill. Most of the drills were by company, after Companies A and F had been detached. Previous to that time a battalion drill was in order every morning, after guard-mounting, either in command of the lieutenant-colonel or the major.

On the seventh General Sherman inspected the regiment in camp and the detachments at Batteries Gentilly and St. John. The number of men under inspection was not large, but they looked well and in good condition. The next day, eighth, to relieve the dull routine of camp life, Companies B and E, then remaining in camp, were marched along the Ponchartrain Railroad to Lakeport, there joined by men from Companies A and F, and an exhibition dress parade gone through with. After lying in the close camp at the bayou, this change, even for a short time, to the cool breezes of the lake shore, was very agreeable.

Orders were received at 9.15 A. M., May 9th, from division headquarters, for all men that could be mustered of the detached portions of the second division to immediately report, in heavy marching order, on Canal Street, in New Orleans, for review. The men were at once got under arms and marched into the city, arriving fifteen minutes too late to take part. One brigade (the Third) was absent on a reconoissance; only the First and Second Brigades were in line. They made a handsome appearance. The One Hundred and Sixty-Fifth New York Infantry (Second Duryea Zouaves), Lieutenant-Colonel Smith in command, carried off the honors for best condition in everything.

Various rumors were in circulation in the city about this review, some people insisting upon it that the army under General Banks had fallen back from the Teche campaign, and the troops under review were a part of that army. Others said that General Banks had met with a bad defeat, and the troops were under orders to reünforce him. Numerous citizens industriously asked questions of the men at every opportunity; but, to give credit where it is due, the news they received must have puzzled if it did not mislead them. The men got the hang very quickly of what they were after, and acted accordingly. If instructions had been issued to cover such an attempt of the enemy's spies to obtain information, they could not have been obeyed any better than was the case.

The true cause of such a hurried review of this division was soon apparent. General Sherman had received orders to report at Baton Rouge with two brigades. His three brigades, assigned to the Defences of New Orleans, were scattered along the various forts and entrances to the city, while the brigade not on review was distant some thirty miles on a reconnoissance; yet, in thirty-six hours after receipt of his orders, General Sherman had been rejoined by his Third Brigade, transferred some regiments of the Second to the First and Third, leaving the Second Brigade in the Defences, and was on his way, *via* the river, to Baton Rouge with two brigades to join General Augur in a demonstration against Port Hudson.

During the entire month men at Gentilly Camp and picket-stations on the lake were kept in a condition to move in twenty-four hours' notice, in obedience to an order issued by the division commander. This was supplemented on the twenty-eighth by a confidential circular issued, to keep a careful watch and supervision at each camp and post, in such a manner as not to attract attention or excite alarm. All officers and men were obliged to remain in camp ready for any duty. Nothing of importance transpired during this time to furnish a key to these instructions. Perfect order and quiet reigned within the limits of the Defences of New Orleans.

Some changes in the commanding officers took place: Colonel Cahill, Ninth Connecticut Infantry, assumed command of the brigade on the ninth, and General Emory assumed command of the Defences New Orleans on the nineteenth.

No changes took place in the stations occupied by the Forty-Second. Companies A and F remained on picket at the lake. By Department General Orders, No. 35, issued April 27th, registered enemies of the United States were ordered, peremptorily, to leave the Department on or before May 15th. Many of them were sent by the provost-marshal-general *via* the lake. This placed extra duty on the men of the Forty-Second stationed there, as all of their baggage had to be overhauled and inspected upon the wharf before leaving, and guards furnished to steamers transporting them to points across the lake and on the Gulf shore. Large numbers were taken to Madisonville, Manderville, Pass Christian, Biloxi, Mississippi City, Pascagoula, and to Mobile.

Many captures were made of small boats endeavoring to get across the lake with supplies for the enemy. The occupants in every case escaped, for Department General

Orders, No. 37, issued April 29th, announced that any person convicted before the commanding general of furnishing supplies to the enemy would suffer the penalty of death. In spite of this order attempts were constantly made, but the parties engaged in such acts lost no time in taking to the swamps when discovered at it.

The routine of guard and picket duty at this time is explained by the following letter to General Sherman:

"HEADQUARTERS 42D REGIMENT, MASS. VOLS.,
"CAMP FARR, BAYOU GENTILLY, LA., May 5th, 1863.

"*Sir,*— I have the honor to acknowledge the reception of your communication of the fourth instant. I would respectfully report the following facts concerning the guard duties at the mouth of Bayou St. John. Captain H. S. Coburn, of Company A, has under his command at that place: one sergeant, four corporals and thirty privates. He furnishes three sentinel-posts: one, a picket of three men at the extreme end of the bayou, who are relieved every twenty-four hours, one man being on duty all the time; the second post is at the quarters of the captain, and the third on the drawbridge across the bayou. These two posts are relieved every two hours by rotation of the men in the command. This manner of relieving the men at the last two posts is resorted to on account of the small command and to allow the men good rest between each tour of duty, for it often happens that six or ten men are called out in the night on extra duty, either to arrest some suspicious character or to watch for smugglers of contraband goods. One non-commissioned officer is detailed each day and has charge of the guard for the twenty-four hours, and his whole duty is to carefully observe all that is going on and to relieve the sentinels at proper hours. The reason of only five men appearing to be on duty at the time of the inspection was because the balance of the command was in line.

"In reference to the absence of the commanding officer at Bayou St. John, I have ascertained that he was away on Saturday afternoon at the lake-end of the bayou.

"Captain Coburn has frequently occasion to visit the office of the provost-marshal-general, and he had been away that day. It is found necessary to keep one commissioned officer at the mouth of the bayou all the time, for the purpose of examining passes, vessels, etc., going into and out of the bayou. Lieutenant Burrell has been in the habit of aiding Captain Coburn at times when he was in the city, and he was absent that day for this purpose, Captain Coburn having returned from General Bowen's office a short time previous to your visit.

"Lieutenant Burrell has at Battery St. John thirty men. In reference to the absence of ten of his men, he reports as follows: two were away at Camp Farr for rations; three were at the lake-end of the bayou for a few days on account of sickness, and the surgeon considered a change good for them; two were in the city for a few hours on a pass; the remaining three were absent for a short time preparing a boat for use, in duty at the bayou.

"In regard to the strength of the guards within my command and the posts, I would respectfully report as follows:

"I have in this camp two companies for duty, viz., B and E. The number of effective enlisted men by this day's report is one hundred and eighteen; commissioned officers, five. At this camp and from these companies I mount a daily guard, consisting of one commissioned officer, five non-commissioned officers and twenty-seven privates. This guard furnishes nine sentinel-posts. Five of these posts are a camp-guard, one at headquarters, one over the quartermaster's stores, one at the crossing of the Ponchartrain Railroad and the Gentilly road, and one picket-station on the railroad in the direction of the city.

"At Battery Gentilly, near this camp, I have a detachment of Company A, consisting of one commissioned officer, two sergeants, three corporals and twenty privates. This detachment mans the guns, and for a guard mounts each day one non-commissioned officer and six men, furnishing two sentinel-posts: one on the parapet over the guns, and one as a picket-guard on the railroad and to prevent people from passing within the lines of the fort.

"At Lakeport Company F is stationed, under command of Captain J. D. Cogswell. He has at the present time eighty effective men, including non-commissioned officers. For a guard he mounts daily twelve men, having four sentinel-posts: two of these posts are on the wharf, for the purpose of observing all that transpires within sight on the lake and to detain all boats and persons from leaving the wharf without a proper pass; the second is at the entrance to the wharf, to keep order in the day-time, and to keep all persons from the wharf after nine P.M.; the third post is a picket-post and is rather more than a mile from the village, on the shore of the lake, at the "White House," so called, for the purpose of observing all that transpires within sight of the lake, and to stop smugglers, etc.

"Besides these he sends a picket of six men and one sergeant to Bayou Cashon (eight miles distant), and these are relieved weekly. This picket is supplied with a small boat and sail, and can thus have communication with the commanding officer at any time.

"The schooner *Hortense* is sent to this picket-station every other day with fresh water and rations. In addition to the above sentinels and pickets, one corporal and four men are kept on the schooner *Hortense* at all times, ready for duty; also, two picket-boats have each a picked crew of one non-commissioned officer and two men, ready for duty at any time; at night they cruise back and forth (one on each side), from a point off the end of the wharf to points two miles from the wharf, for the purpose of intercepting smugglers of contraband goods.

"I believe the number of sentinels and location of all the posts in my command have now been stated, and I respectfully submit this report.

"I have neglected to state the number of sentinels at Battery St. John. At that place a daily guard of two privates and one non-commissioned officer is detailed. This guard is increased by one man every night. The first post is upon the bridge on the west side, the second upon the bridge on the east side of the fort; the extra man at night is placed on the parapet over the guns.

"I have the honor to remain,

"Respectfully, your obedient servant,

"J. STEDMAN, *Lieutenant-Colonel*,

"*commanding 42d Regt., Mass. Vols.*

"To CAPTAIN WICKHAM HOFFMAN, *A. A. General*,

"*Second Division, 19th Army Corps, New Orleans.*"

From the main camp at the bayou various details of men were made for all sorts of duty:

On the seventeenth — Company E proceeded to New Orleans and acted as a funeral escort to the remains of Captain Albert Coan, Company A, Twelfth Maine, who was buried from the St. James Hospital.

On the nineteenth — Sergeant Turner, Corporals Lowey and Turner, and seven privates of Company B, Corporal Lovly and five privates of Company E, in heavy marching order, relieved a guard of the One Hundred and Sixty-Fifth New York at the University Hospital, on Baronne Street, New Orleans; relieved in turn, on the twenty-seventh, by Sergeant Emerson, Corporal Southworth and six privates of Company E, and Corporals Fales, Wales, and six privates of Company B.

On the twenty-second — Two corporals and two privates from Company E, with four privates from Company B, were detailed for guard duty at the headquarters of General Emory, in the city.

The extra-duty detailed men were few:

May 13th — Corporal Henry Mellen, Company E, was made orderly at brigade headquarters, serving until relieved in July.

May 24th — Private Frank A. Smith, Company F, was made orderly at brigade headquarters, serving until relieved in July.

April 28th — Private Chauncey K. Bullock, Company D, was placed on duty as hostler at brigade headquarters until relieved May 19th.

Some men of the paroled camp, to vary the tedium of their life, began to trespass upon private property in the neighborhood. It was trivial in its nature, but, on complaint being made, orders were issued, April 1st, to stop such trespassing. This order not having the desired effect, a Board of Inquiry was held May 10th, at the paroled camp, to ascertain the basis of complaints that were made of destruction of fences and depredations upon property. The result was to locate the breach of orders on a few unprincipled paroled men, and to clearly establish that the greater number were behaving in a most praiseworthy manner.

On the seventeenth of June Privates Thomas F. Igo, Thomas P. Contillon and Thomas Dellanty, paroled men of Company I, were placed in arrest on a charge of disturbing persons and property near the camp; the only cases where discipline had to be enforced to stop it.

The bad feeling displayed by the Ninth Connecticut men at Lakeport towards Company F was renewed by men of that regiment detailed for provost-guard in New Orleans, towards men from the Forty-Second who were in the city on furlough. It culminated in a cowardly attack on Sergeant Waterman, Company D, and was the cause of another complaint being made on the twelfth of May, this time to the provost-marshal. The facts are set forth in the following letter:

"HEADQUARTERS FORTY-SECOND MASS. VOLS.,
"CAMP FARR, BAYOU GENTILLY, LA., May 12th, 1863.

"*Sir,*— I would respectfully bring to your notice and attention the manner in which one of the members of the provost-guard treated several enlisted men of this command after having demanded their passes, seen them, and pronounced them correct. The circumstances are as follows:

"Orderly-Sergeant Waterman, Sergeants Hewins and Sawyer, Corporal Merrill, and two privates of this regiment, paroled but unexchanged prisoners of war, were in New Orleans on Saturday, the ninth inst., for the purpose of witnessing the brigade review on that day, and, when coming down St. Charles Street, a soldier with a musket stopped them and demanded their passes; they were shown and pronounced correct. This man, representing himself as a member of the patrol, made some insulting remarks to Orderly-Sergeant Waterman and then seized him by the throat, whereupon the sergeant shook him off. The patrol then fixed his bayonet and charged upon Sergeant Waterman, striking him in the breast and inflicting a slight flesh wound, at the same time calling the sergeant 'a d—n son of a b—h'; at this point an officer came across the street and sent the whole party away. Up to the time of the officer making his appearance no other members of the patrol had been seen by any of the party alluded to, and the man who stopped them had no stripes or insignia of office on his clothing. The name of this patrol has since been ascertained to be Corporal James Gibbens, Company I, Ninth Connecticut Volunteers.

"The same day of the above occurrence Sergeant Waterman went up to the square to learn the name of the man who had assaulted him, and the lieutenant who commanded the guard that day refused to give it to him. After his interview with the lieutenant, this man, Gibbens, came along, and seizing Sergeant Waterman by the collar pushed him out of the square, at the same time calling him 'a nine-months' conscript son of a b—h,' also using much profane language. Other members of Gibbens' company stood looking on, advising him to kick the sergeant, break his head, etc. All this time Sergeant Waterman did not resist in any manner, or make any retaliatory reply.

"I believe that I can prove that said Gibbens has several times before this stopped soldiers in the street and demanded their passes, even when he had no arms and was entirely unaccompanied by any patrol or member of the provost-guard. Trusting that this matter may receive a rigid investigation,

"I have the honor to remain,

"Very respectfully, your obedient servant,

"J. STEDMAN, *Lieutenant-Colonel*,

"*commanding 42d Regt., Mass. Vols.*

"To MAJOR VON HERMAN,

"*commanding Provost-Guard, New Orleans.*"

The provost-marshal promised to look into the affair and report what was done about it. Nothing further was heard about the matter.

With warm weather rapidly setting in, the unacclimated officers and men of the Forty-Second began to swell the sick list. Assistant-Surgeon Hitchcock, in charge of the regimental hospital, had been ordered to Berwick Bay on special duty April 19th, where a large number of sick and convalescent men from the army operating in the Teche district were in hospitals. On his departure, Assistant-Surgeon Heintzelman assumed charge of the regimental hospital at Bayou Gentilly, with the following organization: Private Charles H. Warren, Company F, acting hospital-steward; Private Thomas M. Lewis, Company D, ward-master; Private James Mitchell, Company B, nurse; Private William F. Lacount, Company F, nurse; Private Edwin Rycroft, Company K, nurse; Private John W. Robinson, Company K, nurse; Private Hiram B. Douglass, Company K, nurse; Private William Harris, Jr., Company I, cook; Private Archibald McDollen, Company E, cook. The arrangements of the hospital under Surgeon Heintzelman were excellent. He won the good opinion of all the men, with the exception of those who failed to play their points upon him by playing sick. His experience and knowledge promptly detected all such cases at surgeon's call in the morning; the men being promptly returned back to their companies as fit for duty. These qualities in any officer never fails to command the good will, respect and confidence of the majority of men over whom he has control, for they feel that no shirks can cause extra duty to fall on other shoulders, because they cannot successfully evade it.

Lieutenant-Colonel Stedman and Major Stiles were on the sick list; the major in May and through June. Lieutenant Harding recovered and went to Port Hudson, May 25th, to join his company.

At the close of May there was present for duty, under orders of the lieutenant-colonel, seventeen officers and three hundred and fifty-seven men. Sick in regimental hospital, twenty-five men; and in quarters, ten men. The average sick per day for the month had been: taken sick, four; returned to duty, four; sick in hospital, twenty-four; sick in quarters, thirteen. On the seventeenth there were fifteen men of Company K in hospital, and on the twenty-third seventeen men of that company; nine of them were returned to duty on the twenty-sixth. About all sickness this month was among the men on duty. The paroled prisoners were in good health. Only one man of Company D was in hospital May 31st. Companies G and I did not have a case.

One death occurred. Private John H. Cary, Company G, May 6th, from delirium tremens, and he was buried near the camp. The case of Private Cary was the result of hard drinking. His body was found, badly decomposed, in the swamp by the roadside, not far from camp, on the thirteenth of May. Cary had been a hard drinker ever since his return from Texas, and shown such symptoms of delirium as to cause a watch to be kept on him. On the evening of the sixth he managed to get out of his tent without attracting the attention of any one, and immediately, it would seem, took to the swamp in the place where found, and there died. He was missed soon after disappearing, and for a week diligent search was made to find him. An impure odor, caused by decomposition of the body, attracted the attention of some members of the regiment passing by upon the road; they searched the swamp and found him. He was sitting at the foot of a tree, grasping with both hands the roots, with his legs immersed in mud almost to the knees. Thick bushes bordering on the swamp edge, by the roadside, screened him from being seen and prevented an earlier discovery. Cary was put in a box by the help of an old colored man, called John, who chopped wood in the camp. No one else could be induced to touch the body; but old John said: "I not afraid of a 'Yankee' soger, sah! No sah, dead or alive, sah!" The remains were buried the same day with appropriate ceremonies.

This negro, John, was a camp follower from the time the regiment went into camp at Gentilly until it embarked for the North. He was formerly a slave, and lived a long distance from camp, but was always on hand at reveille, remaining until Peas on a Trencher, doing all the hard work of camp, splitting wood, getting water, etc., etc., and would work steady in the hottest sun, with perspiration coming from the pores of his skin like water. He worked for small pay; for a small sum of money sang the old religious hymns the negroes in that locality sang at their prayer meetings, danced as plantation darkies can dance, and was the jolliest old negro there was in camp. Old John's wife did a large amount of washing for the boys, which brought additional picayunes to his wallet, and, although he made a few bad debts — some of the unprincipled men taking advantage of his ignorance to cheat him — on the whole, John made a good living from his labor for the Forty-Second. His boy was also a hanger-on at camp, but could not be made to do much work. This boy was a great imitator, and would watch attentively the drummers at practice, and soon became able to handle a drum with skill.

CHAPTER X.

BAYOU GENTILLY — JUNE — FAREWELL TO GENTILLY CAMP — IN NEW ORLEANS.

THE month of May passed rapidly without the occurrence of any event of importance to the regiment. With the commencement of June affairs in the Department began to assume such a shape as to lead officers of the Forty-Second to think the regiment was to get some service.

Affairs at Port Hudson reached a stage when reënforcements were needed to maintain the effective strength of the army, and to continue the siege. Troops from Brashear City and Ship Island were ordered to Port Hudson, and from Key West and Pensacola to New Orleans, while the small garrison in the Defences of New Orleans had to be ready for instant service at all hours. It was evident to all hands the regiment was about to be concentrated, as far as possible, to be able to meet any emergency, and soon was it verified.

The detachment at Battery St. John, about sixty men of Company A, was relieved by a detachment Fifteenth Massachusetts Battery, and returned to the regiment June 1st. On the third the detachment under Lieutenant Martin Burrell, Jr., at Battery Gentilly, about twenty men, was also relieved by a detachment Fifteenth Massachusetts Battery, and returned to the regiment. On the sixth Companies C and H marched into camp with about one hundred and forty men, from Camp Parapet, having been relieved from engnieer service. With the exception of a detachment Company A, about forty men, at Lake-end Bayou St. John, Company F at Lakeport, and Company K at Port Hudson, the regiment was again united.

Upon receipt of orders from brigade headquarters to draw as many men as possible from the post at Lakeport, in case the regiment was ordered to move, leaving only a small picket-guard upon the Lake shore and a camp-guard to look after regimental property and the hospital at Gentilly, drills were immediately resumed to an extent allowed by hot weather, and inspections made to see if every man was in proper condition for duty. All parades of ceremony, drill and guard-mounting had to be made before eight o'clock A. M. or after six o'clock P. M. The sentinels had to have sun shelters erected, or were posted in the shade so far as practicable.

The exact state of affairs was not generally known. A majority of the men refused to believe that any danger existed, or that the regiment would do any field duty, arguing that concentration meant the regiment was to proceed home promptly on the expiration of its time of enlistment, June 25th, as they claimed. This was not so, and could not be.

At this time the entire Second Brigade, Second Division, Nineteenth Corps, composed of two New York batteries, three Massachusetts batteries, not equipped, one squadron cavalry, the Twenty-Sixth, Forty-Second and Forty-Seventh Massachusetts Infantry, Ninth Connecticut Infantry, a detachment One Hundred and Seventy-Fifth New York Infantry and Twenty-Eighth Maine Infantry, with some smaller detachments of troops, composed the garrison in New Orleans and its defences, who were under standing orders to be ready to move immediately with one hundred rounds of ammunition to each infantry-man.

On the ninth, after a mixed detachment of one hundred

men under Captain Cook had left camp for Brashear City, everybody woke up and began to think there was music in the air, causing them to feel anxious for something to come next. Their anxiety was increased when Captain Cook and Lieutenant Clifford reported at the regimental hospital on sick leave, and told what a hole the detachment was in.

The case of Captain Cook was singular. Other than a thick-coated tongue, the captain did not show any signs or symptoms of illness. He did not go into the hospital, but lived in his company tent, ate heartily, and acted in every way like a well man. Surgeon Heintzelman said, as his private opinion, that the case was one of fright. It is true that Captain Cook did not do any more duty during the regiment's term of service, but remained on the sick list.

Two men were noticed lurking around camp on the nineteenth, and were recognized by some of the paroled men as Texans from the Confederate army. They were arrested, and claimed to have left the service and had taken the oath of allegiance. As General Emory had issued orders on the fourteenth to arrest and send to him any person found lurking around the forts or intrenched positions, they were sent to his headquarters for examination. What became of them is not known.

Positive information having been received that the enemy was raiding on the west bank of the river and threatened to cut communication with Brashear City, on the nineteenth all troops of the Second Brigade were again ordered to have two days cooked rations on hand, and be in readiness to move any moment, and Colonel Cahill was ordered to concentrate the brigade as much as possible. All officers and men, of all arms, whether on detached service, provost duty, or other duty, were under orders to hold themselves ready to move, with cooked rations and one hundred rounds each man. All outlying companies were to be ready to move into the city at a moment's notice, except the guard over prisoners at Algiers and the troops at Pass Manchac. All leaves of absence were absolutely stopped, and every officer and man obliged to remain at their quarters.

By the sudden departure of all available troops at New Orleans to reënforce Colonel Stickney at La-Fourche Crossing, orders were received at noon on the twenty-first, at the Forty-Second camp, to immediately report in Lafayette Square to General Emory, in heavy marching order. The picket-posts at Lakeport and Bayou St. John were also ordered to be weakened, that as many men as possible should join the regiment. At two P.M., having packed baggage and struck camp, leaving behind the surplus baggage, a hospital-guard and the paroled men of Companies D, G and I, the regiment proceeded by rail to the city, with a total effective strength of about two hundred men.

On first receipt of marching orders a general impression prevailed in the ranks that they were *en-route* for Port Hudson. The prospect of active field duty was hailed by every one with feelings of lively satisfaction. After lying inactive in camp for nearly the whole term of enlistment everybody thought the regiment was to see a little service before going home, and perhaps taste powder in a different way than by biting cartridges when loading for guard duty. These feelings were dispelled on arriving at Lafayette Square, where the regiment was ordered to take possession of the Ninth Connecticut Infantry camp and to do provost duty in the city; a few days after joined by a detachment Twenty-Eighth Maine Infantry, from Camp Parapet.

All convalescent men and stragglers in the city capable of bearing arms were collected together and made ready for duty in case of necessity. Private instructions were given Lieutenant-Colonel Stedman, by General Emory, to have every available man in quarters ready for any emergency at a moment's notice. The regiment was kept so, for there could not have been over five hundred soldiers in the city from the twenty-first to the twenty-sixth.

The city was remarkably quiet at this time. Movements of the troops were made so quietly the citizens were not aware of what was going on. There was no indication among the populace that the enemy were near, or expected to get near. Some of them must have been aware of it, but gave no outward sign.

When the enemy ceased to seriously menace New Orleans, on the twenty-sixth, most of the troops at Boutee Station, on the Opelousas Railroad, returned to the city, including a part of the detachment Forty-Second, in command of Lieutenant Tinkham, and the Ninth Connecticut Volunteers. They brought with them a small number of Texan prisoners, who looked more like Mexicans than Americans. They looked clean, were well clothed in loose-fitting trousers and jackets of gray cloth, with large, slouchy-looking, gray felt hats. Their blankets, carried slung over the shoulder, were of the best quality, in fact, better than those in use by men of the Forty-Second. The complexion of these prisoners was quite dark, and they had a savage look in their faces.

Some slight disturbances, soon quieted, occurred between men of the Ninth Connecticut and Forty-Second Massachusetts, growing out of disputes as to who should occupy the tents in Lafayette Square. On this occasion the Ninth Connecticut again behaved in a disgraceful manner, more like rowdies and bullies than soldiers, and it appeared as though the line officers had no control over their men.

The Forty-Second marched back to its old camp-ground

at Bayou Gentilly, five miles in a hot sun, on the afternoon of June 27th. Camp was put in order and arrangements made for a long stay, the picket-post detachments rejoined their stations, when, the next morning, twenty-eighth, orders were received, by a mounted orderly, to report at once in the city at the Custom House and occupy quarters vacated by the Twenty-Sixth Massachusetts Infantry. The entire regiment, with the exception of small detachments left on picket-stations, arrived at the Custom House during the afternoon.

This was a final farewell to Bayou Gentilly. The duty detachments left behind on this second breaking up of this camp were: two sergeants, four corporals and thirteen men of Company A, under Captain Coburn (who was not in condition for field duty), on picket at Bayou St. John; four sergeants, three corporals and thirty-four men of Company F on picket at Lakeport; Private Rufus C. Greene, Company G, placed on detached service June 25th, in command of picket-schooner *Hortense;* a hospital-guard of one sergeant, two corporals, and eighteen men of Company A. These picket-posts, the Gentilly Camp and paroled men were under command of Major Stiles, then not well and unfit for active duty. There were fifty-eight men under the surgeon's care June 28th; twelve were returned to duty, and there was left, when the regiment moved, twenty-six men sick in hospital and twenty men sick in quarters.

The accommodations for troops at the Custom House were not good, and it seems a pity and a shame men were obliged to occupy such dark, damp and feverish quarters for any length of time. No surgeon could sanction the quartering of troops in the manner they were placed at this Custom House, except under the most pressing circumstances. The men were distributed in quarters, the guard of the Twenty-Sixth Massachusetts relieved, and by sunset the Forty-Second was in full possession of the New Orleans Custom House, with regimental headquarters established in a room formerly occupied by Major-General Butler. A few officers, who did not like their quarters, provided for themselves elsewhere in the neighborhood. This could not be tolerated at the time, owing to the peculiar position of affairs; General Emory insisted on all officers quartering with their men.

At midnight, on the twenty-ninth, the long-roll called the regiment to arms, and crossing Algiers Ferry to Algiers, a reconnoissance was made for some miles to find the enemy's cavalry, reported to be on the river road below that town. None were found, or any traces of them, and at eight o'clock A.M. next day the regiment was back in quarters again. On this occasion Company C was thrown out in skirmishing order to move down the road and over fields that bordered on a woody swamp, and here they first discovered those watermelon patches which they afterwards despoiled of the luscious fruit. That night march, who can forget it? Awakened from a sound sleep, clothes and equipments put on quick, ferried across to Algiers, and then marched down a lonely road for several miles on a hunt for an imaginary foe. Lucky was the man who wore his overcoat, for the air was damp and chilly, though it was in June. Every sentry on guard at storehouses along the river front of Algiers was dressed in his greatcoat; experience had taught them to fear the treacherous midnight air.

An effort was made by General Banks to reënlist men from the nine months' troops for one, two, or three years, at their option. For some reason it was not successful. From the Forty-Second the only man who reënlisted was Musician Bernard McKenna, Company C, who was discharged May 25th to reünlist as a bugler in the Twenty-Sixth New York Battery. The same date, Lewis Eddy, drummer in Company D, was discharged by Department orders, and returned home.

In connection with this reënlistment attempt, more men from the Forty-Second would have done so but were unable, on account of disqualifications or irregularity on the part of recruiting officers. Privates Diomede Roseline, Company G, Luigi Briana, Company D, and John Brown, Company G, offered to enlist in a battalion called the First Louisiana Sharpshooters. Roseline and Brown were under parole and could not do so until duly exchanged, and Briana was not a member of the regiment. Somebody had given an *alias* to Captain Salla, commanding the First Louisiana; who it was could not be ascertained. Privates Charles Slattery and George Ward, Company C, were claimed by Lieutenant Whitaker, Second Rhode Island Cavalry, as having reënlisted in that regiment, but they changed their minds before they could be mustered in.

At the close of June there was present for duty in New Orleans, twelve officers and three hundred and eighty-two men. Sick in hospital and quarters, five officers and forty-six men. Twenty-nine of the men were in the regimental hospital at Bayou Gentilly. The officers sick and not on duty were: Adjutant Davis, Captain Cook, Company B, Captain Emerson, Company E, and Lieutenant Tinkham, Company B. Adjutant Davis was absent from June 25th to July 9th; Lieutenant Powers, who was relieved from charge of the paroled camp by Major Stiles, acted as adjutant during that time.

The average sick per day for the month had been: taken sick, five; returned to duty, four; sick in hospital, twenty-one; sick in quarters, thirteen.

The extra-duty details for June were:

June 8th — Sergeant T. M. Turner, Company B, and Sergeant George Bell, Company C, as color-bearers.

June 8th — Privates Everett A. Denny, Company E, and John A. Paige, Company B, as clerks at headquarters Defences of New Orleans. Private Paige returned to his company for duty June 26th.

June 14th — Corporal Alfred Thayer was made chief-wagoner, *vice* Wagoner John Willy, Company B, ordered to his company. Private George A. Davis, Company D, on duty in Company E, was made wagoner. Private Warren A. Clark, Company B, was made wagoner.

The deaths in June were:

June 5th — Private Nelson Wright, Company E, typhoid fever.

June 13th — Private Buckley Waters, Company E, chronic diarrhœa.

June 19th — Private Lewis E. Wales, Company B. typhoid fever.

June 30th — Private Benjamin Gould, Company G, congestion of the brain.

The case of Private Waters was not considered fatal up to the time of his death. The surgeons were inclined to think he was suffering more from home-sickness than disease. He died quietly in the evening, as the glee club, composed of Sergeant Hunt, Company I, Sergeant Waterman, Company D, Quartermaster Burrell, and Lieutenant Powers, Company F, were singing an appropriate song in the headquarters office, adjoining the hospital ward. They did not know that Waters was dying, and when the nurse asked some one in the ward to stop it Waters requested them not to do so, as he preferred to listen to the song.

Notwithstanding the general orders issued April 24th by General Sherman, to prevent sending North bodies of deceased persons until after decomposition had ceased, in order to prevent any quarantine to Government vessels, the bodies of Privates Nelson Wright and Lewis E. Wales were prepared and partially embalmed by the regimental surgeons for transportation home.

The operation was performed in the rear of the hospital, a guard being posted to prevent men from coming near who had curiosity to witness it. The skin upon the chest was first cut, and after removing a small bone in the upper part was laid back upon each side a sufficient distance for work. Interior parts of the chest were then taken out and examined, followed by removing the bowels; the vacant space thus left was filled with charcoal, the skin replaced and sewed together. The body was then packed in liquor, with the heart separate, and was ready to be sent home. The parts of bodies removed were properly buried. This process is similar to that of dressing cattle for market.

Private Wright, according to the surgeons' testimony who examined his lungs, could not have lived much more than a year longer, as they were diseased.

Of those men who were curious to witness these operations, some would stand, eyes wide open, with no evidence of any feeling more than of wonder that the surgeons could handle their knives with so much composure; others would evince so much interest and desire to get near, in order to learn such secrets of the human system as they could, that they troubled the guards; while others had a look of sorrow on their countenances, and after a short stay would saunter slowly away in deep thought. No man knew whether he would or not be treated in the same manner in case he sickened and died.

Bodies sent home were invariably escorted a certain distance from camp by the regular Guard of Honor detail, according to the rank held by the deceased, with arms reversed, followed by the regiment with side arms, as mourners, the band playing a' dirge. On arrival at the prescribed distance three volleys were fired over the remains, when the regiment marched back to camp, while the body was carried to New Orleans in an ambulance, attended by a few members of the company to which the deceased belonged, and put aboard some steamer for New York. In all such cases burial service was held in front of the hospital, in presence of the regiment.

The dead that were buried near camp were escorted to the grave, and burial service held there. After the service all passed around the coffin to take a last look of the remains before committal to the earth. Burials were solemn occasions, and it was plain to see such scenes were not without some influence on the men. He must be a hardened man who can gaze upon the remains of a departed comrade, perhaps a few weeks and sometimes only days before as full of life and hope as himself, but now cold, rigid and at rest, without some mysterious sensation creeping over him. The chances were that any one was as likely in a short time to be an inhabitant of the same ground as the one just buried.

All coffins were made of pine board, painted a dark brown color, filled with shavings on which to rest the body. They were very good for the kind, and answered the purpose for which they were intended. Each grave was marked with a head-board, on which was inscribed the name of deceased, rank, company, regiment, age, and time of death.

Privates John H. Cary, Benjamin Gould, and Sergeant Philip P. Hackett, of Company G, Private Buckley Waters, Company E, Private Rufus G. Hildreth, Company C, and Private Thomas J. Clements, Company H, were buried at

Bayou Gentilly. Their graves were situated near three large oak trees, between them and the swamp, at the end of the Gentilly race-course, looking towards it from the Ponchartrain Railroad. Some three or four soldiers of a native guard regiment (Union colored troops) were also buried at the same spot.

Chaplain Sanger officiated at these burial services. His remarks were generally to the point and well delivered. A brief resume of the deceased soldier's life, as far as known, was usually given, and a prayer offered for his relations. The chaplain always attended to notifying relations of their loss, forwarding the personal effects, any rings or valuables, together with locks of hair taken from the person before burial. This duty was done well and conscientiously. It is not pleasant, however, to record that Chaplain Sanger was not popular with the command. A feeling was first manifested by the Galveston prisoners, and by them communicated to the rest of the regiment. The only reason for this, so far as could be ascertained, was that they did not like his behavior when the prisoners were marched from Texas to the Union lines. They accused him of neglect to their sick and suffering when he should have at least tried to do something for them; of currying favor with the Confederate officers in such a manner to lead them to suppose he was deficient in manly bearing.

On this march Chaplain Sanger was sick with diarrhœa, and remained so for some time after reaching regimental headquarters, a fact sufficient to account for any lack of energy he did display. He always spoke well of the men, was anxious to do for their good and to gain their esteem. That he did not do so was a misfortune for both. Many regarded the chaplain as ranking among some of the best that left Massachusetts. Except a rather quick temper, his personal behavior was in keeping with his profession.

Private William F. Lacount, Company F, a hospital nurse, acted as chaplain on Sundays from the time the regiment arrived in Louisiana, in December, until Chaplain Sanger returned with the paroled men, afterwards conducting divine service on the Sabbath at the paroled camp; the chaplain officiating at the regimental camp. It was thought proper to have these separate services on account of the feeling prevalent. Private Lacount deserves much credit, more than he received, for the able and intelligent manner in which he performed these volunteer duties. He displayed a true Christian spirit and was satisfied in doing good.

CHAPTER XI.

BRASHEAR CITY.

ON ACTIVE SERVICE — ACTION OF JUNE TWENTY-THIRD — CAPTURED — PAROLED AND RETURNED TO ALGIERS.

COLONEL CAHILL, Ninth Connecticut Infantry, commanding Second Brigade, Second Division, Nineteenth Army Corps, issued, June 9th, 1863, Special Orders No. 97, for Lieutenant-Colonel Stedman to have Company B, with details from other companies sufficient to make the full strength three officers and one hundred men, with one day's cooked rations in the haversacks and at least forty rounds of ammunition to each man, proceed at once to Algiers and report to Captain Schenck, ordnance officer at the New Orleans, Opelousas and Great Western Railroad depot, for transportation to Brashear City, and there report to Lieutenant-Colonel Stickney, Forty-Seventh Massachusetts Infantry, commanding the post.

Regimental Special Orders No. 107 were immediately issued, detailing Sergeant Charles L. Truchon, Corporal Francis N. Luce and eighteen privates of Company E, Corporals Charles M. Marden, —— Smith and twenty-three privates of Company H, Corporal John F. Cushing and eleven privates of Company A, to report to Captain Cook, commanding Company B. The lieutenants who accompanied the detachment were First-Lieutenant Benjamin C. Tinkham and Second-Lieutenant Joseph C. Clifford, both of Company B.

In heavy marching order this detachment left Gentilly Camp about half-past two o'clock the same afternoon orders were issued, and took the train for New Orleans, proceeding at once to Algiers, where a train made up of box and platform cars carried the men to Brashear City. They started about five o'clock and arrived about midnight, after a tiresome ride of eighty miles. In passing through New Orleans to the Algiers Ferry suspicious actions of two privates in the detachment were noticed, and Sergeant T. M. Turner, Company B, was ordered to keep in the rear and watch them, to prevent their desertion, an object they evidently had in view.

When General Banks made his first campaign through the Teche country towards Red River, in April and May, 1863, a garrison was left at Brashear City, and Berwick on the opposite side of the Atchafalaya River; Colonel Walker, Fourth Massachusetts Infantry, in command of the post, with his own regiment, and the Sixteenth New Hampshire Infantry forming a part of the garrison. The post was a base of supplies for the army in the field, and contained general hospitals to relieve the field hospitals of sick and wounded men, who are always sent to the rear as fast as possible. Naturally, a large amount of army material would accumulate at such a post.

From Algiers to La-Fourche the posts upon the railroad line were occupied by the Twenty-Third Connecticut Infantry, and the posts from Terrebonne to Brashear were in charge of the One Hundred and Seventy-Sixth New York Infantry.

All was quiet at these various posts until the latter part of May, the detachments on duty having what soldiers call "a soft thing." On the twenty-first of May Colonel Chickering, commanding Forty-First Massachusetts Infantry, and other troops, convoying an immense train of six hundred wagons, three thousand horses and mules, one thousand five hundred head of cattle, with six thousand negro camp followers, who expected to locate on Government plantations in La-Fourche and adjoining parishes, left Barre's Landing at daybreak on the march for Berwick, where he arrived May 26th, closely followed by the Confederate forces operating under the command of Major-General "Dick" Taylor. By the thirtieth all of this force under Colonel Chickering had proceeded to Port Hudson, including the Fourth Massachusetts and Sixteenth New Hampshire Regiments. On June 1st Colonel Holmes, Twenty-Third Connecticut, assumed command of Brashear City, with portions of his own regiment and that of the One Hundred and Seventy-Sixth New York in occupancy of the post.

In a few days Colonel Holmes was taken sick, and, as Colonel Nott, One Hundred and Seventy-Sixth New York, was also sick, the command fell to Lieutenant-Colonel ———, Twenty-Third Connecticut. He, frightened by the situation of affairs and deficient in nerve, was relieved by General Emory, who sent Lieutenant-Colonel Stickney from New Orleans to take command. Stickney was on detached service from his regiment, having been made inspector-general of the Defences of New Orleans June 6th, with orders to commence a thorough inspection of convalescent and other camps.

The troops on duty in Brashear under Stickney comprised detachments from the One Hundred and Seventy-Sixth New York, Twenty-Third Connecticut and Forty-Second Massachusetts Infantry, Twenty-First Indiana Artillery, one company of the Corps de' Afrique (colored troops), and various cavalry squads, in all about six hundred effective men. Adjutant Whiting, Twenty-Third Connecticut, was post-adjutant; Quartermaster Kimball, One Hundred and Seventy-Sixth New York, post-quartermaster; Lieutenant Kinsley, Forty-Seventh Massachusetts, was serving as an aide-de-camp.

The post hospital contained many sick and wounded soldiers, who were removed to New Orleans when able to undergo the journey. At one time near one thousand convalescent soldiers, capable of bearing arms in an emergency, were in camp at Brashear. A large amount of baggage, commissary, quartermaster and medical stores, cannon, arms and ammunition was stored in various buildings and places. Part of the baggage and stores was removed to Algiers previous to June 21st.

Passing the night of their arrival in bivouac about the depot, next day the detachment was ordered by Stickney to quarter in the depot building, and do picket duty upon the railroad line and guard a water tank used by locomotives of the road. Excursions across the river to Berwick were in order almost every day, to drive out cavalry scouts of the enemy and obtain cattle. The enemy always returned when the way was clear for them to do so, and an exchange of shots across the river was of frequent occurrence. The weather was extremely hot. There was some movement made by the troops each day, with guard, patrol and picket duty to be done at night. Mosquitos were thick and blood-thirsty enough to cause refreshing sleep to be an impossibility. With difficulty could food be obtained to serve out with any semblance of regularity. Food was plenty, but there was no system in delivering rations. The men were gradually becoming worn out.

The time and energy of all troops at the post was frittered away in this manner without any good accruing from it; instead of devoting the same time and labor to what was absolutely needed, *i. e.*, to prepare defences for use in case of emergency, with plenty of idle convalescent men at hand capable of rendering assistance, besides a large number of negroes whose labor could be utilized. No intelligent attempt was made to organize the convalescent men for service, or to render efficient a number of field-guns that were in Brashear, posted on the river front.

The enemy was active in an annoying sort of way across the river, on the Berwick side, after it had been abandoned by troops of the garrison, and on the line of the Atchafalaya River. Danger of an attack existed from the first day of June.* The officers of the Forty-Second detachment soon learned from various sources that the situation was rather ticklish. Even privates came into possession of information, from the many negroes in and around Brashear, that the enemy was up to mischief, and trying to get in between Brashear and New Orleans, upon the line of railroad.

Lieutenant-Colonel Stickney was not a man calculated to inspire confidence as to his military abilities. He had a habit of riding around, often alone, to give verbal orders for all sorts of petty things, and to find fault with trifles. As to perfecting the organization of what troops he had, or establishing any system out of the chaos that existed, there seems to be but one verdict from those on duty under him. He did nothing. No one knew what the position of other bodies of troops would be in case of an attack; no one knew what was expected or required to be done in case the enemy appeared. No one knew where to expect support in case of need, or to whom or how to render such support if wanted. Lieutenant Tinkham reports that there did not seem to be a head to anything.

* The official report of General Banks mentions the fact that the officials at Brashear City were fully warned of danger, by orders, and the disaster was due to the carelessness and disobedience of subordinates. General Emory sent word by a steamer (after the telegraph line was severed) to hold out to the last. The place was captured before this steamer could arrive.

First-Sergeant Ballou reports that most of his time was occupied in finding food for the detachment, and that it appeared to him as though the Forty-Second were visitors who had remained too long, but did not leave because there was no one to tell them to go. The testimony of all the observing men is of a like nature.

All the various detachments on duty had no knowledge of each other, were acting without concert, had never before co-operated, were entirely destitute of *esprit de corps*, while a half-regiment on duty would have had all of these essentials, so requisite to a body of men expected to defend an important post in daily danger of an attack. It would be safe to say, not in a boastful spirit, had the four or six companies of the Forty-Second Regiment, in camp at Bayou Gentilly and at the posts on Lake Ponchartrain, been at Brashear, that place would not have been lost without a fight of some duration. Under their own officers, the companies well acquainted with each other and of excellent material, cohesion and confidence would have existed, that made a gallant stand not only possible but almost certain. When Sir John Moore organized and disciplined the British army at Shorncliffe, it was on the basis of the regimental system. The object of this system was to make each regiment a living unit, by making officers and men thoroughly acquainted with each other. This engenders a feeling of close comradeship which is exemplified even now in the many regimental reunions that annually take place, where old times are revived and talked over without regard to present station in life.

The Forty-Second Regiment, since the days of Readville Camp, had shown on several occasions this feeling of comradeship. The men knew their officers (some of those officers better than they knew themselves), and with the companies at Gentilly Bayou were officers who had only to say what they wanted done, when the men would have done it without hesitation or fear.

Under the circumstances, as they existed, the congregation of troops at Brashear could not be expected to have done any better than they did.

June 14th Captain Cook obtained sick leave, and returned to the regiment at Bayou Gentilly. The men said, "his boots hurt him." This hit can be appreciated by those who remember the elaborate high-top boots the captain was wont to wear. June 18th Lieutenant Clifford and a few enlisted men did the same thing. Lieutenant Clifford suggested to Lieutenant Tinkham how easily he could obtain sick leave also, if he desired; but Tinkham refused to entertain such an idea, preferring to stand by his men, and remained, the only commissioned officer with the detachment. The same day Clifford left, Sergeant Albert L. Clark, Company B, then at Gentilly, was ordered to his company at Brashear. In view of what subsequently happened, it seems a pity that two officers from the regiment of sound judgment and undoubted courage were not ordered to Brashear also.

The most extended scout in which any part of the detachment participated was on June 17th, when the steamer *Kepper* and gunboat *Hollyhock*, three guns, which had arrived on the sixteenth, carried a company One Hundred and Seventy-Sixth New York, a few cavalry, and a detachment Forty-Second Massachusetts, under Lieutenant Clifford, the entire force in command of a captain, One Hundred Seventy-Sixth New York, for a trip up the Bayou Teche to Pattersonville, on a foraging expedition. This expedition started at four o'clock in the morning. On landing, a skirmish line was formed and marched inland from the bayou. The line was then swung around in half-circle form, driving in all live stock that was found, aggregating some one hundred head of horses, mules, and cattle of all kinds. The day was, as usual, extremely hot, and when they arrived on the bayou the cattle were allowed a rest previous to attempting to make them take the water and be swum across. When a large bull had been caught, and by aid of boat and rope pulled into the water, with an encouraging prospect that the rest would follow, word was given by a lookout on the *Hollyhock*, " the enemy's cavalry are coming!" The usual exaggerated stories were afloat at once. The report gained credence that their force was five thousand strong. A cool head would have known better. As a matter of fact the enemy was not over one hundred strong, probably nearer fifty men, while the Federals numbered about one hundred and fifty men.

Ordered to cease work, the troops hastened on board the *Kepper*, leaving the cattle to roam back to their homes and be picked up by the planters, who had followed the troops, protesting against taking their stock, for they were good Union men; at the same time they undoubtedly conveyed word to the enemy of what was going on. On arrival at Brashear, about five o'clock in the afternoon, it was found that quite a number of men were missing. The *Kepper* took aboard two guns, as an addition to her small armament, and volunteers were called for, to go back as a guard and assist in finding the stragglers. Tired and hungry as they were, without food all day (rations had not been carried in haversacks), volunteers were numerous. Going back a few miles, an exchange of shots with the enemy's cavalry took place. The infantry upon the *Kepper* fired away most of their ammunition without doing any execution, because the Confederate cavalry kept at a respectful distance. A hail from the right bank of the river disclosed all of the stragglers, about twenty and mostly New York men, who were taken on board.

On the way back to Brashear a sad accident happened to a private of the New York company, who was leaning upon his rifle, when it was by some accident discharged; the ball entered his head, causing instant death. There were no other casualties during the day, unless what happened to Corporal Lowery, of Company B, can be so called. The corporal was out with a forage party when they came to a high board fence, and instead of lending a hand to break it down he chose to jump over at a place that was rather low, to land on the other side in a bee-hive. The bees stung him badly before he could get away from them. It was sport for lookers-on, but no fun for the corporal.

On the morning of the twentieth, shortly after midnight, Sergeant Ballou with twenty men was sent upon the gunboat *Hollyhock* to assist in obtaining and removing three heavy cannon that were in battery upon an island in the river, some few miles below Brashear City, where an earthwork had been constructed named Fort Chene, garrisoned by a detachment of the Twenty-First Indiana Artillery, under Lieutenant Sherfy, and one company, about thirty men, of the One Hundred and Seventy-Sixth New York, under Lieutenant Kerby. It was understood that, by orders of Lieutenant-Colonel Stickney, the fort was to be evacuated and destroyed, and the garrison, with the cannon, was to proceed to Bayou Bœuff.

Lieutenant Tinkham, with all the business on his hands that one man would care to undertake, had not been able to obtain any sleep for many hours, and had just lain down to take some needed rest, immediately after the detail of men for the gunboat had started, when a train of cars was run into the depot. Thinking it strange, with his curiosity aroused to learn what was taking place, caused him to remain wide awake while the rest of his men slumbered. Very soon after detachments of the One Hundred and Seventy-Sixth New York and Twenty-Third Connecticut Infantry, without music, quietly filed into the depot in light marching order. Still watching what was going on, Stickney approached and wanted to know why the men of the Forty-Second were not ready to board the train. No orders had been received to that effect from any source, and so Tinkham informed him. Stickney disputed this, and curtly gave the detachment a limited number of minutes to get ready. The time was extremely short, and without rations the lieutenant with about fifty men, all there was with him at the time, took the train and left Brashear City for La-Fourche. Orders were left with the sentries on duty for Sergeant Ballou to follow as soon as possible with the balance of the detachment. General Emory had telegraphed from New Orleans for Lieutenant-Colonel Stickney, with all of his available force, to proceed to La-Fourche, as the enemy might attempt to sever communications.

The departure of Lieutenant-Colonel Stickney left Major Anthony, Second Rhode Island Cavalry, in command of the post. It seems that Lieutenant Colonel Stickney, for some trivial matter, had placed Lieutenant-Colonel Duganne, commanding One Hundred and Seventy-Sixth New York, under arrest on the sixteenth, but had released him from arrest on the evening of the eighteenth, with an understanding that Duganne would report for duty in a few days, that officer pleading illness as a reason for not returning to duty immediately. Abruptly ordered away at midnight, before Duganne was on duty, caused Stickney to place the post in command of Major Anthony, the next senior officer fit for duty in Brashear. This should not have prevented Duganne, by virtue of his senior rank, assuming command the next day, twentieth, when he returned to duty. Lieutenant-Colonel Duganne was in command of troops in the garrison; Major Anthony was not. Even if Duganne had done so, that any prompt measures for defence, backed up by pluck and determination, would have been attempted is very doubtful. The defence of Bayou Bœuff by this officer answers the doubt.

Major Anthony did not possess the qualities to make a successful soldier. There were line officers in the One Hundred and Seventy-Sixth New York, on duty under him, more competent to assume command. A good idea of the kind of soldier Major Anthony was is afforded by an incident that occurred on a scout made on the Berwick side. Some of the Forty-Second detachment on this scout, under Captain Cook, inclined to have some fun out of it, on the sly would dig the pigs in their vicinity, that were running around loose, with the points of their bayonets, causing them to give an occasional squeal. To this amusement the major took exceptions, and because Captain Cook could not detect men in the act, or cause them to stop, he was threatened with arrest by the gallant major.

What did it matter if a few pigs were touched up with bayonets? there was work to do of more importance than to fret and fume over a thing so insignificant; but so it was with the post-commanders at Brashear in June, 1863. Instead of bending their energies and giving their time and thought to the critical situation of affairs, they preferred and did do nothing but put on airs about trifles.

Sergeant Ballou, with his men, arrived at the depot from Fort Chene about daylight with the guns. The guard, about twenty men under Sergeant Turner, that had been sent out early on the morning of the nineteenth for twenty-four hours duty at the water tank, situated nearly a mile from the depot upon the railroad line, came in about the same time. The men were mustered and found to number forty-five.

Everything had the appearance that morning of an intention to vacate Brashear. The remaining cars, about fifty, mostly box cars, were made up into a train, with half of them loaded with stores of all kinds, the other half occupied by all of the men who could go. With the locomotive *La-Fourche* attached, it was about four o'clock in the afternoon when a start was made. Upon stopping at Bayou Bœuff, seven miles out, the rumor was current there, among the troops and people, that the force which left Brashear early that morning had been taken prisoners at La-Fourche, the track torn up, and the enemy waiting for the next train to come along. The train was run some thirteen miles further and then stopped near Chucahoula by some whites and blacks, who signalled the engineer.

As previously instructed, on coming to a stop, one-half of the troops formed upon each side of the train and awaited orders. No reconnoissance was made. A Captain Bailey, deputy provost-marshal at Houma, had arrived at Brashear during the day and reported "rebs" upon the road between Houma and Tigerville. This report was undoubtedly true, for the enemy scouted continually upon all of the roads in La-Fourche Parish; still an armed reconnoissance by the troops might have developed a fighting chance to get through by a bold dash. As it was, no enemy was seen, although they may have been in ambush. Most of the soldiers were chagrined at going back without an attempt to push through to La-Fourche Crossing, eight miles further on. Telegraphic communication had been severed between Brashear and La-Fourche during the day, and the report that a rebel battery and cavalry commanded the track was accepted as gospel truth by some of the officers, and in a short time the train was ran back slowly to Brashear, arriving about ten o'clock the same evening. The Forty-Second detachment again occupied the depot building, without orders from any source.

Berwick City was shelled, set on fire, and partially destroyed by the gunboat *Hollyhock* during the afternoon, after the train left Brashear. The light of burning buildings was visible to those upon the train as they were returning. It is supposed that the gunboat commander considered the evacuation completed when the train started, and that it would run through without any trouble; then shelling Berwick, in retaliation for the annoyance from there by the enemy, and taking on board a few officers and men, had steamed down the river out of the enemy's range and there remained to watch further Confederate movements.

A heavy rain-storm set in the next day, Sunday, June 21st, in the afternoon, continuing that day and all night. Some of the negroes were armed, equipped, and organized into a company, by a few of the non-commissioned officers of the Forty-Second detachment. Late in the afternoon Lieutenant-Colonel Duganne collected all the men of his regiment he could and proceeded to Bayou Bœuff, in accordance with an understanding with Major Anthony. Captain Hopkins, with a company Twenty-Third Connecticut, was stationed at Bayou Ramos, six miles from Brashear, to guard the railroad bridge. These dispositions appear to have been foolishly made. They were thus strung seven miles out from Brashear, without any food supply except what could be daily sent to them by cars, instead of concentrating at Brashear, where danger existed, and all of the necessary equipment was on hand for defence and to subsist, if properly applied.*

When Stickney left for La-Fourche with all of the troops not on duty as guards, pickets, or were straggling, the force of duty men left behind was quite small. When Duganne went to Bayou Bœuff, this force was so reduced that there were in Brashear, on the morning of the twenty-second, the convalescent soldiers, some colored troops, about one hundred men of the One Hundred and Seventy-Sixth New York Infantry and Twenty-First Indiana Artillery Regiments at Fort Buchanan, forty-five men of the Forty-Second Massachusetts at the depot, and various small squads of guards over property. The fort mounted ten heavy siege-guns, for use on the water face only, commanding the rivers Teche and Atchafalaya, from a point above the fort where they make a junction. These guns were of no use whatever to repel a land attack, as they could not be swung around. No attempt was ever made to throw up breastworks to cover the open rear. The only guard against a rear attack was to station pickets in the wooded swamp.

During the twenty-second, the Forty-Second men subsisted as best they could, appropriating provisions found in the depot and vicinity. No orders from any officer were received by Sergeant Ballou, who was in a quandary as to what he should do. The post-commandant had two platform cars arranged with a barricade of railroad sleepers, with two 12 Pr. howitzers mounted upon them. These cars were sent out late in the morning, under command of

---

* Duganne, on his arrival at the Bœuff, received information from Lieutenant Robens, One Hundred and Seventy-Sixth New York, who was deputy provost-marshal at Tigerville, that a Union fugitive from Alexandria had, on the preceding Thursday, informed him that General Taylor, with fifteen thousand men (how figures do swell as they travel), was moving down the Teche River for a movement upon New Orleans.

Lieutenant Stevenson, One Hundred and Seventy-Sixth New York, with a small force of infantry acting as sharpshooters, to reconnoitre upon the railroad. This train returned in about two hours, after proceeding to Terrebonne, three miles from La-Fourche, where the enemy was found tearing up rails, and a few shots exchanged with a battery commanding the track.

About nine o'clock that night, Lieutenant Robens, One Hundred and Seventy-Sixth New York, was sent by Duganne from Bayou Bœuff to report to Major Anthony that a scout had brought in the intelligence of boats seen crossing Lake Pelourde; a movement which threatened both Brashear and the Bœuff, in the rear, but no steps were taken to meet it.*

Near sunrise on the morning of the twenty-third the four-gun Confederate (Valverde) battery opened fire from Berwick upon the depot building, situated upon the river front with a wharf attached. A few solid shot crashed through that structure, and some shells reached the wharf and convalescent camp. The men under Sergeant Ballou turned out promptly, attempting to silence the battery by opening fire from the railroad wharf, but their Springfield smooth-bore guns would not carry bullets across. The gunboat fired a few rounds and then proceeded down the river without further effort to silence the battery. Some Confederate riflemen, in support of the battery, joined in the fun, blazing away lively, sending some shots well across the water (about eight hundred yards), without inflicting any serious loss. Of the Forty-Second, Sergeant Turner, Company B, had a bullet go through his blouse sleeve at the elbow. An old iron 6 Pr. gun, which was

* The Confederates, under Major Hunter, started at six P.M. on the twenty-second, in forty-eight skiffs and flats, from the mouth of the Teche, up the Atchafalaya into Grand Lake, where oars were muffled, and then a pull of about eight hours landed them in rear of Brashear City.

mounted upon the wharf, trained upon the Berwick side, was put into use without effect.

About an hour after this amusement commenced a few men of the One Hundred and Seventy-Sixth New York, under Lieutenant Stevenson, commander of the provost-guard, hauled a 24 Pr. gun, from the river front below, to the depot, and placed it into position, opening a fire with shells, which soon caused the Confederate battery to limber up and get out of the way. At this period there was a mixed assemblage around the depot, composed, in part, of infantry men belonging to the Forty-Second, yet Sergeant Ballou received no orders or instructions. He was ignorant of how matters stood, or the positions of what few troops remained at the post, and as to any knowledge if the post-commandant was in existence an unborn child was as learned.

Not long after this, about six o'clock, Privates Lovell and Redmond, Company A, who were on their regular tour of duty watching the surrounding country from the cupola of the depot building, saw the Confederates dash out from the woods between Fort Buchanan and the convalescent camp. Fort Buchanan was about two miles from the depot, while the camp was about one-quarter of a mile away. Giving the alarm, they joined their comrades below. In not over thirty minutes the enemy was seen coming from the direction of the fort, while some of the convalescent soldiers ran down from their camp at the same moment, shouting: "the rebs are coming!"

Major Sherod Hunter (of Baylor's Texas Cavalry), with a small force of three hundred and twenty-five Texans (picked men), had got in from the swamps, situated in rear of the tented camps that were between the depot and fort, meeting with a slight resistance. Hunter got through about four o'clock A.M., when, on arrival in view of an imposing display made by the tents of the convalescent camps and those occupied by the One Hundred and Seventy-Sixth New York and Twenty-Third Connecticut, left standing when the men went to La-Fourche and the Bœuff, with all of their baggage in them, including knapsacks, blankets and extra clothing, his men fancied a large army was before them, and fled back to the swamps from whence they came, but Hunter succeeded in rallying them in season to make the attack as stated.*

When the alarm by the lookout was given, Sergeant Ballou did not know what to do. Neither himself or the detachment had been under fire at close quarters. He thought of the train upon the track, loaded and ready, to be moved to Algiers if an opportunity offered, but could not find any matches handy with which to fire it. Then he thought of deploying the men as skirmishers, hold the enemy in check, retreat gradually, and try to escape capture. Not knowing the country, he finally concluded to get his men into line upon the railroad track and do the best he could with them.

What defence was made by other troops seems to have been in the use of artillery by small detachments, and scattered squads of infantry. All of these isolated attempts to fight showed good pluck and courage, a sure sign that if handled properly in a body it would not have been a holiday affair for the enemy. Captain Cutter, One Hundred and Seventy-Sixth New York, on the sick list and in hospital, was killed while rallying men among the tents. The isolated squads of brave fellows were soon put to flight. Major Anthony had been down to the depot when the battery opened fire from Berwick, also Captain

* Major Hunter does not mention this fact in his official report. His men did say so, however, and it is the enlisted men who state facts seldom found in official reports. All of the Confederate documents relating to Brashear City, Bayou Bœuff and La-Fourche are an eulogy of their own prowess.

Noblett, artillery commander at Fort Buchanan, but both started for the fort when the dash was made from the woods. Major Anthony got there; Captain Noblett had his horse shot, was dismounted, and sought refuge in the hospital. Beyond an endeavor, crowned with success, to get a gun from the fort into position to use upon the land side, and firing a few shots, no defence was made by troops in the fort. Lieutenant Stevenson and his men in charge of the 24 Pr. gun attempted to use it against the enemy, but were shot down and captured.

The Forty-Second detachment, with a number of other soldiers on duty, also some convalescent men, took position in a small ditch alongside the railroad track, behind box cars, while what colored troops were on the right occupied the barricaded platform cars, and a few men were left in the depot building to defend the door.

The enemy skirmished up to within ten paces of the train; a skirmish fire continued for about half an hour. On the Confederate side, their firing was wild for a time, most of their shots going over the cars. From the Federals the firing was also rather wild, but they managed to do some execution, about forty of the enemy being killed and wounded.* At the end of a half hour the colored troops suddenly stampeded to the woods, the enemy got into the depot and around the head of the train, opening a fire upon the flanks and rear. A few men had fallen previous to this time, and now, under this cross-fire, they commenced to drop quick, most of the casualties among convalescent men.

In the absence of any orders, with no sign or hope of

* Hunter says he lost three killed, eighteen wounded. His orders were to concentrate at the railroad buildings. He says the forts made but a feeble resistance, and each column pressed on the point of concentration. At the depot the fighting was severe, but of short duration. He claims the Federals lost forty-six killed, forty wounded.

assistance, Sergeant Ballou sang out: "Boys, take care of yourselves!" when the men broke, some for the woods and swamp, a short distance away, a few to fall back, under Sergeant Turner, maintaining a fire from behind trees and buildings until they reached a saw-mill on the river, where a number of unarmed sick and convalescent men had taken refuge to be out of danger. Here an officer of the One Hundred and Seventy-Sixth New York with some men of that regiment were found, and a fusillade with the enemy was kept up for some time. Two convalescent men were wounded by this scattered fire, when the officer, who did not stand up to his duty (preferring to lie down), raised a white handkerchief upon his sword-point and surrendered the party about nine o'clock.

Privates Redmond, Company A, and Albee, Company B, in company with a few One Hundred and Seventy-Sixth New York soldiers, fell back to a breastwork to make a further stand. As there was no possibility of making a successful defence, and no way of escape except by swimming the river, it was decided to surrender, in turn. A handkerchief was raised by Albee, attached to his musket, from which the lock had been shot off without his knowing it, and a surrender was made of this knot of men.

Private Lovell, Company A, and six men of the One Hundred and Seventy-Sixth New York escaped in the only boat to be found at this point, landing at Fort Chene, thence going aboard the gunboat. Lovell jumped into the boat just as it was pulled off and nearly capsized the party. Little Franklin Borden, fourteen years old, fifer for Company B, who was on duty with the detachment, managed to get a small skiff and also escaped to the gunboat. He was fired upon by Texans, shot striking the water all around him, their only effect to cause the little fellow to hurry up and get out of range as soon as possible and to yell like an Indian. The eight men who escaped were put on board a steam-transport from New Orleans that was met in the river, bound for Brashear to assist in removing material of war, and were brought to New Orleans.

Before he ordered his men to take care of themselves, Sergeant Ballou was severely wounded by a rifle-ball in the left arm, near the wrist, and Private Cook received his fatal wound. Ballou asked Private George Kingsbury, Company B, to assist him in binding up his arm, and while doing so about twenty Texans made a rush upon them, with a demand for their surrender. A Confederate lieutenant gave orders to shoot them down, because there was a flag of truce displayed while the firing continued. An appeal to Major Hunter was necessary to prevent this barbarity, the sergeant not being aware of any flag of truce having been raised, and informed the major that he did not raise one. This was settled satisfactorily, and the few men left with Ballou were taken prisoners.

Corporal Fales, Company B, had noticed the flag of truce when it was raised near the railroad wharf, by whom nobody knew, either at that time or after. If it was not a trick of the enemy, famous at such games in small actions, then it must have been done by some of the other men on duty, or from convalescents who wished to surrender. In either case it had no reference to or binding force upon the men who had the courage to make a fight. Each knot of men act for themselves in an action of this character. Fales spoke to Private Young, Company B, saying: "It is foolish to stand where we are and be shot down or to surrender with the flag of truce," and both fell back behind a house near by, from there ran into the woods and swamp, and were joined by Privates Nathaniel Ide, David Robinson, George S. Rice, a private of the

Twenty-First Indiana, and a sergeant of the Twenty-Third Connecticut. They endeavored to travel southward in the swamp, with an idea of reaching Shell Island, expecting to be able to escape from there towards Algiers. Their food gave out, and finally, after trying to live upon uncooked green corn with salt pork, not daring to make a fire, they surrendered to Colonel Baylor at Bayou Bœuff, on Sunday, the twenty-eighth, after five days' life in the swamp. About eleven men escaped by the railroad track to Bayou Bœuff, and reported for duty to Lieutenant-Colonel Duganne, commanding post.

The casualties to the detachment were:

Private Lawson Comey, Company H, twenty-five years old, shot in the head and killed before the detachment scattered.

Private William E. Cook, Company B, twenty years old, wounded in abdomen, dying the same day.

First-Sergeant George W. Ballou, Company B, severely wounded in left arm just before the detachment scattered.

Private George E. Clark, Company B, severely wounded in calf of left leg.

Several men had narrow escapes from wounds or death, for bullets grazed clothing, muskets, and accoutrements.

At Bayou Bœuff, on the morning of the twenty-fourth, Lieutenant-Colonel Duganne found he had only seventy-two infantry and forty artillery men for duty, instead of two hundred and fifty men with him the day before. This does not speak well for the officers on duty, that over one hundred men should have disappeared during the night. Everything was entangled. When an engineer ran two locomotives into the Bœuff the morning before, bringing news of the capture of Brashear City, and men who had escaped capture came straggling in and corroborated the engineer's story, the post-commander made some preparatory measures for a proper defence. He had three siege-guns and one brass howitzer. Slight earthworks were thrown up. Captain Hopkins burned the bridge at Bayou Ramos early on the evening of the twenty-third, and joined Duganne with his men. The situation of the post was bad, with an enemy in front and rear. An officer of experience and courage who, when his determination was fixed to defend the post, had decision of character sufficient to make the attempt, could possibly so arrange his plans of defence as to enable him to have kept the enemy at bay for a few days at least. The men were reliable, if under an officer in whom they had confidence. The food supply was one day's rations to each man, but this could have been eked out to last two or three days, if any skill had been applied. The ammunition was plenty for a proper defence. Many times in the history of wars have small bodies of soldiers been placed in worse positions, yet, by a heroic defence, saved themselves and prevented the intentions of an enemy from being carried out. There was no defence of Bayou Bœuff. The fact that relief was likely to come from New Orleans was ignored. On the very day Lieutenant-Colonel Duganne surrendered, a force of five companies Ninth Connecticut Infantry, under Lieutenant-Colonel Fitzgibbons, advanced to Chucahoula in the afternoon, within nine miles of the Bœuff, before a Confederate force was met. Had Duganne kept them at bay for one day, letting his guns tell the story, their reverberation along the narrow, densely-wooded railroad line would have brought down upon them the whole Federal force then at La-Fourche.

Early on the morning of the twenty-fourth a council of officers was held and decided to surrender. A sugar-house with outlying sheds, filled with army supplies, officers' baggage, arms, and military appurtenances of all kinds, stored by some of the brigades of the army, was burned during the evening of the twenty-third. The two locomotives were rendered unfit for immediate use, but not destroyed. What negroes had been armed to assist in the defence were disarmed, that the enemy might have no reason to maltreat them. Some of these negroes were excellent shots, anxious and ready to fight.

Shortly after dawn the Confederates appeared from Brashear and opened a parley. While debating whether to accept the terms of unconditional surrender demanded, Colonel Major and his men appeared on the other side; a parley was opened, Colonel Major crossing the railroad bridge with a flag of truce, and while discussing the preliminaries of surrender, before the truce was withdrawn, Major's men got into the post without a gun being fired, and the Federal troops were prisoners before they knew it. The enemy appropriated everything, as usual, and the prisoners were marched to Brashear the same day, joining their comrades at Fort Buchanan the same night. To use an expression frequently made by the enlisted men, it was a "sell out," and they expected it from the method adopted to organize and prepare for defence.

About two hundred and fifty enlisted men were taken prisoners at Bayou Bœuff, and the following officers:

   Lieutenant-Colonel A. J. Duganne, 176th New York.
   Lieutenant Charles Kerby,   "
    " John F. Kimball,   "
   Captain Julius Sanford, 23d Connecticut.
    " A. D. Hopkins, "
    " Alfred Wells, "
   Lieutenant John F. Peck, "
    " Charles D. Hurlbutt, 23d Connecticut.
    " John A. Woodward, "
    " Frank Sherfy, 21st Indiana.

The following officers were made prisoners at Brashear City:

Major R. C. Anthony, 2d Rhode Island Cavalry.
Lieutenant Caleb Brennan, "
Colonel Charles C. Nott, 176th New York.
Captain William P. Coe, "
" S. E. Thomason, "
Lieutenant John Babcock, "
" David G. Wellington, 176th New York.
" J. D. Fry, "
" J. P. Robens, "
" Daniel G. Gillette, "
" T. Foster Petrie, "
" Louis W. Stevenson, "
" Charles Sherman, "
Captain F. W. Noblett, 21st Indiana.
" Albert Allen, 1st U. S. Vols., "Corps d'Afrique."
Lieutenant Charles E. Page, 4th U. S. Vols., "
Captain S. G. Bailey, 23d Connecticut.
" George S. Crofut, 23d Connecticut.
" James R. Jenkins, "
Lieutenant O. H. Hibbard, "
" John G. Stevens, "
" Charles Bailey, "
" John W. Buckingham, 23d Connecticut.
" James DeLamater, 91st New York.
" Charles Avery, 25th Connecticut.
" George W. Hugg, "
" Henry W. Morse, 4th Massachusetts.
" James M. Sampson, "
" Henry Humble, "
Surgeon James Waldock, "
" David Hershy, 4th U. S. Volunteers.
" A. J. Willets, 176th New York.
Assistant-Surgeon —— Throop, 176th New York.

After a full list of the prisoners was made up for parole, there was found to be between twelve and thirteen hundred, including officers, enlisted men on duty, sick and convalescent men, some few citizens, and about one hundred railroad laborers.

The following men of the Forty-Second Regiment detachment were paroled:

Company A.

1. Corporal John F. Cushing.
2. Private Charles S. Redmond.
3. Private James G. Raymond.
4. " George W. Tirrell.
5. Private Charles S. Williams.

Company E.

6. Corporal Francis N. Luce.
7. Private Robert Whiteside.
8. " Francis T. Jones.
9. Private David F. Cummings.
10. " John H. Hildreth.
11. " Patrick Fitzpatrick.

Company B.

12. 1st Serg't George W. Ballou.
13. 2d " Thaddeus M. Turner.
14. 4th " Frederick D. Morse.
15. Corporal Henry J. Daniels.
16. " Silas E. Fales.
17. Private Daniel Akley.
18. " Erastus Adams.
19. " D. Newton Blake.
20. " Albert E. Bullard.
21. " George E. Clark.
22. " Sewall J. Clark.
23. Private Frank L. Fisher.
24. " George H. Fisher.
25. " Harrison E. Harwood.
26. " Nathaniel Ide.
27. " George A. Kingsbury.
28. " Charles M. Morris.
29. " George S. Rice.
30. " Henry S. Richardson.
31. " David Robinson.
32. " Orson D. Young.
33. " Albert Albee.

Company H.

34. Private John Davis.
35. " James Healey.
36. " William A. Ragan.
37. " Calvin W. Woods.
38. Private Lovett B. Hayden.
39. " Charles McLaughlin.
40. " John Barrett.
41. " Henry A. Watkins.

And Private Joseph P. Snow, Company K, sick in hospital.

After fighting at Brashear City was over the prisoners were collected at Fort Buchanan and wounded sent to the hospital, where appearances indicated that as many of the enemy were wounded as upon the Federal side. The

Confederate troops at once commenced to loot the town and camps, and get drunk. The rank and file were a good-natured, motley crowd, apparently without discipline or organization. After General Taylor arrived (twenty-fourth) with the balance of his command, the force was seen to be well mounted and armed, most of the men owning their horses and equipments. The general understanding among them was that each man was entitled to keep what he captured. No attempt was made to maintain uniformity in dress or arms. Privates were seen wearing the uniform of a Federal officer, with sword, belt and sash, while officers were seen dressed in a red shirt and striped trowsers.

Sergeant Turner got Major Hunter to allow him, with a guard for protection, to look around the post and find the missing men of his detachment. Visiting the hospital first, Private Cook was found laid out upon the grass beside a dozen others, having died from his wound. Sergeant Ballou was found back of the hospital, suffering great pain from his wound. His blanket had been stolen, and he was very thirsty and hungry. Turner obtained a blanket and did what he could for his comfort. At the depot, where he expected to find the knapsacks, the enemy's troops were in force, and had seized everything left there. In the village a few dead New York soldiers were to be seen and one soldier of the Fourth Massachusetts, supposed to have been shot down where they lay. Private George Clark was found at a house, in comfortable condition, receiving good care from two pretty girls. They were told to keep him there, and kept their promise to do so, baffling all attempts made to take him to the hospital.

On the way back to the fort a Confederate officer halted the party. During a conversation that ensued he noticed the figures forty-two on Turner's cap, and inquired if he belonged to the Forty-Second Massachusetts. Turner answered, "Yes;" the officer then said he was present at the capture of Galveston with the Forty-Second Regiment; that the men were paroled, and he would have to look into his case. It was hard work to make the fool understand that only three companies of the regiment were made prisoners at Galveston, and not the entire regiment.

Sergeant Ballou went to the hospital about ten o'clock in the forenoon to have his arm looked after, and was informed that it was done up so well he could wait better than other wounded men, for an amputation. It was late in the afternoon and dark when the surgeon requested the sergeant to get upon the table and have his arm taken off. A request to save the arm, if possible, caused the surgeon to make another examination, but he gave an opinion that it was impossible to save it. Ballou, however, insisted upon making the attempt, and the surgeon proceeded to its attention. He found about two and one-half inches of the large bone in the wrist was shot away and the small bone broken. With the cavity made by the wound stuffed with lint and bound up, the suffering that night from pain endured by Ballou was terrible. He fortunately found Surgeon Willets, One Hundred and Seventy-Sixth New York, the next morning, who carefully removed the lint bandage, examined the wound, set the broken small bone, put on a board support, and attended to it assiduously. Sergeant Ballou saved his arm and hand, but the hand has never been of use to him. In refusing to submit to the loss of his arm it is probable that he also saved his life, for with one exception every man died who suffered amputation. Hot weather and no ice to be had, gangrene would set in and the patients die. With the exception of a short allowance of food, the wounded were well treated while in the enemy's hands.

On Saturday, June 27th, the enlisted men having been paroled, searched, and deprived of everything except what they wore, a haversack and woollen blanket, started at five o'clock in the afternoon to march for the Union lines. A curious feature in regard to prisoners taken at Brashear is that no negro soldiers were among them. As no one saw or heard of any cut-throat actions towards colored Federal soldiers, the supposition would seem to be well founded that they all èscaped capture in some way through the wooded swamps. Sergeant Turner, on receiving his parole, was complimented by an officer who represented the United States forces, and thanked for what defence the detachment made. The tenor of his remarks were, that if there had been a few more men like those composing the Forty-Second detachment the shameful surprise, with attendant consequences, would not have occurred.

The following men were left at Brashear, not able to march:

First-Sergeant George W. Ballou, Company B, wounded.
Private George E. Clark, Company B, wounded.
Private George H. Fisher, Company B, sick.
Private Patrick Fitzpatrick, Company E, sick.

Many convalescent and sick soldiers not able to march, but anxious to reach the Federal lines, attempted to do so with their fellow prisoners. They gave out day by day from sickness and fatigue, caused by debility, hot weather, poor drinking-water, and insufficient rations, to be left on the line of march all the way from Brashear to New Orleans. Quite a number died. Many were in a condition to give out any moment, but pluckily kept on and reached the lines. From the Forty-Second detachment Privates Henry Richardson and George Kingsbury, Company B, sickened, and had to be left at Thibodeaux.

At first the Confederate guard was a company of Louisiana infantry, soon relieved by a cavalry company of Colonel Baylor's Rangers, because the infantry could not keep up with the impatient prisoners. The guard was kind in treatment of their charge, while under strict orders to shoot down any man attempting to straggle or forage without permission. As to rations, they fared no better than their prisoners, making an equal division of what they had so long as it lasted.

The route of march was upon the railroad road-bed which ran through a swampy, thickly-wooded country a greater part of the way. The atmosphere was stifling. The first night was passed at Bayou Ramos, about six miles out from Brashear; the second night upon a plantation beyond Bayou Bœuff, where Corporal Fales and five men came in and surrendered. Starting at four o'clock on the morning of the twenty-ninth, after a march of eighteen miles, the prisoners reached Terrebonne, remaining over night. On the thirtieth they continued on to Thibodeaux and beyond, to remain over night near the La-Fourche railroad bridge. July 1st, after an early start in the morning, while *en-route*, the men found the hospital in which was Private Woodman, Company B, wounded in the action of June 21st. A halt for the night was made at Raceland, midway between Brashear and Algiers. Very little progress was made the next day as rations had given out, causing a delay until provisions expected from Brashear should be forwarded; meanwhile the men had to get along with what they could forage. July 3d the Federal pickets were found just before reaching Boutte Station — where the advanced troops were stationed charged with the Defences of New Orleans — and the prisoners delivered over to Federal officers.

The Confederate guard attempted to play a sharp trick that night. After turning over their prisoners, with a

Texan yell they departed, but not to go far, for they hung around until night, when they made a raid upon the picket-posts. Their design had been suspected and the posts were on the alert, prepared for them; the consequence was that instead of capturing the posts many of them were made prisoners instead, and sent to New Orleans, where they arrived before the paroled men whom they had under guard from Brashear to Boutte.

The duty performed by this Forty-Second detachment, with all the necessary exposure attending it, told upon the men. On their return, July 4th, to Algiers, where they were quartered in the Iron Works building (a very dirty place), receiving poor treatment, most of them were suffering from diarrhœa, dysentery, or chills and fever, some men having a combination of these complaints. Efforts were at once made to have the Forty-Second Regiment men sent to the paroled camp at Bayou Gentilly, which was not accomplished until July 8th.

Sergeant Ballou, with Privates Clark and Fisher, remained at Brashear City five days after the Confederate troops departed, on July 22d, when two Federal gunboats arrived. These men proceeded to New Orleans by water, going into the University Hospital, and then reported to the regiment at Algiers July 28th.

With one dollar and forty cents in his pocket when made prisoner, the sergeant was fortunately enabled to borrow twenty dollars from a soldier of a Connecticut regiment. With this money he was able to subsist until carried to New Orleans, securing board with a German woman, who furnished him with one meal a day for twenty-five cents. Several of the Texan troops took meals at her house, for which she made them pay one dollar a meal. She claimed to be a good, true Unionist, and was not at all backward in saying so. Unlike many of the so-called

Southern Unionists with whom the army often came in contact, this woman was as outspoken before Confederates as she was before Federals. She made no attempt to disguise her sentiments.

At Brashear Sergeant Ballou had excellent opportunities to see what was going on. Taylor and his men came down the river to Brashear in five steamboats, except the artillery, which marched overland. They had several batteries; one called the Valverde Battery they considered the best equipped in the Confederate service. They were five days removing contents of railroad cars and other material found at Brashear, carrying the same across the river to Berwick, thence to their various depots. The cars, when emptied, were ran about half a mile out upon the track and set on fire. After the fire was well under way the locomotive *La-Fourche*, under a full head of steam, was started from the depot and ran into the burning train, jumping some ten feet in the air when it struck.

The spoils obtained by the enemy consisted of heavy cannon and field-guns (about fifteen), small arms, ammunition, tents, baggage, commissary and quartermaster stores, with large medical supplies of great value to them. The colors of the One Hundred and Seventy-Sixth New York Regiment were also lost.

The gift of Brashear City to the enemy, with this valuable property, was without an excuse. There is but one explanation of the failure to properly defend the post: incompetency and cowardice of the senior officers. A determined stand by half the number of the raiding force under Major Hunter would have easily driven them back. Had the naval vessel remained in the river to co-operate whenever an opportunity offered Hunter would not have had easy work in forcing his men to make the attack; many of them declared that if the gunboat had not moved down the river they would not have attempted to get in. This may or may not have proved to be the case. The Texans under Colonel Green, when they attacked Donaldsonville upon the twenty-eighth, were not deterred from it even with three gunboats present, but a defeat was given them there, with severe loss to them.

A repulse of the attack made by Hunter's raiding party would have given time to decide upon a course of action to be adopted before General Taylor made his appearance. Had it been decided to evacuate, then the train with its valuable load and other property in Brashear could have been destroyed, the garrison, with all sick men able to be moved, could have been taken by water to New Orleans, for ample facilities were at Brashear. On Monday the *Hollyhock* had brought around from Bayou Bœuff a number of flatboats, which were added to those already at Brashear, then there was the gunboat, the small ferry steamers used to ply across from Brashear to Berwick, with the transport-steamer that was coming up river on the morning of surrender. The flatboats were put in use by the enemy to remove captured property.

The entire force of duty men were nine months' troops. They were what are termed raw troops, with unseasoned officers. The freshness of troops does not matter so much if they can be officered by men of experience. What fresh troops need most, in action, is to be informed of the situation of affairs, the location of other troops, and general instructions as to what they have got to do, or what is expected of them. Old troops soon acquire the art of finding out all this without being told, understanding that the least danger lies in holding together, face to the enemy, and that a stampede is running headlong into danger.

In consequence of the loss of medical stores in Brashear,

the medical purveyor's stock became too small for army necessities, with men rapidly swelling the sick lists and the hot weather in season. To replenish supplies, the transport-steamer *New Brunswick*, a light-draft side-wheeler, nine hundred and thirty tons burthen, manned by a fine crew, was loaded with coal and despatched to New York in July or August. Her captain had orders to drive her with all possible speed and spare nothing in order to make a quick passage North, and return. Fortunately good weather prevailed, with the exception of a stiff blow off Hatteras and a short gale on the return trip. This transport made what was then called "the famous passage." The exact time is now lost, but it was between six and seven days. Everything on board that could be utilized was used for fuel; her chief-engineer, Wesley Allen, to whom the credit is due for her quick passages, although he had as assistants two efficient men, stood by his engines almost the entire time, pushing the wheels to twenty-two revolutions a minute, and so maintained them. They ordinarily made from seventeen to nineteen. Allen is said to have slept not more than twenty hours on each passage. He fully understood that many lives could be saved by each day gained, and was a man, every inch of him.

The *New Brunswick* arrived at New York early one morning, was loaded with medical and hospital stores the same day, and at night was on her way back to New Orleans, passing a mail steamer at Sandy Hook, bound in, that she parted company with and left at the Passes of the Mississippi River. Coal and stores were rushed on board with a run. Coal was dumped upon the open deck forward, instead of wasting time to fill up her hold. Fires were not drawn from the boilers, and they only had the water blown out while fresh water ran in. No time was lost in fancy oiling of machinery, for it was slapped on without regard to appearances, in order that no part should become heated. Among the firemen life below deck was a hard lot, as her blowers were never turned off from the boiler fires.

The round trip was made in a little less than two weeks, ruining her boilers in so doing.

CHAPTER XII.

ACTION AT LA-FOURCHE CROSSING.

ABOUT six o'clock Saturday morning, twentieth June, 1863, the train which left Brashear City for La-Fourche a few hours before, arrived at the railroad bridge crossing Bayou La-Fourche, twenty-eight miles from Brashear, fifty-two miles from Algiers, then a suburb of New Orleans, upon the west bank of the Mississippi River.

Lieutenant-Colonel Stickney had under his command on the train: one hundred and fifteen men One Hundred and Seventy-Sixth New York Infantry, Major Morgans in command; seventy-five men Twenty-Third Connecticut Infantry, Major Miller in command; forty-six men Forty-Second Massachusetts Infantry, Lieutenant Tinkham in command; and two pieces of artillery, a 6 Pr. gun and a 12 Pr. howitzer. This force was in light marching order, having left at Brashear City all knapsacks, extra clothing, and many of them their blankets.

There was posted at Terrebonne and La-Fourche, guarding the railroad bridge, a force of about two hundred and fifty men with one 12 Pr. gun and one 12 Pr. howitzer. This force, joined with the reënforcements from Brashear, made Stickney's command about five hundred and two men, as follows: — companies, one hundred and ninety-five men, Twenty-Third Connecticut Infantry; — companies, one hundred and fifty-four men, One Hundred and Seventy-Sixth New York Infantry; one company, forty-six men, Forty-Second Massachusetts Infantry; one company, thirty-seven men, Twenty-Sixth Maine Infantry, under Captain Fletcher; one company, fifty men, First Louisiana Cavalry, under Captain Blober; and about twenty artillerymen, mostly from the Twenty-First Indiana Artillery.

Upon disembarking from the train, the commanding officer of the post appeared to be much surprised at this appearance of additional troops, and asked what was to be done. When informed that the post was threatened by the enemy he laughed heartily, and told Stickney no enemy had been seen around there for six months.

Captain Blober, on his return from a scout made the day before, ordered by Lieutenant-Colonel Stickney by telegraph from Brashear, reported no signs whatever of any force on the Bayou La-Fourche. Blober, ordered to be sure and scout as far as Napoleonville, and beyond if possible, only proceeded a mile or two beyond Labadieville, about twelve miles from La-Fourche and nine miles from Thibodeaux. He reported that people from Napoleonville *said* no force was in that direction; the reason, probably, why he did not carry out his orders. This company of the First Louisiana Cavalry was composed of raw recruits, without much drill or discipline. In his official report of the action Stickney says: "Had their scouting been properly done, there was no necessity whatever of the infantry force at Thibodeaux being captured."

Colonel Major[*] with three regiments of Confederate

---

[*] Colonel James P. Major commanded the Second Cavalry Brigade, composed of mounted infantry, artillery and cavalry. His official report, dated June 30th, 1863, does not give the strength of his command, but enough is gleaned from it to know that he had regiments commanded by Colonels W. P. Lane, B. W. Stone, and Joseph Phillip, Colonel C. L. Pyron's Second Texas Cavalry, and Captain O. J. Semmes' battery.

Major captured Plaquemine June 18th, was at Bayou Goula at daylight on the nineteenth, at dark sent a force under Colonel Lane through a swamp direct to Thibodeaux, and at midnight followed with the rest of his men, arriving at 3.30 A.M. on the twenty-first. The rest of his report on this action does not agree with

Texan mounted men was at that very moment on his way down from Plaquemine — forty miles from Thibodeaux — and could not have been many miles away. On the nineteenth June General "Dick" Taylor was at the Fausse Riviere, an ancient bed of the Mississippi, some miles west of the present channel and opposite Port Hudson, in company with Colonel Major and his men. He had heard from some ladies of his acquaintance there, recently from New Orleans, that the Federal force in that city was not over one thousand men, and with the exception of a small garrison in the fort at Donaldsonville there were no troops on the west bank of the river. This was not true. There was scattered in the Parish towns on the west bank a respectable force of detached Federal troops on guard and provost duty. Taylor ordered Major to proceed at once, for the express purpose of reaching the rear of Brashear City by the twenty-third, and to pass Plaquemine at night to escape observation. Major could not do this. His men, hungry for spoils, raided into that town, capturing some prisoners and burning two steamers. Lieutenant White, of the Forty-Second Massachusetts, with his unarmed colored engineer troops barely escaped capture at the time.

The men lay around carelessly until afternoon, as it was extremely hot and nothing could be had to eat. Lieutenant-Colonel Stickney, when he left Brashear, did not apprehend any attack on that place for some days, and intended to return as soon as possible. Not hearing from Captain Blober, who had again been ordered to scout and cover the roads about Thibodeaux, about four o'clock he got ready to go back to Brashear upon the same train that brought him. An order was given Lieutenant Tinkham to remain at La-Fourche with his detachment, as a reünforcement to the post; Stickney remarked he did not d leave without doing so. Orders had also been received from New Orleans to return two companies infantry to Brashear.

As the men were about to board the cars up rode a cavalry-man in hot haste, with bare breath enough to say, "the rebs are coming, three divisions of them," and told that they were already at Thibodeaux. Blober's cavalry detachment came in shortly after, with a loss of two men in a close pursuit by the enemy. With no wish to weaken his force just then, but desirous to increase it, the train was hastily despatched to Terrebonne, three miles distant on the railroad, with orders for Captain Barber, Company K, One Hundred and Seventy-Sixth New York, posted with about sixty men and one piece of artillery in a stockade, to evacuate. The gun and detachment of gunners left for La-Fourche during the morning.

Throughout the morning crowds of colored people kept coming along the road, from the direction of Thibodeaux, with reports that the enemy were coming. Failing to obtain satisfactory news from these people Captain Barber rode to that town to find out the facts, arriving just as the cavalry scouts started for La-Fourche, and with them the captain went. This left young Lieutenant Phœbus W. Lyon, One Hundred and Seventy-Sixth New York, in command, without proper information of what to expect. When the Confederate troopers appeared they did not dare to attack the stockade, as they expected that the field-gun was there. They showed the convenient flag of truce. To the sergeant who was sent out to meet it a demand was made to see the commanding officer. Lieutenant Lyon, alone, went to meet them some three hundred yards from the stockade, and refused their demand for a surrender of the post, when the Confederate commander pulled out a revolver, placed it behind an ear of the lieutenant and demanded that he should go along with him. To the charge of violating a flag of truce by such a demand no attention was paid, and entirely at their mercy Lieutenant Lyon had to go with them, a prisoner of war. The enemy made a feint to charge upon the stockade, and then withdrew some distance. Without molestation the Federal troops embarked upon the train, which arrived shortly after all this occurred, and Lieutenant Lyon had to witness the evacuation, from the woods where he was held, with chagrin.

At Thibodeaux the Confederates captured all the infantry stationed there, also about one hundred men upon plantations in the vicinity (forty-seven men of the Twelfth Maine, with Lieutenants Freeman H. Chase and John W. Dana, convalescents sent by Stickney from Brashear; forty others, also convalescents from Brashear; about ten men Company D, One Hundred and Seventy-Sixth New York; and a few plantation guards). At Terrebonne Captain William H. May, Twenty-Third Connecticut, was taken prisoner.

When the cavalry-man had made his report all of the troops were ordered to "fall in," and a line of battle was formed. The position taken is described by Lieutenant-Colonel Stickney in his official report as follows: "The levee of the Bayou La-Fourche is about twelve feet high; the railroad crosses the bayou over the top of the levee, nearly in a direction perpendicular to that of the bayou, and is about twelve feet above the level of the surrounding country. For five or six miles to the east of La-Fourche Crossing a carriage-road runs up and down the bayou on both sides close to the levee, passing under the railroad on both sides of the bayou. We were on the east side of the bayou and north of the railroad, our front being parallel with the railroad, extending about one hundred and fifty yards from the levee, and being about two hundred yards from the railroad. From the right of our front I had a line of defence running perpendicular to and resting upon the railroad. I was obliged to have my front farther from the railroad than it otherwise would have been, on account of trees standing, which could not be cut down. The country around was level, affording full play for the artillery, and was covered with tall grass, which I subsequently had cut down, as it concealed, in a measure, movements in our front.

"A detachment of about fifty men of the Twenty-Third Connecticut, under command of Major Miller, was posted in the tall grass on both sides of the road along the levee, lying down, about four hundred and fifty yards in advance of the battle line.

"The remainder of the infantry was drawn up in line, with the right flank in reverse, excepting the company of convalescent men, under Captain Fletcher, Twenty-Sixth Maine, who were posted at the railroad bridge.

"Captain Blober and his cavalry-men were posted so as to guard against the turning of the right flank, with the detachment Forty-Second Massachusetts in their front, and to the rear of the centre of the battle line.

"The artillery was posted as follows: a 12 Pr. gun upon the railroad bridge, near the left bank of the bayou; two 12 Pr. howitzers and one 6 Pr. gun on the battle line front, one of the howitzers being so placed upon the extreme right so that its fire could be directed to the front or right flank."

These movements were the first indication of an action in which this detachment of the Forty-Second had seen an opportunity to participate. Not without reason Lieutenant-Colonel Stickney rode up to Lieutenant Tinkham and asked him what he thought about the behavior of his men under fire; the lieutenant answered, he did not know, but thought they would fight. Cavalry-Captain Blober, a plucky little German, was boiling over for a fight. He was just the man to put courage into any one a little weak in the knees. Later in the day this captain captured a Confederate bugler upon the road.

With nothing to eat since the evening before, a hot, dusty and tedious ride in the cars early that morning, lounging around all day in a hot sun, no wonder there were many anxious inquiries, at all hours of the day, for some stimulant. Those who had it in their possession kept still, and the welcome friend was hard to find. However, no sooner had position in line been taken to meet the expected enemy, when out came the secreted whiskey, and was passed around to those in need of it.

About five o'clock the enemy came marching down the bayou road, mounted, in column of fours, and as soon as the head of the column was in sight a shot was fired from the gun upon the bridge, causing them to halt and retire. They soon advanced about one hundred skirmishers, who drove in the Federal pickets and moved on until encountering the detachment Twenty-Third Connecticut, hid in tall grass, who, after an exchange of shots, fell back upon the right flank of the main line without loss.

The artillery gave them a few solid shot and shell, when the enemy retired towards Thibodeaux with their killed and wounded.

Even here, almost before a gun was fired, the malady which seemed to have attacked some officers on duty in this section was made manifest. Major Miller, Twenty-Third Connecticut, during the day had spoken to Major Morgans and Lieutenant Tinkham about a surrender to the enemy; said he was in favor of it, and that it was of no use to make a fight. He got an unfavorable response from these officers, but the major continued panic-struck, for, after the first fire by the enemy upon the Twenty-Third Connecticut in the grass, as Lieutenant-Colonel Stickney says in his official report: "I found Major Miller, some distance to the rear of his command, crouching in the high weeds on the levee. I ordered him under arrest, and put in command of this detachment the next senior officer, who faithfully executed my order."

Soon after the enemy's disappearance, instead of promptly throwing out his skirmishers to follow up their retrograde movement and ascertain what they were doing, Stickney sent a flag of truce to obtain permission to remove his hospital stores and sick from the hospital, which was in front of his lines and exposed to his fire. The truce party went two and one-half miles on the road before meeting the Confederate pickets. True to their own cowardly use of flags of truce, they refused to comply with Stickney's request. This made no difference, however, as they could not interfere where they were, and the hospital contents were removed to the Federal rear, and, just before dark, the building was burned, to prevent interference with the range of fire. A building upon the other side of the bayou was also set on fire, to enable movements of the enemy to be seen, as it was feared they might come down on that side and attempt to cross the railroad bridge.

The position in line of battle was maintained all night, ready to repel at any moment an attack: the men rested upon the ground as best they could; pickets were thrown out about four hundred yards to the front; squads of cavalry kept scouting to the right and rear; everything upon this Johnson Plantation that could be used for fuel was torn down to keep fires going.

About eleven o'clock at night a train arrived from Algiers

with five companies, three hundred and six men, Twenty-Sixth Massachusetts Infantry, under Lieutenant-Colonel Sawtelle. Being the senior officer, Stickney tendered him the command, which Lieutenant-Colonel Sawtelle refused. The Twenty-Sixth Massachusetts went into line on the front. No demonstrations were made by the enemy during the night.

The next morning, Sunday, June 21st, Captain Grow with one section of the Twenty-Fifth New York Battery and thirty men arrived from Algiers. One gun went into position on the extreme left of the line to cover the bayou road, and one gun was held in reserve, where it could be moved to the front or upon the right flank, as occasion should require. Slight earthworks were thrown up, at no point over two feet high, but they extended only a few yards in either direction from the angle formed on the right flank by the two fronts.

During the morning Confederate mounted troops appeared in small bodies within range of the outposts, to reconnoitre the position. About four o'clock in the afternoon nearly one hundred and fifty Confederates, mounted and dismounted, attacked the outposts and pickets, but made no attempt to advance in force. A desultory fire was maintained for one hour and a half, when the enemy retired.

Shortly after noon a heavy rain commenced, and continued until about half-past six o'clock, drenching the men to the skin, who maintained a battle line the greater part of the day as they had during the night. Stickney claims this was necessary, as he could not depend on the men falling into position with sufficient alacrity at the least warning.

The Federal position at dusk was about the same as on the previous day, except that two companies of the Twenty-

Sixth Massachusetts were added to the front line, two companies on the right flank in reverse, and one company upon the railroad bridge in support of the gun placed there.

Between five and six o'clock Lieutenant Tinkham was ordered to advance on the road to a point about one-quarter of a mile in front, with his Forty-Second Massachusetts detachment and some fifty negroes, to take down a rail fence that somewhat obstructed the view. While engaged in this work the enemy could be seen about another quarter of a mile up the road, somewhat covered by the woods. Captain Blober tried his best to draw them on, by riding towards them and circling around as the ground would permit, without effect. Lieutenant-Colonel Stickney rode up and wanted a volley fired at them, but Lieutenant Tinkham informed him it would do no good, as his men were armed with Springfield smooth-bore guns that would not reach the distance. Finally a volley was fired, without effect, when Stickney told the lieutenant to hold on and he would send out a field-gun, which was done.

It was shortly after this fence was levelled that the enemy, dismounted, with a yell, and opening fire at the same time, made a charge. The field-gun, after three discharges of canister shot, was abandoned by the Twenty-Fifth New York artillery-men, although Lieutenant Tinkham suggested to the gunner in command to fire in retreat. The gunner was either a coward or too frightened to listen to any orders or suggestions, and the gun was left. As the gunners retreated Lieutenant Tinkham, who had his men in line to the rear in support, upon one side of the road, wheeled the detachment into line across the bayou road and gave the enemy a volley from his smooth-bores, carrying a ball and three buckshot to each musket, almost point-blank in their faces. They were not over ten paces distant. This volley staggered them for a few minutes, as well it might, for an uglier weapon to face at close quarters than those Springfield smooth-bore muskets, even in the hands of raw troops, could not be found in the entire army at that time.

Promptly faced about, the detachment was double-quicked back to the battle line as fast as the mud and slippery condition of the road would allow, for the rain had caused the Louisiana soil of that region to assume the consistency of a sticky paste, so well known to all campaigners in the Gulf Department. With this uncertain footing, the close proximity of the enemy, fairly on their heels,* yelling and firing, and the balance of the Federal force in line of battle also opening fire, placing the detachment between two lines of fire, it is remarkable that the casualties were so few at this time. Not a man was taken prisoner. Major Morgans did not expect the detachment would be able to get back, but reserved the One Hundred and Seventy-Sixth New York fire as long as he dared, and then opened an oblique firing, to prevent any harm to the detachment, if possible.

The Forty-Second detachment was not out as skirmishers, and did not have that formation. It was on a special duty and had performed that duty. No orders were given the lieutenant except to support the field-gun. What had become of the pickets and outposts Lieutenant Tinkham did not know. The enemy were upon him almost without warning, for they had crept up in the tall grass on his front. In his official report Lieutenant-Colonel Stickney says: "The enemy advanced rapidly and soon

---

*One of the curious events of the action, which also proves the close proximity of the enemy, was that a Confederate lieutenant-colonel, mounted upon an iron-grey horse, who must have distanced his men in the charge they made, got around and ahead, by the flank, and led the Forty-Second detachment on its retreat to the main line. This officer came in contact with men of the Twenty-Sixth Massachusetts, who made him a prisoner, as related later on in this chapter.

compelled the pickets to fall back on the main line, which they reached in rather a straggling condition at our left wing." This could not mean the detachment Forty-Second Massachusetts, for they did nothing of the kind. The detachment ran in, maintaining as good an alignment as the slippery soil would allow.

A ridiculous proceeding occurred just after the detachment reached the line. A second-lieutenant, an acting staff-officer, came up in an excited manner and ordered Lieutenant Tinkham to go back and retake the abandoned gun. Tinkham replied he would see him d—d first, and to go and get it himself. With the darkness, fire opened on the enemy in front, the bad condition of the ground and the uncertainty just where the gun was at that moment, made the undertaking foolhardy, without a chance for success; in reality giving the enemy a present of so many prisoners. It was another instance of that want of judgment in an inexperienced officer, of which many examples were furnished in the whole history of General "Dick" Taylor's raid towards New Orleans.

After reaching the line the detachment was posted on the extreme left, resting on the bayou and covering the road. Firing was continuate until about eight o'clock. The artillery used canister; there not being any canister for the 6 Pr. gun, packages of musket ammunition were used instead. The infantry were ordered to fire by rank, and opened in that manner, soon substituting firing at will. The smoke became quite dense and would not lift readily, on account of the dampness of the atmosphere. Nothing could be seen in front, not even flashes of the enemy's guns; nothing to be heard, except continued reports of artillery and musketry-firing.

When the order was given "cease firing," pickets were thrown out, and the abandoned gun, near the rail fence, left by the enemy when they withdrew, was brought in to the Federal lines. The wounded within reach were carried to a field-hospital that had been established in a planter's house, about one-quarter of a mile in the rear. The Federals rested upon their arms, remaining in line of battle all night, with what sleep they could obtain under the circumstances. Moans and cries of the wounded, well to the front, could be distinctly heard. Totally destitute of provisions, and hungry, having been without food of any consequence for forty-eight hours, worn out by loss of sleep and fatigue, nothing but the excitement could have held the men up so long and prevented them from breaking down completely.

That many of the Confederates were crazy drunk and in no condition to continue a steady fight seems to be fully established by the information obtained on Tuesday, when an advance to Thibodeaux was made. They were capable of making a bold dash, but no more; repulsed, they could not maintain a destructive fire. What firing came from their side was wild and high, as the total casualties to the entire Federal force engaged amply testifies.

Notwithstanding General "Dick" Taylor, in his book called "Destruction and Reconstruction," says that Colonel Major had no artillery with him, they fired a few shots from one field-gun while Tinkham and his men were at the rail fence. Whether they ceased firing because their ammunition was bad or damaged by rain, or compelled to do so by shots from a gun of the Twenty-Fifth New York Battery that was placed in position upon the right to engage their gun, is not known. Prisoners stated that they had other guns in position, but the rain prevented their use.

There were many sensational stories told next day of what was done along the line. Some men of the One

Hundred and Seventy-Sixth New York claimed to have performed special feats of valor. A careful inspection of the ground in front soon put to flight all belief in these camp yarns. The enemy never got dangerously close, except in a few individual cases. An attempt made by them to gain the rear and turn the right flank caused the gunners of the Twenty-Fifth New York Battery to become panic stricken and abandon their gun, a 12 Pr. howitzer, posted at the angle made by the front and right flank thrown in reverse. This made two guns that the Twenty-Fifth New York artillery-men abandoned in this action, though only one came into possession of the enemy.

The actual Federal force in this action was eight hundred and thirty-eight men; about six hundred were engaged; the balance were posted upon the railroad bridge and to protect the right. The Federal loss in this action was: three killed, ten wounded, Twenty-Sixth Massachusetts Infantry; two killed, twelve wounded, One Hundred and Seventy-Sixth New York Infantry; one killed, three wounded, Forty-Second Massachusetts Infantry; two killed, sixteen wounded, Twenty-Third Connecticut Infantry.

Lieutenant Starr, Twenty-Third Connecticut, was the only commissioned officer injured in the action. He was wounded in the thigh, and afterwards died in consequence of amputation.

The force of Confederates engaged is estimated to have been six hundred men of the Second Texas Mounted Rangers, Colonel Pyron, claiming to be the oldest regiment in the Confederate service, and that they never before had been whipped in action.

As General Taylor has published that only two hundred men under Colonel Pyron made an attack on La-Fourche Crossing, the attack being repulsed with a loss to the

Confederates of only fifty-five killed and wounded,* the official report of Lieutenant-Colonel Stickney is again quoted: "The enemy were engaged during the night in carrying away their killed and wounded who were outside of our lines, and the following morning fifty-three of their dead were counted inside of our pickets. When we entered Thibodeaux, Tuesday morning, nearly sixty wounded were found in the hospitals, from which I conclude that their loss in killed and wounded must have been three hundred, taking fifty as the number of their killed, and reckoning the ratio of killed to wounded as one to four."

* General Taylor relies on the official report of Colonel Major for this statement. As a specimen of Confederate reports on their operations west of the Mississippi River during June and July, the following *extract* of Major's report of this action is given:

"At Paincourtville received a despatch from Colonel Lane stating he had captured the town, taking one hundred and forty prisoners and a large amount of stores, also a small force at Terrebonne Station, and that there was a force in strong position, with artillery, at La-Fourche Crossing. I pushed on and arrived at Thibodeaux at 3.30 A.M., on the twenty-first. Pickets reported reënforcements from New Orleans during the night, and at sun-up reported the enemy advancing. I posted Pyron's regiment, West's battery and two squadrons cavalry on east bank La-Fourche, and moved them down towards the railroad bridge. Lane, Stone and Phillip were posted at Terrebonne Station, and they were moved forward to La-Fourche Crossing. The enemy fell back, and my pursuit was checked by one of the heaviest rains I ever saw fall. It rained until five P.M., and having only thirty rounds of ammunition to the man when I started, and not over one hundred cartridge boxes in the entire command, my ammunition was nearly all ruined, and I found myself with an enemy in front, rear, and on the flank, with only three rounds of ammunition to the man. I directed Pyron, as soon as it stopped raining, to strengthen his picket and feel the enemy, find his position, and test his strength, giving him some discretion in the matter. He advanced his picket, driving the enemy into his stronghold, and then charged his works, taking four guns and causing a great many of the Federals to surrender. But night had come on; it was very dark, the ammunition nearly all gone, and just at that moment a train with about three hundred fresh men arrived from New Orleans, and Pyron was forced to retire from a position won by a daring assault, unequalled, I think, in this war. Had I known his intention to assault the works I could have sent him such reënforcements as would have insured success. Pyron's strength in the attack was two hundred and six. The enemy's force, reported by themselves, was over one thousand."

Some of these statements will cause a smile to spread o'er the face of men on the Federal side who were in this action.

Probably this is not an exaggeration, but many of the wounded must have been slightly so, not going into the hospitals, except for occasional treatment, else a larger number would have been captured. They left some badly wounded upon the field. One poor fellow was found bleeding to death from wounds, in a trench not over fifty feet in front of the line.

Whether Lieutenant-Colonel Stickney is correct or not, in regard to the Confederate dead, Lieutenant Cooke, Twenty-Sixth Massachusetts, reports the following facts, viz.: "On the morning of the twenty-second, when a lookout, stationed upon a house, reported a flag of truce coming, I happened to be standing near Stickney, who immediately turned to me and said: 'Meet them as far outside of our picket line as you possibly can, and I will despatch another officer immediately to act as messenger.' I was upon my horse instantly, and galloped up the bayou road, running my sword-point through my handkerchief corners to make a flag of truce, meeting the party so far from our lines as to cause, I fancied, a shade of disappointment to pass over the face of an officer in charge, which quickly changed to a smile as we drew rein and saluted; he introduced himself as Captain Johnson, of Texas, and remarked that it was a singular coincidence that both sides should start out at the same time for a truce, and was much astonished when I said that I had come to meet him, having seen him approaching. He stated that he was sent by Colonel Major to ask permission to drive upon the battle field with their wagons and carry away their dead. The request was carried to Lieutenant-Colonel Stickney, who replied that it was impossible to grant it, but if they would send their wagons to the point of negotiation he would receive and return them to the same point loaded. This was a necessity, for the majority of their dead lay so near our battle line had they been permitted to come near they would have gained an accurate knowledge of our position and numbers. Colonel Major assented to this modification of his request, and wagons soon began to arrive and the work went on. After the transfer was made I inquired of those who were engaged in the work how many dead they found, and was told one hundred and sixty. These are the figures written in my diary at the time. I was also told that in one place fifteen bodies were found in such close proximity as to justify the statement that they were slain in a heap. At my interview with Captain Johnson, he complimented our forces in very flattering terms for the courage and steadiness with which they met and repelled the assault; that had it been known we had such a large and well-disciplined force their action would have been less hasty and impetuous."

The ground was cut at regular intervals by irrigating ditches, a probable reason why the enemy made their attack dismounted. These ditches made the ground unfavorable for cavalry.

Two of the unwounded prisoners captured (sixteen in number) came in and surrendered to Lieutenant Tinkham, after the firing had ceased. They must have secreted themselves under the lee of the bayou bank.

The killed and wounded of the Forty-Second detachment were:

Private Reuben Dyson, Company E, wounded fatally in the abdomen and hip, and died in a short time after he was carried to the rear. When wounded he clasped both hands across his abdomen and exclaimed: "What have I done that they should hit me!"

Sergeant Edmand A. Jones, Company B, was slightly wounded in the left shoulder.

Private William Whiting, Company B, was wounded by

a bullet in the back of his neck which passed out of his mouth, taking three teeth in its course.

Private Daniel S. Woodman, Company B, was wounded in the right hand, losing one finger and part of the thumb joint; also, shot in the right breast, the ball entering about two inches above the right nipple, passed through the upper part of his lung and came out through the shoulder blade.

Private Dyson was buried on the field at La-Fourche. Private Woodman, too dangerously wounded to be removed, was left in an abandoned planter's house in care of an old planter. Woodman had lain upon the field all night; was carried to the hospital about noon next day, where his wounds were dressed by surgeons of the Twenty-Third Connecticut and Twenty-Sixth Massachusetts. His clothes were removed, as they were very bloody, and he lay naked almost a week, when a comrade procured some old, ragged clothing for him. He was brought from La-Fourche July 31st, and came home with the regiment.

Early on the morning of Monday, June 22d, the enemy were found to have retired near to Thibodeaux. Among the debris picked up upon the field was found some muskets that were indentified as belonging to the three companies Forty-Second, captured at Galveston. The wounded were cared for and the Federal dead buried.

A Confederate flag of truce came with a request for permission to bury their dead and carry away their wounded. This was granted on condition that all of their wounded men outside the camp lines should be paroled, that none of their drivers should come within the outposts, and that all wounded within the camp should be retained. They agreed to these conditions, and men were engaged throughout the morning, with carts and wagons furnished by the enemy, in carrying their dead to Thibodeaux.

Very early in the morning there reached the crossing about six hundred men Fifteenth Maine Infantry, Colonel Isaac Dyer, a fresh regiment from Pensacola and Key West, under orders to reünforce the troops at Brashear City, and about eleven o'clock Colonel Cahill arrived from New Orleans with the Ninth Connecticut Infantry, two additional companies Twenty-Sixth Massachusetts, and another section of the Twenty-Fifth New York Battery. Colonel Cahill assumed command of the forces at La-Fourche.

The men who comprised the detachment Forty-Second Massachusetts behaved admirably in this, their maiden action, with the exception of Sergeant Albert L. Clark and Private John Donnelly, both of Company B, who attempted to desert from their comrades, without leave, and board a train about to start for Algiers. They threw away their guns, and did not report to the detachment until Tuesday.

Lieutenant Clifford was not in this action, as he rejoined the detachment from leave of absence after the action was over.

Other men, attached to the several commands, showed the white feather, and the official report of Lieutenant-Colonel Stickney says: "Their wounded in our hands thought that our troops must be regulars, so steadily did they stand at their posts; but I regret to say that the train in waiting on the track left at the commencement of the fight, without orders, carrying away some cowardly soldiers, and that during the battle some few left their ranks and sought shelter near and behind the railroad."

Among those who left by this train was the Twenty-Sixth Massachusetts color-bearer with his flag. He was ordered back to his regiment in a peremptory manner by General Emory, commanding the Defences of New Orleans. A word of defence is due this color-bearer. A brave, honorable and worthy man; when the darkness came on he was ordered by his commanding officer to retire from the line and remain with his color at a house just to the rear. Those panic-stricken men who ran away from the ranks passed this house towards the railroad, shouting: "All is lost, the rebs are inside of our lines and gobbling up the whole force." He supposed it to be true, and animated with a desire to save his flag also ran to the railroad, tearing his flag from the lance to secrete it upon his person. He felt the disgrace keenly, suffered mental agony, and died from the effect upon him in September following. None of his comrades thought him guilty of cowardice, rather a victim to circumstances, for he could not see the true situation.

Lieutenant-Colonel Stickney officially makes special mention of two officers and one private. He says: "Major Morgans, commanding the One Hundred and Seventy-Sixth New York Regiment, through the action encouraged his men, and to him is due, in a great degree, the fine conduct that they showed. Captain Jenkins, commanding the Twenty-Third Connecticut, displayed the greatest bravery and coolness. A Confederate officer seized him by the throat, demanding a surrender. The assault was immediately returned in precisely the same manner, when one of Captain Jenkins' men bayoneted the Confederate. I desire particularly to mention Sergeant John Allyn, Company A, Forty-Seventh Massachusetts Regiment, who has been with me since I was ordered to Brashear City, and has at all times rendered the most valuable service, going on dangerous scouts, once inside the enemy's lines, and showing at all times the greatest courage and remarkable sound judgment. His thorough knowledge of the country and habit of reporting facts only were of the greatest assistance to me."

Two companion incidents to the hand-to-hand scrape of Captain Jenkins are these: Lieutenant Cooke, acting adjutant Twenty-Sixth Massachusetts, the action still in progress, was startled by the sudden appearance before him, inside of the battle line, of a Confederate lieutenant-colonel, who said: "Captain, I am badly wounded, will you be kind enough to take me to the rear." The lieutenant informed him he would do so, when he felt justified in taking men from the ranks to act as a guard, and conducted the wounded officer to a tent, standing not more than twenty yards to the rear, and saw him comfortably stretched out upon the straw. After the action was over, with no prospect of its renewal, Lieutenant Cooke went to this tent for his prisoner, to find him gone, without a clew to be obtained of his whereabouts. On the reconnoissance to Thibodeaux, twenty-third, this wounded officer was found in hospital, and paroled. He stated that while lying in the tent it occurred to him that in the darkness he might walk out of our lines, and did so without difficulty.

Another case of foolhardy bravery was exhibited by a fiery Texan lieutenant, who rushed up to a field-gun, placing his hand upon it, in face of a dozen men, and demanded its surrender. Three men answered him; one with a bayonet, one with a musket ball, the other with the butt of his gun, to send him down to mother earth fatally wounded, and with curses upon his lips of the men who did their duty. He was carried to the hospital, and lived four hours.

No further hostile movement was made by either combatants on Monday, except at about dark the Confederates fired a few rounds from one field-gun. On Tuesday, June 23d, an advance was made to Thibodeaux by a part of the troops, now commanded by Colonel Cahill, to find the enemy had gone. Colonel Major with his Texans were well on their way towards the rear of Brashear City. At night the Fifteenth Maine Infantry was sent back to New Orleans.

Wednesday morning, June 24th, at eight o'clock, five companies Ninth Connecticut, under Lieutenant-Colonel Fitzgibbon, proceeded to Terrebonne Station as guard to a construction train, repairing the track for one mile beyond. Proceeding towards Chucahoula, twelve miles from Bayou Bœuff, the bridge, one mile from the station, was found to be on fire. This was extinguished, and the bridge repaired. Skirmishers were then deployed and advanced towards the station, where the enemy was found on the open land, behind buildings and fences, who at once commenced a sharp fire. Confined to the narrow track, a thickly-wooded swamp upon both sides, after engaging the enemy for one hour Lieutenant-Colonel Fitzgibbon deemed it prudent to retire, also being recalled by a signal-gun fired at La-Fourche Crossing, nine miles distant, which the lieutenant-colonel says he heard. The Federal loss was three wounded, and two men taken prisoners by the enemy.

Port Hudson still holding out, with work enough in prospect to occupy the attention of all the available forces in the Department, the troops that composed the force under General Emory, charged with the defence of New Orleans, reduced to a low number, and Brashear City lost, with all of the troops on duty between that place and La-Fourche Crossing, there existed no further necessity for holding the railroad line to Brashear. The ill-luck experienced by General Emory in losing post after post, through cowardice and inefficiency of regimental officers, surrendering without firing a gun, was not assuring as to how far he could trust the balance of his force. Prudence dictated to withdraw his troops close to the city where protection of the navy could be given.

The Confederates pushed up from Brashear, bold and fearless, offering many opportunities to inflict some hard blows against their undisciplined troops if any equally bold officers had been with the Federal soldiers. This was not the case, and on June 26th the Federal force fell back to Boutee Station, twenty-four miles from Algiers, after they had spiked and abandoned three field-guns and some old iron guns; an absurd gift to the enemy, without any valid excuse.

With the energy displayed by the enemy, which the Federals did not meet with counter efforts, it was undoubtedly sound policy to allow them to dash against the fortified defences whenever they felt so disposed. They moved quickly from place to place, leaving stragglers and scouting squads occupying all of the roads in the region of country upon the left bank held by them, looting where they could. Many of them could easily have been bagged by small forces equally as bold; by so doing thrown them into much the same state of uncertainty where to look for a blow as existed among the Federal officers.

While at Boutee Station orders from Colonel Cahill directed the Forty-Second detachment to be temporarily attached to the Fifteenth Maine and to proceed to the Metairie race-course, in New Orleans, where a camp was formed, comprised of detachments One Hundred and Seventy-Sixth New York, Twenty-Third Connecticut and Fifteenth Maine, with Grow's battery; Lieutenant-Colonel Stickney in command of the force. These orders were countermanded on the same day and the detachment ordered to rejoin the regiment, then in New Orleans, and did so June 29th, bringing under guard to the provost-marshal some sixty prisoners taken at La-Fourche and vicinity.

On the thirtieth June the Federal force drew back to Jefferson Station, eight miles from Algiers, where fortifications of a formidable character were thrown up by large gangs of negroes. This station was an outpost to the Defences of New Orleans for some weeks, with pickets upon the roads and railroad line back to Algiers, and the river patroled by gunboats between Company Canal and Donaldsonville.

While the Confederates under General Taylor raided on the various posts in the Parishes between the Atchafalaya and the Mississippi Rivers, picking up all scattered troops found, to send them on parole to New Orleans, the garrison in the defences of the city was quite small. General Banks had drawn all the men he dared to take in front of Port Hudson, even bringing troops from Ship Island and Pensacola. To offset this General Emory had all troops in the garrison, on whatever duty, kept ready from the nineteenth June until all danger was over to move readily at any moment with two days cooked rations and one hundred rounds per man. The Second Brigade, Second Division, was concentrated as far as possible; all passes or leaves of absence were absolutely stopped; convalescent soldiers were got together and organized, and colored regiments, recruited from intelligent blacks of the city, were organized for sixty days service, under colored officers. In this manner were sufficient troops obtained to do the needed garrison duty, furnish required guards and patrol service, while the regular forces attended to the extreme outposts. The First Texas Cavalry, Colonel Davis, did all of the scouting service, under direct orders from General Emory.

This action at La-Fourche Crossing must not be confounded with the disastrous engagement of July 13th at Bayou La-Fourche, in which the Forty-Eighth, Forty-Ninth and Thirtieth Massachusetts Regiments formed a part of the Federal forces; Colonel Dudley in command.

CHAPTER XIII.

JULY — IN NEW ORLEANS — AT ALGIERS.

NEW ORLEANS on a Sunday during the summer of 1863 would have shocked those staid old New Englanders who believed in a proper observance of the day. Army and navy officers, soldiers and sailors, who could obtain furloughs, did not hesitate to use the day for a grand spree. All the elements were there to have a merry time, and upon the Shell-road there was seen a cosmopolite crowd bent on enjoyment of the day. The colored population was always out in full force. Until one got so used to it that the novelty was gone, all this excitement, in endless variety, was not to be lost by those who could take part.

The Fourth of July was made a gala-day. Salutes were fired morning, noon and night. A street parade was made by the Forty-Second Massachusetts and a few small companies from the One Hundred and Seventy-Sixth New York, Twenty-Third Connecticut Infantry and Twenty-Fifth New York Battery, with two squadrons cavalry, as an escort to a procession of citizens, mostly dark colored. Fireworks in front of the Custom House at night closed the jubilations of the day.

At the Custom House the regiment remained until July 14th, on provost duty and on guard over Confederate prisoners, confined in the best part of the building. The treatment of these prisoners was good; their food was the same furnished to the regiment on guard, and except deprivation of their liberty they had no reason to complain. It was a hot time the day these Confederate officers arrived from Port Hudson. A large crowd of sympathizers were on hand to welcome them, so boisterous in behavior the cavalry-men, who assisted the infantry guard, in a number of cases lost their temper and drove the people into stores and houses by backing their horses into the crowd; sabres were also used a few times. The crowd threatened at one time to make an attempt to seize some stacked arms in a street near the Custom House, after the prisoners were placed in quarters. In a day or two quiet was restored and all expressions of sympathy ceased.

While on duty in the city all drills were suspended; parades of ceremony, guard-mounting and dress parade, took place on the reserved ground in the centre of Canal Street. These parades were gone through with in an indifferent manner on account of hot weather and debility, which began to affect a great majority of the men. Not being acclimated the extreme hot weather told on their health in a marked degree; not exactly in a condition to be called sick, they did not feel well; what duty had to be done was made easy as possible. Guards for hospitals, men for patrol, funeral escorts, and regular sentry duty at quarters kept at work every man able to do duty. One funeral escort was furnished every day, always at six o'clock in the afternoon.

After several assaults had been made upon solitary unarmed soldiers by the rough element in the city, an order was issued July 11th for every officer and soldier to wear his side-arms whenever upon the street. Several men had been roughly handled, and reports were current of the assassination of two men in the suburbs, but of the truth of this report there is no definite knowledge. The night patrol had orders to prevent more than three persons assembling together and to arrest all officers and men of the army without side-arms. The patrol furnished by the Forty-Second consisted of one lieutenant and eighteen men, who covered all streets within the limits of — from St. Mary's Market to Eliseum Field Street, to Dauphin Street, to Canal Street, to St. Charles Street, to Julia Street, to Tchoupitoulas Street, and to Custom House Street. These limits covered many questionable places of resort and afforded night patrols an opportunity to see very curious incidents. At reunions of the regiment these incidents form the basis of a large number of amusing anecdotes.

To while away care and to lighten the burden of duty a few officers and men conceived an idea of forming a mock Sons of Malta Lodge. Prominent in this amusement were Captain Leonard, Lieutenants Sanderson and Phillips, Sergeant-Major Bosson, Sergeants Nichols, Vialle, Attwell, and others. The first move was to secure a victim for an initiation ceremony. It was decided to try Sergeant John Binney, of Company A, a man well known to all on duty at the Custom House. After broaching the subject in a careful way to the sergeant, he was anxious to join such a lodge, which he was informed had already been formed, and thought it an excellent idea. He was kept in suspense a few days on the plea that his name would have to go before the lodge, and if not black-balled he would be admitted on a certain evening. Binney caught at the bait like a hungry fish.

When everything was ready the *pseudo*-lodge members assembled, masked, in a dimly-lighted room in the Custom House, prepared for fun. A bugle, trombone, bass-drum and cymbals were procured from the band, officers appointed, and the sergeant, blindfolded, was admitted after passing through certain mock forms at the door. All worked well; the questions and answers and chorus from lodge members were carried out with due decorum until the moment the embrace of fellowship was to be given.

There was attached to Company C, as cook, an immense large negro, a regular old plantation hand, tall, burly looking, black as coal, with an odor about him as bad as from a skunk. With some difficulty, and not without threats, this negro was got into the room and made to strip naked to the waist. As the arms of Binney were placed around this negro and his head laid upon the bare, black breast the whole ceremony came near being spoiled by those present bursting into a roar of laughter; fortunately this was stifled, and amid a crashing din, made by band instruments, gas was turned on and the bandage removed from the eyes of candidate Binney. For a moment dead silence reigned, while Binney stared around and then at the negro in such a manner those present can never forget. Suddenly he kicked him, and with an exclamation more forcible than polite he proceeded to kick him out of the room amid peals of laughter. The negro did not lose any time in escaping from Binney's wrath, for the poor fellow had been almost frightened out of his wits during the initiation; large drops of sweat stood out upon his face and breast like moisture on a well-filled ice pitcher.

Binney was mad. It was some time before he was cooled down. Finally he saw the joke, took it good-naturedly, and had his revenge in assisting at the initiation of others. Quite a number were "put through," but as the proceedings leaked out candidates became scarce, and the lodge adjourned *sine die*.

While at Bayou Gentilly there was much discussion among some officers and men about their time of enlistment, caused by a regimental order, issued May 19th, promulgating the time of service for the regiment to expire on July 14th. Opinions varied, and naturally the men inclined to believe that theory which made their time for discharge come early. Some company officers allowed themselves to display their ignorance by agreeing with the short-term men, and did all in their power to keep up that belief. Those who knew better did not try to stop this short-term theory by informing the men of the true facts in the case. By a decision of the War Department, promulgated at the time when nine months regiments were called for, and modified at various times so that it was at last expressly stated that companies could be mustered when full, the men to draw pay from time of enlistment, though it be a month or two before their company was mustered; that when ten companies were mustered and formed into a regiment, then the field and staff were to be mustered, and the time of the regiment would date from the time the tenth company was mustered into service. This should have been known by all officers. Men in the companies who did not have the correct information imparted to them had an idea their term expired from date of muster of each company, and thought they could be sent home by companies. These men seemed to think of nothing but to get home as soon as possible, and they did not show any pride in the duty of a soldier, nor any regard for the cause they were in service for.

A few company commanders sent in to Department headquarters a notification their time would be out on a certain date — which was required by regulations — and received for reply the information, in substance, as issued by the War Department. Notwithstanding this official information they still refused to believe such to be the case, and took no steps to quell a mutinous sentiment which prevailed to a great extent; men swearing they would rather be shot than do another day's duty, and similar foolish remarks.

This feeling reached a climax on the morning of July 14th. In the morning orders had been received to have the companies in readiness to move at a moment's notice, in light marching order. The men and a few officers declared the time of the regiment had expired, and refused to do further duty. It was necessary to notify General Emory. The day before it was with difficulty a detachment of seventy-three men was furnished Lieutenant-Colonel Fitzgibbon, who ordered the detail.

The men on duty were assembled upon the top of the Custom House and addressed by Lieutenant-Colonel W. D. Smith, One Hundred and Tenth New York Volunteers, acting assistant-adjutant-general on the staff of the general commanding. The trouble was mortifying, besides interfering with plans of the general, and it is no wonder Lieutenant-Colonel Smith could not control his temper, and used threats, combined with entreaty, to bring the men to a proper sense of their duty. The state of affairs was told to them, with a warning of what to expect if a refusal to do duty was persisted in. One officer, Lieutenant Duncan, Company F, protested, claiming that his time had expired, and asked in the name of *justice* that he and his men be sent home. He was promptly placed in arrest and his sword taken from him. This summary action was well-timed, for Lieutenant Duncan was a special champion of the "want to go home" men. It was proof to the men to butt against the Government was not an easy matter. When the Twenty-Sixth Massachusetts marched into the Custom House in the afternoon, to occupy their old quarters and relieve the Forty-Second, ordered to Algiers, the men thought and so expressed themselves that the commanding officer intended to coerce the regiment into doing duty, if it was found necessary. Fortunately, without further difficulty, the regiment went over to Algiers in the afternoon. Lieutenant Duncan was released from arrest and his sword returned, after an apology for his hasty, ill-timed behavior.

A history of the regiment would not be correct, and the truth not told, without recording these events, though it is unpleasant to do so. All true friends of the Forty-Second have every reason to be thankful nothing further took place to bring discredit on the regiment. This ebullition of sentiment about expiration of time of enlistment is the only act the enlisted men, as a body, have reason to feel ashamed about during their term of service.

From the fourteenth to the twenty-ninth the regiment was on picket duty upon the Opelousas and Gulf Railroad. Headquarters of troops on the west bank of the Mississippi River were at Company Canal, Brigadier-General McMillan in command (from July 21st, when he relieved Colonel Plumley) of all troops from Algiers to Des Allemands, and troops were pushed forward to La-Fourche Crossing, repairing the track and bridges to that point. The picket-detail usually consisted of from thirty to forty men, who were out on duty forty-eight hours, carrying rations for that time, their blankets and mosquito bars. The bars did not prove effective protection, and it was generally the case these men could not obtain any sleep, for they were obliged to keep awake and fight the terribly annoying insects. This was all of the fighting done on picket.

This picket duty extended to Jefferson Station, eight miles from Algiers, where two companies of Colonel Desanger's regiment of sixty-day free colored troops and a battery of artillery were on duty. These colored troops were neatly dressed in the United States regulation uniform, and to all appearances were doing their duty well.

Besides this picket-detail a guard was retained on duty, comprising nine men from Company A, eight men from Company B, nine men from Company C, five men from Company E, seven men from Company F, seven men from Company H, forty-five men in all, and acting Lieutenant George G. Nichols, Company G, under the command of Lieutenant White, Company C, who were sent to the Bellevue Iron Works in Algiers, July 13th, to relieve a guard from the Ninth Connecticut over Confederate prisoners of war confined there.

Another permanent guard was detailed for duty at Canal Street and French Market Ferries from New Orleans. Their duty was to prevent soldiers or citizens from crossing over without passes and to arrest suspicious persons.

Algiers and vicinity would not have pleased a tourist, with its delapidated and uncared-for buildings, abandoned and neglected plantations and small population. All drills were stopped. Men not on duty could stroll where they pleased. A mixed contraband camp, not far away, was a favorite spot for many men to pass their spare hours. The men raided on all watermelon patches within a radius of several miles until complaints were made to the provost-marshal. In more than one case did these melons effect a cure of that scourge in armies — chronic diarrhœa. Singular as it may seem several men with this complaint, unable to get relief from the surgeons, were completely cured by eating these melons.

Quarters were taken in an old salt warehouse close to the river, with all the companies located in the building, space allotted each company, every man making himself comfortable upon the floor. Doors and windows torn out, there was no trouble about ventilation in the extreme hot weather that prevailed. The guard occupied tents on the opposite side of the road; the company cooks* and kitchens were in tents upon the levee. A house situated within a fine orchard, not far from the men's quarters, was used by the surgeons for a hospital, the grounds in front for the field and staff-officers' tents.

Each night, after taps, the men made this salt warehouse ring with fun and music up to midnight. Many rough remarks were passed to and fro with special reference to the lieutenant-colonel, who, the men thought, was not exerting himself to obtain transportation home. As great injustice was done Lieutenant-Colonel Stedman while at Algiers, it is proper some of the correspondence in relation to securing passage North should be read by the regiment. At first he endeavored to have the paroled men sent home; affairs in the Department would not warrant an application to send home those men able to do duty, as every man was wanted.

"HEADQUARTERS 42D REGIMENT, MASS. VOLS.,

"CUSTOM HOUSE, NEW ORLEANS, LA., July 5th, 1863.

"*Sir*,— I would respectfully present the following facts to the attention of the commanding general of the Defences of New Orleans:

"January 1st, 1863, three companies of the Forty-Second Massachusetts Volunteers, viz., D, G and I, under Colonel I. S. Burrell, were taken prisoners at Galveston, Texas. These men were taken to Houston and kept

---

* One day a negro cook of Company C (the same man who took a part in the Sons of Malta ceremonies at the New Orleans Custom House) got into a difficulty with a camp-follower colored boy. Bantered into frenzy by this little devil the cook got a small dagger, and would have committed a murder had not the sergeant-major and Private John Davis, Company H, seized him, as he was about to stab the boy. A short struggle took place before this dagger was obtained. For punishment the negro cook was kicked for some distance down the road. Whatever became of the burly, quick-tempered negro has often been a subject of speculation among those who remember him.

several weeks, when they were sent to our lines at Baton Rouge and paroled. February 25th they arrived in New Orleans and were ordered by General Sherman to report to me at the camp of the Forty-Second Regiment at Gentilly Crossing, on the Ponchartrain Railroad, since which time they have been in camp at that place.

"These men have had nothing to do or to engage their attention, and as a consequence they have become very low spirited and much reduced in bodily vigor. Several of them have lately died very suddenly, and several are daily taken sick. One sergeant taken sick July 3d was buried July 4th.

"The time of this regiment expires the fourteenth of this month, according to the rule established by the War Department for the service of the nine months troops, this date being nine months from the date of muster of the last company in the regiment. In view of these circumstances and of the fact that these men have been of no service to the Government in their present condition, I would respectfully ask the commanding general that they be sent to their homes as soon as possible.

"Many of these men are from the best families in Boston and vicinity, and their friends are deeply anxious that they should be sent North, and personally I am deeply interested that their case may be acted on at an early day, for if they are kept in this climate even a few weeks longer many more will be lost by reason of sickness, not only to their friends but for future use to the country.

"There are also at Algiers forty-four men from different companies of this regiment who are paroled, having been taken at Brashear City; these with those first spoken of make a total of two hundred and seventy-six paroled men of this regiment.

"By allowing these men to be sent to their homes not

only a humane act will be accomplished but a great and never-to-be-forgotten favor will be bestowed on these men, who faithfully served their country when in service, and on many true friends of the Union in Massachusetts.

"With the highest consideration,

"I remain, your obedient servant,

"J. STEDMAN, *Lieutenant-Colonel*,

"*commanding 42d Mass. Vols.*

"To LIEUT.-COL. W. D. SMITH, *A. A. General*,

"*Defences New Orleans.*"

The transport-steamer *F. A. Scott* was partially promised by Provost-Marshal-General Bowen, but on July 11th he wrote Lieutenant-Colonel Stedman as follows: "General Emory, in view of the altered condition of affairs since the fall of Vicksburg and Port Hudson, revokes the order for the transportation of the paroled soldiers of the Forty-Second Regiment Massachusetts Volunteers to New York." This letter was the first intimation that an early return North could be expected of all nine months regiments whose time had expired. Until the two Confederate strongholds surrendered they would have been retained in the Department.

As a matter of form a letter was sent to the Department commander June 19th, stating the time of expiration of service, with a request for transportation to Massachusetts.

The two following letters explain themselves:

"HEADQUARTERS FORTY-SECOND REGT., MASS. VOLS.,

"LAFAYETTE SQUARE, NEW ORLEANS, June 21st, 1863.

"*Sir*,— I have the honor to report that your communication of the eighteenth instant, relative to the muster into service of this regiment, is received.

"I would respectfully state that no formal muster was ever made of this regiment, and the field and staff were mustered on the eleventh November, 1862. But the War Department have decided that in the case of the nine months' troops their time was to expire nine months from the date of muster of the last company, which in this regiment was the fourteenth of October, making our time, as above, the fourteenth of July next.

"I received a short time since an official order from Governor Andrew, based on an order from Secretary Stanton, that the time would be reckoned as above stated.

"I have the honor to remain,

"Very respectfully, your obedient servant,
"J. STEDMAN, *Lieutenant-Colonel*,
"*commanding 42d Mass. Vols.*

"To LIEUT.-COL. R. B. IRWIN, *A. A. General*,
"*19th Army Corps.*"

"HEADQUARTERS FORTY-SECOND REGT., MASS., VOLS.
"CAMP AT ALGIERS, LA., July 27th, 1863.

"*Sir*,— The time of service of the Forty-Second Regiment Massachusetts Volunteers having expired the fourteenth instant, I would respectfully request that transportation be furnished the regiment for their return to Massachusetts. I would state for the information of the commanding general that the aggregate strength of the regiment at this time is as follows: on duty with the regiment and on detached service, including sick, five hundred and eighty; paroled enlisted men, two hundred and seventy-five; this making a total of eight hundred and fifty-five officers and enlisted men, for whom I apply for transportation. Of this number from twenty to thirty will be unable to travel with the regiment on account of sickness and these will need separate transportation. Of the above number I have only about two hundred men fit for duty Many have become debilitated from exposure and from the effects of the climate (fever and ague being quite prevalent), which incapacitated them for duty at the present time.

"Of all the commissioned officers I have only the adjutant, one captain and nine lieutenants for duty, the balance being either sick, on detached service, or prisoners of war at Huntsville, Texas.

"I have five captains sick, who will probably never get well in this climate. In view of the present condition of the regiment I would urgently request that this matter receive an early consideration from the commanding general, on the ground of humanity, if for no other reason.

"The paroled men have done no duty since their capture at Galveston January 1st, and they have become much debilitated from this constant inactivity, and they have lost a large percentage of their number by death and many more will be lost, not only to their friends but to their country, if a change of climate is not granted them soon.

"Nothing has yet been asked of the Forty-Second Regiment that they have not fully carried out, and if Port Hudson still remained in the hands of the enemy there is not a man but would volunteer to stay to assist in any manner in accomplishing so desirable a result, as its capture.

"But having been informed that the exigencies do not now exist for our services that prevailed previous to the fourteenth of July, and our time having expired, as above stated, every member of the regiment is more or less anxious that the Government should allow them their right of returning to their homes and friends.

"I have the honor to remain,

"Very respectfully, your obedient servant,

"J. STEDMAN, *Lieutenant-Colonel*,

"*commanding 42d Mass. Vols.*

"To LIEUT.-COL. R. B. IRWIN, *A. A. General*,

"*19th Army Corps.*"

A letter from Brigadier-General McMillan, dated July 28th, stated that the major-general commanding the Department would send all nine months men home in such order as he would select, and as fast as transportation could be obtained; that he would send all at once if he could, and that all petitions and representations would fail to expedite the sending.

July 17th — Paroled men of Companies D, G, I, A, B, E and H arrived at Algiers from Gentilly Camp and were assigned quarters in the warehouse.

July 21st — Company K rejoined the regiment.

On one occasion while at Algiers an act of insubordination had to be summarily dealt with. Details for picket duty had been ordered, and first-sergeants had notified their men for that duty. When the hour arrived to "fall in" and report to the adjutant, the men from Companies C, H and E refused to do so. Their company officers proved powerless to enforce the orders, and the case was reported at regimental headquarters, when the lieutenant-colonel, major, adjutant and sergeant-major went to quarters to straighten matters out. Most of the trouble was in Companies C and H. Lieutenant-Colonel Stedman ordered the first-sergeant of Company C to order his detail to "fall in," fully equipped. The first man called absolutely refused to do so. He was given five minutes to obey by the lieutenant-colonel, who held his watch in one hand and a pistol in the other. This man reluctantly did as ordered before the time expired, and the rest followed suit. No difficulty was experienced with other company details, and the picket on duty was regularly relieved. This ended all serious trouble of this kind, although Private Lawrence Mannocks, Company I, was placed in arrest July 19th for inciting to mutiny and indulging in blasphemous remarks; it was also necessary, on the twenty-eighth, to reduce to the ranks Corporal Thomas P. Hobart, Company A; a regimental special order was issued to that effect. At Battery St. John Captain Coburn reduced to the ranks Corporal E. C. Crocker, Company A, June 5th.

The guard-house was filled each day by men temporarily placed there for being drunk. They were old, hard, chronic cases, poor soldiers, unfit to be in service. Captain Leonard, Company C, found it necessary, in June and July, to arrest and confine quite a number of his men for disobedience of orders. Of his men, Private Charles F. Towle was in arrest from June 10th to July 13th, for desertion; Private John Myers, for same cause, from July 1st to the 10th. No further action was taken in either case.

Confinements in the guard-house while at Gentilly were few. Privates Owen Fox, Michael Bresneau, Company A, and Thomas Matthews, Company D, frequently got placed there for drunkenness, disobedience of orders, and insolence. Private Fox was once sentenced to carry cannon balls for two days (February 25th and 26th), without a proper hearing into his case in the regular manner. Private Bresneau was once confined a week for insolence. At other times they would be released in a few days, when sober.

At Algiers the men suffered more from sickness than at any other period of service. The regimental hospital was at Bayou Gentilly until July 18th, Surgeon Heintzelman in charge, leaving that part of the regiment at Algiers without a medical-officer, as Surgeon Hitchcock was at Port Hudson on a visit, without orders. Hitchcock always claimed permission was granted him to go there, but the only order received at regimental headquarters which authorized his absence was Special Orders No. 207, Defences New Orleans, issued April 19th, 1863, ordering him to report for duty at Berwick Bay, where he remained for a short time. Department Special Orders No. 185, issued July 30th, read: "Relieved from duty at Berwick Bay." This want of a surgeon caused a letter to be sent the medical director, Defences New Orleans, which read: "I would respectfully bring to your attention the following facts: many men of this command are sick at this camp, and without any medical attendance. Unless a surgeon can be sent us some of our men will die in forty-eight hours. The reason of our being destitute of a surgeon will be explained by Chaplain Sanger, the bearer of this note. Please send us a good surgeon for temporary service." Surgeon Hitchcock allowed a personal matter with the lieutenant-colonel to interfere with his duty.

The medical director had the regimental hospital removed to Algiers on the nineteenth, in order to secure the services of Surgeon Heintzelman.

The hospital record tells the following story of sickness in July. At Bayou Gentilly, July 2d, forty-four men were taken sick, most of the cases among the paroled men recently arrived from Brashear City. On the third, of sick in quarters: fourteen were in Company A, twelve in B, six in C, two in D, fourteen in E, and eight in H. July 4th, ninety-five men were sick: twenty-seven in hospital and sixty-eight in quarters. The average sick per day at Gentilly up to July 11th was: taken sick, twelve; returned to duty, ten; in hospital, twenty-seven; in quarters, fifty-five. At Algiers, July 20th, one hundred and seven new cases were reported on the sick list; nearly all were sick in quarters. The largest number sick on any one day was reported by the surgeon in his morning report of July 22d, when one hundred and forty-five men were sick and unfit for duty, in and out of hospital, viz.: Company A, twenty-one; B, twenty-two; C, seventeen; D, two; E, twenty-seven; F, fifteen; G, two; H, eighteen; I, five; K, sixteen. Not until the twenty-third did the paroled men from Galveston begin to show signs of breaking down, when eleven men of Company D, six of G, and eight of I were taken sick. After this date sick in quarters gradually diminished, but the sick in hospital kept that building full. The average sick per day at Algiers was: taken sick, twenty-three; returned to duty, seventeen; in hospital, thirty; in quarters, sixty-two.

Had the regiment remained in the Department another month the deaths would have doubled those in July, owing to the debilitated condition of many men. The deaths were:

July 4th — Sergeant Philip P. Hackett, Company G, congestion of the brain. At Gentilly.

July 7th — Corporal Uriel Josephs, Company A, jaundice. At Marine Hospital, New Orleans.

July 8th — Private Rufus G. Hildreth, Company C, dysentery. At Gentilly.

July 12th — Quartermaster-Sergeant Henry C. Foster, suicide. In New Orleans.

July 17th — Private Thomas J. Clements, Company H, chronic diarrhœa. At Gentilly.

July 17th — Private Welcome Temple, Company H, disease not known. At United States Barracks.

July — Private Patrick Fitzpatrick, Company E, chronic diarrhœa. In New Orleans.

July 26th — Private Ezekiel W. Hanaford, Company H, chills and fever. At St. James Hospital, New Orleans.

July 25th — Private John M. Gates, Company K, chronic diarrhœa. At Algiers.

July 26th — Private William H. Bickers, Company G, swelling of glands. At Algiers.

Sergeant Hackett (at one time an active member of old Barnicoat Engine No. 4, of Boston) was a clever man, full of life and good spirits. His disease was the result of hard drinking.

Corporal Josephs was a thorough believer in the cold-water cure. When his disease first showed its symptoms, about one month before he died, while on duty as ordnance-sergeant, he refused to report to the surgeon, but got permission to hire a room in a house not far distant on the Gentilly road. Every day he would bathe in a tub of water and then go to bed wrapped up in a wet sheet, until the landlady complained at headquarters about the corporal acting like a crazy man in her house, and asked for his removal. As Josephs was found to be very sick, he was removed to the Marine Hospital in the city.

Poor Hildreth lost all courage and hope a month before his death. He was then able to move about, and was cheered up by those who met him, without any effect. Had he shown some strength of will, as others did, he might have reached home and recovered.

The case of Private Gates was sad. Although blind in one eye and quite old when mustered into service, being a good marksman, very enthusiastic to serve, the officers and men of his company assisted him to deceive the mustering officer that he was only forty-two years old. He did duty manfully until his disease took such a hold upon him that he gradually wasted away. At his death he could not have weighed more than fifty pounds.

Private Bickers was unconscious when he died. He was placed on an operating chair in an upright position, a nurse standing near with a fan to stir the air for him to breathe, and drive away swarms of flies infesting the place. Around the room were beds arranged upon the floor, occupied by sick patients, all watching with intense interest poor Bickers draw his last breath. The sight was not calculated to give them courage, for Bickers was sick in the hospital only a short time.

Privates Temple, Fitzpatrick and Hanaford were sent to the general hospitals for better treatment than could be given them in the regimental hospital. During the latter part of July medical supplies became scarce. With difficulty were sufficient quantities of proper medicines obtained to treat a majority of cases; the supply of quinine gave out completely. Such a large quantity of medical stores lost at Brashear City could not be replaced until supplies from New York were received.

Private Hanaford lay upon the warehouse floor for some days, suffering with chills and fever, and nothing could be done for him. When taken with chills, it seemed as though he would shake the breath out of him. His removal to St. James Hospital was not made until nearly dead. This case caused much comment among the men, who freely charged he had been neglected.

About noon, July 12th, word was brought in to the headquarters room by a corporal in charge of the guard stationed at a house on Canal Street, corner of Magazine Street, occupied by the regimental quartermaster, quartermaster-sergeant and commissary-sergeant, that Quartermaster-Sergeant Foster had committed suicide a few minutes before. The news was hardly credited, but an immediate visit to his room, in which the sad event happened, proved it to be a fact. Foster lay upon the floor near the centre of the room, not far from a bureau, feet towards the door, dressed in his flannel shirt, pants and socks, just as he fell; a small pool of blood upon the floor near his head, a small bullet wound in the centre of his forehead, encircled by a small black-and-blue ring, and a pistol upon the floor by his side. Sergeant Foster had not been in good health for some time, and latterly shown great despondency. The reason was not known. His sickness was nothing more than came from extreme debility, and was not dangerous. For a few days previous he had given some evidence of not being exactly in his right mind, but there was nothing exhibited to lead any one to think him not capable of taking care of himself. He occupied a room with acting Quartermaster-Sergeant Hodsdon, both men sleeping in the same bed.

That morning Hodsdon thought Foster spoke and acted queer, without exciting any suspicion however, and when obliged to go out on business Hodsdon, contrary to his usual custom, laid his belt, containing a holster and pistol, upon the bureau, intending to be back in a moment and then wear it. He left the room, leaving Foster upon the bed, and had barely closed the door when he heard the report of a pistol and immediately opened the door again, to see Foster lying upon the floor as described. He never spoke, dying in a few moments.

His effects were taken in charge by the chaplain and sent to his parents, then residing in Dorchester, Massachusetts, from which place Foster enlisted. From a partial examination of his knapsack, where a few letters were found, it was thought the sad act was caused by unwelcome news from home.

The weather being hot, by orders of the commanding

general all bodies had to be buried the same day that death occurred. Quartermaster-Sergeant Foster was buried in Greenwood Cemetery, at dusk, on the twelfth, escorted to the cemetery by a proper detail becoming to his rank, under command of Sergeant-Major Bosson, and the customary volleys fired over his grave. The burial party started at half-past three in the afternoon, and reported back to quarters at nine o'clock same evening.

Corporal Alonzo I. Hodsdon was made quartermaster-sergeant, July 13th, *vice* Foster, deceased.

Special-duty details in July were few :

July 18th — Private William A. Clark, Company B, was placed on duty as a wagoner.

July 23d — Private Leavitt Bates, Company A, was made clerk at regimental headquarters in place of Clark K. Denny, returned to duty with Company F.

July 25th — Private Lewis Buffum, Company B, to be a locomotive engineer on the Opelousas and Great Western Railroad.

CHAPTER XIV.

Companies C and H on Detached Service at Camp Parapet.

SPECIAL ORDERS No. 16, issued from headquarters Defences of New Orleans, January 15th, 1863, detailed Companies C and H for duty in the Department engineer service. The two companies made a skeleton battalion, under command of Senior-Captain Leonard, who, after reporting to Major D. C. Houston, chief-engineer Nineteenth Army Corps, for instructions, on the seventeenth marched them to Camp Parapet, three miles up river, with their camp equipage, and pitched tents upon a level piece of low, muddy land, formerly used as a burial place for soldiers. This Camp Parapet was so called because a large number of troops were in camp near earthworks thrown up a few miles above Carrollton. These works then consisted of a parapet and other fortifications on the east bank, between the river, the swamps and Lake Ponchartrain, with an abandoned Confederate redoubt upon the west bank, re-named Fort Banks.

The camp was moved to a fig grove January 21st, tents provided with floors, and here the battalion remained until relieved from detached duty, without suffering any inconvenience except, when a portion of camp was drowned out, February 15th, by a terrible thunder shower that forced men to seek shelter in barns not far away. Regular Sunday and monthly inspections were maintained, with an occasional drill. The inspections were thorough, as they should always be, and more drills would have been ordered had the details been less heavy. The companies suffered from a lack of commissioned officers. In Company C, Captain Leonard, as battalion commander, occupied the best quarters obtainable in the vicinity, and exercised command as such. Lieutenant White, absent on detached duty a greater part of the time, left but one company officer on duty, Lieutenant Sanderson. In Company H, Captain Bailey took things easy until placed in arrest April 16th, leaving Lieutenant Phillips the only company officer on duty; Lieutenant Gould was on detached service as an acting quartermaster.

There was little sickness among the men in this detachment during their stay at the Parapet. The position of their camp was more favorable for health than others at the post, with the additional good feature of being kept scrupulously neat; the prettiest camp at the post. On the extreme right of the earthworks, near the Jackson Railroad track, ground was so unhealthy it was nicknamed "Camp Death." Here the One Hundred and Fifty-Sixth New York suffered severely from sickness. This ground, near the railroad, was also a risky place for the troops there stationed on account of shells exploding in the neighborhood, fired from the gunboats when practising to obtain a range of this road. All shells had time fuses and would explode high in air, but fragments occasionally fell where not wanted. On one occasion, March 31st, a shell from the *Portsmouth* went over the One Hundred and Fifty-Sixth New York camp to explode nearly half a mile away, as every one thought, yet a large fragment was flung into camp and took off the head of a Zouave, who did not dream his death was so near. At another time a shell in passing over Companies C and H camp prematurely exploded overhead; pieces were flung into camp, fortunately without injury to anybody.

Among the few inhabitants who lived near Camp Parapet must have been some treacherous, be-deviled secessionists. Ammunition was occasionally stolen, the empty boxes afterwards found in places where they had been thrown. An attempt was once made by them to cause a break in the levee above the fortifications, by removing pickets placed to keep the levee embankment from giving way. This attempt was discovered before any damage resulted, and guards were afterward placed upon the river banks to prevent other attempts of a like nature.

Private Charles E. Warren, who had been an apothecary clerk in Boston, was detailed by Captain Leonard to act as medical-officer for the two companies. Warren did not take the position from any love for the medical profession, but did so to advance his personal interest and comfort. He was a social, jolly, good fellow, with a certain amount of acquired knowledge how to use medicines, but had no diploma as a graduate from any medical institute authorizing him to assume the practice of medicine.

Other details from the enlisted men were made to serve in various capacities, viz.:

Sergeant Frederick C. Blanchard, Company C, acting adjutant.

Sergeant Edward P. Fiske, Company C, acting sergeant-major.

Sergeant Edward L. Jones, Company H, acting commissary-sergeant.

Sergeant Dennis A. O'Brien, Company H, wagon-master.

Private David N. Phipps, Company H, carpenter.

Corporal William A. Hinds and Private Reuben Smith, Company H, clerks in Commissary Department.

Privates John Davis, Company H, Larry O'Laughlin,

Company H, James Haley, Company H, Daniel E. Demeritt, Company C, Solomon Kennison, Company C, and Henry C. Dimond, Company C, overseers of contrabands. Private Henry C. Dimond was also clerk in the superintendent's office.

Corporals Charles E. Loring, Company H, Charles M. Marden, Company H, and George H. Smith, Company H, clerks in office superintendent of contrabands, Engineer Department.

Private Henry A. Fenner, Company H, orderly to Major Houston, United States Engineers.

Companies C and H contained a queer mixture of men, that made it hard to handle them in good shape. No other companies in the regiment were like them in their *personnel*. There were good men, with excellent reputations at home and from families of high standing; many men whose reputations were known to be bad, taken from the rough element of cities and towns, whose faces and behavior were enough to stamp them what they were; also many excellent fellows who did their duty manfully, though they did come from the ordinary ranks of society. This much must be said about the tough characters: fight as often and hard as they could among themselves, a frequent occurrence, whenever an outsider molested any comrade belonging to their companies, they came to his rescue, and would stand by each other to the last.

The duty performed by these companies was not arduous. It mainly consisted of guard duty and acting as overseers to gangs of contrabands at work on the fortifications. There was plenty of this kind of work to keep in good order earthworks already finished, change the lines of some portions, raze and rebuild other portions, cut and haul wood, and, under direction of Mr. Long, volunteer United States engineer (the same young officer who was at Galveston), a bastioned redoubt, to form a part of the earthwork defences, was commenced January 30th, and completed before the companies rejoined their regiment.

There were several large contraband camps maintained at the Parapet, known as colonies number 1, 2, 3, 4 and 5, the Greenville colony and Brickyard colony. Women and children were kept in camps separate from the men. These camps received additional negroes brought from abandoned plantations by details of men sent up river to collect them. A number of men from C and H were detailed in various capacities to assist such officers as were in command of these negro camps, for they had to be governed and fed by the military authorities.

No guard was kept over these contraband colonies, the negroes in them allowed to go and come as they pleased; but over those able-bodied negroes in the engineer camp a line of sentinels was placed, whose orders, at first, allowed them considerable liberty after their day's work was done. A great many had what they called wives, who were domiciled in the colonies, and at dusk would go to see them, frequently remaining out of camp all night. Sometimes they got on a carouse, and made things lively. A considerable number would attend the numerous religious meetings held every night in the swamps. This exodus, at times, was so great that detachments of men from Companies C and H, mounted upon mules, would be started to hunt them up and bring them into camp, a fact Sergeant Meserve well remembers, because on one of these night hunts his mule became stubborn, and refused to obey the reins or the sergeant, finally landing him upon a tree-limb, where he hung until assisted to get down.

It was thought necessary to have more stringent orders than those in force, and by directions from General

Sumner, Engineer Department, the sentries were ordered to shoot any one that attempted to leave without authority to do so. Naturally, this created considerable dissatisfaction among them, especially those who had wives and children in other camps. This state of feeling led some officers to apprehend acts of insubordination several times, and the orders caused an unfortunate affair to happen on the evening of April 17th, when a negro man, while attempting to creep out of the engineer camp, was detected in the ditch and challenged; not responding, he was shot in the back by a sentry from Company H. His wound was an ugly one, and he died the next day, after receiving every attention that could be given. The negro camp was thrown into great excitement by this event, requiring a large force of soldiers on the spot before quiet was restored. Many officers expressed their indignation at the manner in which negroes were restricted and guarded in this camp, as they did not consider these strict rules necessary. To get the case before a court, where their views could be ventilated, Lieutenant White placed the sentry in arrest, insisting that he should stand an inquiry into his conduct; by such action he incurred the displeasure of Company H. The man was released next day by Captain Leonard, for the case was clear that the orders compelled him to fire as he did.

Eleven days later, April 28th, an uproar of voices within this same camp alarmed Private Martin, on sentry duty, who thought trouble was brewing in the camp and raised an alarm, which caused both guard-reliefs to turn out and double-quick to the spot, while the rest of the men also ran down, some with arms, others without, seizing for a weapon anything they could lay hands on, ready and willing to fight anybody if their comrades were in danger. An investigation showed that the contrabands had built a large bonfire, and were singing around it. After these two events no further trouble was given by the negroes on engineer duty.

Thrown in contact with such large numbers of contrabands of both sexes as they were, it would not be Companies C and H if the men did not manage to find amusement in their surroundings. Perhaps the officers could tell a good story in connection with the marriage of Captain Bailey's negro servant, an occasion they graced with their presence; while enlisted men could spin startling and true tales of pranks they played in these camps when off duty.

First-Sergeant Henry C. Mann, Company C, met with a serious and curious misfortune March 26th. It is surmised he had imbibed freely during the day, a fault common to many enlisted men at this camp, and as acting officer of the guard slept at night in the guard tent, upon the ground, without covering. At daylight he was quite sick from a cold thus contracted, and was unable to speak above a whisper. Nothing was thought of this at the time, as every one supposed upon a recovery from the cold his voice would return. It did not, and Sergeant Mann was incapacitated from further duty with his company during the term of service on account of this infirmity. One year after, while walking on Washington Street, Boston, Mann was seized with a violent coughing spell, and coughed up two pieces of gristle-like matter, when his natural voice suddenly returned. Sergeant Mann afterwards served in an unattached heavy artillery company. He died from consumption several years ago.

Of the officers from the regiment on detached service, Lieutenant White had more adventure than the rest. Immediately after the two companies arrived at Camp Parapet he was detailed, by orders from General Banks, to visit any abandoned plantations he could find within or without the Federal lines, gather together what negroes he could and bring them to the Parapet to work on the fortifications. He usually took from the two companies a detail of ten men as a guard, finally reducing this detail to seven men, for his own convenience and to obviate some difficulty he had experienced in obtaining rations. All of his trips were successful.

The first trip was made January 17th, and resulted in bringing in about four hundred on the nineteenth. The second trip was made on the twenty-seventh, when about six hundred were obtained and brought in January 30th. The third and last trip was made early in February to Donaldsonville and below. The detail for this trip consisted of: Corporal Augustus H. Young, Privates Elbridge G. Martin, Jr., Cornelius Dougherty, and Francis Droll, Company C; Sergeant Joseph J. Whitney, Company H; Private George H. Brown, Company C; and John Scroder, a Boston boy, who had been servant to Captain Leonard.

Complaints had been made by old resident planters in the parish, who remained to work their plantations, that many negroes were gathered on the plantations committing depredations. Major W. O. Fiske, First Louisiana Infantry (white troops), suggested to Lieutenant White that a trip to those plantations be made, and he would be able to get together a considerable number of negroes to bring down; by so doing benefit the planters, if they told the truth in their complaint, and also the Government. Caution was to be exercised, however, as the major did not fully believe the planters wished to have these negroes disturbed, as they had work for them to do upon the plantations. What occurred on the trip would seem to prove this view of the case was correct.

There was a detachment of thirty men, under a lieutenant from the One Hundred and Tenth New York, stationed at Magnolia Plantation, in St. John Parish, for what purpose Major Fiske said he did not understand, but did know this officer was having a fine time there and was on good terms with the planters, a fact that would make it probable he could not be counted on to render any assistance. This proved to be so.

Taking a river boat White and his men arrived at a landing two miles below this plantation about ten o'clock at night. On visiting this lieutenant a pleasant evening was passed without any mention made of the business in hand. Quarters were furnished for the night. Early next morning Lieutenant White, in company of the New York officer, made a round of adjacent plantations to look over the ground carefully. Upon their return White explained what he was after, when the lieutenant stated his position: he was pleasantly situated, well treated, on good terms with the inhabitants, and did not feel like doing a thing to disturb his pleasant life. Lieutenant White at once made up his mind the work must be done without assistance. He quietly gathered his men together and informed them there was considerable work to do, with a hint how easier it was to ride than to walk, then left them for the night. After breakfast, next morning, when he reached the place where his men quartered, he found seven horses ready, bridled and saddled. To his inquiry: "What does this mean?" one of the men replied: "It is White's cavalry." As he said it was easier to ride than walk, his men acted on the suggestion and equipped themselves in the night. Without difficulty he procured a mount for himself and proceeded to make a tour of the surrounding plantations, collect the negroes together, and explain what he wanted to do with them. They received the intelligence with delight, and were told to bring all of their effects and families with them, occupy a large storehouse situated by the river bank, where they could live until he could take them down river. They came in large numbers.

White left two men to look after matters at the storehouse, with instructions how to find him in case of need, and with five men started upon another tour on the succeeding day. While absent, a civilian provost-marshal, named Marmillon, or calling himself by that name, rode up to the storehouse, accompanied by a squad of hard-looking characters, fully armed, and demanded to see the lieutenant in charge. Word was despatched to White, who returned and confronted the gang. After some parley, Marmillon demanded that the detail should get out of the parish; said they had no business there; that he had orders of a later date than White's instructions, which stated that all officers on such detailed duty as his should cease their operations and forthwith join their commands, insisting that White should read the orders, which he refused to do in a positive manner, but informed Marmillon no such orders had been received by him, furthermore, he could not receive them through him as official, and that he was on a service he meant to put through to the best of his ability.

The following orders were all that Marmillon could have had at the time, issued from headquarters of the Department, viz.: a circular of February 16th, 1863, which explained a system of labor adopted for the year in utilizing unemployed negroes, and General Orders No. 17, issued February 18th, 1863, that reads: "No negroes will be taken from the plantations until further orders, by any officer or other person in the service of the United States, without previous authority from these headquarters."

While the conversation was at its height, with sharp

questions and answers upon both sides, the men of "White's cavalry" became uneasy and were ready for a fight, intimating to Lieutenant White their desire to "clean out" the provost-marshal's gang. They were held in check, until finally Lieutenant White notified Marmillon it was of no use to talk further about the matter, he did not intend to leave the parish and should not, but the best thing he (Marmillon) could do was to get out himself with his crowd of scallywag cut-throats, about as rascally a set of men as he ever saw, for his own men were a little excited, and if he did not clear out he would not hold himself responsible for the consequences. This appeared to settle the matter, for the provost-marshal and his men went away saying they would be heard from again. That night Marmillon, or somebody, sent to Lieutenant White a threatening letter, with peremptory orders to leave the parish.

The negroes were attentive listeners to all that passed between the two parties. During the evening one of them quietly asked White to go with him to the storehouse, where he found these negroes had made a barricade, with their bedding, baggage, and sundry traps of all kinds, on the three sides approached by land (the fourth side was on the water front), so as to make the building almost bullet proof. In the vicinity were about two hundred negroes, armed with long sugar-cane knives, very excited and full of fight. They said, let the provost-marshal and his gang make an attempt to use force and they would wipe them out of existence.

The situation was not pleasant to contemplate, not knowing what Marmillon with his men would attempt to do, and they could not get away. Repeated attempts to stop boats on the river were failures. The boats hug the east bank as though they feared some trick was attempted upon them. This uncertain state of affairs continued for several days without interference from any quarter, White and his men in the saddle most of the time, raiding around to prevent any attempt to surprise them. Finally Lieutenant White and Corporal Young seized a horse and wagon, drove to Donaldsonville and, by pluck combined with CHEEK, compelled a steamer bound down river to land at the storehouse and take the negroes on board. They were landed at the Parapet and turned over to the proper officers. This detail was absent about thirteen days, unable all that time to communicate with Captain Leonard, who thought the party had been captured by the enemy.

Several other short trips after negroes were made at various times by Lieutenants Phillips and Sanderson without any trouble while performing that duty.

Preliminary steps were taken in March towards enlisting from the negro camps a sufficient number of men to organize the First Regiment Louisiana Engineers, to form a part of the "Corps d' Afrique," then under consideration, and later on ordered to be organized as proposed in General Orders No. 40, from headquarters Nineteenth Army Corps, issued May 1st, 1863, at Opelousas. In those orders Major-General Banks proposed to organize a *corps d' armee* of colored troops, to consist ultimately of eighteen regiments, representing all arms — infantry, artillery and cavalry — organized in three divisions of three brigades each, with appropriate corps of engineers, and flying hospitals to each division.

Considering the character and standing of many men who received commissions in these regiments the following part of General Orders No. 40 sounds like *buncombe*. The extract is as follows:

"In the field the efficiency of every corps depends

upon the influence of its officers upon the troops engaged, and the practicable limits of one direct command is generally estimated at one thousand men. The most eminent military historians and commanders, among others Thiers and Chambray, express the opinion, upon a full review of the elements of military power, that the valor of the soldier is rather acquired than natural. Nations whose individual heroism is undisputed have failed as soldiers in the field. The European and American continents exhibit instances of this character, and the military prowess of every nation may be estimated by the centuries it has devoted to military contest, or the traditional passion of its people for military glory. With a race unaccustomed to military service, much more depends on the immediate influence of officers upon individual members than with those that have acquired more or less of warlike habits and spirit by centuries of contest. It is deemed best, therefore, in the organization of the Corps d' Afrique to limit the regiments to the smallest number of men consistent with efficient service in the field, in order to secure the most thorough instruction and discipline, and the largest influence of the officers over the troops. At first they will be limited to five hundred men. The average of American regiments is less than that number.

* * * * *

The chief defect in organizations of this character has arisen from incorrect ideas of the officers in command. Their discipline has been lax, and in some cases the conduct of the regiments unsatisfactory and discreditable. Controversies unnecessary and injurious to the service have arisen between them and other troops. The organization proposed will reconcile and avoid many of these troubles."

The First Louisiana Engineers comprised twelve companies of sixty-five men each, in three battalions, under command of Colonel Justin Hodge, U. S. A. This regiment was conceived in the following manner: all negroes employed at work upon the fortifications were in a camp by themselves, styled "the engineer camp." These negroes were organized into gangs of one hundred and twenty-five men each, commanded by two enlisted men from Companies C and H, each gang numbered one, two, three and so on, the same as companies in a regiment. The gangs were further subdivided into squads of twenty-five men, commanded by the most intelligent negro to be found. Before recruiting for this regiment was thought of, acting under orders these gangs were often drilled in marching, the facings, and other exercises without arms, by the detailed men who commanded them. Contrary to expectation, they took a great interest in these drills and improved rapidly, manifesting considerable intelligence for slaves, one reason why it was easy work to handle them, for they obeyed all orders without causing trouble, accustomed as they had been to doing so for their late masters.

Opinions differ in regard to whether the negroes enlisted of their own free will, fully understanding what they were about, when this regiment was determined upon. Lieutenant White says, that the two companies taken by him to Brashear City were sent away in a hurry, and the manner in which they were mustered into the service was this: the men were drawn up in line, when a German officer, who spoke poor English, said something to them that White could not understand, though he stood near him, and then declared the two companies mustered into service. These negroes afterwards asked what had been going on, and appeared ignorant of the nature of the ceremony. No enlistment papers had been made out or signed that White ever knew. On the other hand, soldiers who were engaged in recruiting for this regiment say, that the men signed enlistment rolls, nearly all by affixing their mark, and that they fully understood what was wanted of them, enlisting of their own free will. This is probably true so far as other companies than the first two are concerned. At all events, it is a fact, none of them ever protested against their enlistment, or mode of muster in, and were wonderfully tickled at the idea of becoming soldiers, proud to belong to the "machinery department," as they termed it, in their ignorance supposing as a matter of course anybody called an engineer must have something to do with machinery in some manner.

After passing an examination early in April, the following men of the Forty-Second were appointed officers in this engineer regiment, and received their commissions a month later, viz.:

Sergeant Moses Washburn, Company C, to be captain. Commissioned May 23d.

Sergeant Frederick C. Blanchard, Company C, to be captain. Commissioned May 23d.

Private William E. Melvin, Company C, to be captain. Commissioned May 23d.

Sergeant Edward L. Jones, Company H, to be captain. Commissioned May 23d.

Sergeant Samuel H. Everett, Company H, to be captain. Commissioned May 23d.

Sergeant John G. Meserve, Company C, to be first-lieutenant. Commissioned May 21st.

Corporal Joseph McField, Company C, to be first-lieutenant. Commissioned May 21st.

Sergeant James G. Hill, Company K, to be first-lieutenant. Commissioned March 27th.

Sergeant William H. Shepard, Company K, to be second-lieutenant. Commissioned March 27th.

Corporal Augustus H. Young, Company C, to be second-lieutenant. Commissioned May 21st.

Private Edwin G. Sanborn, Company C, to be second-lieutenant. Commissioned May 23d.

Private Charles E. Warren, Company C, made assistant-surgeon, June 24th.

Private George F. Clark, Company C, appointed quartermaster-sergeant, June 26th.

Other men in Companies C and H had commissions tendered to them, which they declined for personal reasons. Some of the above-mentioned promotions were good — men adapted to carry out the spirit of Major-General Banks' order.

An expedition made February 12th by the Third Division down Plaquemine Bayou, for the purpose of capturing Butte a la Rose, at the head of Grand Lake, was obliged to abandon the attempt on account of timber drifts in the swollen bayous, that made a passage through them impracticable, and returned February 19th. Lieutenant Swift, Thirty-Eighth Massachusetts, had got an idea into his head that he could, with a proper force, remove the greatest obstacle encountered by the Third Division: a completely-packed drift of wood like a raft, about three miles long, situated at the upper end of Bayou Sorrel, in St. Martins and Iberville Parishes, a narrow sheet of water about nine miles long. Swift had received permission, with orders from General Banks, to attempt it.

In winter months it had been the custom for light-draft river boats to make a short cut from Berwick Bay by way of Grand Lake, Lake Chilot, Bayou Sorrel, the Atchafalaya River, and Bayou Plaquemine to the Mississippi River. In summer months this route is almost dry in places, and not navigable for local boats. From Brashear City, via Grand Lake, to Lake Chilot is about thirty miles;

Lake Chilot to Bayou Sorrel, about eight miles; through Bayou Sorrel, nine miles; and from Bayou Sorrel to Plaquemine, upon the Mississippi, is about twelve miles.

On April 26th, at the earnest request of Colonel Hodge, Lieutenant White consented to take command of two companies, about one hundred and thirty men, from the colored engineer regiment, under orders to proceed to Brashear City to assist Lieutenant Swift in his project.

The officers in command of these two companies were: Captain Samuel H. Everett, Captain William E. Melvin, Acting Lieutenant David C. Smith and Acting Lieutenant James S. Lovejoy, from Company C, Forty-Second Massachusetts Volunteers, Acting Lieutenant —— Purrington, from Twelfth Maine Volunteers, and Acting Lieutenant —— McCown, a clerk to Colonel Hodge.

At Brashear City the expedition had to remain some three weeks, until suitable steamers could be furnished from boats in use by the army, then advancing up the Teche. Two small tug boats and two barges were finally provided, with all the equipment and rations supposed to be sufficient for the time it would occupy, calculated by Lieutenant Swift to be ten days. A start was made about May 20th. No surgeon was detailed or medicines provided, although an attempt was made to obtain both in Brashear City. The post hospital officers refused to do anything in the absence of direct orders to do so, although White had a personal request from General Banks to get a couple of panniers, with a full set of surgical instruments and medicines. The bags were obtained, but no instruments and but few medicines. Lieutenant Swift had with him a detail of thirty men, Twelfth Maine Infantry, all practical river lumber drivers. He did not conceal his opinion, that the negro troops were of no use to him in this scheme, and that the men from the Twelfth Maine would make short work of the obstacle.

On arrival at Bayou Sorrel, where they were attacked the first night by guerillas, they went to work with a will for some days, sending the logs right and left floating down towards Lake Chilot, where they again collected together to form a formidable obstacle in their rear, and before they were aware of it they were caught between the obstructions; they could not go ahead or go back. The weather was extremely hot, with mosquitos and flies terribly annoying, and before many days Lieutenant Swift was obliged to call upon Lieutenant White to assist him with the negro troops.

The expedition lay in this bayou between three to four weeks, the water falling steadily until there were places in their rear fordable over sand bars. The men sickened rapidly, measles appeared, and all of the Maine detachment, except five or six men, were on the sick list unfit for duty. Fortunately none died. About sixty-five of the negro detachment were also sick and unfit for duty; seven of them died. Provisions ran short. The few inhabitants in the vicinity gave information that the Confederates were operating around their rear to cut them off, not expecting they could get through in front and must eventually abandon the boats to try and work back by land towards Brashear.

In this emergency Swift appealed to White for a trustworthy man to go to Brashear City for provisions, and arms for the negro companies. Acting Lieutenant McCown was selected, who, with two negroes, managed by travelling at night to work their way back to Brashear, where they obtained provisions, also forty muskets, without bayonets or ammunition, and brought them up upon a small steamer.

Work was pushed day and night by all of the available

hands to break through the obstacle in front, as it had become impossible to work back. This was at last accomplished, and with a clear passage beyond this obstacle the steamers were rushed through to the Mississippi, reaching that river late in the afternoon of June 19th, and the men were landed on the east bank, opposite Plaquemine.

One boat struck a snag while entering the Mississippi and sank in water almost up to her deck cabin; all hands, except the captain with a few of the crew, were taken on board other boats. Next morning Confederate soldiers appeared on the river bank and captured those who remained upon the wreck. It was afterwards ascertained that a force of about two thousand cavalry reached a point on the Bayou Plaquemine very soon after the expedition had passed, to find they were too late, when they pushed for Plaquemine Town, capturing the small force stationed there, burning the hospital building, and committing other acts of vandalism.

At the season of the year it was undertaken this expedition was a farce. Had an intelligent officer first made proper inquiries to ascertain the true state of that line of water course, when it was navigable and when not, the probabilities are that the expedition would not have started.

Lieutenant White, Acting Lieutenants Smith and Lovejoy proceeded immediately to the regimental hospital at Bayou Gentilly, sick with fever, and for a time it was doubtful whether they would recover. The two companies went to Port Hudson to rejoin their regiment.

The First Louisiana Engineers received orders to proceed to Baton Rouge May 20th, with General Neal Dow's brigade. The brigade passed up river May 21st; on the twenty-second the engineer regiment had its first dress parade, with music furnished by the Forty-Seventh Massachusetts regimental band, that regiment having arrived at the Parapet a few days before. Without arms, clothed in straw hats and uncouth clothing (regulation uniforms had not been issued), this regiment made an appearance that agreeably disappointed the military spectator.

On Sunday, May 24th, camp was struck, transports taken, and the First Louisiana passed up the river for Port Hudson, where it did some hard work, received well-merited praise for duty actually performed, and praise for what it did not do. At Port Hudson this regiment did about all of the engineer hard labor of the army, divided into detachments to cover the whole Federal front (about five miles), to throw up temporary fortifications, dig approaches and mines. On the extreme left a work for twenty-one guns was made by these colored troops. In the first assault this regiment carried fascines to fill the ditch, and to their credit it must be said they ran forward, threw them in helter-skelter, expecting to receive the enemy's fire every moment. The enemy did not fire on them (that was reserved for the assaulting columns of white troops), and they got back without loss. During this siege the regiment was as much under fire every day as any white regiment, suffered a loss of about seventy men, and displayed good pluck for untrained men.

While convalescent, Lieutenant White, disregarding the advice of Surgeon Heintzelman, returned to his company in New Orleans the last of June. From there he started for Port Hudson to report to Colonel Hodge. At Springfield Landing, the base of supplies for the army, an attack was made on the post July 2d, by a raiding party of Confederate cavalry, just as a party, including Lieutenant White, were about to start in a sutler's wagon for Port Hudson, seven miles distant.

The Confederates dashed through a force of some

ninety men from a New York regiment on duty at the landing, and then divided into squads. One of these squads rode down to the river bank where White, with a dozen other men, had taken refuge in an old trading boat. After discharging a few volleys, from the saddle, they rode away. They did not dare to dismount, because a sharp musketry-fire was springing up behind them from the New York infantry-men, who rallied, behind shelter, by twos and fours, as they saw a chance, until they drove the Confederates away, after a half hour's skirmish, and before the Thirtieth Massachusetts, ordered down from Port Hudson, could intercept them.

From the boat Lieutenant White witnessed the capture of his old companion, Lieutenant Swift, by a Confederate squad who rode up to look inside a tent occupied by Swift a few moments before busily engaged in writing, and who had hid, with two men, in bushes close by. They would have been safe had not one of the men incautiously looked out to see what was going on and been seen by the enemy, who ordered them out and made them prisoners.

Lieutenant White was relieved from duty with the engineer troops July 7th, to rejoin his company.

To sum up what these two companies did is to say that they done their duty well. They were once, April 24th, under orders for Port Hudson, and held in readiness for two days to proceed there; the nearest they ever came to going into active field service.

June 5th, Companies C and H were relieved from duty in the Engineer Department, and marched seven miles to Bayou Gentilly, accompanied by the regimental band (sent them at the request of Captain Leonard), and rejoined the regiment.

CHAPTER XV.

COMPANY K IN CHARGE OF PONTOONS — BATON ROUGE — TECHE CAMPAIGN — SIEGE OF PORT HUDSON — DONALD-SONVILLE — RETURN TO REGIMENT.

COMPANY K, under command of Lieutenant Henry A. Harding, a talented young officer, twenty-one years old, in obedience to Division Special Orders No. 51, issued February 16th, proceeded to New Orleans on the eighteenth from Gentilly Camp, and reported to Major Houston for duty in the engineer service. Quarters were assigned in Shippers' cotton press, already partially occupied by the Twenty-Sixth New York Battery, one hundred and fifty men, eight brass guns and one hundred and ten horses. This battery remained at the cotton press until March 8th, the two commands fraternizing without any trouble.

Company K was ordered to take charge of the pontoon train. The pontoons, in two sizes, were made of rubber, inflated with air by hand bellows in lieu of air pumps, when all ready for use. Such miscellaneous articles as planks, guy ropes, oars, etc., occupied a large amount of space. Thirty wagons, drawn by four mules to each wagon, were used to transport this bridge and material. Negroes were employed as drivers, "bossed" by a large, powerful Irishman called "Big Slattery." Slattery was a bully, always ready to curse and whip his negro drivers.

His brutality assumed such proportions men of Company K had to interfere and put a stop to it. The company wagoner, in charge of the wagon used to convey company property, was Private Jotham E. Bigelow, until Wagoner Porter Carter was ordered to join his company.

At first sight the men made up their minds they were to see hard service in handling this cumbersome, clumsy-looking pontoon bridge. To bridge a river or bayou the requisite number of pontoons were inflated by hand-bellows, then launched and placed in position, afterwards planked, and fastened by ropes to remain steady. Company K had eighty men for this duty, until sickness and death gradually reduced the number to about fifty. They learned how to handle the pontoons without instruction from an engineer officer, by practice drills with sections of the bridge, and gained much valuable knowledge of the property confided to their care by odd jobs of necessary work done to have everything in complete order.

Two accidents happened that, for a short time in March, left the company without a commissioned officer. Lieutenant Harding, kicked by a horse about a week previous, had to go into hospital March 1st, on account of the injury. In the afternoon Lieutenant Gorham was thrown, his horse fell upon him, and he was insensible until taken to the St. James Hospital next day. He returned to duty March 9th, in season to command the company ordered to Baton Rouge with the pontoons on March 10th. They went up river upon the steamer *Eastern Queen* and arrived at Baton Rouge March 11th at three o'clock P.M, going into camp about half a mile from the river.

All signs pointed to a forward movement by the large body of troops massed at this place, commanded by General Banks in person. Great activity was observed on board naval vessels, which caused the men to understand they were about to do active field duty and gain some practical knowledge how to use pontoon bridges for service. Early on the twelfth the pontoon train was marched to Bayou Montesino, five miles from Baton Rouge, and the men commenced to throw a bridge seventy-seven feet long across this bayou. Picket lines were established some two miles in front until next morning, when the Forty-Eighth Massachusetts and Second Louisiana Infantry, with unattached Massachusetts cavalry companies, commanded by Captains Godfrey and Magee, were sent up river on transports to Springfield Landing, proceeding to the junction of Springfield Landing and Bayou Sara roads, driving in Confederate pickets and clearing the roads down to where the bridge was thrown. At night, work was suspended, but Company K kept on the alert, as pickets were firing throughout the night and alarms frequent; the men were formed into line three times, ready for a defence of the bridge. By noon of the thirteenth all was made ready, and at night troops commenced to cross on the advance towards Port Hudson.

The men remained on duty at their bridge until the seventeenth, with the Forty-Ninth Massachusetts Infantry on guard for a part of the time, witnessing the constant movement of troops, accompanied by baggage trains, and listening to the guns from the fleet while Admiral Farragut succeeded in pushing two gunboats past Port Hudson batteries March 14th. The retrograde march towards Baton Rouge commenced on the fifteenth, a rainy day, and on the seventeenth Company K commenced to take up, load their bridge upon wagons and go in the same direction, ordered to accompany the Third Brigade, First Division, Colonel N. A. M. Dudley in command, under orders to reconnoitre the west bank of the river.

On the eighteenth teams went to the levee and remained

until five A.M. the next day (all hands sleeping upon the levee), when they embarked on the *Sallie Robinson* and proceeded to within five miles of Port Hudson, landing in the afternoon at Hunter's Plantation. The brigade foraged, scouted, and opened communication with Farragut, while naval vessels below Port Hudson kept the Confederate steamers well under the protection of their own forts. Without having to make any use of the pontoons, the brigade returned to Baton Rouge on the afternoon of March 22d, and Company K left the next day, still upon the *Sallie Robinson*, for New Orleans, where they arrived on the twenty-fourth at four P.M., and marched immediately, with their train, to Shippers' Cotton Press. Several men were taken sick from exposure to damp atmosphere at night, which almost penetrated their blankets as they slept upon the river bank.

For two weeks the company was kept busy in making alterations in the pontoons, found necessary during the short service they had seen, preparatory to moving with the army, about to commence a campaign in Western Louisiana towards Red River.

Hospital-Steward Charles J. Wood was detached from the regiment March 31st, by Department special orders, and joined April 3d, to act as medical-officer. First-Sergeant J. Gilbert Hill and Sergeant William H. Shepard were detached, by Department special orders, March 26th, and ordered to Baton Rouge to report to Captain Justin Hodge, assistant-quartermaster, on recruiting service for the First Louisiana Engineers, colored troops. They afterwards received commissions as first- and second-lieutenants. The following sick men were sent to hospitals: Sergeant George L. Johnson to St. James Hospital in New Orleans; Privates W. J. Bacon, C. B. Bacon, Samuel Johnson and S. M. Stafford to the regimental hospital at Gentilly Bayou.

Preliminary movements of troops were in progress as follows: the Second Brigade, First Division, under General Weitzel, had advanced to Brashear City from Bayou Bœuff April 2d; the Third and Fourth Divisions were *en-route* from Baton Rouge by transports to Algiers, thence by rail, a portion marching from Donaldsonville *via* Thibodeaux, when orders were received by Company K, April 5th, to move with the pontoons. At eight o'clock P.M. next day, the detachment took cars at Algiers for Brashear City, where they arrived early next morning. The bridge was unloaded, piled compactly near the track, and tents pitched close at hand.

Weitzel's brigade was transported across the river to Berwick on the ninth, and the Third Division followed as fast as limited facilities at hand would admit, occupying two days in crossing. The bridge was put together about a mile from camp, below the city, on the ninth, using all of the material, that made a bridge two hundred and eighty-seven and ten-twelfths feet long. This took an entire day, and completely tired out everybody. Next day an attempt was made to tow this pontoon bridge to Bayou Teche, but the tide proved too strong for a tug-boat, and the steamer *St. Mary's* was called on to render assistance, and then the *Sykes* had to assist before it could be moved and brought up to the railroad wharf at Brashear. This day was lost. The *Sykes*, at two P.M. on the eleventh, took the bridge in tow, with all hands upon it, bound for Pattersonville, three miles above Brashear. After a hard pull, obliged once to make fast to the shore, the bridge reached Pattersonville in the evening and remained all night. The men remained upon it, in readiness to obey any orders. On the twelfth the bridge was thrown across the bayou, and one infantry regiment, one cavalry company and five artillery guns crossed over. While at work Company K was fired on, and seven men were thrown forward to ascertain if a force was in the vicinity; a small guard was found, who beat a hasty retreat. Lieutenant Harding, with a boat's crew, went up river at night for orders; Lieutenant Gorham, left in command, tried to execute an order to bring up the bridge to a spot about three miles from his position, where a bridge was destroyed by the enemy, but the captains of steamers *Sykes* and *Smith* thought it unsafe to try it, and the bridge was not towed up until next day, the thirteenth, when it was placed in position about three-quarters of a mile from the battle-field. Gorham was placed in arrest by Major Houston for the delay, and released and ordered to duty on the fifteenth, as it was not his fault.

The Third (Emory's) Division, the Second (Weitzel's) Brigade, First Division, advanced to Pattersonville, threw out pickets, and went into bivouac on the eleventh. The enemy was posted behind breastworks on the Bisland Plantation, about four miles above Pattersonville. On their left were six hundred men, with six guns, defending the ground from Grand Lake to the bayou. The gunboat *Diana* defended the bayou main road, and there were two 24 Pr. guns in position upon the bank, on their right, to assist the *Diana*. Sixteen hundred men, with twelve guns, held the line of their right to a railway embankment, where General Green was posted with his dismounted men.

After this position was reconnoitred on the twelfth, with skirmishing and considerable artillery firing in the afternoon, an advance on the enemy was made about ten A.M. April 13th, by a strong line of skirmishers, supported by artillery. No attempt was made to assault. This movement on the enemy was evidently made to occupy their attention until Grover's division could gain the roads in their rear at Franklin. At noon the gunboat *Clifton* pushed up river to aid the troops, until she ran afoul of a torpedo. For fear of being blown up by these machines, she anchored until afternoon, and then commenced to throw shot and shell dangerously near the Federal troops. This was soon stopped, for the *Clifton* was not in a proper place to render any service. The bridge was in constant use during the day, soldiers and ambulances crossing and recrossing. The company remained under arms, on guard, until the fourteenth, squads of men going up river in small boats to witness the army movements on the twelfth and thirteenth, collect small boats and carry orders. The enemy retreated to Franklin on the fourteenth, after destroying their one gunboat on the bayou (the *Diana*), to escape a threatened rear attack by Grover's fourth division, that had by way of Grand Lake, on transports, effected a landing with difficulty near Hutchin's Point, not far from Franklin, and advanced to the Bayou Teche.

In this first Western Louisiana campaign the pontoons did not see much service. Bridges over the small watercourses General Taylor attempted to burn or otherwise destroy were repaired without difficulty, as the pursuit was close enough to prevent much destruction. A great flood existed, but saving the bridges obviated a call for use of pontoon-sections. The labor done by Company K was not heavy, but kept them constantly at work on the river for ten days, exposed at night to foul air and bad vapor from swamps. This exposure caused a large proportion of the men to be taken sick. Serious cases were sent to post hospitals at Berwick Bay, a portion distributed among hospitals in New Orleans, and those who could travel were sent to Bayou Gentilly.

The company proceeded to Franklin, April 14th, upon the *Sykes*, with gunboat *Clifton* for an escort, leaving their bridge where it was in position, with a detachment on guard. From Franklin the men were kept moving down and up the river, on the lookout for torpedoes, and at work to try and remove the wreck of the Confederate gunboat *Cotton*, blown up by the enemy in January, obstructing free navigation where she sunk. Plenty of opportunities were found to go ashore on foraging expeditions.

Orders were received on the twenty-third to join the army, well on its way towards Opelousas. Small boats took the men down to where their pontoon bridge lay, when it was taken in tow for Brashear City, and arrived there in the afternoon. The bridge was taken up on the twenty-fifth, loaded upon wagons, and transported on the steamer *G. A. Sheldon*, that left Brashear City on the twenty-sixth for Barre's Landing, *via* Grand Lake, the Atchafalaya and the Cahawba Rivers, stopping at Butte a-la-Rose to leave supplies for the gunboat *Calhoun*. On arrival at Barre's Landing on the twenty-eighth, wagons were sent ashore and the command went into camp. Bustle and excitement ruled the hours. A large amount of cotton kept coming in to the army, and was stored or shipped by steamers to Brashear.

From exposure upon the bayou Lieutenant Harding became sick with malarial fever, that forced him to leave his company April 21st and return to the regimental hospital for treatment. The command fell on Lieutenant Gorham, who was not equal to the task. With a weakness for liquor he could not control, this one fault completely unfitted him for such a position as he held. He was reprimanded once by a general officer, who noticed he was inebriated while on duty and cautioned him not to repeat the offence. Gorham failed to obey the caution, was found by the rear guard in a state of intoxication at a rebel's house on Carnell's Plantation, and at Alexandria, May 9th, was placed in arrest. Captain Smith, First Louisiana Engineers, was placed in command of Company K until

Lieutenant Harding should rejoin. The option was given Lieutenant Gorham to resign or stand trial by court-martial. He chose the former, and was discharged from the service of the United States by Department Special Orders No. 115, issued May 13th.

General orders were issued to prevent straggling and pillage. As these orders were not promulgated to Company K, and many men never heard read General Orders No. 29, it is here given:

"HEADQUARTERS DEPT. OF THE GULF,
"19TH ARMY CORPS,
"OPELOUSAS, April 21st, 1863.

"GENERAL ORDERS NO. 29.

"The exigencies of the service, and safety of the troops, imperatively demand that the disposable force of the corps shall march in column, except where necessary detachments upon special duty are ordered by superior officers. The desertion of the column upon the march, or straggling, for the purposes of pillage and plunder, is an offence made punishable with death by the Articles of War. The honor of the flag, and the safety of the men who faithfully discharge their duty, demand that this law be enforced; and the commanding general gives notice, absolute and positive, that this punishment will be executed upon those men, of whatever command, who violate the army regulations and dishonor the service by inexcusable and attrocious acts of this kind. All officers, of whatever grade, who shall allow the men under their respective commands to leave the line of march or the camp, without authority, will be summarily and dishonorably discharged the service, as unworthy to participate in the triumphant march of this column. The army is now hundreds of miles from its base of operations, in the enemy's country. The campaign may be made one of the most creditable of the war, or it may disgrace the troops and dishonor the country. The commanding general appeals to officers and men to reflect upon their position, to consider their duties, and faithfully to discharge the obligations which rest upon them, and is, for himself, determined to execute the severest sentence of military law upon those who basely betray the service and dishonor their country in this regard. Whatever property may be necessary for the support of the army, or may be prostituted to support the rebellion, will be taken by the Government, and due reparation will be made therefor. But we do not war upon women and children, however much and in whatever way they may have erred. Our contest is with the men and the armies of the rebellion.

"Information has been received at these headquarters that the lives of officers as well as of the men of the line have been endangered by the unauthorized and criminal discharge of firearms by persons engaged in pillage. Notice is given to all officers and soldiers that the parties engaged in these practices will be held responsible for the consequences of their acts, and that such offences will be punished with the severest penalties prescribed by the Articles of War. This order is not a matter of form, but will be rigidly enforced during the campaign.

"Officers in every division, brigade and regiment of this command are directed to place a rear-guard for the purpose of preventing stragglers from falling to the rear of the column. Where men are sick or foot-sore, upon the certificate of the surgeon, they will be allowed such conveyance or provided with such hospital accommodations as their situation may require. The captured straggler is the best source of information that the enemy possesses. A soldier who deserts his column in the face of the enemy will not hesitate to betray his comrades, and deserves the penalty which the law provides for his great wrong.

"By command of
"MAJOR-GENERAL BANKS.
"RICHARD B. IRWIN,
"*Assistant Adjutant-General.*"

Several men of Company K got permission of Sergeant Johnson to forage, and went down the river on the twenty-eighth for the express purpose of pillage and plunder, returning next day with silver spoons and jewelry they had taken from a dwelling, whose owner promptly reported this case of burglary to General Grover. Lieutenant Gorham was ordered to parade his company in front of Grover's headquarters, where the property owner indentified Sergeant Baker, Corporal Bates, Privates E. G. Bacon, Luke Bowker, A. J. Thayer, E. M. Thayer and James Mins as connected with this affair. They were placed in arrest, sent to Algiers, and confined for twenty days before released from their dilemma with a reprimand, because they could give conclusive proof Orders No. 29 had not been promulgated to them.

Under orders to proceed to Alexandria the company and pontoon train left Barre's Landing May 5th, with a column of troops under Grover, reaching Washington at half-past six in the evening, after a twelve-mile march, and remained over night. On the sixth, after a march of twenty-four miles over a rough road, a halt was made at a large sugar-house for the night. This was a tough day for the men; wagons broke through small bridges crossing ravines, had to be unloaded, bridges repaired, wagons repaired and reloaded, fences taken down to facilitate passing across plantations, and other innumerable vexatious accidents that make soldiers swear. On the seventh an early start was made; twenty miles marched before a halt for the night was made at a sugar-house two miles from Chanaville. On the eighth the march was continued to Carnell's Plantation, sixteen miles from Alexandria, and on the ninth, after an early start, Company K reached Alexandria at noon. Nothing was done at this place except to guard a ferry across Red River, where forage parties, negroes and horses were constantly coming over.

Ordered to Simmsport, with troops destined to invest Port Hudson, the pontoon train again joined a column that left Alexandria May 13th, about two o'clock in the afternoon. Fourteen miles were marched that day; about twenty miles to Cheneyville on the fourteenth; eighteen miles to Evergreenville on the fifteenth; to Moreanville on the sixteenth, twelve miles from Simmsport. Simmsport was reached about noon on the seventeenth, after an average march of fifteen miles a day. Two pontoon rafts and an abutment were built next day for a part of the army to cross the Atchafalaya River to take transports at points on Red River for Port Hudson. The current was too strong and river too wide to permit the bridge to be used, and flatboats had to be brought into requisition. A portion of the troops marched to Morganza, on the Mississippi River, and took transports there.

Lieutenant Harding and Private Austin Hawes rejoined the company on the twenty-first to find the army had departed that day, leaving a guard over baggage and trains, that were moved as fast as transportation could be provided. It was on Sunday, the twenty-fourth, before Company K could proceed upon the steamer *Forest Queen*, arriving at Bayou Sara about ten o'clock the same night. The pontoon teams did not arrive until late in the evening of the twenty-fifth, when they were loaded, ready for an early start next morning.

The first assault on the enemy's works at Port Hudson was arranged for May 27th. On the twenty-sixth Company K, with the pontoon train, started from Bayou Sara at four o'clock A.M., under orders to bridge Bayou Sandy (or Sandy Creek) on the Federal right. They arrived at two o'clock P.M., after a terrible hot and dusty march of sixteen miles. A light footbridge had been built over the bayou by pioneers, and one colored regiment was on the other side skirmishing with the enemy in a cool, collected manner. Work was at once commenced on a pontoon bridge two hundred and eighty feet long. Shot and shell from the Confederate works, less than a mile away, would occasionally fly over the heads of men at work, who ran for shelter when they could. The enemy's infantry retired when the Thirty-Eighth Massachusetts Infantry and Eighteenth New York Battery put in an appearance. At night the Third and Fourth Regiments Louisiana (colored) Native Guards relieved the Thirty-Eighth and the battery. Everybody not obliged to be on picket or guard, slept through the night as only worn-out men can sleep, without a thought of the morrow, undisturbed by the continual boom from heavy guns fired by naval vessels bombarding the enemy.

Next day, Wednesday, at half-past five o'clock A.M., two negro regiments (First and Third Louisiana Native Guards), with other troops from Colonel Nelson's brigade and two brass guns Sixth Massachusetts Battery, crossed both bridges to assault a redoubt. The battery-guns were handled in the road until withdrawn, with a loss of three horses killed and two men wounded. The infantry, with great bravery, pushed up close to the earthworks, where they found an overflow of water from the bayou a serious obstacle to success, and were obliged to retreat to cover of woods. One brave mulatto officer was left dead in the water near the redoubt. Five ineffectual advances through this water were made by Nelson's colored brigade to scale a high bluff on which the redoubt stood, suffering heavily (about four hundred in killed and wounded), before approaches could be commenced on advanced ground that was gained and held. A cavalry detachment arrived late in the afternoon, dismounted and skirmished forward without any result. On their return an orderly-sergeant was killed while recrossing the bridge. During the day shells from the enemy came fast, and were exploding lively among the tree tops about Sandy Creek, where Company K remained as a bridge-guard. The enemy had the range, but could not depress their guns to make shot do any execution.

Corporals Lovegrove, Alden and a private were stationed at night on the exposed end to cut the lashings, so the bridge could be swung to the other shore by guy ropes, in case the enemy came down in force. The men not on guard slept in sheltered places, behind trees, anywhere to escape from shells fired by the enemy throughout the night. Early in the evening Lovegrove picked out a place, spread his blanket and was about to lie down when a shell went under his temporary sleeping bunk without exploding.

In this general assault of May 27th the following (nine months) Massachusetts troops were engaged at various points on the lines, with credit to themselves:

Forty-Eighth Infantry, in First Brigade, First Division, had seven killed, forty-one wounded.

Forty-Ninth Infantry, in First Brigade, First Division, seven companies engaged, had sixteen killed, sixty wounded.

Fiftieth Infantry, in Third Brigade, First Division, had one killed, three wounded.

Fifty-Third Infantry, in Third Brigade, Third Division, had none killed, several wounded.

The Thirtieth, Thirty-First and Thirty-Eighth Infantry (three years troops) were also in the action.

After this first assault the pontoon bridge was taken up, loaded upon wagons for an immediate start to any portion of the lines, and Company K went into camp, near other camps, about one and one-half miles to the rear. In preparation for a second assault the entire train was moved, June 4th, to a position near General Banks' headquarters. On the tenth three detachments from the company, with sections of bridge work, were detailed to several division commanders, with orders to be prepared to bridge the ditch in front of the enemy's works. Lieutenant Harding, with about twenty men, remained in camp near general headquarters as a guard over material not in use.

Corporal Lovegrove, with three men of Company K, was assigned to the First Division, General Augur. Forty-two men from the Forty-Ninth Massachusetts and One Hundred and Sixty-First New York Regiments were sent to him and placed under his orders for practice.

Corporal Bates, with a squad of nine Company K men, was assigned to the Second Division, General Dwight, until the fourteenth, when Corporal Hall relieved him.

Sergeant Howe, with about fifteen men of Company K, was assigned to the Fourth Division, General Grover. Forty men from other commands were detailed to assist Howe.

A flag of truce was sent to General Gardner on the thirteenth, demanding a surrender of Port Hudson, which he refused, and the bombardment recommenced along the entire line from new batteries, a prelude to an assault on the fourteenth, when an attempt was made by the Second Division to work up quietly through a ravine and rush over the works, while the Fourth Division assaulted the enemy's left, near Sandy Creek. At daylight Corporal Lovegrove was ordered to load his bridge on a wagon, and the detachment went to within a short distance of the works, where they waited for orders. A siege battery in front and two light batteries maintained a fire nearly all day. The smoke became so dense nothing could be seen in front. No assault in force was ordered, and at five o'clock P.M. this detail returned to camp. Sergeant Howe and his detachment was with a brigade commanded by General Paine, in the third line, ready to bridge the ditch immediately after the storming party obtained a foothold within the intrenchments. This assault was repulsed. After General Paine was wounded, just as the ditch was reached, the men were ordered to lie down until chance enabled them to creep away in safety towards the rear. For hours the men lay in a burning hot sun, shot and shell flying thick around them. Fortunately none of Company K were killed or wounded; three men received slight scratch wounds. Two men of other regiments, in the bridge detail, were killed. Some of the men of Company K with Sergeant Howe on this day were: Privates Giles Blodgett, Warner E. Bacon, Benjamin F. Bacon, Amos D. Bond, Asa Breckenridge, Austin Hawes, R. W. Homer, Samuel King and Charles S. Knight. The Thirty-Eighth Massachusetts took two hundred and fifty men into this assault, and lost one officer, seven men killed; five officers, seventy-seven men wounded; or about thirty-five per cent. of its strength. Eight companies of the Fifty-Third Massachusetts were engaged, three hundred men, and lost one officer, thirteen men killed; six officers and sixty-six men wounded; or about thirty per cent. of its strength.

Other Massachusetts troops at Port Hudson, in this second assault, suffered as follows:

Fourth Infantry, in First Brigade, Third Division, had two companies detailed, with three companies from other regiments, to carry hand grenades in advance of the attacking column. Captain Bartlett, Company K, had command, and was mortally wounded upon the breastworks. Other companies of this regiment were in the reserve line. This regiment lost six killed, sixty-two wounded, a number mortally. Most of the casualties were in Companies A and K. Captain Hall, Company A, was wounded.

Thirtieth Infantry was in the reserve column and did not participate. The color-sergeant was wounded.

Thirty-First Infantry was in the Third Division assaulting column. Lost thirty men out of two hundred and fifty engaged.

Forty-Eighth Infantry was in the assaulting column and lost two killed, eleven wounded.

Forty-Ninth Infantry was in the brigade, First Division, that made a feigned assault, losing eighteen killed and wounded.

Fiftieth Infantry was in the reserve column and did not participate.

Fifty-Second Infantry was deployed as skirmishers between Weitzel and Grover, to prevent any flank movement on the assaulting columns. Lost three killed, seven wounded; one officer mortally.

For these two assaults many gallant men volunteered to lead the several columns. After the second failure it was at once decided to try a third time, and orders were issued to organize a storming column, after this style:

"HEADQUARTERS 19TH ARMY CORPS,
"BEFORE PORT HUDSON, June 15th, 1863.
"GENERAL ORDERS NO. 49.
(*Extract.*)

" For the last duty that victory imposes, the commanding general summons the bold men of the Corps to the organization of a storming column of a thousand men to vindicate the Flag of the Union and the memory of its defenders who have fallen; let them come forward.

"Officers who lead the column of victory in this last assault may be assured of the just recognition of their services by promotion, and every officer and soldier, who shares its perils and its glory, shall receive a medal fit to commemorate the first grand success of the campaign of 1863 for the freedom of the Mississippi. His name will be placed in General Orders upon the Roll of Honor.

"By command of
"MAJOR GENERAL BANKS.
" RICHARD B. IRWIN,
"*Assistant Adjutant-General.*

Between the three years and nine months troops from Massachusetts, engaged at Port Hudson, there was no choice as to which behaved the best. They all did well in the positions they were placed.

The entire day of the fifteenth was occupied in removing dead and wounded men to the rear. All sick and wounded who could bear transportation were sent to Springfield Landing, thence by steamers to New Orleans, for distribution in the general hospitals. Hot weather made heavy inroads on the effective strength of besieged and besiegers.

Sergeant Perry, Corporal Bryant, Privates McIntosh,

Johnson, Bruce, Desper, L. Barnes, Wheeler, Flagg and Sibley, who had been in hospital at Gentilly Bayou, with six other men that were in New Orleans, rejoined Company K June 15th, in obedience to orders issued June 11th. Hospital-Steward Wood was sent with them from the camp at Gentilly. The effective strength on duty during June was: one officer, four sergeants, seven corporals, one musician and fifty privates — total, sixty-two enlisted men.

From June 14th to July 8th the duties of Company K were easy. Several men volunteered and served in the batteries, while the detailed detachments and sections of bridge work remained with each division, ready for any movement that should be ordered. News that Vicksburg surrendered July 4th was heralded to the troops early on the morning of July 7th, by a heavy artillery salute given by the left battery. This was followed by an intended salute to the enemy, at noon, by all of the Federal batteries engaged in the siege. The Confederates answered by displaying a flag of truce, and an armistice for twenty-four hours was arranged between the two commanding generals. Soldiers on each side then met each other half way between their respective lines, without arms, during the night and morning, and had a jolly good time together, until a formal surrender took place in the afternoon of July 8th.

Receiving orders to get ready to take the field, the bridge was packed upon the wagons, and Company K marched into Port Hudson at five P.M. July 9th, all ready to embark at once on transports from the landing. For three days, under orders and counter-orders, the company remained in Port Hudson, while other troops were embarked and sent down the river.

To open river communication, the entire First Division, General Weitzel in command (General Augur was ill), was embarked at Port Hudson upon transports, at night, July 9th, and sent down to Donaldsonville, disembarking on the morning of July 10th. Other troops marched to Baton Rouge, for transportation to the same place, and the pontoon train was ordered to follow at midnight July 12th. Roused from slumber the men worked hard until morning, when the steamer *St. Maurice* carried them to Donaldsonville, arriving in the evening, July 13th, too late to take part in a reconnoissance made that day by the Third Brigade, First Division, under Colonel N. A. M. Dudley, Thirtieth Massachusetts.

What few particulars can be gathered of this second action on the La-Fourche are here recorded:

General Taylor heard of the fall of Vicksburg and Port Hudson during the night of July 10th. He immediately concentrated his troops on the La-Fourche, at Labadieville and Donaldsonville, to offer resistance if pressed, until sufficient time was gained to clean out his spoils in Brashear City.

July 11th, the Thirtieth Massachusetts skirmished down Bayou La-Fourche about four miles, when they met the enemy's cavalry in force, and returned to Donaldsonville towards night. At noon the next day this regiment again marched down the bayou road about one mile before meeting the enemy's pickets, who retired after an exchange of shots, a lieutenant of the Thirtieth being wounded. After proceeding nearly four miles, this regiment, with four guns Sixth Massachusetts Battery, went into bivouac on Kock's Plantation.

Early on the morning of July 13th a few shells dropped into the woods where General Green's dismounted cavalry and Semmes' battery were under cover, served to elicit a reply from that battery; an artillery-fire was maintained on both sides for about two hours. Under orders not to bring on an engagement, the First and Third Brigades advanced down the right side of the bayou, accompanied by an additional battery (First Maine), while a detachment from Grover's division, commanded by Colonel Morgan, Ninetieth New York, advanced down the left bank. Had the pontoon bridge been on hand to facilitate the carrying of orders across, perhaps the disaster of this day would not have occurred. The bayou was not wide, but no boats or skiffs were to be found. There was a stupid disposition of the Federal forces, who must have outnumbered the Confederates, with an absence of intelligent orders from the colonel in command, that has never been satisfactorily explained.

Upon the left bank, in front of Colonel Morgan, was a wide, open plain. In front of troops upon the right bank were sugar-cane fields, the stalks grown about seven feet high, with scattered trees, thick shrubbery and houses, both on and off the road, completely obstructing a view of what was taking place along the line. The Thirtieth Massachusetts, covering the bayou road, could not see beyond two hundred yards or so. While artillery-fire continued the men were nonchalant, paying little attention to shells, as they did no material damage. Some of the men improved the opportunity to bathe in the bayou and wash their underclothing.

Until two o'clock P.M. skirmish lines engaged the enemy; companies from the Thirtieth Massachusetts supported a section First Maine Battery, the One Hundred and Seventy-Fourth New York supporting another battery. At two o'clock Confederate cavalry on the left bank were seen to deliberately form line on the open plain and swoop down in fine style, with a continual yell, on the men under Colonel Morgan, who fell back rapidly, exposing Federal troops on the right bank to a flank fire. About the time this cavalry charge was made Confederate infantry and dismounted men, without the customary yell, carefully skirmished through the cane fields on the right bank, towards the Federals, who opened an infantry-fire in support of the artillery. No connected account of what happened along the line can be obtained, but it is well known that the Thirtieth Massachusetts suddenly found themselves receiving a sharp fire from across the bayou, a hot fire in front, and stray bullets from the cane fields to their right. Part of the regiment lay down behind a provisional breastwork made by the levee bank, which was also extended by them over the bayou road, and tried to silence the enemy seen in their wide-brim slouch hats on the other bayou side.

Though the enemy steadily crept along in front, to rise, fire and drop, to continue creeping up, no one seemed to think of a retreat. The two guns, First Maine Battery, were in an open space between the bayou road and levee bank, just back of the Thirtieth Massachusetts men. Exposed to the enemy's fire from across the bayou, the cannoneers sought shelter by laying upon the ground under their guns. Lieutenant Healy, in command, was obliged to use his sword on his men to force them up and serve the pieces; without aid, he loaded and fired a gun several times. This state of things continued until about three o'clock, when these guns became heated and could not be used; all the artillery horses were killed or disabled, with but four artillery-men left fit for duty, as the rest were killed or wounded.

Orders had been given to retreat, obeyed by some men who heard them, while others did not obey because they did not hear on account of the noise made by the musketry, artillery and bursting shells. The men who remained fought on for a short time, when two small companies One Hundred and Seventy-Fourth New York Infantry crowded in on them, pell-mell from the right, and completely filled the space that sheltered the Thirtieth Massachusetts, leaving bare enough elbow room to work in; still they kept on fighting (these One Hundred and Seventy-Fourth New York and Thirtieth Massachusetts men) to hold their ground, and at this time the heaviest loss of the day occurred.

When it was seen men were in retreat and the enemy was closing in rapidly, Captain Fiske, Lieutenant Barker, with some dozen men of the Thirtieth Massachusetts, endeavored to save the battery-guns by hauling them over a levee bank to the roadway with drag ropes. One gun was saved; one gun was abandoned, or thrown into the bayou. All of the troops upon and near the road then retreated in good order, exchanging shots from behind house corners and such shelter as could be found; in a few cases individual soldiers almost crossed bayonets with men of the enemy. The Thirtieth Massachusetts colors were defended by a handful of men until safe to the rear.

Colonel Dudley endeavored to rally his men for another stand, or check the enemy's advance, and succeeded in forming a line of about seventy-five men. This line fired a few rounds and then continued the retreat. On the retreat Private Horace F. Davis, Thirtieth Massachusetts, was cut off in a cane field by Confederate cavalry, made a prisoner about six o'clock, and with about fifty more prisoners was coralled under a cluster of trees, guarded by sentries. A rain-storm set in at night, accompanied with heavy thunder and sharp lightning, which enabled Private Davis to pass between two Texans, who were leaning upon their rifles on guard, and escape by crawling along in the darkness between the lightning flashes, avoiding the enemy, whose location was shown by their camp fires, around which they congregated, until he joined a flag-of-truce party, sent out after the dead and wounded. With this party he remained on duty, no one supposing he did not come out with them, finally rejoining his regiment at one o'clock A.M.

Private Davis, while firing from behind the breastwork across the road, was in range of a battery-gun First Maine. His attention was called to the fact, and at the moment he looked behind a shell was fired from this gun, the concussion as it passed over him causing a prickly sensation in his right eye. Nothing was thought about it at the time, or for some time after, until he discovered the sight was gone. Not daunted by this discovery, Davis remained on duty with his regiment, and reënlisted, with one eye, when his first term expired. The sight to his right eye has never been restored.

Other Massachusetts troops in this action were the Forty-Eighth and Forty-Ninth Regiments, attached to the First Brigade, and the Sixth Battery.

The Forty-Eighth was posted in sugar-cane fields to the extreme right, with a skirmish line out. In retreating, no orders were sent to the skirmishers, who were surrounded before they knew it, and lost two officers and twenty-one men taken prisoners.

The Forty-Ninth was posted in a lane that ran at a right angle with the bayou, and were lying down when the fight commenced. The regiment was soon ordered to a sugar-house, seen above the sugar-cane, about five hundred yards to the right and front, to reënforce a regiment and battery supposed to be there. No troops were found on arrival at the place. This regiment caught a moderate infantry-fire from the front, and saw a mounted force upon its right. Confederate infantry got in on the left of them, when the regiment fell back to the lane, and there remained until a staff-officer, Lieutenant Weber, got to them by the rear and ordered the regiment to save itself, as it was cut off. This was done by making a detour of some three miles through cane fields before it could rejoin the command.

The Sixth Battery lost one gun, dismounted and carried a short distance to the rear for repairs, where it had to be left, because sudden orders to retreat were given before it could be mounted to bring away.

Total casualties to Massachusetts troops in this action were:

Thirtieth Infantry — Eight killed; thirty-seven wounded; one missing.

Forty-Eighth Infantry — Three killed; seven wounded; twenty-three missing.

Forty-Ninth Infantry — One killed; twenty wounded; one missing.

Sixth Battery — One wounded.

Other regiments in the two brigades and Colonel Morgan's detachment lost in about the same ratio as above, because the enemy must have captured at least two hundred prisoners, probably more, and men in Company K saw at Donaldsonville, laid out for burial, about forty Federal soldiers, picked up on the field by a flag-of-truce party. Most of these men were shot in the head.

July 14th and 15th baggage and teams were unloaded from the steamer. On the sixteenth two hundred and thirteen feet of bridge was thrown across Bayou La-Fourche, under the direction of Sergeant Austin Hawes. The company remained on guard until July 20th, when they parted from their pontoons, relieved from further engineer duty by Captain John J. Smith, with one company First Louisiana (colored) Engineers.

Camp was struck July 21st, when the company proceeded to New Orleans upon the steamer *Sallie List* and reported to the regiment at Algiers late in the afternoon. Department Special Orders No. 181, issued July 25th, formally relieved Company K from detached duty in the engineer service.

During this tour of active field service sick men of Company K were left in hospitals at Berwick, Brashear City, New Orleans, and many men were sent to Gentilly Bayou regimental hospital. Deaths from sickness were as follows:

March 31st — Private Albert N. Bliss, fever, at Marine Hospital, New Orleans.

April 26th — Private Charles L. Atwood, fever, at Brashear City Hospital.

May 1st — Private Charles B. Bacon, fever, at Brashear City Hospital.

May 3d — Corporal George H. Shepard, congestion of bowels, at Berwick City Hospital.

May 24th — Private Samuel A. Knight, ——, at Baton Rouge Hospital.

May 28th — Private Elias H. Cutler, fever, at Brashear City Hospital.

July 4th — Private George H. Allen, dysentery, at New Orleans Hospital.

July 5th — Private William Stone, typhoid fever, in camp at Port Hudson.

CHAPTER XVI.

August — At Algiers — Bound North — On Board "Continental" — Arrival Home.

MAJOR-GENERAL BANKS having decided to send the regiment home in a few days, July 29th was devoted to cleaning guns and equipments, and turning over material to the regimental quartermaster. Orders came on the thirtieth to embark August 1st on the steamer *Continental* for New York, thence proceed to Readville, Massachusetts, and report to the United States mustering officer in Boston. The thirtieth and thirty-first July were busy days for the quartermaster, who turned over to proper Department officers arms, ammunition, equipments, camp and garrison equipage, unissued clothing, transportation and quartermaster stores, surplus medical and hospital stores. Twenty-five muskets and five hundred rounds of ammunition for the guard was retained.

All detached service men and convalescent sick men able to travel were ordered, by Department orders, July 25th, to join the regiment. Surgeon Hitchcock and Lieutenant Proctor reported back to the regiment. Major Stiles and Lieutenant Duncan, Company F, were relieved from court-martial duty July 30th. The detachments from Companies A and F reported July 25th from picket duty at Bayou St. John and Lakeport, relieved by Company H, Twenty-Sixth Massachusetts Volunteers. The sick in regimental hospital not able to travel were removed to New Orleans and distributed among the general hospitals.

The reveille was sounded at three A.M. August 1st, and every man was busy putting his personal effects in shape until the time arrived to eat his last breakfast in Louisiana. At eight o'clock the embarkation commenced. The *Continental* lay alongside the levee, near the warehouse, so no difficulty was experienced in placing aboard what little baggage was to be transported and the sick men supposed to be able to undergo the voyage. After all had got aboard, the *Continental* steamed up to New Orleans for Brigadier-General Cuvier Grover and his staff officers, Brigadier-General Paine, and a number of officers going North on leave of absence.

An attempt was made by General Grover to have his horses and those of his staff sent North upon the steamer. The only place where they could be accommodated was below the upper deck, where all available space was already taken up by the men, crowded well together, while space in immediate vicinity of the main hatch had been fitted up to accommodate the sick, as it was handy to have communication with the cabin; yet General Grover insisted that his horses should be taken on board. No amount of expostulation would change his determination. Captain Cogswell, Company F, swore that if they did come on board not one would be alive after one day at sea. His men below deck, packed like sheep in a railroad car. would have made short work with the animals before they would suffer the nuisance to remain. By a united remonstrance to General Banks, from surgeons and officers of the regiment, a Board of Survey was ordered and soon decided the matter. The horses did not get on board. General Grover's conduct in this affair was not humane.

While tied up at the levee until a decision was reached on this horse business, Sergeant Vialle, who was ashore on some errand, saw a drunken cavalry-man fall from his horse, and in a kind manner assisted him. The fellow was on a troublesome drunk, and turned on Vialle, accusing him of stealing his property. This was all that was wanted to set the devil at work in a patrol-guard from the Ninth Connecticut, who had a guard-station near the spot. They arrested Vialle and conducted him to this station, with an intention to hold him until after his regiment left. Word reached the boys that one of the regiment had been seized by the Ninth Connecticut, and on shore a drove of them rushed and went direct to the guard-station and demanded his release. This was refused, with a threat to fire into the crowd if they did not go away; but the boys held their ground, coming in contact several times for a scuffle with men on the patrol, who used their bayonets once or twice. While in the act of tearing up paving stones from the street to hurl at the guard, for the Forty-Second men were now thoroughly aroused, Lieutenant-Colonel Stedman, in a carriage, drove between the two bodies of men and put a stop to it. The patrol-guard set Vialle free by a back-door entrance of their quarters, when they saw what threatened them.

Hawsers were finally cast off, and the *Continental* headed down river bound for South West Pass. No cheers were given as the steamer got under way; all hands felt too happy now they were bound home to care a picayune for Louisiana. The following officers and men were left in Louisiana sick or on detached service:

Captain George P. Davis, Company K, on provost-marshal duty.

Lieutenant Augustus L. Gould, Company H, acting-quartermaster of a colored engineer detachment, to render his final accounts.

Private William H. Gilman, Company C, as hospital-steward in General Ullman's brigade colored troops.

Private Everett A. Denny, Company E, on duty at division headquarters. He came North by way of the river, in charge of a sick officer.

Private John Nolan, Company B, sick in hospital with chronic diarrhœa. Died in New Orleans.

Private Lewis Buffum, Company B, on detached service as locomotive engineer.

Private Jonathan Brown, Company C, in hospital with both ankles broke. Came North by way of the river.

Private Charles McLaughlin, Company H, sick in hospital with dysentery.

Sergeant Chauncy B. Sawyer, Company I, was sent to St. James Hospital July 31st, sick with typhoid fever. He was sent to New York, August 17th, on the *Cahawba*.

Private Thomas P. Contillon, Company I, sick in hospital.

Private Thomas F. Igo, Company I, sick in hospital.

Private Amos B. Howard, Company G, sick in hospital with a fever.

Private Franklin Hall, Company E, sick in hospital.

After remaining all night at South West Pass, for a high tide to cross the bar, early on the morning of August 2d the *Continental* put to sea. Fine weather the entire trip, with scarcely a cloud to be seen in the sky and a sea almost as smooth as glass, was what kind fortune favored the Forty-Second this time. In spite of all this, Lieutenant Powers, Company F, was again very sea-sick. He lay day and night upon the deck, close by the cabin's side, covered by his blanket, not wishing any nourishment, and took very little of what was forced on him, the picture of misery. Not another man on board suffered much from sea-sickness; a slight nausea for one day.

Mounting a guard every day was the only duty done on board ship. The men were allowed to enjoy themselves in any proper manner without restraint. Many of them slept on deck at night, instead of in the close, crowded deck below. The food furnished was plain, though not so good as when on land, while the drinking water was bad. Without storage capacity for enough fresh water to last the trip for the number of men on board, condensed sea-water had to be used. When drank fresh from the condenser it was not palatable, but if left to stand ten to twelve hours was not bad to the taste, and answered for drinking purposes. The difficulty was to get enough supply ahead to let it stand these hours, consequently most men had to drink it warm or get none at all. Music was freely given by the regimental band during the trip, and enjoyed for the want of better.

Details on board ship were: Lieutenant White in charge of receiving and delivering rations and of men detailed to assist the cook. Lieutenant Tinkham had charge of giving out water.

The strength of the regiment on board was — twenty-two officers and four hundred and six men for duty; three officers and one hundred and thirty-three men sick, with two hundred and seventy-two men paroled prisoners of war.

During seven nights the *Continental* was at sea, gambling was carried on in the cabin by a few young officers on leave of absence. The hours chosen were between ten P.M. and two A.M., when those not interested in the game had retired. Rolls of bills and small piles of gold pieces upon the table was not an unusual sight, while any one who had any curiosity, by lying upon the floor (a custom followed by some, instead of sleeping in their cabin berths), could witness the double dealing done by all the players and the passing to and fro of cards underneath the table between partners. It was interesting to witness, by outsiders, but the players frequently lost their temper as the play went against them, and open accusations of cheating and fraud were frequent, sometimes almost leading to a fight.

In the improvised hospital every attention possible was given sick men by the surgeons. The following deaths occurred however, and the bodies were committed to the deep ocean with usual appropriate ceremonies, viz.:

August 5th — Private Patrick O'Day, Company H, of acute dysentery.

August 6th — Private Charles H. Poole, Company I, of dysentery.

August 6th — Private Andrew J. Fisher, Company F, of heart disease.

In the cases of Poole and Fisher, their comrades did all in their power to give them comfort, but O'Day was shamefully neglected by his company officers and comrades, none of whom took the slightest interest in his case.

On the trip Corporal Andrew P. Olson, Company C, sick with chronic diarrhœa, and Private James A. Knight, Company F, sick with dysentery, rapidly grew worse. By their will power, they lived to reach New York. Corporal Olson died August 9th, Private Knight, August 10th, Private Benoni H. Calvin, Company E, August 12th, and Private Thomas Curran, Company C, August 19th, after they reached home.

Cape Hatteras was passed on the night of the sixth; a pilot was taken on board the next evening, and the *Continental* arrived in New York Harbor early on the morning of August 8th. The sick were at once transferred to the New England rooms. The steamer *Commodore* came alongside the *Continental* in the afternoon, and men and baggage were transferred, to proceed on to Boston, *via* Providence, Rhode Island.

As the *Commodore* did not start until seven o'clock in

the evening, a day was passed in New York. Most of the men remained quietly on board these steamers, or upon the pier. Permits to pass the guard, stationed at head of the dock, were granted in cases where it was well known the privilege would not be abused. The guard, Lieutenant Martin Burrell, Jr., in command, was under strict instructions, and did their onerous duty well. All precautions taken did not prevent some turbulent spirits from getting beyond the dock and supplying themselves with liquor. No serious cases of intoxication were to be noticed, however, until late in the afternoon, when Private Con. Dougherty, of Company C, was rolling about the dock, insulting everybody in his way, and spoiling for a fight. About the same time the guard passed in from the street Private John Davis and Sergeant Joseph J. Whitney, both of Company H, very drunk and very ugly. Before many minutes elapsed the three men came in contact, and a savage fight took place.

Nobody seemed to have the courage to put a stop to it. As it occurred in the immediate vicinity of the guard, a few officers near by presumed Lieutenant Burrell would at once arrest the men. Unfortunately he was absent from his post, and the sergeant on duty lacked proper knowledge of what he had authority to do. Word was sent to the lieutenant-colonel, who immediately came on the scene, accompanied by Major Stiles. Davis and his companion were ordered to stop their rioting, as Dougherty was badly punished and at this time upon his back. Davis, now full of fight, savagely turned upon Lieutenant-Colonel Stedman, and threatened to serve him in the same way he had Dougherty, at the same time shaking his fist very close to Stedman's face. For at least a minute the parties looked at each other: the colonel pale in the face, without showing signs of fear, only a little hesitation as to what was the proper thing to do; Davis and Whitney uttering blasphemous and insulting language, with threatening manners. The sergeant-major drew, cocked his pistol, and held it behind his person ready for use, and if either of the men had struck their lieutenant-colonel one blow they would have been shot down. Lieutenant Burrell soon arrived; he ordered a detail of his guard, with fixed bayonets, to arrest the three men — if they resisted, to use their bayonets freely. This diverted the attention of Davis, who at once started for the steamer; the other two men were arrested, but soon after released on promise of their company companions to take care of them.

The principal offender, Private Davis, on reaching the *Continental*, proceeded to whip the steward of that boat, whom he owed a grudge, and for a time made things hot for everybody. He was not taken in charge at this time, nor during the night, notwithstanding he made himself very offensive until the effects of bad rum were gone. This leniency towards Davis should not have been permitted. He had placed himself in just such positions many times during his service, and should have been taught a lesson. As far back as when in camp at Readville, he was reduced from the rank of corporal on account of his rowdyism.

A heavy fog set in before the steamer was well in Long Island Sound, continuing all night. The men slept in every nook and corner they could obtain a chance to lie down. General quiet prevailed, except such noises as were made by a few drunken men, the aforesaid Davis among the number.

Using due care, with a thorough knowledge of Sound navigation, the pilot supposed Point Judith was passed and steered a course to carry the steamer up Narragansett Bay, when at five o'clock A.M. Sunday, August 9th, the

Commodore struck upon the rocks of Point Judith, hard and fast. When she struck it was with sufficient force to throw men partly from their berths. There were two distinct shocks, with a grating sound as if timbers were being crushed and broken. No confusion followed the event; every one was cool and collected as though nothing had happened; when it was definitely ascertained that the steamer was fast upon the rocks, many men went to sleep again.

Upon deck it was impossible to see a hand or any object a few feet distant, the fog was so dense. The water was smooth and at high tide. After ineffectual attempts to back off, boats were lowered to make an examination of the hull near the water line, and a careful inspection made of the hold. While making water freely there was no danger, for the bow was hard and fast upon the rocks, and when the tide receded would leave her hull upon solid bottom; still all was done that could be to stop the leak.

The fog lifted gradually and by seven o'clock A.M. entirely disappeared, when the steamer's position was seen to be within a stone's throw of the shore. Adjutant Davis and Quartermaster Burrell went ashore, got conveyance to Kingston, and with some difficulty opened telegraphic communication with Providence, for assistance, also sending word to Boston. Fortunately the commissariat was in condition to keep the men from hunger. With the exception of grumbling on account of disappointment at not being able to eat a good breakfast in Boston, the men took the accident philosophically. The morning passed without any event of importance.

Early in the afternoon steamer *City of Newport* arrived from Providence, and after attempts were made at high tide to float the *Commodore* into clear water, without success, numerous heavy hawsers being broken, it was decided to transfer the men to the *City of Newport* by life-boats from both steamers, each boat-load hauled hand over hand along a hawser prepared for the purpose, instead of using oars. This operation was slow, the boats carrying a small number at a time. As darkness came on the tide receded and obliged the *City of Newport* to let go her end of the hawser and keep farther off from shore, to prevent grounding; the wind freshened up and caused a heavy swell on the sea and surf on shore. This took place before the transfer of men was complete, and made the rest of the operation tedious and tiresome, as oars had to be used to pull more than a mile.

Officers and men behaved admirably until afternoon, when boats were ready to transfer men; then came the tug of war in an endeavor to fill these boats. Orders and in some cases entreaty had to be used in forcing men into them. Men who would face an enemy without fear were afraid to trust themselves in small boats upon the water. The last boat to reach the *City of Newport* contained seven or eight men, who were saved from capsizing, in an insane endeavor they made to reach the steamer's deck together, by the coolness of two men.

When all were on board that could be induced to take to the boats, the *City of Newport* proceeded to Providence, arriving there at two o'clock Monday morning, August 10th. No time was lost in taking cars, held in readiness, and the train started for Boston without delay, arriving at the Boston and Providence depot at five o'clock. Had the regiment arrived home on Sunday morning, as expected, a rousing reception was ready for it.

The Forty-Second marched to Faneuil Hall, where breakfast was waiting, and the regiment formally welcomed home by prominent citizens. At half-past ten o'clock A.M. the regiment formed line and marched to the parade ground on Boston Common, where the men were dismissed until the twentieth.

August 20th, 1863, one year after the first detachment went into camp as a nucleus to organize the regiment, the men assembled upon the old ground at Readville and were mustered out of the United States service.

The following officers and men remained in the enemy's hands, prisoners of war: Colonel Burrell, Surgeon Cummings, Captains Sherive, Proctor and Savage, Lieutenants Cowdin, Eddy, Bartlett, S. F. White, Newcomb and Stowell, Corporal H. W. McIntosh, Privates Dennis Dailey, Edwin F. Josselyn, Francis S. Morrill, James O'Shaughnessy, of Company D; Corporal David L. Wentworth and Private Joseph W. D. Parker, of Company G; Private Joseph W. McLaughlin, Company I; and Private Samuel R. Hersey, Company C.

CHAPTER XVII.

Adventures of Corporal Wentworth and Private Hersey.

CORPORAL DAVID L. WENTWORTH, Company G, Private Samuel R. Hersey, Company C, and Frank Veazie, officers' cook, with about three hundred men (including Lieutenant Hamilton, Master Hannum, Engineers Plunkett and Stone, of the *Harriet Lane*), left Camp Groce, December 9th, for Shreveport. Long captivity in restricted quarters left them in such a debilitated condition that a march of any duration completely prostrated them.

The guard, some fifty men, under a good officer, was composed of a clever set of men, who made it easy for the prisoners so far as lay in their power, occasionally helping some poor fellows along by allowing them to ride their horses. Those too ill to walk (Hersey was among them, and towards the journey's end Wentworth, sick with dysentery) were allowed to ride in the baggage wagons, five in number, an uncomfortable conveyance, none provided with springs, and the roads in poor condition.

Cooking utensils were scarce. Living principally upon "mush," each mess, when they arrived at camping places, would try all sorts of tricks to secure a "dodger-pan" from some other mess, in spite of orders, "first come, first served." Some would have to wait until late at night for their turn to come, while others, too tired, would retire to their bed of leaves and go to sleep hungry.

Every morning a start was made soon after daybreak, in order to reach each day's destination as early as possible. On an average fifteen to twenty miles constituted a day's march, and was done every day until December 22d, when a halt for several days was made, one mile beyond Tyler, to rest the weary prisoners. While here the officers left at Camp Groce passed them on their way to Camp Ford, without an opportunity being given to converse. Pleasant, cool weather was experienced the first four days, then came cold, windy weather for two days, then rain for one day, clearing off cold and windy and remaining so until the march ended, varied with a few rainy and many cloudy, damp and freezing cold days. It took six days to reach Trinity River, and several days more before arriving at Tyler. The march was resumed on Sunday, December 27th, crossing Sabine River during the morning, and continued each day until about sunset December 30th, when it ended, after an eighteen days' tramp, and four days' rest at Tyler, twenty-two days after leaving Camp Groce.

Even the negro drivers, rollicking jolly as they appeared to be, singing and yelling all day long, could not enliven this small regiment of marching sufferers. A favorite song, because it was constantly sang, and in a manner impossible for any white man to imitate, "Rock me Julie, rock me," rang in the prisoners' ears long after they had parted company with their ebony-colored singers.

The following account of what occurred while at Shreveport was written by Private Hersey, who claims that there is no exaggeration in his statements — facts alone are stated:

STATEMENT OF PRIVATE HERSEY.

"The last two days of the year 1863 will long be remembered by those members of our regiment who, with some three hundred other Federal prisoners, were wending their toilsome way over the rough, frozen roads leading from Marshall, Texas, to the Louisiana border, in expectation, when arriving there, of being exchanged or paroled. December 29th a fierce 'Norther' set in, which was soon accompanied by a severe storm of rain, hail, snow and sleet. Through this terrible storm we plodded on over a dreary region of woodland and prairie, with the icy hurricane piercing our tattered, scanty garments, the pelting rain and sleet drenching us to the skin. At night there was no shelter from the pitiless storm, excepting such as we could find under the wet, dripping branches of the forest trees, or form by twisting their limbs into arches and covering them with moss gathered from the cypress trees. Those who could creep in under the awnings of the army wagons, which the guard had appropriated for their own quarters, were fortunate indeed. Sleep or rest there was none, and for two days and nights our lives dragged on in utter misery.

"A dozen or more of our number were shoeless, and many a footprint stained with the blood of these unfortunate ones could be traced along the snow-covered ground. A score at least had no clothing, except an improvised suit made by tieing their well-worn army blankets around their waists. The hope of release urged many a poor captive forward, who otherwise would have succumbed to the fatigues and hardships of the long marches. Even the Confederate soldiers who guarded us, although much better provided for than ourselves, were scantily and meanly clothed, and suffered severely.

"On the thirtieth of the month, after a day of intense suffering from the severity of the weather and the length and fatigues of the march, we reached the end of our journey, or rather the place where we were to await the arrival of the agents of exchange or parole. We were halted in the depths of a snow-covered wood; there left to ourselves to find such shelter as leafless, dripping branches of the trees afforded. This locality was known as 'Four Mile Springs.'

"Beyond this wood was a camp of Federal prisoners, who had arrived some time before us, occupying long, frame barracks, crowded so as to afford no shelter for fresh arrivals. The appearance of these prisoners was wretched, and so filthy were their quarters our men declared that some of the vermin, or 'graybacks' as they were called, had inscribed upon their backs the words, 'in for the war.' These poor fellows had been quartered since their capture, some six months previous, at Camp Ford, Texas, but were marched to their present quarters a few weeks previous to our arrival, to await exchange. They were chiefly Indiana troops.

"The weather was extremely cold for this latitude, resembling more the rude, bleak winter of our Northern clime than the soft, genial atmosphere we had always associated in our minds when thinking of the sunny South, and was said to be the severest ever known in this region.

"For a few days after our arrival we were allowed to roam at will through the woods and vicinity without a guard, for the reason that in daily expectation of proceeding to our lines the men were not likely to attempt any escape. Days passed by in this partial state of freedom, until finally, as the days passed into weeks without any indications of a speedy release, our hopes again began to darken; the men grew restive, and numbers of them were daily missing at roll-call. Every man who attempted escape was recaptured before he got far away and brought back to be placed under guard.

"During our long captivity in Texas our hopes and

expectations had so often been raised only to fall again, we got somewhat accustomed to disappointments of this nature, but never since our capture had we been quite so sure of immediate release, or felt the bitterness of 'hope deferred,' as we did then. In our prison days at Houston and Camp Groce we had regular *quotations of exchange*, and the stock was as fluctuating as any in the markets of Wall or State Streets; our days were made cheerful or gloomy according as the stock advanced or fell.

"One morning, at roll-call, we were all summoned to the headquarters of Colonel Théard, commanding the prison-guard, and informed that our Government refused to receive us as paroled prisoners, also refusing to negotiate for our exchange. The colonel made us a neat little speech, in which he expressed his sympathy for us in our deplorable condition, and informed us he had sent a letter to General Kirby Smith, commanding the Confederate Trans-Mississippi Department, asking him to issue clothing, and describing our destitution and sufferings. He also stated he had written to the general, that in case he could not comply with the request for clothing he should feel impelled, from an aversion to seeing so much distress continually before his eyes, to ask to be relieved of his duties as commander of the prison camp. As we never received any clothing from General Smith, or any other quarter, and as the Confederate soldiers were sadly in need of supplies, I was convinced that the Quartermaster Department of the Trans-Mississippi army was in a wofully depleted condition.

"In front of Colonel Théard's headquarters was an extensive plateau, and here we were ordered to encamp, a guard again placed over us and the dead line traced out. This broad plain was perfectly barren of shrubbery or trees; not even a plot of grass could be found upon it. To make shelter for ourselves we were allowed to go into the woods in squads, under guard, and cut timber and gather leaves. In a few days there sprung into existence, upon this plateau, a village of huts and nondescript structures of the quaintest and most original designs imaginable. Many of these habitations consisted simply of a few bent twigs, arched so as to form a burrow just large enough to creep into head foremost, suitable only to sleep in. Those who from sickness or weakness were unable to erect a domicile depended upon the generosity of their more fortunate comrades, or slept in the open air. Our rations consisted chiefly of coarse corn meal, coarse salt, sugar, and occasionally beef. Having a limited number of cooking utensils, we were often obliged to wait for hours before we could cook our food. Our guards at this camp were a good-hearted set of fellows, and, with a few exceptions, inclined to favor us whenever they could.

"About the middle of January Colonel Théard was relieved of his command, much to our regret, for his treatment of us had been kind and considerate. His heart was evidently not much in sympathy with the rebellion, for we heard a short time after his removal he had left the Confederate army and taken the oath of allegiance to the Federal Government, in New Orleans. He was succeeded by Colonel Harrison, whose administration of affairs while not particularly harsh was lacking in the kindliness which we had always met with under Théard.

"Rumors of the opening of cartels for exchange were as rife here, and received almost as often, as in our former days at Houston and Camp Groce. 'Exchange stock' rose and fell with almost its former regularity; our daily advices from Shreveport caused a constantly-fluctuating stock board. Our own Government was universally condemned for its indifference or neglect of our welfare, and many an imprecation was hurled against those who had it in their power to exchange or parole us and would not. We frequently heard of the exchange of other Federal prisoners, and knew that the Confederates captured at Vicksburg and Port Hudson had all, long ago, been released, and therefore it was we complained so bitterly against our fate.

"About the middle of March rumors of General Banks' advance towards Shreveport with a large army came thick and fast, greatly elating us with a hope they might soon encircle the place of our imprisonment. Suddenly, on the morning of March 26th, the prison camp was broken up and the prisoners, excepting Wentworth, Williams and I, were started on the road towards Texas, destined for Camp Ford.

"Upon our arrival at Four Mile Springs Wentworth and I discovered on the roadside, in the woods and beyond the place where the command had been halted, a log hut, in which we found quarters for the night. The hut was a small, dilapidated structure, like old log cabins of the early settlers, and evidently been standing for many years. We found it occupied by three Confederate soldiers, fitted up as a blacksmith shop for the cavalry forces in the vicinity. The exposed condition of the building rendered it only a partial shelter from the storm, for through chinks in the roof and walls the wind and sleet came in freely, and the smoke from the smouldering fire filled the space within almost to suffocation; however, it was a better refuge than the other prisoners could find. Upon lumps of coal and bits of iron on the rude forge I endeavored to find rest in vain; the wind blew through the log crevices in furious blasts, and that side of my clothing exposed to the hut walls was covered with a thin coating of ice, making sleep or comfort impossible. It was a terrible night for the half-clad, shivering wretches outside, and a most cheerless, uncomfortable one for those inside.

"The next morning broke clear, but cold and windy. A thin surface of sleety snow covered the ground, causing the landscape around us to look anything but Southern. The men were huddled around slowly burning camp fires, waiting patiently for the distribution of their meagre rations and trying to get warmth into their almost frozen limbs.

"The three soldiers occupying the hut were no better off as to accommodations, and not a whit better provided with rations than ourselves. We lived with them during our stay at Four Mile Springs, and became in that time greatly attached to them. Their names were Ramsey, Dick Fickling, and Stanley. Mr. Ramsey, or 'Pap' Ramsey, as he was familiarly called, was an old man, about sixty years of age, a splendid specimen of our ideal western backwoodsman. His life had been passed on the wild borders of the Indian Territory and Western Louisiana, knowing little of life in cities and towns. He had never strayed beyond his native prairies and forests until the Southern Confederacy, in its distress for every able-bodied man, brought him forth from his peaceful cabin, compelled to enter its service. He was conscripted some few months previous to our arrival, but being too old for the routine duties of a soldier's life was detailed to serve as blacksmith for the regiment in which he was placed. A tall, broad-shouldered, well-built man, with gray hair and beard, and an eye as bright and keen as any young person; he was simple-hearted, unskilled in the ways and observances of the world, but with a vast experience of the rough, free, adventurous life of a pioneer. Stanley, his assistant, was a young man, about twenty-five years old, large-hearted, good-natured, and always ready for sport, but with a natural aversion to work. His comrades gave him the name of 'Fox,' on account of the cunning and shrewdness he displayed in stealing away from camp to visit his home, sixteen miles away, on every possible occasion. He seldom applied for a furlough, deeming such sort of discipline, as he said, entirely unnecessary and too much like slavery. When called to account by his officers for his absence from his regiment, he generally appeased their wrath by presenting them with a fine turkey or shote. A conscript, he managed to evade camp duty by getting detailed as assistant-blacksmith, though wherein his assistance was of any value or service to Mr. Ramsey would have been difficult for an observer to tell. The only labor he was ever known to perform was to occasionally wield the sledge, when the other assistant was absent. His ideas in regard to the cause or object of the war were vague and indefinite, but as far as he knew them they were altogether opposed to the Southern Confederacy. He was the owner of one slave, who took charge of his little farm while he was away.

"Anxious to continue our abode with these kind-hearted soldiers, Wentworth and myself called upon Colonel Théard, when the prisoners were again placed under guard, prevailing upon him, after considerable pleading, to allow us a *pass*, granting the liberty of the camp until further orders; a phrase we construed to mean any distance within five miles of the hut. When Colonel Harrison succeeded Colonel Théard he was disposed to revoke this *pass*, condescending, after some persuasion, to let the order 'remain for the present.' He was a strict disciplinarian, severe and often harsh in his treatment of the prisoners and his own men; it was a surprise to all that we had won such favor.

"'Time wore on pleasantly; the weather grew mild and

genial, and about the middle of January the short Southern winter was over. Our hut was romantically situated, and since our occupation of it we had closed up the chinks in the sides and patched the roof, so that the rain could no longer gain entrance. The road in front of us wound through a broad tract of beautiful woodland, and stretched on in one direction to Shreveport, in the other to the prison lines. Beyond this forest was a vast waste of swamp land, covered with a prolific growth of cypress and gum trees, and intersected in every direction by dark, coffee-colored bayous, in which the finest species of the 'Buffalo' fish were found. Along the banks of these streams and scattered over the bottom-lands were clusters of impenetrable thickets, where countless numbers of bright-plumaged birds made their nests, and where the venomous mocassin and deadly scorpion found hiding places. All day long, in the deep recesses of these lonely wilds, the air was resonant with the music of feathery warblers. We caught many of them in traps, which Stanley was expert at making, but remembering our own prison experience we never kept them long 'in durance.'

"The hut soon became a popular rendezvous for Confederate soldiers passing to and from their camp, and we became acquainted with most every one belonging to the regiment acting as prison-guard. With some we formed friendships that lasted long after the war closed. Political questions were seldom argued, but when they were it was always with good humor on their part at least, and we were invariably treated with courtesy and kindness, often with generosity.

"Life at the hut was by no means monotonous; each day found us enjoying ourselves in a free and easy way. Mr. Ramsey was owner of a fine horse, and valued him highly. The old man gave me permission to ride the animal whenever I felt inclined, leaving the whole care of the horse to me. With Stanley, always ready for a drive, I took many an excursion through the woods and swamps and to the different plantations in the neighborhood; thus became acquainted with about every planter within a radius of five miles from camp. Amongst them was Mr. Elliot, owner of a plantation at Bayou Pierre, with whom I formed a most intimate and pleasant acquaintance. With him and his family I often passed a delightful hour, always entertained as a welcome guest. Mr. Elliot had formerly been in the Confederate army. While with his regiment in Tennessee, just after the battle of Perryville he purchased a furlough for a large amount of money, returning home, and had not again rejoined his command. In order to obtain exemption from conscription he purchased the position of superintendent of a Government planing-mill in Texas, but had not reported at his new field of service. He was a thorough Union man, and a bitter enemy of the Confederacy. His service in the army was compulsory, and although engaged in several battles said he had never fired a gun during the actions except in the direction of the sky. He was, like many others of the South, an owner of slaves, but not an advocate of slavery. Through him I became acquainted with many loyal men, and was surprised to find the Union sentiment so strong. Of the half-dozen or more planters living within four miles of the camp not one was an advocate of secession, but all were anxiously longing for the approach of our army to this portion of the State. Even amongst our prison-guard we found many a secret friend of the Union, who only waited for an opportunity to place themselves in the ranks of its army. The number of such was by no means small, although the great majority were loyal to the 'Stars and Bars.'

"During the latter part of January I obtained of Colonel Harrison permission for two other prison comrades to live with us at the hut. They were Williams, whom we called 'Transport,' and the carpenter of the United States ship *Morning Light*, who went by the name of 'Chips.' Their arrival rendered it necessary for us to enlarge our dwelling. Through the soft persuasiveness of Wentworth, the quartermaster was prevailed upon to grant us a small supply of timber and nails, and in a short time we built a small addition to the hut, in which we erected sleeping bunks for the accomodation of us all.

"My acquaintance with the quartermaster's clerk, young Finney, enabled me to obtain a much larger supply of rations than I was lawfully entitled to, and, as I was usually allowed to attend to the weighing of them, I did not hesitate to take advantage of this privilege for the benefit of us all. By going a short distance into the woods we were sure to find a stray hog or pig wandering around, and our stock of pork was always well kept up. It being against orders to kill any of them, the undertaking was always attended with considerable difficulty, and we were obliged to hunt our game at night. As we never could get near enough to kill them by any other means than shooting, the report of our gun at midnight was frequently heard at camp, the officers invariably causing inquiries to be made concerning the reason of the untimely firing. To prevent discovery we concealed our game in a small cellar, dug under the floor of our hut annex, with the boards so arranged that they appeared nailed down to the uninitiated. Our cooking of this food was done when no prying eyes were upon us and the savory odor would not be likely to betray us. Besides this sort of fare, costing nothing, we had frequent opportunities of purchasing sweet potatoes, eggs and butter, with money obtained by the sale of our *tricks* and watches when leaving Camp Groce. Our table was unrivalled by any of the 'messes,' either of the prisoners or the guard. The *ne plus ultra* of cookery were the 'corn-dodgers' Wentworth made to perfection, and which were certainly worthy the skill of the finest French cook. Old 'Pap' Ramsey refused to indulge his appetite with this rich food, claiming that such delicacies would inevitably bring on gout or dyspepsia, and that his palate, accustomed to the coarse, homely fare of the backwoods, was unfitted for the luxurious compound which Wentworth made. Through the colonel's orderly, George Cole, I was usually the recipient of some dainties from his table, after an entertainment had been given by that officer to visiting friends.

"One day during February Wentworth obtained permission of Colonel Harrison to visit Shreveport on one of the army wagons, which made daily trips to that place. His stay there, for a few hours only, was quite long enough for him to get disgusted with the appearance of the city, and especially with the fabulous price they charged him for his dinner; a small piece of pork, with bread and butter, and a tiny cup of coffee cost him six dollars.

"A few days after Wentworth's return 'Transport' made the same trip without obtaining the requisite permission. The day previous, while strolling in the woods, he met in a quiet nook a few Confederate teamsters with a supply of Louisiana rum, which they invited him to drink. The temptation was too strong for his feeble powers of resistance, and the potations were so deep and frequent that he was soon exalted to a state of complete recklessness. In this condition he remained with his jovial friends over night, accompanying them the next morning to Shreveport. On reaching the city he was so muddled for awhile he was unable to clearly comprehend the state of affairs, and even in doubt as to his own identity, whether he was a Federal prisoner or a Confederate soldier. The following morning he was found at the entrance to a hospital, standing guard for a soldier whom he had succeeded in making even drunker than himself. An hour or so later he found himself on board the ram *Webb* (then lying in the river abreast of the city), in the presence of a recruiting officer, who endeavored to persuade him to join the vessel, by offering him tempting inducements in the shape of pay and bounty. 'Transport,' though very drunk, was not to be enticed by any proffers which they could make him to desert his flag.

"Late that evening he returned in company with his convivial friends, reckless of consequences and unable to give a satisfactory account of his trip. That same night he was sent for, to explain his absence without leave, failing in which he was deprived of his liberty and placed under guard again. The next morning I met him in camp, and a more pitiful-looking object I could hardly have imagined; no wonder the poor fellow was disconsolate after his recent experience of partial freedom with us. He begged me to intercede with Colonel Harrison and obtain his release, swearing eternal gratitude if I would, and promising not to be overcome by such a temptation again. I found the colonel in good humor and had no difficulty in persuading him to grant 'Transport' a new lease of freedom; only he proposed, he said, to hold me personally responsible for my comrade's good behavior in the future. His demonstrations of joy, when I carried him the good news, were unbounded, but his promises of good behavior were short-lived, for the same day he again fell in with his festive friends, and during his spree so far forgot himself as to make a visit to the colonel, at his headquarters, to request the loan of a horse. The utter ridiculousness of such a request, coupled with the jovial good nature with which he made it, so amused the colonel that he allowed him to return to the hut with a slight reprimand. A few days after this 'Chips' was remanded to the lines for drunkenness and insulting an officer of the guard while in that condition.

"For several days during the latter part of March the prison camp was kept in a continuous state of excitement by a variety of conflicting rumors concerning the disposition to be made of us, on account of the approach of our army up the Red River, under General Banks. An occasional report would reach us that we were to be sent at once to our lines and transportation down the river was being prepared; but the gist of these rumors indicated a removal of all prisoners in this vicinity to Camp Ford, in Texas. We were on the alert for any news of a definite description; our only fear was that we would be suddenly ordered into camp with the other prisoners.

"While standing by the fire-place in the hut, early on the chilly morning of March 26th, I saw a squad of cavalry pass along the road in front, and a few of their number dismounted and entered, to warm themselves by the fire. I saw at once they were not Colonel Harrison's men, and inquired where they were going so early in the morning. Not knowing I was a 'Yankee' prisoner, they replied that they had come from Shreveport for the purpose of taking the 'Yanks' to Camp Ford, and said the 'Yankee' army was *booming* along up the Red River and had already reached Natchitoches, and would soon reach Shreveport unless defeated. The prisoners were to start at nine o'clock, under orders to make forced marches until their destination was reached. I pretended to be much pleased at the idea of being relieved from guard duty, and gave utterance to a few other justifiable prevarications to conceal my identity, fearing all the while a guard or summons should come for us from the camp.

"When they had gone I went to the bunk where Wentworth, who heard the conversation, was lying, and urged him to start immediately for the swamp in rear of Elliot's Plantation. As he was undecided what to do, I started for the woods, meeting 'Transport,' who joined me, until a deep ravine near the swamps was reached. I left 'Transport' and started for the hut for my money I forgot to bring away. Meeting Mrs. Gupton, an acquaintance, she volunteered to procure my money while I awaited her return. She soon came back with it and the information that Wentworth was alone at the hut, still undecided what to do. I made my way to Elliot's Plantation, and waking Elliot up, for it was yet early, I explained the situation of affairs and asked his advice. He told me to return to the ravine, secrete myself until I should hear from him, and that he would visit camp to obtain all the information he could.

"Finding 'Transport' where I left him, we lay for hours expecting every moment to be discovered or trailed by hounds, which we could hear yelping in the distance. Late in the afternoon Mr. Elliot sought us, bringing a substantial supply of food, the more welcome because we had eaten nothing since the day previous. He reported that on his way to camp he found the prisoners already drawn up in the road, near the hut, answering to rollcall. He was unable to state whether our names had been called, but thought they had been omitted or some one had responded for us. He found Wentworth inside the hut, seated upon a log, smoking, and apparently in deep thought. He advised him to strike for liberty at once, and Wentworth jumped out of the window in the rear, hurrying to a thicket that bordered a small stream back of the hut. Shortly afterwards line was formed and the command given to start. We passed the night in a woody hollow between the trunks of two fallen trees, every now and then alarmed by a pack of hounds barking near by, who we feared were on our track, but we afterwards learned belonged to a neighboring planter, a Union man.

"Early next morning Mr. Elliot sent a servant to us with breakfast, and shortly after appeared himself. We held a consultation as to the best mode of procedure, and concluded that the safest plan would be to remain concealed near or in the swamp-lands, until Banks' army approached, which we then had no doubt would soon be in this vicinity. Mr. Elliot offered to supply us with food and to give us such information as he could obtain. The weather being now mild and pleasant, our open-air quarters were rather pleasant than otherwise."

The statement of Private Hersey ends here. The following account of wanderings and adventures in the attempt of Wentworth, Hersey and Williams to reach the Federal lines is compiled from Private Hersey's diary, and verified by him:

Hersey and Williams remained concealed in the swamp, at "Fort Hersey" (so named), until April 17th, their wants provided for by Mr. Elliot, when they found Wentworth, who had been kindly befriended by a Confederate soldier named Leeds, afterwards by a Mr. McGee, owner of a plantation. They knew of reënforcements for the Confederates arriving from Texas and Arkansas, and saw a portion of General Price's Arkansas men marching along a road crossing the margin of the swamp, on their way towards Mansfield. They heard heavy firing in that direction April 8th, and the next day were informed by Mr. Elliot of the total defeat of the Federal troops at *Sabine Cross-Roads* and their retreat to Alexandria.

At McGee's Plantation a conference was held by Hersey, Wentworth, Williams and several Unionists, Mr. Elliot, Mr. Dickinson, Mr. Bell, and Mr. McGee, when it was decided the safest course was for them to make their way down the country by following the river until Alexandria was reached, and watch for an opportunity to cross into the Federal lines. This meeting was held April 17th, and the *tramp* was commenced April 20th (declining to allow a deserter from the Confederate army to join them), by Wentworth, Hersey and Williams, who crossed the Red River to the north bank at Bell's Plantation, to follow the plan decided upon, viz., to cross the river, follow its course down, keeping in the swamps and woods as much as possible, claim to belong to Harrison's regiment if questioned or suspected, and that they were on their way to rejoin from the hospital at Shreveport. Harrison's regiment was then on the north bank operating against the Federal navy, under Admiral Porter. They felt confident their clothing would not betray them, as it was entirely of homespun material.

The first day, while being entertained by Union people, Monsieur Lattier and his two granddaughters, Mrs. Scopenie and Miss Sophia Hall, they escaped capture by three cavalry-men, who rode up to the house, by hiding in one of the rooms until they had departed. The ladies thought it was a very romantic episode, but the prisoners did not. Travelling sometimes all night, or all day, or partly by day and night, in the swamps, with their course lying in a south-easterly direction, they were guided by the North Star when the nights were clear, occasionally losing the way when the sky was clouded. Food was obtained by going to houses and asking for it; water, by filling their canteens at rain-water cisterns; and sleep, in deserted cabins, corn cribs, or under trees.

They were always enabled to trace the windings of the

Red River by tall trees that grew along its banks and marked its course. Most of the planters' residences were situated near the river road, facing the river; the plantations extending back to the swamp-lands or forests. The land in this region was as level as a prairie, and the soil of the farms a rich, black earth, with scarcely the smallest pebble to be found upon it. They crossed Loggy Bayou on the twenty-second, went through Springville Village at night on the twenty-fourth, reaching the pine woods on the twenty-fifth, where it was almost impossible to conceal themselves from the eyes of anybody they chanced to meet, on account of the absence of undergrowth or shrubbery. In passing through the town of Compti, on the twenty-sixth, recently burned by the Federals, Hersey says: "We stopped in a ravine on the edge of the town until after midnight, and then quietly and cautiously went forward. The few houses remaining look deserted, and the whole scene, as we viewed it in the darkness of the night, was the picture of desolation. The silence of death reigned over the place, except now and then when an owl would hoot in the woods that fringed the suburbs. We had just reached a bridge crossing a little stream in the centre of the town when we were terribly alarmed by the sudden sound of horses hoofs on the road behind us. On looking back we saw through the darkness a number of horses galloping towards the bridge at a terrific rate, so rapidly as to give us no chance to escape them. The scare was of short duration, for when they rushed by we saw that they were riderless, and probably had taken us for their masters. The shock produced a sense of timidity upon us we could not shake off with all the assumption of gayety and laughter that we outwardly manifested, and we felt greatly relieved when we reached the woods and left the desolate town far behind us."

They frequently saw officers and men, but managed to evade them, until on the night of April 27th they reached a bayou and were dismayed to find a soldier on guard at the only fording place they could discover. Hersey says: "This was the worst obstacle we had yet encountered, and we were at loss to find a way to overcome it. The banks of the stream were high and steep. We crept onward to get a better view of the situation, and could plainly see the sentry by the light of his bivouac fire. He was sitting or reclining upon an old log with the light shining upon his face, his gun across his shoulder. We soon saw he was fast asleep, and decided to cross while he was wrapt in slumber. The distance from bank to bank was short, but the fording place was narrow and almost barred by the form of the guard. The undertaking was venturesome, but there was no other way out of the difficulty, so we determined to run the gauntlet. Arranging to go one at a time, Wentworth started first, passed the sentry safely, climbing the opposite bank. As I drew near I felt a strange fascination which almost deprived me of action, and when I reached him was compelled to stop and gaze into his face before the spell was dissolved. Williams, who came last, was also successful, but we could not resist our suppressed laughter at the comical figure he cut in his endeavors to deaden the sound of his footsteps. With a sense of relief we made haste to gain the woods, and travelled on until morning."

On the twenty-ninth of April, when within thirty miles of Alexandria, they accidently stopped at the house of a Jayhawker (a name given to those secret bands of Southern Unionists who resisted by force the conscription acts and were the deadliest foes of the guerrillas), who provided *them* with food and excused himself from giving breakfast to a Confederate lieutenant of cavalry and three privates, who rode up while the three escaped prisoners were talking with their host upon the door-porch. By advice of this Jayhawker they endeavored to find a Madam Nowlan, who lived near the river, and who, he said, would find a way to assist them across the river into the Federal lines.

The next day, April 30th, while proceeding in the direction given them how to find Madam Nowlan's Plantation, they encountered an army wagon and learned from a soldier that Harrison's cavalry was not far away, stationed on that side of the river. This fact decided them to represent Texans, knowing they were on the south side, and they were well acquainted with the history of many Texas regiments. About noon they called at a house to procure a dinner, introducing themselves as Texas soldiers attached to Captain Clipper's company, of Elmore's regiment, on their way from Shreveport hospitals to rejoin their company. While awaiting dinner, conversation was carried on with the host, under some shady trees, about army matters, until Williams asked the nearest way to reach Madam Nowlan, when a red-headed man came from the house and demanded in a rough tone: "What do you know about Madam Nowlan?" The question was so abruptly asked, Wentworth and Hersey were disconcerted for a moment. They were subjected to a series of questions and cross questions, which were answered as best they could; Hersey's information, gathered while visiting Colonel Harrison's headquarters, about the Confederate troops in Louisiana and reënforcements expected from Texas and Arkansas coming in very opportune.

The red-headed man was a "courier," named Harris, attached to the "courier line" carrying despatches between army headquarters and Shreveport, on the north bank of Red River. He suspected the three prisoners were spies, and was not to be duped. Disappearing for a short time, he returned followed by three soldiers, who apparently dropped in one at a time, as if by chance. Courier Harris laid his plans well. Offering no opposition to their departure, they started for the river road, when he followed them and began conversation, intimating a desire on his part to desert. They were not to be caught by this trick and resented such proposals, when he rode away, after directing them how to reach the river crossing. Feeling that the end was near, they kept on until a deserted log house built upon piles, beneath which was a little grass plot, tempted them to rest under its cool shelter.

While resting a pack of hounds surrounded them, soon followed by a cavalry squad, headed by Harris, who levelled their guns and ordered a surrender. The prisoners were taken to the house of Mr. Swafford, said to be the headquarters of the courier line, and there kept until their case was reported to Brigadier-General Liddel, commanding Confederate forces.

On Monday, May 2d, Captain Micot, chief of the courier line, arrived to take them to General Liddel, whose camp was about twenty-five miles distant, opposite Alexandria. Captain Micot was sociable and friendly, expressing his sympathy and promising to do what he could for them. He did so, returning from an interview with his general exclaiming: "Well, boys, I've got good tidings for you," handing them a piece of paper, torn from the blank leaf of a printed book, upon which the following lines were written in pencil:

"Guards and pickets will pass Samuel R. Hersey, David L. Wentworth and Charles Williams outside the Confederate lines.

"BRIGADIER-GENERAL LIDDEL,
"Per ———, *A. A. A. G.*"

A verbal provision was attached to the pass, that they must not attempt to reach the Federal lines on Red River, but return by way of Harrisonburg, thence to the Federal forces on the Mississippi River. This pass, Captain Micot informed them, would be respected by all regular Confederate soldiers, but probably not by the guerrillas, as they were not subject to the discipline of the army. Thus was Williams' oft-repeated prediction, "Our journey is only a round-about road to Texas again, it would be better for us if we had gone with the crowd," not likely to be realized.

The three prisoners returned to Swafford's house, accompanied by Captain Micot and a private named Meecum. Meecum, who found an opportunity to unbosom himself, advised them to call upon his father, a Baptist clergyman and member of a league of Jayhawkers, residing about seventeen miles from Swafford's, directly on their way, who would mark out a course to pursue that would be of assistance. He had a brother serving in the Federal army, and his sympathies were with the Union cause; his service was compulsory with the Confederates.

Wednesday, May 4th, Wentworth, Hersey and Williams again commenced a tramp of one hundred and seventy-five miles, after an adieu to their Confederate friends who had treated them very kindly; since their recapture it appeared to them as though they were friends upon a visit, so considerate had been the treatment they received from everybody with whom they came in contact. Mr. Swafford presented Wentworth with a blood-hound "pup" of fine breed, as a remembrancer of him, and also as a reward for those songs Wentworth sang at his house and the marvellous yarns he told, the like of which they never heard before and will probably never listen to again.

They were hospitably entertained that night by Rev.

Mr. Meecum, the next night by Mr. Paul, twenty miles beyond, and then travelled onward carefully in order to avoid guerrillas, especially a band known as "dog" Smith's (a name given them on account of their use of bloodhounds in hunting victims), until May 8th, stopping each night with some friendly Unionist, to whom they were directed by the preceding host.

It was on Sunday, May 8th, after remaining over night with a Mr. "Jack" Wharton, as he was called, they walked into a guerrilla camp, situated in the dense woods near Tensas River. The "pass" did not satisfy the motley crowd of ill-clad, villainous-looking men, who heaped the vilest epithets upon them, and several men threatened to shoot them down but were held back by their comrades.

The guerrilla chief, Captain Smith, was absent, and the prisoners were taken before a Lieutenant Eddington, a young man about twenty-five years old, tall and well shaped, with features indicative of refinement and intelligence, whose parents lived in Missouri. The prisoners told their story and plead for their lives. After talking the matter over, Eddington was satisfied the "pass" was genuine, and told them the only thing he could do was to pass them out of his tent by the rear, while his men were ordered away, and advised them to "run for it" to the river bank, where they would find a regular company of Confederate cavalry, commanded by a Captain Gillespie. His men, so he said, were much exasperated over the loss of some of their comrades, captured in a recent skirmish with colored troops, and who had been shot.

A Colonel Jones, an officer in the Confederate service, wounded at Shiloh, owner of some four thousand acres of cleared land along the Tensas River and vicinity, invited them to his house and provided supper and sleeping apartments. Colonel Jones knew they were paroled Federal prisoners on the way to Natchez, and the reason of his hospitality was unfolded when he called Hersey aside and requested him to inform General Tuttle at Natchez, with the utmost secresy, *that three hundred bales of cotton were on the way down Black River, coming from Colonel Jones.*

The three men started shortly after sunrise, on Monday, May 9th, for Natchez, expecting to walk the distance that day. The danger of again encountering guerrilla bands was all they had to fear. By nightfall they were within hearing of the evening guns from the forts around Vidalia. While walking rapidly along the road three United States colored cavalry-men, in a menacing manner, ordered them to halt, and demanded to know who they were. No explanation would be believed by these wide-awake soldiers, who marched the prisoners into town to the provost-marshal's office, where the mistake was rectified, and they received good treatment at the only hotel in the place. At Natchez, the following morning, their appearance in such ridiculous clothes as they wore created considerable commotion in the streets. Whenever they stopped a crowd of curious people gathered around, enabling Wentworth, with his fertile genius for story telling, to relate in a most thrilling manner the story of their escape, embellished with a few deeds of bloodshed and heroic action. A Mr. Marsh, in charge of the New England Aid Society store, offered to clothe them, but the offer was declined, as the Quartermaster Department provided for them.

From Natchez the three escaped men were sent to Vicksburg, and from there got transportation to Washington, by way of Cairo. Williams parted company with Wentworth and Hersey at Cairo, not desirous to go on to Washington, and remained to seek employment upon the transport-steamers on the river; Wentworth and Hersey proceeded to Washington, obtained their pay without trouble, and reached Boston, home again, June 1st, 1864, having passed over sixteen months of their lives as prisoners of war.

Charles Williams, "Transport," was last heard from May 24th, 1864, when he was furnished transportation from Chicago to Utica, New York, by a United States quartermaster, as Williams claimed to be a private of Company D, Forty-Second Regiment, Massachusetts Volunteers, on sick leave, granted by Brigadier-General Tuttle.

CHAPTER XVIII.

OFFICERS IN CONFEDERATE PRISONS — HOUSTON — STATE PRISON — CAMP GROCE — CAMP FORD — EN-ROUTE HOME — AT HOME.

SOON after the enlisted men (Galveston prisoners of war) were paroled and left for the Federal lines, the officers retained at Houston were joined (January 25th) by one hundred and nine prisoners taken at Sabine Pass, officers and crews of the U. S. sailing vessels *Morning Light* and *Velocity*. Among them were Acting Masters Dillingham, Fowler and Washburn, Masters-Mates Chambers and Rice, Acting Assistant-Surgeon J. W. Shrify, and Captain Hammond of the *Velocity*.

These two successful ventures (Galveston and Sabine Pass) elated the Texans, giving them a confidence in their prowess that expressed itself in constant jubilations. "We Texans are whales," remarked by one of them to a prisoner, was but an index of opinions they all entertained.

The officers were allowed liberty of the city, on their parole-of-honor, for about a week or ten days after reaching Houston, when this privilege was withdrawn, and they were kept in close confinement. This freedom was not improved further than to purchase supplies. Union men had secretly cautioned them not to go out in the then excited state of feeling among the people, who thought hanging was good enough for Federal officers. A watch was upon every one who evinced a desire to show the Federals any attention. One man, who gave them a stove, was thrown into confinement. Another man, a storekeeper, had Colonel Burrell dine with him at home, but did not dare to visit the officers in their quarters. In conversation with the provost-marshal on this state of feeling, that official said they were safe from any trouble while under guard, for the army did not wish any harm to come to them, because there was no telling when they would find themselves in the same predicament; still the prisoners were chary of trust in either army or people, and at night barricaded their prison-apartment door with what chairs they had; each man armed himself with a stick of wood for defence, if an occasion arose.

There were men in Houston who secretly passed into the officers' hands a sufficient amount of Confederate bills to supply their needful wants. Prominent in this good work was a Mr. H. W. Benchley, who was lieutenant-governor of Massachusetts in 1855. The money thus obtained was of the greatest benefit at the time, enabling many necessaries to be procured. The names of all these men are not known. Many were former citizens of Massachusetts, whose hearts were not alienated from the old Bay State. There was a slumbering affection for the United States Government, kept in abeyance from fear of the Confederate authorities, who, it has been proved beyond a question, were wont to treat with severity every man suspected of sympathy with the Federal Government.

The prisoners' quarters would have been tolerable comfortable had any decent arrangements been made to take care of excrements, made by Confederate soldiers and Federal prisoners. The lower stories were occupied by troops, the upper story by prisoners, who had to stand all bad odor that ascended from below. Rations issued, while not what the prisoners would like, nor, in fact, such as Northern people would consider fit to eat, were quite as good as the authorities issued to their own troops, accustomed to that kind of food. To become accustomed to "corn-meal coffee" and coarse "corn-dodger" was hard work. Food was issued to last ten days at a time, and had to do so. Each man was expected to fare no better than his fellows. No trouble occurred until Stone and Dillingham helped themselves one day, out of meal hours, to ginger-bread laid aside. Some personal feeling was engendered when they were remonstrated with, and the Confederate provost-marshal issued an order that made Colonel Burrell commander of the Federal prisoners. An effort was made to draw up a code of regulations all would agree to be governed by, but no committee could be found to do this duty. Colonel Burrell was obliged to exercise a supervision over all matters material to their welfare, until he left Houston.

Ennui of confinement, in January, February and March, was somewhat abated by singing, card playing, drills in sword exercise, with sticks of wood for weapons, and gymnastic exercises. On and after February 12th they were allowed two hours a day, under guard, to stroll around the city and outskirts, generally to cross Buffalo Bayou and play ball upon the prairie land, free of annoyance from citizens. This privilege was granted on a medical certificate from Surgeon Cummings, stating such liberty was absolutely necessary, and consent obtained of General Magruder, through Surgeon Peples, medical director of the Department, with whom Cummings was on intimate terms.

The *Houston Telegraph* was eagerly read every morning, and each item relating to exchange of prisoners or their parole was sought for and noted. They could get little satisfactory information from its columns concerning the situation of military affairs; according to its "pony express news," victories were always with the Southern arms, and such victories! *Bombastes Furioso* could not have done better than did the publisher of this newspaper.

Among the frequent visitors was Major Shannon, C. S. A., who did his best to make everything pleasant, also a Captain Chubb, formerly from Charlestown, Mass., then a resident of Texas. Chubb was captured early in the war by Federals, and confined in Fort Lafayette for over a year. He was much given to boasting, and could utter more oaths in one sentence than any man the prisoners ever heard. Notwithstanding his boasts, bluster, and intense fire-eating proclivities, he was always found to be pleasant, agreeable company, kind and generous at heart, ever ready to do the prisoners a favor. He did contribute money to the officers' fund in a quiet way. Other visitors were a Mr. Whitcomb, formerly of Roxbury, Mass., and a Mr. Stearns, of Waltham, Mass., then an engineer on the Galveston and Houston Railroad.

Acting-Master Munroe, wounded upon the *Harriet Lane*, died January 30th, and was buried next day, the funeral being attended by all of the naval officers present. Corporal McIntosh, Company D, died February 10th, in hospital, at six P.M., and was buried next day in the afternoon. The officers made a neat head-board to mark his grave. March 26th Private O'Shaughnessy, Company D, made his first appearance, on crutches, since losing his leg at Galveston. April 6th Private Josselyn, Company D, wounded at Galveston, was discharged from hospital.

On the twenty-ninth of April an order came from General Magruder to send all commissioned officers to the State Penitentiary at Huntsville, there to be kept in close confinement until further orders. This order, so it was stated, came from Richmond, and was to place in confinement all captured officers that were in General Butler's army, and was said to be in retaliation for a similar act of the Federal authorities. None of the officers came from Butler's army; General Banks had superseded him, and the 42d Mass. was acting under Banks' orders. Without any regular order from General Banks in his possession, Colonel Burrell was unable to make the authorities understand this fact, or more likely they chose not to understand it. All colored men in the captured crews of the *Harriet Lane* and *Morning Light* had previously been sent to this prison, to do convict duty. An intimation of some proceeding like this was given on the nineteenth.

Under escort of a cavalry detachment the officers proceeded to the Texas Central Railroad depot to take a special freight car, at nine o'clock A.M. Dinner was eaten at Cypress City, twenty-five miles from Houston, and at half-past four P.M. they reached Navasota, where quarters were provided for nineteen officers in one room eighteen feet square, at the Morning Star Hotel. Supper and breakfast cost them two dollars each. After breakfast next morning, and a friendly shake of the hand by General Sam. Houston, who promised to call at their new quarters and see them, at quarter-past six o'clock they took four wagons, with mule teams, provided to make the journey to their destination, forty-five miles distant, and arrived at the prison about noon May 1st, where the information was imparted that they were to be confined in separate cells. A protest was drawn up, signed by all, and Surgeon Cummings, with Frank Veazie, non-combatants, returned with the same to Houston. This was not a May-day festival for the prisoners.

In this old-fashioned prison, with none of the conveniences now in use, convicts were employed at the shop in manufacturing cotton cloth for the Confederate Government, a Mr. Chandler, from Massachusetts, acting as superintendent of the factory. Life was enjoyed somewhat after this routine: after the convicts had gone to work, the officers were released from their cells and allowed to do as they pleased in the yard until dinner hour, when they returned to their cells, to be released again after the convicts had eaten their dinner and returned to work. This rule was in force for nine days only, when Colonel Carruthers obtained a supply of lumber, had cots made in a room in the upper story of the prison building facing the street, and this room, on and after May 9th, was occupied by all of the officers for a sleeping apartment. Regular prison fare was provided on the first day, when Colonel Carruthers, in charge of the prison, a humane man, informed his military prisoners he would shoulder the responsibility and give them meals at his own table, although without authority to do so. After this no complaint could be made on that score. Confined a few nights in small, hot cells, afterwards in the large room, was the extent of their inconvenience until released from prison June 27th, nearly two months from the day they entered prison walls. General Houston, Mrs. Houston, their two daughters and son, Andrew Jackson Houston, frequently visited the officers and entertained them so far as lay in their power. Old Sam, seventy years old, straight as an arrow, was a very interesting entertainer, with enlivening conversation of his experience in the United States Senate.

The officers subjected to the indignity of a prison confinement by the Confederate officials were: Colonel Burrell, Captains Sherive, Proctor and Savage, Lieutenants Cowdin, White, Eddy, Newcomb, Bartlett and Stowell, 42d Mass. Vols.; Masters Hamilton and Hannum, Engineers Plunkett and Stone, of the *Harriet Lane;* Masters Dillingham, Fowler and Washburn, Masters-Mates Chambers and Rice, Purser's Clerk Van Wycke, of the

Morning Light; Captain Hammond, of the *Velocity*. The three last-named were not brought to prison until May 14th.

Engineers Plunkett and Stone were taken to court, held in Houston June 10th, to testify in the case of a man who was on trial for repairing the boilers of the *Harriet Lane* while she lay in front of Galveston. Plunkett refused to testify and was placed in jail for contempt of court, but soon after released.

After Magruder sent these officers to Huntsville prison, with orders to have them treated as prisoners of war in confinement and not as felons, a controversy arose between the State and military authorities over the right of the latter to send prisoners of war to the penitentiary. The result was their transfer to a new camp established for war prisoners at Hempstead, called Camp Groce.

Leaving behind Colonel Burrell, sick with rheumatism, under care of Captain Sherive, the other officers left Huntsville June 27th for Camp Groce, under escort of a cavalry guard commanded by Captain Cundiff. Transportation back to Navasota was in wagons, with three extra wagons, hired at ten dollars a day from each man, to carry their baggage. Twelve miles were made on the first day, and sleeping accommodations found at night in an old school-house, having dinner and supper from rations provided by kind Mrs. Carruthers. Twenty-one miles were travelled the second day, at night bivouacking under trees in a splendid moonlight, and Navasota was reached on the twenty-ninth, about noon. There they remained until the thirtieth, when cars were taken for Camp Groce, which place was reached at eleven o'clock in the forenoon.

Until removed to Camp Groce the few enlisted men 42d Mass., left behind at Houston, were quartered in a large warehouse used for storage of general merchandise, in company with sailors composing the *Morning Light* crew. These sailors were a motley crowd, comprising men from nearly every nation: Irish, English, Dutch, Spanish, Greek, Italian, and two South Sea Islanders. They did not mind captivity, apparently thought of nothing beyond amusement. Occasionally they got put in irons for some misdemeanor or violation of rules, but no sooner were the irons riveted upon their ankles than off they were filed by comrades, to be again put on when an officer of the day came around to call the roll. One night three of these rollicking sailors broke away from the building and went on a spree, with some of Captain Clipper's men. While on a raid through the city, mounted on horses, they all rode into a bar-room and were captured by the provost-guard, brought back to quarters, and placed in irons that had no terrors for them.

Several prisoners recently captured in Louisiana were brought in June 1st, and three more June 9th, taken at Franklin, La. One of these new prisoners, Hugh Dolan, became a great favorite with the sailors immediately on arrival on account of his wonderful vocal abilities, so they thought, and light-hearted manner. One of his favorite songs was "Bowld Jack Donahoe," and whenever he sang this song his nautical audience would listen with the most profound attention.

What the "boys" considered an affliction was the removal of their kind-hearted and friendly "old guard," Captain Clipper's company, ordered to Galveston June 9th. Another company, commanded by Captain Buster, had for some time assisted Captain Clipper in guarding the prisoners, and remained to do that duty. The men of this company were not liked very much by any of their charge; none of that cordial feeling existed as had been the case with the "old guard." They were a despicable set of fellows. Captain Buster, a mild, pleasant man, lacked energy and was too indolent to pay much attention to the discipline of his men. His first-lieutenant, Morgan, was a bombastic and disagreeable man, who paid little attention to his prisoners. This guard remained on duty until September 18th, when militia relieved them.

Floating rumors in regard to removal up country were verified on the thirteenth of June, when all prisoners in Houston were taken by railroad to Camp Groce, enjoying an all-day ride upon platform freight cars, without shelter from a hot sun. Their new home was a long, narrow frame barrack, leaky in rainy weather, divided into three compartments, situated about three hundred yards from the railroad, in the centre of a dry, sandy clearing, with a few trees left for shade. This clearing was surrounded by a belt of woods on all sides but one, and near by was a sluggish body of swamp water bordered by cypress trees. The place was supplied with bad water from two deep wells. Another row of barracks, occupied by the guard, ran almost parallel to those occupied by prisoners, at about two hundred yards distance. A few frame buildings between these barracks and the railroad served as quarters for Confederate officers.

The location of Camp Groce was decidedly unhealthy, and had been abandoned by Confederate troops as a camp of instruction for this reason. Arrangement of sinks was bad, not at all conducive to health. Sickness prevailed to such an extent there were not enough men able to watch and properly attend their sick companions. When a person stops to think of what has to be done in cases where patients are too weak to move themselves, with primitive utensils at hand to perform necessary acts, it is a wonder how prisoners in this hospital camp managed to exist. Each sick man remained with his mess for care and attention. Hospital accommodations were not provided, except what was in the town reserved for exclusive use of Confederates.

All through August, September, October and part of November, the dull monotony of prison life wore on unattended by any hopeful news or enlivening sensations. Communications were forwarded to General Banks, the Secretary of War, and General Meredith, Federal Commissioner for the exchange of prisoners, on the subject of being paroled or exchanged. None of the prisoners then understood why the Federal Government did not do something in their behalf. They were informed by Colonel Sayles, who formerly commanded at Camp Groce, that repeated efforts had been made by the Confederate authorities to induce the Federal Government to exchange them, but the Federal authorities repeatedly refused to listen to any propositions towards that end, also stating that the Confederates were as anxious to get rid of their prisoners as they were to go, and placed the responsibility for their continued captivity on the Federal Government. This misstatement of facts naturally caused some animosity of feeling among the prisoners towards their own Government, losing strength each day, with sickness and death constantly staring them in the face. They were not aware of the obstruction existing to interrupt an exchange of prisoners; that the Government was fighting with the enemy for a principle, the placing of negro soldiers on a par with white troops, entitled to the common usages of war when taken prisoners.

On the eighteenth of October a strict search was made through the barracks, for what purpose the prisoners were not informed, but surmised it was to ascertain if any parties in the State, Houston in particular, had compromised themselves by writing them. News of the arrest of Union men, especially in Houston, was often heard. In this search all money was taken away under a promise of return, and a receipt given. Writings, diaries and letters were seized, never to be seen again.

A stockade was built in October completely encircling the camp, made so high escape by climbing would be impossible, and the prisoners became down-hearted at this indication of a possible lengthy stay, when, on the sixteenth of November, after most of the men had retired for the night, Colonel Burrell entered the barracks with news that all were to be paroled as soon as the papers could be made out. Wild excitement prevailed on the announcement of these joyous tidings, and the night was passed without sleep, amid cheers, yells, and frantic demonstrations of delight.

All hands commenced to get ready, by disposing of "traps" they could spare to purchasers easily found among the guard and citizens. Parole papers were signed by the enlisted men November 20th, and the march for three hundred miles to Shreveport, La., commenced December 9th. On December 11th the officers were removed to Camp Ford, Tyler, Smith County, Texas, well understanding they must keep up courage until the new year came in, and manage in some way to get through approaching winter, ill-prepared as they were to stand cold weather, from having disposed of many necessary articles of clothing to obtain money to purchase food while on their way to the Federal lines, when they expected to go with the enlisted men.

The following record of sundry events at Camp Groce was culled from several diaries:

"July 4th — Celebrated in the best manner possible under the circumstances, and was dull enough. The day was not recognized by the Confederates. July 11th — A battalion of conscripts arrived in camp; most of them

Germans and Mexicans. July 30th — Barracks look like a hospital. Six officers sick abed, and out of one hundred men sixty are in the same condition. Not a man is in good health; all are ailing, though those not in bed have to keep up and about to attend the others. Impossible to procure suitable medicines even with money collected among the prisoners to obtain medical supplies; none furnished by the authorities. August 1st — Colonel Nott, Lieutenant-Colonel Duganne and Lieutenant Sherman, 176th N. Y.; Captain Van Tyne, 131st N. Y.; Lieutenants Bassett and Wilson, 48th Mass.; Lieutenant Humble, 4th Mass.; and seven civilians, captured at Brashear City and on the La-Fourche, arrived in camp. After these arrivals Sunday services were held, Colonels Nott or Duganne officiating. August 6th — Colonel Burrell and Captain Sherive arrived from Huntsville State Prison. September 14th — Two hundred and twenty prisoners arrived in camp, taken at Sabine Pass on the tenth instant. The wounded arrived September 30th. Particulars of this engagement, furnished by the captives, caused everybody to feel sorrowful and chagrined. September 26th — A sailor was fired on while playing ball, because he went too near the picket line; he was not hit. October 5th — Twenty officers attached to the U. S. gunboats *Clifton* and *Sachem* arrived in camp from Sabine Pass and were confined in separate quarters, not allowed to hold any conversation or communication with other prisoners for some time. October 27th — Four prisoners arrived, captured in Louisiana.

A total of four officers and eighteen men died at Camp Groce; ten or twelve were sailors. Ship Carpenter Morris, of the *Harriet Lane*, sixty years old, died July 19th. Lieutenant Ramsey, 175th N. Y., died October 11th; he was sick with consumption, but dysentery was the immediate cause of death. Lieutenant Hayes, 175th N. Y., was found dead in his bunk October 16th.

The following officers and men of the 42d died at Camp Groce, viz.:

August 1st — Private Dennis Dailey, Company D. He was a great favorite with sailors of the *Morning Light*, with whom he generally associated.

August 22d — Lieutenant Bartlett, Company I, at one o'clock A.M., of dysentery, after a short illness.

September 3d — Private E. F. Josselyn, Company D, in the afternoon, of dysentery, after a long illness.

September 9th — Surgeon Cummings, in the afternoon. He was in failing health for a month, and was unconscious for some days previous to his death. The burial took place next day with Masonic rites, attended by Federal and Confederate Freemasons. Lieutenant-Colonel Duganne conducted the ceremonies.

Private Parker, Company G, was left sick in Hempstead Hospital. He died December 14th, 1863.

The guard over the officers who marched from Camp Groce to Camp Ford was commanded by Captain Davis, who marched them sixteen to seventeen miles a day over the sandy and hilly roads. The march usually commenced at seven A.M. and ended for the day between two and three o'clock P.M. The weather was pleasant and cool nearly every day, but cold at night. They got caught in two rain-storms, and wet through. The officers arrived at Camp Ford about two o'clock P.M., December 22d, after a twelve days' tramp.

At Camp Ford the prisoners already there, mostly Western men, had built log cabins and were quite comfortable under the circumstances. The so-called 42d mansion was built in a few days, with help and aid from two officers of the 19th Iowa who understood the way to construct log cabins. Within this cabin, before a roaring log fire, while rain, snow and hail reigned without, were passed the closing days of 1863. Snow blew into the cabin, wetting blankets through, and fell an inch deep upon the ground outside.

The first three months of 1864 were wearisome, with constant and conflicting rumors of parole or exchange, and occasional news of officers who had been exchanged, a subject of all-absorbing interest to everybody. No description of the life they led can afford an adequate idea of the torments to mind and body, their hopes and fears for the future, and constant struggle to make the best of their situation until a change came. Northern papers frequently found their way inside the stockade to be greedily devoured for news, as they were passed around from one to another. A newspaper from home was like a visiting angel. Southern papers were in camp every week. A tolerable correct idea of what was going on in the outside world, political and military, was sifted from these papers, aided by information obtained from Confederate officers.

To kill time the prisoners occupied themselves in repairs and improvements on quarters for business, and visits to brother officers, singing and dancing, for recreation. A violin, purchased by subscription for one hundred and ten dollars Confederate money, Captain May, 23d Conn., as violinist, and a banjo made in camp and played by Engineer R. W. Mars, of the gunboat *Diana*, accompanied by a flute manipulated by Captain Thomason, 176th N. Y., and a fife by E. J. Collins, made a select orchestra to furnish appropriate music for the dances. Gardens were started early in February, when corn, mustard, lettuce, watermelons, squashes, onions and cotton was planted. Corn and onions showed above ground early in March. A system of barter and exchange in various articles was carried on among the prisoners, affording a means to keep their wits at work if no money was made out of the transactions. A newspaper was published, *The Old Flag*, edited and printed by Captain May, the printing done with a pen. Editions were issued February 17th, March 1st and 13th, that afforded great interest to the camp. Only one copy was issued of each number, to be passed around, read and returned to the captain. It has yet to be recorded at what post, where Confederate prisoners were confined, did they show so much versatility in amusing themselves as was shown by Federal prisoners in all parts of the South.

The birthday of Washington, February 22d, was duly celebrated. All expenses were met by a subscription among the officers in confinement. Lieutenant-Colonel J. B. Leake, 20th Iowa, delivered an oration, followed by an original poem, written in camp by Lieutenant-Colonel Duganne. In the afternoon an election was held for Governor, Lieutenant-Governor, and Inspector of Insane Asylums of Camp Ford, to carry on a species of fun concocted at the expense of half-witted Sam Morton, a Kansas soldier. Sam was elected Governor, and then taken in a chair through the camp with great *eclat*. Fine singing by a glee club and a grand ball in the evening closed the celebration.

Pending the result of efforts constantly made to obtain a parole or exchange, attempts to escape were made at various times. Two officers of the 26th Indiana, Lieutenants Greene and Switzer, were missed at roll-call January 12th, and a pursuit made. The escape of these two officers, some two weeks before this, was known to a few comrades, who concealed their absence from roll-calls by answering for them. At last it was decided to let their escape become known. At roll-call their names were not answered, when a Confederate officer innocently asked: "Does any one know where Greene and Switzer are?" An answer was given, with a laugh, "Guess they have gone for a pair of shoes." The two officers were afterwards heard from as having arrived in New Orleans after a walk of some three hundred miles, done in a month and two days. They gave newspaper men, for publication, a detailed account of their tramp, with names of parties who had helped them along. This published account came into Confederate hands, and was used as an excuse for persecuting those Union friends.

On a rainy night, March 24th, Colonel Rose and fourteen other officers escaped early in the evening, by sliding aside a stockade post. From a neglect to replace the post discovery of the escape soon followed, and an alarm at once sounded. Mounted men, with bloodhounds, were immediately on their track. Four men were brought back next day, recaptured after they had walked twenty miles, and nine more were retaken on the twenty-seventh. One man succeeded in making good his bold dash for liberty. This attempt to escape was contemplated for some time; those in the plot secretly prepared parched meal and dry beef to carry for food. Another attempt was in progress, suggested by reading in a paper of an escape by officers from Libby Prison, Richmond, Va., by the tunnel process. From the 42d cabin, it was calculated a tunnel fifty feet long would carry them outside of the stockade. It was a double cabin, one-half occupied by Captain May's mess, also the editor's *sanctum* of the *Old Flag*. A commencement was made March 21st, the earth taken out secreted underneath bunks and carried outside when an opportunity offered; the opening was covered by a bunk when work was suspended. Men in this plot had worked a hole twenty-one feet under ground March 24th, when the original stockade line was removed to enlarge the camp, and an order was received by Colonel Allen, the commandant, to shoot at sight any prisoner caught in attempting escape. These two facts caused the attempt to be abandoned.

Colonel Allen was an old engineer officer in the United States Army, and like all regular army officers disposed to treat his prisoners as men. This disposition to do all in his power to ameliorate their sufferings probably caused his removal May 27th, a Colonel Anderson assuming command of the post. The policy pursued by Anderson, or rather a drunken lieutenant-colonel under him who took charge of all matters appertaining to the prisoners, was in an opposite direction.

Camp Ford was blessed with good water and situated upon high ground, an improvement over Camp Groce. Yet the stockade interior was filthy, without any system of sinks or police of grounds. This was the fault of the prisoners, a lazy, careless, motley crowd, not disposed to take hold of such work. Colonel Allen left such matters to those inside the stockade. Officers who saw the necessity of a system in hygienic matters soon gave up in disgust the attempt to force an organization for this purpose. As is usual in such a collection of men, refusing to recognize any superior authority except their guards, it was each man for himself and the devil take the hindmost.

Among the imprisoned officers were several lieutenant-colonels and majors. Colonel Burrell was one of the three officers of his rank. As a matter of pride, to uphold the dignity of his commission, what many officers signally failed to do, Colonel Burrell was always scrupulously polite to Colonel Allen, never visited him except in full uniform, transacting all business with that officer in a business manner, and so gained his esteem and regard. Burrell maintained that the rules in force should be respected and obeyed — he would insist on their obeyance were he in command of such a camp — and by maintaining dignified relations with the commandant was enabled several times to secure a rescission of harsh orders issued by Colonel Allen, in consequence of foolish speeches and acts done by brainless fools in the stockade.

No medicines, no special accommodations nor post surgeon were provided at Camp Ford. Surgeons Sherfy, 1st Indiana, and Hershy, U. S. Colored Volunteers, did all in their power for the sick, and that could not be much. An old surgeon in the Confederate service, formerly of the U. S. regulars, would occasionally visit the stockade and render some service. To him Colonel Burrell owes his life, when threatened with an attack of typhoid fever.

The commandant's wife, Mrs. Allen, was a visitor to the officers' quarters at various times, frequently accompanied by other ladies. The good impression this lady made by her visits resulted in a poem, written by Lieutenant-Colonel Duganne, published in *The Old Flag*, issue No. 3, March 18th, 1864.

The arrival of captured prisoners to increase the inhabitants of this stockade town, taken from various soldiers' diaries, were: January 22d — Captains Coulter and Torrey, 20th Iowa, captured at Arkansas Bay, Texas, December 19th, 1863. March 5th — Six enlisted men captured at Powder Horn, January 22d. March 30th — Between six and seven hundred prisoners arrived from Shreveport, where they were awaiting exchange. They were a hard-looking lot of human beings, many without shirts or shoes, with trousers torn, ragged, or hanging in shreds. Among them were Privates Morrill, O'Shaughnessy and McLaughlin, of the 42d. They left Shreveport March 26th. Frank Veazie was sick in a Shreveport hospital. He died the following May.

About sixteen hundred prisoners, captured at Pleasant Hill, La., arrived April 16th, 17th, 18th and 20th. To accommodate these hungry men all hands had to keep their cooking apparatus at work on corn meal until they were fed. The appearance these prisoners made could not have been equalled in Falstaff's time. Confederate soldiers robbed them of clothing, sometimes with threats of violence if property wanted by these greedy men was not handed over for the asking. The prisoners did not seem to mind it, and laughingly said they would square accounts whenever the Confederates fell into their hands as prisoners of war. They thought it rather rough to be placed in a pen like a flock of sheep, without food or shelter. Still, nothing better could be expected, because the Confederates had no other safe place to guard their prisoners. When arrangements could be completed, they were made as comfortable as the limited means at hand would allow.

During May about eighteen hundred prisoners came in, thirteen hundred captured in Arkansas; June 6th, one hundred; and July 6th, another batch of one hundred and eighty prisoners from Banks' army were brought in. The old prisoners commenced to think, from the continued arrivals of officers and men of the 19th Army Corps, perhaps the entire corps would eventually be captured.

Through May, June, and up to July 9th, it cannot be said the death rate was large, received as the men were in all conditions of health and sickness. Six privates died in May, and one was killed by a sentry; five died in June; five died July 1st.

With the prisoners were Chaplains Robb, 46th Indiana Vols., Hare, —th Iowa Vols., and McCulloch, 19th Kentucky Vols., who labored hard among the men to excite a religious sentiment, holding frequent prayer meetings, and administered the rites of baptism to several, among them Lieutenant Brown P. Stowell, 42d Mass., on May 22d. These religious services met with the approval of Colonel Allen, who was a devout Free Will Baptist.

Some talk was made about overpowering the guard, nearly one thousand men, composed of poor material. An insurmountable difficulty was to provide a store of food, for use when free, and a sufficient supply of arms and ammunition, for they were nearly three hundred miles from any safe place. Nothing was done, as it was useless to try it. Next to parole or exchange the idea of escape occupied the most attention. Naturally officers in command of guards were always on the lookout for anything tending towards preparations in that direction. In February about one hundred officers were drilled in the sabre exercise by Major Anthony, 2d R. I. Cavalry, for instruction and pleasure, using sticks in lieu of swords, but the post-commander summarily put a stop to it within a few days after these drills commenced.

Attempts to escape commenced again with fresh arrivals; five men got away at night June 9th, to be recaptured and returned next day. Several officers succeeded in making a break for freedom at night, July 2d, but were discovered and fired on by the guard. Nearly all of them were recaptured next day. Captain Reed, Missouri Vols., was made to stand bare-headed upon a stump near the guard-house for several hours in the hot sun, as punishment for his attempted escape.

Early in June rumors of parole and exchange again began to be circulated within the stockade. Confederate officers from Shreveport visited the prison camp more frequently than they had heretofore done, to make out lists and rolls of prisoners and time of capture. News brought by Colonel Allen and the tenor of letters received from surgeons, gone forward for exchange, raised a hope within the breasts of those long confined that there would not be a disappointment this time. When the chaplains, surgeons, and citizens not connected with the army, were paroled and started for Shreveport June 19th, hope grew into certainty. On the fifth of July, after what was termed a glorious Fourth-of-July celebration, the joyful news was brought in the stockade, by Colonel Burrell, that a paroling officer had arrived, and their day of deliverance was at hand.

Through this captivity letters from home came at long intervals, with news they were anxious to receive. Dates when letters were received by the 42d officers are as follows: March 12th, July 29th and August 26th, 1863; March 18th, June 10th, 13th and 23d, 1864. Letters received June 10th were for Captain Savage and Lieutenant Newcomb, dated February 28th and March 4th. Captain Proctor had letters from his father and wife dated May 12th and 23d, 1863, over a year old, as they were not delivered to him until June 13th, 1864. After men arrived from Banks' army, men who belonged in Boston and vicinity made themselves known to Colonel Burrell and brother officers, some of whom had within a few months arrived from home and could give them tolerably late news from that section.

Clothing was furnished once by Confederate officers, at Hempstead, October 17th, 1863; from that time onward what the prisoners wore had to stand the wear and tear of time and use. Previous to July, in anticipation another winter would not be passed as prisoners, whoever had overcoats and extra clothing sold the garments for high prices in Confederate money, and thus obtained means to purchase extra supplies for their messes.

One thing should not be forgotten in connection with

this long, tedious imprisonment: the love of country existing in every manly heart, despite his feeling at times the Government did neglect him. This patriotism was not the kind flaunted before audiences by spread-eagle political orators, all froth and no substance, but an honest, earnest, deep-seated love, ready to suffer for her cause at all times, resenting any flings or insults to its flag, giving voice to sentiments within them by singing national songs and celebrations of important days in her history.

July 7th and 8th were devoted to baking hard bread, for use on the march, and at last the prisoners, who were up at three o'clock in the morning preparing breakfast and getting their few "traps" ready, left the stockade to march for Shreveport, homeward bound. There were nine hundred and thirty officers and men, divided into one column of officers and two columns of enlisted men, with a kind and considerate Confederate cavalry guard, commanded by Major Smith and Captain Tucker. Guard and prisoners fared alike in food and slept in the open air at night: tents were not carried with them. Extreme hot weather prevailed, yet the prisoners managed to cover a respectable number of miles each day, crossing the Sabine River on the first day and sleeping upon its banks at night, with a record of twenty-one miles. The marching column reached Shreveport about noon on the thirteenth, without the loss of a man by death, having made nineteen miles July 10th, twenty-three miles on the eleventh, twenty-four miles on the twelfth, and sixteen miles on the thirteenth. Sick and worn-out men were sent by the Marshall and Shreveport Railroad on the twelfth, and this railroad also transported a portion of the prisoners on the thirteenth. About twenty officers hired a six-mule team for five hundred Confederate dollars, to carry them on the last day's journey, and rode into camp in great style. Each morning the men were up between three and four o'clock, commenced the march within an hour after, plodding steadily along until eleven, when a rest was taken until two o'clock, then the march again resumed until evening.

At Mugginsville, one mile from Shreveport, the prisoners remained until July 16th, when they were sent on board steamers *Osceola, General Hodges* and *B. L. Hodge*, bound for Alexandria, where they arrived at dusk July 18th, above the dam built by Federals to save their naval vessels in April and May, 1864, and were disembarked to camp in woods by the river side until the twenty-first, when steamers were ready below the dam to carry them on to the journey's end. Three men died July 18th, and were buried near a spot upon the banks where lay the remains of several Federal sailors.

All hands were up at daylight July 21st. At seven o'clock they marched two miles to Alexandria, crossed Red River on a pontoon bridge and embarked upon steamers *Champion No. 3* and *Relf*, bound for the mouth of Red River. An extract from a diary, kept by an officer of the 42d Mass., is here given:

"July 22d, 1864 — We started about noon yesterday, and ran all night; arrived at the mouth of Red River as the sun was about one and one-half hours high, and were brought to a stop by a shot from one of our gunboats on blockading service. None of our transports were there, and we began to have some misgivings. All eyes were turned down the Mississippi, with anxiety depicted on many faces. About one o'clock smoke was seen coming up river, indicating a river steamer was on her way, and the prisoners began to cheer. Soon, sure enough, there was our flag flying within hailing distance, but we are still prisoners; perhaps no exchange after all, but be turned back to the tender care of "Johnny Reb" again. But no, it proves to be the *Nebraska* with rebel prisoners on board. We landed and went aboard the *Nebraska* as soon as we could, and gave six rousing cheers for the 'Old Flag.' Stop and look at the comparison of the two squads of prisoners. Those coming from our lines for the Confederacy are loaded down with clothing, boots and trunks. Our men are bare-footed, shirtless and hatless; but I thank God I am once more a free man. None but those that have been placed in like circumstances can appreciate the change. We were given a feast on the *Nebraska*. We had plenty of coffee, real 'Lincoln" coffee, no parched rye; and butter! real butter, and bakers' bread! Well! I have had some good dinners before and since then, but that feast took the cake. Good-by to corn-dodger and bull-beef. It all seemed like a dream. The boys were up until about three o'clock next morning, singing and enjoying themselves."

The exchanged officers of the 42d Regiment arrived in New Orleans at midnight July 23d, where they remained until the thirty-first, receiving two months' pay from a paymaster to meet their immediate wants. None of the officers got back their swords they were entitled to retain by the terms of surrender. The swords were taken from them by a provost-marshal at Houston, properly marked with each man's name, with an understanding they would be given up when each officer was paroled or exchanged. It is needless to say they were soon appropriated by any Confederate officer who was in need of one.

Taking passage upon the steamer *Matanzas*, July 31st, bound for New York, after a pleasant run of seven days they were once more within easy communication with families and friends, who met them on arrival in Boston, August 9th, *via* the Fall River route from New York. All were in tolerable fair health except Lieutenant Stowell, who was in bad condition, and Lieutenant Cowdin, sick with chronic diarrhœa. An escort in waiting, with music, consisting of past and present officers and men of the 42d Regiment and the Boston Independent Fusileers, escorted their guests to the American House, where breakfast was served and a cordial welcome tendered by His Honor Mayor Lincoln and the military committee of the City Government.

Governor Andrew could not be present, and sent the following letter:

"COMMONWEALTH OF MASSACHUSETTS,
"EXECUTIVE DEPARTMENT,
"BOSTON, August 9th, 1864.

"COLONEL W. W. CLAPP, JR., &C., &C.:

"*My dear Colonel*,— I have this moment received your note of invitation to attend the breakfast at ten o'clock this morning, given in welcome of Colonel Burrell and his associates. The long captivity of those brave and patriotic men has earned for them every consideration, even if their qualities as soldiers had been less conspicuous than they are. In all respects, however, deserving gratitude and honor, and deserving all the sympathy of true and manly hearts for what they have suffered in our common cause, I shall, though absent in person, unite in heart with your expressions of grateful applause and welcome for these honored guests. My return to headquarters yesterday, after a valuable work of service elsewhere, leaves me, for the present, not an hour which during the daytime I can withdraw from the accumulated work which brooks no delay.

"I am faithfully your friend and servant,

"JOHN A. ANDREW."

With repeated disasters attending expeditions to Western Louisiana and Texas, that are a part of history, and failures attending every attempt to permanently occupy such territory, the following remarks at this breakfast, made by Colonel Burrell, are not without reason. He said: "I hardly know what to say. I thank your Honor for your kind expression of welcome. We have suffered long, but I do not know as we have done more than our duty. I can hardly be expected to make a speech, for I have been living a half-civilized life among half-civilized people for nearly the last two years. I know our friends at home were doing all in their power to obtain our release, but fate has seemed to be always against us. For my soldiers and officers I can say that they have behaved with courage and cheerfulness; their fortitude has been worthy of men of Massachusetts. They have behaved with credit to their state and to their country. I come home prouder than ever of my native city. As soon as we are somewhat recovered from our fatigues and sufferings, we will be ready to put on the harness and return to the field again.

"I have enjoyed much opportunity of communication with men from all parts of the Southern Confederacy, and I believe that you entertain an erroneous opinion of them. You believe that there exists among the masses an extended Union sentiment. It is not so. They go into this war with all their heart and soul. The little Union feeling among the class of poor whites amounts to nothing. They are opposed to us, man, woman and child. They are fighting with the spirit of '76, for their rights, homes, liberties. They put up with every privation to sustain their army — and every man is in the army. The quicker we understand this the better for us. I do not think we shall accomplish much until we take hold of the work in earnest.

"In the section where I have been the enemy is three times stronger than they were two years ago. Now an army of 40,000 men cannot penetrate the country one hundred miles. They have an army of 40,000 men. They carry no equipage — they sling their blankets with a bit of cotton rope, and are all ready for an expedition. We must take our blankets on our shoulders — we cannot fight with army trains. I repeat, in order to carry on this war to a successful termination, we must fight them on their own ground and fight them in earnest."

After this breakfast Colonel Burrell and his officers were escorted to Roxbury by the Roxbury Artillery Association, where another reception was given them by their townspeople.

August 10th the officers met at the Parker House, proceeded to the State House and reported to Adjutant-General Schouler, then to Major Clarke, U. S. Army, to receive their final pay, then to Major McCafferty, U. S. mustering-officer, and were mustered out of service, after being in "Uncle Sam's" employ about twenty-one months — eighteen months and twenty-one days of the time as prisoners of war.

CHAPTER XIX.

IN SERVICE FOR ONE HUNDRED DAYS — ORGANIZATION — READVILLE — OFF FOR WASHINGTON — AT ALEXANDRIA — AT GREAT FALLS — RETURN HOME.

A SCARE existed in Washington, caused by Confederate operations under General Jubal Early, who threatened an invasion of Pennsylvania in order to mask a contemplated dash on Baltimore and Washington.*

Adjutant-General Schouler casually informed Adjutant Davis, whom he met on the street, a call had been received from Washington to send troops immediately for one hundred days' service. The adjutant had kept up a correspondence with all of the old line officers, for an ultimate purpose of again calling the regiment together when Colonel Burrell was exchanged. Davis mentioned this fact to General Schouler, who at once advanced the idea of again going into service and advised an attempt

---

* Governor Andrew was in Washington at the time, and telegraphed his adjutant-general (received July 5th) as follows: "I have arranged with the Secretary of War that men who volunteer for one hundred days' service, as requested by him to-day, shall be exempted from any draft that may be ordered during such hundred days' service, not from any future draft, but only from such as may be ordered during the term of hundred days for which they are asked. I direct you, at request of Secretary, to issue an order calling for four thousand one-hundred-days' infantry, on the terms above mentioned. The details in connection with the project will not differ materially, otherwise, from those heretofore prescribed in like cases. I shall have another consultation to-morrow. Have sent home Peirce to-night." General Orders No. 24, calling for five thousand hundred-day men, was issued July 6th, 1864, by Adjutant-General Schouler.

to do so. The old line officers were consulted, and, as the idea was favored by a majority of them, official orders were issued to go into camp at Readville, Mass., July 18th, 1864.

The following companies were designated to compose the regiment:

Company A, Captain Isaac Scott, of Roxbury; Company B, Captain Benjamin C. Tinkham, of Medway; Company C, Captain Isaac B. White, of Boston; Company D, Captain Samuel A. Waterman, of Roxbury; Company E, Captain Augustus Ford, of Worcester; Company F, Captain Samuel S. Eddy, of Worcester; Company G, Captain Alanson H. Ward, of Worcester; Company H, Captain F. M. Prouty, of Worcester; Company I, Captain James T. Stevens, of Dorchester; Company K, Captain Benjamin R. Wales, of Dorchester.

Active measures were at once instituted to clothe, arm with Enfield rifles, and equip these companies, to be in readiness for a quick departure. Complete uniforms, with equipments, were issued at Readville. Many companies went into camp several days previous to July 18th, gaining recruits every day until ready for muster in for service. Captain Scott failed to recruit more than thirty men. Captain Prouty failed to recruit his company, although at one time it promised well; from some cause his men scattered to other companies or went home. Companies commanded by Captains French and Stewart, already mustered into service, were assigned to the regiment as Companies A and H.

The first regimental morning report was made up July 20th, and showed a strength of thirty-five officers, seven hundred and thirty-eight enlisted men, present and absent.

The regiment was ready for marching orders July 23d, with the following strength :

	Officers.	Enlisted men.	Mustered in.
Field and Staff,	5	3	July 22d.
Company A,	3	95	" 14th.
" B,	3	81	" 22d.
" C,	3	93	" 14th.
" D,	3	97	" 20th.
" E,	3	90	" 22d.
" F,	3	98	" 15th.
" G,	3	87	" 21st.
" H,	3	88	" 16th.
" I,	3	84	" 19th.
" K,	3	90	" 18th.
Total,	35	906	

The roster of the regiment was as follows :
Colonel — Isaac S. Burrell.
Lieutenant-Colonel — Joseph Stedman.
Major — Frederick G. Stiles.
Adjutant — Charles A. Davis.
Quartermaster — Alonzo I. Hodsdon.
Surgeon — Albert B. Robinson.
Sergeant-Major — Jediah P. Jordan.
Quartermaster-Sergeant — Charles E. Noyes.
Commissary-Sergeant — Augustus C. Jordan.
Hospital-Steward — Robert White, Jr.
Principal-Musician — Thomas Bowe.

Company A — Captain, Warren French; Lieutenants, Charles W. Baxter and Joseph M. Thomas.

Company B — Captain, Benjamin C. Tinkham; Lieutenants, George W. Ballou and George E. Fuller.

Company C — Captain, Isaac B. White; Lieutenants, Joseph Sanderson, Jr., and David C. Smith.

Company D — Captain, Samuel A. Waterman; Lieutenants, George H. Bates and Almon D. Hodges, Jr.

Company E — Captain, Augustus Ford; Lieutenants, James Conner and Frank H. Cook.

Company F — Captain, Samuel S. Eddy; Lieutenants, Henry J. Jennings and Edward I. Galvin.

Company G — Captain, Alanson H. Ward; Lieutenants, Moses A. Aldrich and E. Lincoln Shattuck.

Company H — Captain, George M. Stewart; Lieutenants, Julius M. Lyon and Joseph T. Spear.

Company I — Captain, James T. Stevens; Lieutenants, Edward Merrill, Jr., and Charles A. Arnold.

Company K — Captain, Benjamin R. Wales; Lieutenants, Alfred G. Gray and Charles P. Hawley.

Officers who resigned and did not accompany the regiment on this second term were: Quartermaster Burrell, Surgeons Hitchcock and Heintzelman, Chaplain Sanger, Sergeant-Major Bosson, Commissary-Sergeant Courtney, Hospital-Steward Wood, Principal-Musician Neuert.* Of the thirty line officers who served during this second term, Captains Tinkham, White, Waterman and Ford, Lieutenants Sanderson, Ballou, Smith, Cook and Merrill were with the regiment in 1862 and 1863. Colonel Burrell arrived home, from Texas, August 9th, was mustered in for this second term August 10th, and reported at Alexandria September 1st.

The Dorchester Cornet Band volunteered to enlist and become the regimental band. The members were: Leader, Thomas Bowe; Privates Conrad H. Gurlack, Company

---

* Neuert was known as "Dick." By mistake he was enlisted and borne on the rolls as Richard A. Neuert. Young in years, he never thought of correcting the error, and retained the name when he reënlisted in the 11th Battery as a bugler. His right name was Charles A. Neuert.

A; Perham Orcutt, Company B; Horace A. Allyn, George Burleigh, William A. Cowles, John W. Capen, Nathaniel Clark, Lewis Eddy, Edward Lovejoy, Fred. H. Macintosh, Henry B. Sargent, Phillip Sawyer, Andrew J. Wheeler, of Company D; Wells F. Johnson, Company H; Jesse K. Webster, Company I; William A. Cobb and Edward H. Marshall, of Company K.

Two men deserted at Readville, viz.: Private Frederick D. Goodwin, Company C, July 15th; Private Robert Bryden, Company D, July 22d.

The rank and file were a true representative body of Massachusetts citizen soldiery. Three-fourths of the men were born in the State; seventy men were foreign born. Men from a great variety of professions and trades enlisted. About one-half of the regiment were as follows: one hundred and seventy-six salesmen, book-keepers and clerks; twenty-seven students; one hundred and twenty farmers; one hundred and twenty-four journeymen boot and shoe workmen; twenty-seven mill operatives.

The old regimental colors were received in camp July 23d, and under orders to take transports for Washington, promptly at five o'clock A.M., July 24th, the regiment left Readville by special train for Boston, and marched down State Street, about half-past six o'clock, to Battery Wharf, where Companies C, D and E, two hundred and seventy-one men, under command of Major Stiles, embarked on steamer *Montauk*. The other companies and the band, under command of Lieutenant-Colonel Stedman, embarked on steamer *McClellan*. At nine o'clock both steamers sailed for Washington, and arrived there at noon July 28th, after a good passage, without an important event occurring. This landing the regiment in Washington in ten days after being ordered into camp to recruit and organize can be called quick work.

Reporting to General Augur, commanding Department of Washington, the regiment was sent to Brigadier-General Slough, Military Governor of Alexandria, who ordered it into camp on Shuter's Hill, near Fort Ellsworth, about one mile from the city. On the morning of July 29th, after breakfast was eaten at the Soldiers' Rest, in Alexandria, the regiment marched to the ground assigned and occupied log huts, built by other troops when stationed on this hill. In Slough's command were Battery H, Indiana Light Artillery, one battalion First District Columbia Volunteers, the Second District Columbia Volunteers, the Fifth Wisconsin Volunteers, the Twelfth Regiment Veteran Reserve Corps and the Forty-Second Massachusetts Volunteers. These troops were soon organized into a provisional-brigade and attached to the Twenty-Second Army Corps.

Details for guards and for provost duty were immediately ordered by General Slough, as follows: July 29th — Two officers and one hundred and fifteen men for provost duty. July 31st — Eighteen men every day for patrol duty in Alexandria; thirty-one men to relieve a detachment Veteran Reserve Corps at Sickel's Barracks Hospital. July 30th — Lieutenants Sanderson, Company C, and Spear, Company H, were detached for duty at headquarters provost-marshal-general, Defences South of Potomac.

At the close of July there was present for duty thirty-two officers and eight hundred and seventy-three men; twenty-eight men sick; three officers and six men absent.

During August the officers and men were kept busy at drill, on guard, provost and patrol duty, which inured them to endure fatigue and become acquainted with the tedious side of a soldier's life. Train-guards were furnished for trains on the Orange and Alexandria Railroad, to protect working and construction parties in constant danger of attacks from guerrillas and obstructions placed upon the track to delay trains; at Fairfax Station, August 15th, the enemy greased the rails, and a train could not proceed — the enemy decamped, not waiting for the train-guard to get a blow at them. Details were sent to Burke's Station and other places for logs, used to build additional huts for the men. What duty was done in August is shown by the following details, ordered by General Slough:

August 2d — One hundred and thirteen men detailed each day for grand-guard line.

August 6th — Two officers and one hundred and fifty-seven men relieved the Twelfth Regiment Veteran Reserve Corps, in Alexandria; next day this detachment was relieved by the Second Regiment District Columbia Volunteers.

August 7th — A regimental camp guard of fifty men was established.

August 7th — Seventy-five men for train-guards to Fairfax Station, detailed each day until the twenty-third.

August 4th — Seventeen men were detached for permanent duty on the military police in Alexandria.

August 28th — Seventy-five men were detached for duty as hospital attendants in the general hospitals in Alexandria. The hospitals were full of patients.

Details for August were:

4th — Sergeant Alfred Davenport, Company K, clerk at headquarters Department Washington, Twenty-Second Army Corps. Relieved October 29th.

For duty at general court-martial rooms in Alexandria:
1st — Private George S. Partridge, Company B, orderly.
3d — Corporal Thomas J. Rooney, Company B, clerk.
4th — Corporal Edwin H. Holbrook, Company B, clerk.
— Private Alfred Noon, Company H, orderly. — Private Richard M. Sabin, Company G, orderly. 9th — Private

Ellery C. Bartlett, Company K, clerk. 13th — Private J. H. S. Pearson, Company C, clerk.

On detached service at headquarters provost-marshal-general: 1st — Private H. W. Tolman, Company A, orderly. 2d — Private William S. French, Company F, orderly. — Private Alvin S. Pratt, Company F, orderly. 10th — Private Jno. R. Graham, Company A, orderly. 24th — Private William G. Kidder, Company C, clerk. — Corporal George Dunbar, Company D, clerk.

On detached service at headquarters military governor: 4th — Private Herbert W. Hitchcock, Company H, orderly. 5th — Private Fred. S. Dickinson, Company G, orderly. 11th — Private Hiram E. Smith, Company H, clerk. 13th — Private J. Clark Reed, Company C, clerk. — Private Thomas J. McKay, Company F, clerk.

The officers on detached service were: 2d — Lieutenant Shattuck, Company G, on permanent duty with city patrol in Alexandria. 9th — Lieutenant Hodges, Company D, on permanent duty at headquarters provost-marshal-general. 10th — Lieutenant Thomas, Company A, on permanent duty in command of guard at Hunting Creek Bridge blockhouse, under the orders of provost-marshal-general. 12th — Lieutenant Ballou, Company B, was detailed for permanent duty with the military police of Alexandria, to relieve Lieutenant Shattuck, who was not active and experienced enough to suit General Slough.

The officers detailed for general court-martial duty were: Captains Tinkham, Waterman, Ford and Ward, from July 31st; Major Stiles, Lieutenants Baxter and Jennings, from August 6th.

The enlisted men on detailed daily duty were: Private W. A. G. Hooton, Company A, nurse at regimental hospital; Private Mathias F. Chaffin, Company E, nurse at regimental hospital; Private Albert H. Newhall, Company E, nurse at regimental hospital; Private Henry C. Chenery, Company F, nurse at regimental hospital; Private Seth Albee, Company E, nurse at regimental hospital; Private Simon C. Spear, Company C, nurse at regimental hospital; Private Ezra Abbott, Company A, chief wagoner; Private George A. Harwood, Company B, wagoner; Private Thomas Belton, Company C, wagoner; Private Elma H. French, Company F, wagoner; Private Samuel W. Whittemore, Company I, wagoner; Private George W. Abbott, Company I, wagoner; Privates Oliver C. Andrews, Alonzo D. Crockett, Mark Heathcote, of Company G, as a permanent guard at the reservoir in rear of camp near Fort Ellsworth, from August 6th; Privates William G. Kidder, Company C, James Allen, Company E, Hermion J. Gilbert and Charles E. Chase, of Company F, orderlies at regimental headquarters; Private Henry R. Gilmore, Company F, acting drum-major.

It was necessary to discipline one man in August — Private Samuel Young, Company E, for firing his musket without permission or orders. He had to carry a forty-pound log of wood tied to his back for a stated number of hours each day for two days.

At the close of August there was present for duty: twenty-nine officers, seven hundred and forty-eight men; one officer, forty-two men sick. Absent: five officers, one hundred and seven men on detached service, four men sick, two men in arrest.

Duty in September was about the same as in August, the regiment constantly furnishing details of men for grand-guard and other guards. Drills were maintained with what few men were in camp and some progress made in this direction, but all efforts to advance the regiment in drill could not be satisfactory to officers in command, because of this absence of men each day.

September 14th — Company G, Captain Ward, went

on duty as a permanent guard at the Soldiers' Rest in Alexandria.

September 16th — All troops in the command were paraded to witness an execution of a private Fourth Maryland Volunteers, shot for desertion, at eleven A.M., in the open field northwest of Sickel Barracks Hospital. The negroes in and around Alexandria made a gala occasion of the affair, with tents pitched near the spot for sales of cake, pies, lemonade, etc. So far as appearances went the man to be shot, a thick-set fellow, with heavy, black whiskers, was more indifferent to his fate than the soldiers formed to occupy three sides of a square, obliged to be unwilling witnesses. On the open side were gathered a curious crowd of colored people. The condemned man was marched upon the ground, a band playing a dirge. He was followed by a faithful Newfoundland dog, who had to be taken away when his master took position in front of his coffin, face to the firing party. In a speech he confessed to being a professional bounty-jumper, worth at that moment near twenty thousand dollars, the proceeds of his work in jumping sixteen bounties. When the detail of soldiers fired upon him he fell lengthwise upon his coffin. The troops were then filed past him, and had just commenced the movement when signs of life were shown, necessitating a second file of men to be ordered up and put another volley into him.

At nine o'clock P. M., September 22d, orders were received to march four companies at once to Great Falls, on the Potomac, above Washington, and relieve the Eighty-Fourth N. Y. S. V. Militia, on picket duty for protection of the water works. This order came from headquarters Department Washington, and urged promptness in its execution. A guide was also sent to pilot the detachment. Companies B, C, D and E, with enough detailed men to fill up the ranks, with three days' rations, and forty rounds of ammunition in the boxes, were at once started on a march of about twenty-five miles, under command of Lieutenant-Colonel Stedman. This march was not made in a manner creditable to the regiment. At first it was believed a fight was in progress or imminent, and while such belief lasted the men should have been kept well in hand to be of any use. The facts are: a halt was made about one o'clock A.M., and the men slept on the ground until after daylight, and then straggled into Great Falls during the afternoon and evening in a manner not suggestive of a well-conducted march. Fortunately no fight took place, and no harm resulted. Officers and men of this Eighty-Fourth New York (an Irish regiment) were found loitering around a tavern, more or less under the effects of liquor. This tavern was kept by a Mr. Jackson, brother to the Jackson who killed Colonel Ellsworth in Alexandria at the commencement of hostilities.

Lieutenant-Colonel Stedman reported on the twenty-fourth that so far as he could ascertain the duty at Great Falls would be to take care of themselves as well as they could, to keep a few pickets out on the roads leading to his camp, with a few men on the canal to prevent smuggling. The colonel Eighty-Fourth New York said he never had any orders, and acted as his judgment dictated in all matters at the post; he never made any reports to any one, and had been visited by a staff-officer but once. Stedman also reported the place extremely unhealthy, with chills and fever a prevailing complaint. Stedman's strength was then three hundred and fifty-six men. The Eighty-Fourth numbered six hundred and fifty men, and did have, at one time, two hundred and fifty men sick.

Stedman wrote Colonel Burrell, on the twenty-fifth, as follows: "Captain Stewart has arrived, and I learn that arrangements have been made for four companies to remain here permanently, and that the balance of the men belonging to these four companies are soon to be sent here. Allow me to inquire if the balance of the officers have been thought of — viz., Lieutenant Sanderson, Company C, Lieutenant Ballou, Company B, and Lieutenant Hodges, Company D? I cannot get along without the full complement of officers for these companies, and I trust they will be relieved at once and ordered to report to me at this post. I shall be obliged to have one for adjutant and one for quartermaster, thus leaving me only ten others for duty; hence the necessity of these officers above named being sent.

"We shall have to secure some transportation here, but as yet I do not know what arrangements we can make for this necessity. We have a post-commissary here, but have to go eleven miles for soft bread. The nearest post-quartermaster is six miles away, at Muddy Branch. After a few days we can make the men quite comfortable, but the place is not a very agreeable one to be in."

Company C, Captain White, was sent to Orcutt's Cross Roads, three miles away, September 30th, where was stored a quantity of quartermaster's property. Guerrillas were operating in the vicinity. A stockade was set on fire and destroyed by them, and an attempt made to blow up the aqueduct, frustrated by tavern-keeper Jackson, who was well known to the Confederates and on good terms with them. General Sheridan, by his operations in the Shenandoah Valley, caused a lull in the fun carried on by these guerrillas, so that the Forty-Second Massachusetts detachment did not have much to do beyond picket and guard duty.

Lieutenant-Colonel Stedman remained at Great Falls until October 15th, when he was ordered back to his regiment with three companies. Captain Tinkham, with Company B, was left at the post. A suggestion from Colonel Burrell, October 18th, to build a stockade, as the position invited an attack, brought the following reply:

> "HEADQUARTERS COMPANY B, 42D MASS. VOLS.,
> "GREAT FALLS, MD., October 19th, 1864.
>
> "*Colonel*,— I received your dispatch of the eighteenth, for which I am very grateful. My company is small, and what men I have are getting sick very fast, so that I have not men enough to carry out your advice. However, I will do the best I can, and shall not leave here until I know what I leave for. There are several of my company still in Alexandria, whom I wish could be sent to me. Would like to have General Slough informed of my situation.
>
> "Very respectfully yours,
> "B. C. TINKHAM,
> "*Captain commanding post.*"

The enemy began to make trouble immediately after the three companies left. Guerrillas would stop canal boats, untie the horses and make off with them, until this nuisance was partly abated by the use of old, worn-out mules that did not present such temptation. The canal traffic was seriously interrupted, and caused Captain Tinkham to picket the canal for two miles, until ordered back to his regiment October 28th. Pennsylvania troops relieved Company B, and a short time after were attacked by the enemy.

Cases for discipline in September were as follows: 1st — Private Martin Monighan, Company E, for firing his musket without permission, was sentenced to carry a forty-pound log of wood tied to his back for a stated number of hours each day for three days. 17th — Corporal Pond, Company B, and three privates on duty with him in Alexandria, were sent to that city, by orders from General Slough, to serve sentences for neglect of duty. 27th — Private Elisha Atwood, Company A, was sent to Alexandria for confinement in the slave pen, for neglect of duty. 30th — Corporal William Bacon, Company A, was reduced to the ranks for intoxication, by regimental Special Orders No. 78.

This is not a bad record for a raw regiment of short-term men. A practice had been in vogue for captains to assume the power to order punishment of men in their companies guilty of trifling indiscretions. Captain French was noted for this stretch of power. This was stopped by the colonel on assuming command. He maintained that no man should be punished without a hearing.

Details in September were as follows:

On detached service at headquarters military governor: 6th — Private Sidney W. Knowles, Company C, clerk. 20th — Corporal John Stetson, Jr., Company K, clerk. — Private Herbert W. Fay, Company F, clerk. —Private Edward S. Averill, Company B, clerk. 22d — Private Frederick A. Clark, Company K, clerk. — Private Christopher F. Snelling, Company K, clerk.

On detached service at general court-martial rooms in Alexandria: 1st — Private Ansel F. Temple, Company I, clerk. 13th — Private Davis W. Howard, Company I, clerk. — Private Edward L. Harvey, Company B, clerk. — Private Benjamin W. Kenyon, Company E, clerk. — Private James L. Martin, Company C, clerk. — Private Arthur E. Hotchkiss, Company B, clerk. — Private William L. Gage, Company I, clerk. — Private George E. Sparr, Company H, orderly. 14th — Private Charles Curtis, Company D, clerk.

On detailed duty with the regiment: 7th — Corporal James L. Prouty, Company D, clerk at headquarters. 14th — Privates W. F. Adams, W. H. S. Ritchie, George E. Buttrick, of Company A, were placed on permanent guard at the reservoir, relieving Privates Edgerton, Heathcote and Andrews, of Company G. 16th — Private George L. Simpson, Company F, hospital attendant. 21st — Private George W. Brooks, Company K, hospital attendant. 24th — Private Albert S. Barpee, Company E, hospital attendant. 29th — Private Ezra K. Garvin, Company F, with quartermaster.

Officers on detached service in September were: Lieutenants Sanderson and Spear on permanent duty with grand-guard, a line of sentinels stationed between the Forty-Second camp and Alexandria. Lieutenants Hodges and Ballou on permanent duty with provost-marshal-general. Lieutenant Thomas with a permanent guard at Hunting Creek Bridge, where an artillery block-house was built. Lieutenant Hawley was detached on mounted patrol service, in answer to a request from General Slough for an experienced cavalry-officer. Captain Ward, Lieutenants Aldrich and Shattuck, Company G, on guard at Soldier's Rest since September 14th. On detached service at Great Falls were Lieutenant-Colonel Stedman, Captains Tinkham, White, Waterman and Ford, Lieutenants Fuller, Smith, Bates, Conner and Cook. Lieutenant Galvin was absent in Philadelphia on sick leave.

At the close of September there was present for duty: seventeen officers, three hundred and seventy-eight men; twenty-six men sick. Absent: eighteen officers, four hundred and sixty men on detached service; one officer, twenty-two men sick; three men in arrest.

There was no chance for any camp fun in October, for officers and men were constantly on duty, day and night, in obedience to orders for guards, patrols and pickets, that came thick and fast. Details of men were called for by mounted orderlies, with verbal orders, at all hours of the day and night, in addition to details mentioned later on. Adjutant Davis, not in good health, manfully stood to his duty in exceptionally trying circumstances. To fill these constant requisitions from among grumbling men in a raw regiment, already overworked, was not an easy matter. To do so, men who just reported in camp from some long tour of guard or patrol service were obliged to again depart from camp, swearing like troopers, on a like service. After four companies left for Great Falls, members of the band were made to resume duty in the ranks and go on the regular camp guard; at one time not relieved for sixteen days, men were so scarce and the difficulty so great to comply with these orders.

Duty done by the regiment, required by written orders, was: September 29th and 30th — One officer and forty men sent to guard stores to Fairfax Station. October 2d — One officer and fifty men as train-guard on Orange and Alexandria Railroad. October 2d — Captain Ward, with fifty men, to guard a telegraph construction party running a line of wire from Manassas or Warrenton Junction, on the Manassas Gap Railroad. Captain Ward and his men had a skirmish with the enemy's cavalry, on the fourth, near Gainesville, and drove them back without loss. October 3d — One officer and fifty men, with detachments First and Second D. C. Volunteers, as guard for a construction train on Orange and Alexandria Railroad. October 4th — One officer and forty men on same service. October 5th — One officer and fifty men on same service. October 5th — Seven men as permanent guard at coal wharf. October 6th — One officer and twenty-five men to guard a special train. October 12th — One officer and thirty picked men on duty for three days with mounted patrols and pickets, to be relieved every three days. This order was in force until October 27th. October 13th — One officer and twenty-five men for train-guard. October 17th — Four officers and one hundred men, with two days' rations, were sent every day, until October 27th, for train-guards. Of this detail two officers and fifty men went on duty at 3.45 A.M., and two officers and fifty men at ten A.M.

These details were in addition to the regular camp-guard, men for grand-guard duty and men for the pickets stationed outside the grand-guard line. Nearly all the trains were freighted with supplies for General Sheridan, after communication with him was opened. Every two or three miles along the railroad were guard-stations, in block-houses, on account of the guerrillas who infested the line of road. None of the Forty-Second detachments had a chance to test their mettle with the enemy, except the slight skirmish by Captain Ward's men. At Rectortown one train came along just in time to allow the Forty-Second guard to help get a cavalry-post out of an unpleasant position; the enemy retreated without a fight.

Details in October for daily duty with the regiment were: 1st — Private Peter Broso, Company F, on duty with quartermaster. 1st — Private A. W. Mitchell, Company A, orderly at headquarters. 1st — Private Edwin H. Alger, Company D, as wagoner.

One case for discipline occurred: Corporal Albert F. Burnham, Company A, was reduced to the ranks October 24th, for leaving camp without leave. On an appeal for a hearing, made by Burnham, an inquiry was held in his case by officers detailed for the purpose. They justified the degradation.

The officers detailed on court-martial duty in September were: Lieutenant-Colonel Stedman, Captains French,

Eddy, Stewart, Stevens and Wales, and Lieutenant Gray. Every captain in the regiment, except White, did service on general court-martial duty. Major Stiles was constantly on general court-martial duty by details of August 6th and September 20th, and not relieved until October 15th, when the following order was issued:

"HEADQUARTERS MILITARY GOVERNOR,
"ALEXANDRIA, VA., October 15th, 1864.
"GENERAL ORDERS NO. 84.

"1 — The general court-martial convened by paragraph 2, General Orders No. 57, headquarters Military Governor, Alexandria, Va., dated September 20th, 1864, of which Major Frederick G. Stiles, Forty-Second Regiment Massachusetts Volunteers, is president, is hereby dissolved.

"2 — This court has since its first organization (August 8th, 1864), disposed of over six hundred cases, and the general commanding desires to compliment the members composing it for the energetic, faithful and satisfactory manner in which they have transacted the business referred to them.

"By command of
"BRIGADIER-GENERAL SLOUGH,
"W. M. GWYNNE,
"*Captain, and A. A. General.*"

At the close of October there was present for duty (all officers and men were relieved from detached or detailed service) thirty-five officers, seven hundred and ninety-nine men; one officer, seventy-five men sick. Absent: nine men sick in hospitals.

The term of service expired October 29th. A request was made for transportation *via* Baltimore, Philadelphia, New York and Boston to place of muster out, instead of returning home by a sea voyage. The regiment vacated camp and quartered in the Soldier's Rest, Alexandria, October 28th, until relieved from duty in the command. This was on Sunday, October 30th, after a review by General Slough. Monday morning, thirty-first, the regiment marched to Washington, and was received by President Lincoln in front of the White House at nine o'clock. Cheers from the men, a few remarks by the President, and then the march was resumed to the depot to take cars *en-route* home, arriving in Boston late on Thursday evening, November 3d, and quartered in Faneuil Hall. After breakfast next morning the regiment marched to Boston Common and was there dismissed, to assemble on Friday, November 11th, for muster out of service.*

This journey home was full of discomfort for those officers who did their duty. It was a time of great political excitement in New York City. On this account the regiment retained its arms, and twenty rounds of ammunition was in each cartridge-box. In New York the regiment remained at the Battery all day, and marched up Broadway about five P.M. Crowds of people lined the street and cheered alternately for Lincoln and McClellan, the men answering these cheers impartially to avoid trouble. While in Forty-Second Street, where the men remained until late next morning, when a train was made up to proceed on to Boston, there was bad behaviour by various men of the regiment, who became drunk and disorderly. Some of these men fired their muskets, which, coupled with a fire that broke out in the vicinity, was sufficient to cause con-

---

* Before dismissal on Boston Common, Governor Andrew requested Colonel Burrell to take the telegraphic address of every officer, and instruct his officers and men (the men retained their arms until mustered out of service) to hold themselves in readiness for further service. The Governor telegraphed to New York he had a reliable regiment, just arrived home, at the service of the military authorities, if wanted to preserve order. No further service was required.

siderable alarm among people who resided near. Much blame is attachable to officers for their lukewarm endeavors to stop this unsoldierlike conduct.

About one hundred sick men were brought home, some of whom ought not to have left Alexandria, but they were anxious to go home with their comrades. To properly look out for these men was no easy matter. A delay of several hours occurred in Baltimore before transportation across the city could be found for the sick, Colonel Burrell positively refusing to move his regiment and leave them to follow after, as he was advised to do by some of his officers. Orders were given that in case any sick man was obliged to be left at any place *en-route*, one man was to be detailed to remain with him.

At Alexandria the aqueduct was out of order, and well-water was used for drinking purposes; but so bad was this water, a limited quantity of beer was allowed to be sold in camp. Train-guards, hurriedly called for and immediately sent away, had no time to fill haversacks with ample rations, often obliged to start with hard bread as their chief eatable. Of course, this had an effect on the men, a large proportion being under twenty-five years of age, many of them under twenty years, who did not have the advantage of a few months in a camp of instruction and get well seasoned to a soldier's life before they were called upon to endure the arduous and exacting service they saw in Virginia.* During the last weeks in September and through October there was an average of fifty men sick in camp, and forty men absent sick in Alexandria hospitals.

---

* The colonel called the attention of General Slough to the fact that his regiment was overworked, and flesh and blood could not stand the strain without some rest, which the general admitted, but claimed he could rely on the Massachusetts men, while some raw Pennsylvania men in his command (there were several full regiments just arrived), were not reliable.

The regimental hospital tent, of limited accommodations, was always full, and all surplus sick men who required hospital care were sent to Alexandria. The weather was favorable in August and September; October was stormy, and nights cold.

The regiment lost sixteen men by death during this term of service. The bodies of those men who died in Alexandria were sent home. The deaths were:

August 14th — Private George H. Rich, Company B, in third division hospital, from accidental wounds while on guard.

August 24th — Private Richard M. Sabin, Company G, in third division hospital, from acute dysentery.

September 11th — Private Edwin A. Grant, Company B, in third division hospital, from typhoid fever.

September 11th — Private Lyman Tucker, Company F, in regimental hospital, from typhoid fever.

September 18th — Private Samuel Stone, Company F, in third division hospital, from typhoid fever.

September 20th — Private George G. Harrington, Company F, in third division hospital, from typhoid fever.

September 23d — Private Herman J. Gilbert, Company F, in third division hospital, from typhoid fever.

September 25th — Private Edward H. Aldrich, Company G, in Soldier's Rest Hospital, from typho-malarial fever. (Aldrich was a student, borne on the rolls, but never mustered in.)

October 4th — Private Patrick Riley, Company G, in third division hospital, from pyæmia. Riley was shot in the leg by a secessionist of Alexandria, on August 27th. Amputation was necessary, from which he did not recover.

October 5th — Private Henry H. Lowell, Company F, in second division hospital, from typhoid fever.

October 8th — Private Walter Foster, 2d., Company D,

in second division hospital, from suicide by drowning; insanity.

October 24th — Private William T. Cutler, Company F, in third division hospital, from typhoid fever.

October 26th — Private Calvin S. Haynes, Company C, Slough Barracks Hospital, from typhoid fever.

October 30th — Private John J. Bisbee, Company H, Slough Barracks Hospital, from chronic diarrhœa.

November 7th — Private Thomas E. Flemming, Company A, at Roxbury, Mass., from sore leg.

November 17th — Private William H. Perry, Company A, at Boston, Mass., from consumption.

There were eight men discharged from service, by Major-General Augur, Twenty-Second Army Corps, for disability, viz.: Sergeant William H. Alexander, Company C, September 10th; Private Willard L. Studley, Company D, September 10th; Private Wendell Davis, Company H, September 13th; Corporal Jerome P. Thurber, Company G, September 13th; Private Nathan Washburne, Company C, September 16th; Private Jason Whitaker, Company E, September 19th; Private Henry W. Dean, Company I, September 20th; Private Albert E. Frost, Company K, September 20th.

One man reënlisted for one year in the Thirty-Eighth Massachusetts Volunteers: Private Andrew C. Hale, Company H, September 8th.

By regimental General Orders No. 111, issued November 6th, at Roxbury, Mass., the following men were relieved from detailed daily duty at headquarters, with a complimentary notice for their faithful service: Private Ezra Abbott, Company A, chief wagoner; Private James Allen, Company E, orderly; Private Ellery C. Bartlett, Company K, clerk.

As Chaplain Sanger could not get permission from his

church people in Webster, Mass., to serve one hundred days with his regiment, an attempt was made to obtain a commission for Second-Lieutenant Galvin, Company F, a regularly ordained clergyman from Brookfield, Mass., who was unanimously elected by his brother officers, August 10th, to fill that position. Through unavoidable delays and informality in the proper papers, no progress was made towards securing his appointment until late in September. Lieutenant Galvin was then absent in Philadelphia on sick leave, and it was doubtful if he would be able to rejoin his regiment before the term of service expired. Difficulties also existed in obtaining a muster dated back, so his appointment was abandoned. He officiated as chaplain for a few weeks only.

One payment was made to the regiment, the last week in September, when the men were paid for July and August. The following ladies, wives of officers, boarded at a hotel in Alexandria, and saw what constitutes camp life in time of war: Mrs. Burrell, Mrs. Stedman, Mrs. Stiles, Mrs. Robinson, Mrs. Ford.

This brief sketch is sufficient to prove that the one-hundred-day men did not have a picnic during their service. To be sure, the regiment did not get into an action: a stroke of good luck. The various train-guard detachments were liable to have a fight at any moment, and, until back in camp, were kept ready for such a contingency.

In conclusion the writer would add: Let no man who enlisted in a three years regiment sneer at the nine months troops, or those who served a shorter term. A large number reünlisted later on in other organizations, and served to the end of the war. Their previous service was of great benefit wherever they went; in fact, they were not raw recruits. The three years man who served continuously with his colors is a rarity.

It does not follow that every man who enlisted in the army is entitled to credit for so doing. "Bummers" and shirks were plenty. When a thousand men are got together there must be a percentage of this element among them. The most worthy and deserving men do not have much to say about their army experience, and never drag it into prominence for selfish reasons.

No undue importance is intended in naming men who were on detached daily duty as clerks, orderlies, etc.; such places were considered "soft berths," although much hard work was done by many of the detailed men. The soldier who remained with his colors, and did duty like a man, is the one to whom most praise is due.

www.ingramcontent.com/pod-product-compliance
Lightning Source LLC
Chambersburg PA
CBHW051849300426
44117CB00006B/323